David Sedaris is the author of twelve previous books, including, most recently, *A Carnival of Snackery, The Best of Me,* and *Calypso.* He is a regular contributor to *The New Yorker* and BBC Radio 4. In 2019, he was inducted into the American Academy of Arts and Letters. He is the recipient of the Thurber Prize for American Humor, the Jonathan Swift Prize for Satire and Humor, and the Terry Southern Prize for Humor.

'Grumpy, bitchy, sympathetic, sad and welcoming all at once.' *Guardian*

'The humorist's eye for the peculiar is as sharp as ever.' *The Times*

'The second volume of the American humorist's diaries is full of his trademark wit.' *Observer*

'Throughout the colorful, caustic yarns that fill his best-selling essay and story collections, he's maintained league-of-his-own status by staying light on his feet: just when you're expecting a wry jab, he clocks you with a poignant gut punch.' *Washington Post*

'His diary entri͏ aggressive post off   cy
and the non sec
he elevates to th
humor.' *Net*

D1334173

'Uproarious … a must for Sedaris fans.' *CNN*

'A rich trove for hardcore Sedaris fans.' *Kirkus*

Also by David Sedaris

The Best of Me
Calypso
Theft by Finding
Let's Explore Diabetes with Owls
Squirrel Seeks Chipmunk
When You Are Engulfed in Flames
Dress Your Family in Corduroy and Denim
Me Talk Pretty One Day
Holidays on Ice
Naked
Barrel Fever
A Carnival of Snackery
Happy-Go-Lucky

A Carnival
of
Snackery

Diaries (2003–2020)

David Sedaris

LITTLE, BROWN

First published in the United States in 2021 by Little, Brown and Company
First published in Great Britain in 2021 by Little, Brown
This edition published in Great Britain in 2022 by Abacus

1 3 5 7 9 10 8 6 4 2

Copyright © 2021 by David Sedaris

A CIP catalogue record for this book
is available from the British Library.

Paperback ISBN 978-0-349-14190-9

Printed and bound in Great Britain by Clays Ltd, Elcograf S.p.A.

Papers used by Little, Brown are from well-managed forests
and other responsible sources.

Little, Brown
An imprint of
Little, Brown Book Group
Carmelite House
50 Victoria Embankment
London EC4Y 0DZ

An Hachette UK Company
www.hachette.co.uk

www.littlebrown.co.uk

For Ken Shorr

Author's Note

Occasionally in this book I have changed people's names or altered their physical descriptions. I've rewritten things slightly when they were unclear, but most everything was left intact.

A Carnival of Snackery

Introduction

In reading the eighteen years' worth of material that went into this second volume of my diaries, I noticed a few things. For starters, I have a lot of mice in my life. There must have been at least three hundred mentions of them, maybe more. I came across them in my home and in my yard. In restaurants and banks. I even ran into mice on vacation! (Mine, not theirs.) Then there are the ones described secondhand by friends or thrown to snakes and snapping turtles in YouTube videos. If combined, these entries would make for a whole separate book—an edge-of-your-seat thriller for cats. The only place I don't have a mouse problem is New York, where I have rats instead—not in my apartment, thank God, but surrounding it, trying to get in. One of the mentions I had to cut involved one I saw near Times Square at two a.m. with a Cheeto in its mouth. A few weeks later, while walking in West Sussex, I found a wounded rat in a paper bag. I swear, I could move to the moon and still find rodent droppings on my countertops.

There were also an inordinate number of entries that concerned travel of one sort or another. *Why so many airport stories?* I used to wonder as I watched comedians on TV back in the 1980s. *Can't you talk about something else for a change?* Then I started touring and realized just how much time those people spent getting from one place to another. Where there are cars and trains and buses and planes, there's going to be tension and ugliness. There's nothing I find more compelling, so of course my diary is filled with travel stories, many of which involve hired drivers. That makes me sound very grand, but I'm only ferried around when I'm on tour. Sometimes I'm taken from one city to the next, but more often I'm picked up from some airport or other and carried to my hotel. If I had a license I suppose I could rent a car and make the trips myself, but oh, the lovely encounters I would have missed, the hundreds of men and women I've fallen into conversation with and who have surprised and delighted me.

There are also a great many entries about litter. From 2010 on, I mentioned it every day, at least when I was in the UK — exhaustive reports on how many cans and bottles I'd picked up that afternoon, the bags of household trash I'd found dumped by the roadside, the toaster ovens and construction waste. Then I'd travel to another country and write about the litter I *wasn't* seeing. There's only so much of that a reader can take, I suppose.

Left out altogether are the countless quotes taken from books and magazine articles I've read, lines and paragraphs that struck me as beautiful or precise. I've transcribed great chunks of Mavis Gallant's diaries, for example, but none of them made this collection, as reprinting them would involve getting permission. The quotes made me look smart, so I hated to lose them. Likewise, I've left out reviews of the many books that have disappointed me over the years. I've always been excited by authors who disparage their contemporaries, the sort who forever have their dukes up, spoiling for a fight, but I don't want to *be* one of those people.

If a number of these entries seem overproduced, it's because they are. When something especially interesting happens — a monkey is spotted at the Cracker Barrel, a woman tells me that her cousin had his arms chewed off by pigs in Mexico — I take extra care when writing it up in my diary, knowing I'll likely be reading it onstage. These entries, by and large, have taglines. They wave little flags—*Hey, look at me!* Many of the ones that work well in front of an audience I wound up cutting just because they seemed too self-conscious, too eager to please. Others I kept because, come on, his arms chewed off *by pigs*?

As with the first volume, I've included a great many jokes in this book, ones I heard at parties and book signings. I wanted to put them all in—the good and the bad—but times being what they are, I don't know that my publisher could withstand the vast amounts of hate mail they would engender. Oh, offensive jokes...when, if ever, will your time come around again?

As in my first volume of diaries, *Theft by Finding,* I'll remind the reader that this is *my* edit, a tiny fraction of what I've written to myself over the past eighteen years. I haven't gone out of my way to appear thoughtful and virtuous but could easily look much, much worse than I do in these pages. Again, I chose entries that I thought were funny or startling in some way. *Theft by Finding,* which covered 1997 to 2002, had a narrative arc. "David Copperfield Sedaris," Hugh called it. If there's an arc to this book, I don't know what it is. The me that I was when the first volume ended has certainly grown older, though no wiser. It's a safe bet that I've become more spoiled and impatient. Often while rereading my source material, I've thought of Dorothy Parker's "From the Diary of a New York Lady During Days of Horror, Despair, and World Change." Here is war and calamity—natural disaster, mass migration, racial strife—and I'm complaining that the sale at Comme des Garçons starts the day *after* I leave Paris for Zurich, where I am to receive an award. Of all the rotten luck! In fairness to myself, I do mention politics and current events. I follow the news quite closely, as a matter of fact, though you wouldn't know it from reading this book. If I didn't include many of those entries, I guess it's because other people cover that sort of thing much better and with a lot more authority than I do. Plus, if I'm honest, given a choice between writing about the Arab Spring uprisings and a beggar calling out— as one recently did to a woman walking ahead of me—"Hey, you got a hole in your ass," I'll go with the latter.

Though I suspect you already knew that.

2003

Drinks and dinner in Fulham with Jane's friends Allison and Ian. She's fifty-two, an American with thick, shoulder-length hair and the flat eyes of a chronic alcoholic. Allison had been drinking before we arrived, and her mouth was purpled with wine. "Hey," she said. "Guess what? I was walking down the hall and my tooth fell out! Dropped out just like that! Do you believe it? Now I've got a big hole." She picked the tooth off the mantel and offered it for our inspection. It was a molar capped with a heavy gold crown. "Don't ever, ever, *ever* move to England," she warned. Then, "Hey, you want it?"

The strange part was that it hadn't even bled. There was no pain or swelling, just a dry pit. Allison tended toward big, clownish gestures. In the middle of a sentence, she'd stop talking and point from one person to another, shrugging like a mime. She'd say the word *damn* or *hell* and then cover her mouth with both hands. Every story was interrupted by shenanigans. Ian, her Scottish husband, was a little older, and handsome. He'd been drinking as well, but held it better. "All right, old stick," he said as it neared the dinner hour. "It's time to go. These people are hungry." He took the bourbon from Allison's hands and she called him Bossy Boots.

"But *Jane's* here," she whined. "This is *important*!"

We ate at an Indian restaurant around the corner from

their home. I sat next to Ian, who explained the intricacies of reward and punishment offered at the boarding school he'd gone to. If your rugby shirt fell off its hook more than twice a semester, you were roused out of bed and taken to the piffery, a high-ceilinged room that was empty but for a Ping-Pong table. Once there you'd remove your dressing gown and offer your buttocks to the cane. "I don't think it was bamboo," he said when I asked what sort of wood it was made of. "No, I believe it was hickory or perhaps birch."

While Ian talked to me and Hugh, Allison went from wine to brandy. By the time we left the restaurant she was staggering, partly due to alcohol and partly due to bad knees.

January 21, 2003
London
Last night I spoke with (my literary agent) Don, who seems to have forgotten the word *page*. "They want at least two hundred chapters, I mean, no, not chapters but ... oh ..."

This is happening more and more often, and I never know if, in trying to help, I'm like a French person breaking into English. "Two hundred *pages*?"

"That's it."

January 23, 2003
London
Hugh and I walked to Maida Vale yesterday. Close to Bayswater we found a tile shop and were looking at samples when a man entered. He was Jamaican and approached the counter to ask for directions to a particular street. "The next road over is one-way," the saleswoman told him. "So you need to go one up and take a hard left. It isn't far, really it isn't."

The man then asked if the woman would ride with him. "As a passenger, and point it out in person."

"Well," she said warily, "I can't really do that, you see, as my supervisor is on the phone and I'm the only one watching the floor."

"Fine," the man said. "We'll just wait until your supervisor gets *off* the phone."

It was an outlandish request, and I could see the woman begin to panic. "It's honestly not far at all," she said. "Anyone can find it. It's easy, really."

February 18, 2003
London

While walking to the Tesco on Sunday afternoon I felt something strike me in the middle of my back. It wasn't sharp, but flat, like the feeling of someone congratulating you a little too hard. I was wearing a Walkman and looking at the ground, so it took me a moment to realize I was being passed by a group of boys riding their bikes on the sidewalk. I'd just accepted the idea of them when a second kid came from behind and hit me against the side of the head. *Wait a minute,* I thought as they scattered. *You can't do that. I'm a grown-up!*

Further up the sidewalk they hit two other men and, beyond that, a woman walking her dog. I imagined what I'd do if I ever got my hands on them, but it was tricky, as they were children. The thought of punching a ten-year-old is rough, at best, and so I left the boys alone and concentrated on their bikes, mentally puncturing the tires and destroying the spokes with the heel of my shoe. Mainly I wondered if, a year from now, they'd remember hitting a small man upside the head. Would I stick out in their minds or might they have hit so many people that a single episode was impossible to recall?

In 1970, while riding bikes up Shelly Road, Dan Thompson and I gave a driver the finger. He'd crowded us, or at least we felt that he had, and the moment our gestures registered, he stopped the car and got out. The man didn't touch me personally but grabbed the bars of my bike. "Son," he said, "I ought to knock those braces right down your fucking throat." Had he simply continued on his way I would have forgotten about the whole thing, but instead he threatened me, thereby setting up permanent camp in my memory.

The boys were there when I reached the Tesco, the entire group of them. I thought of saying, *Excuse me, but one of you accidentally hit me on the head, and now I'm guessing you'd like to apologize.* They were kids. There would be no brawl, no switchblade pulled from a boot, but instead I chickened out and spent the rest of the day hating myself for being such a coward.

February 26, 2003
London

On my way home from Wandsworth, I saw an Indian man cut in front of a black passenger who was standing before the driver, paying for a bus ticket. "Fuck off," the Indian man said when the black man gave him a look. "Just fuck off." The Indian man was tall and slender. The crown of his head was bald, a barren field surrounded by shining, shoulder-length hair.

"No," the black man said, "you fuck off."

"You fuck off."

"No, you fuck off."

The two men moved toward the back of the bus and I thought for a moment that it would come to blows.

"Fucking n—," the Indian man said.

"Hey, if it weren't for me you wouldn't be here," the black man said. I guessed he was speaking of Africa as the cradle of civilization.

"Fuck you," the Indian man said. "If you want to know where you came from, ask your mother. I fucked her."

"No, I fucked *your* mother," the black man said.

"No, you didn't."

"Yes, I did. Just ask her."

"Your mother's a monkey."

"*Your* mother's the monkey, not mine."

"Fuck off."

"No, you fuck off."

The bus stopped to accept more passengers and the men fell silent. I wondered if, throughout the rest of the ride, they reflected upon the argument. Did either wonder what might happen next, or did they both accept that it was over? Had I been the black man I would have skipped that whole "I fucked your mother" business and gone straight for the bald spot, which was obviously the Indian man's Achilles' heel. The way he arranged his hair suggested that he was very sensitive about it, while who knows how he actually feels about his mother.

March 21, 2003
Paris, France

They've closed all the train lines running beneath the American embassy. A wall has been erected and police now line the Concorde. I arrived early for my periodontist appointment and watched a group of students march up rue Royale to the Madeleine. It was hard to make out but it sounded as if they were yelling "Boom Chaka Khan."

On my way home from Dr. Guig's, I saw the demonstrators again and realized they were chanting *"Bush est un assassin."* There were manifestations all over town and I sort of followed them throughout the day. If this is the reaction to France sitting out the war, I can't imagine what might have happened had Chirac committed troops.

*　　*　　*

Last week Hugh was interviewed by the *Orne Combattante,* which wanted his view on the Iraq War. Pierre brought a copy of the resulting article to dinner last night at a Vietnamese restaurant he likes in the sixth and tossed it on the table, saying that Hugh, who had trashed Bush, was a disgrace to his country. I wanted to hear what Pierre thought of Jacques Chirac, but he was too caught up in flirting with the young American woman at the next table. "Just so you will know how charming I am, my two favorite movies are *Sleeping in Seattle* and *There Is Mail for You,*" he said.

March 23, 2003
Paris
While the *International Herald Tribune* follows American efforts to remove French words and products from their restaurant menus, the BBC reported that Jordanians are giving up their American cigarettes in exchange for harsh-tasting Gauloises, which is really much more of a sacrifice. In Thursday's paper there were pictures of angry Midwesterners emptying bottles of Bordeaux into the Mississippi River. On TV I watched a French news report on a handful of middle-aged anti-war demonstrators living in a small town in Massachusetts. It doesn't take much to join a crowd of thousands, but these people are basically alone, and their neighbors now despise them. The group was marching in front of city hall when a man ran up and started pushing them, shouting, "I hate the French. I want to kill them." It was a strange thing to see translated into French.

March 24, 2003
Paris
They cut the red carpet from this year's Academy Awards ceremony and as late as yesterday there was talk that certain

stars would not be attending, some for security reasons, some because they were against the war, and some because they thought this a time for quiet reflection. In yesterday's *Financial Times* the president of the Academy was quoted as saying it was our patriotic duty to carry on with the Oscars. He didn't explain how, but then again, no one does. They just say it's your patriotic duty and everyone kind of goes along with it.

French's Mustard has issued a press release explaining that French is a family name and has nothing to do with France or the behavior of that country's president or UN ambassador. "We're baseball games and Fourth of July picnics," they say. "We are America in all its glory."

Our cabdriver from JFK was disappointed. It seemed he'd wanted a female passenger but instead he wound up with us. "I love the ladies," he said. "They remind me of my baby's mother. They remind me of Mommy."

Traffic was heavy and during the ride he listened to Hot 101. The afternoon show was hosted by Wendy Williams and between songs she accepted calls from listeners eager to tell her how great she was. We hadn't even left Queens and already Hugh was threatening to return to France. "I know how to drive the Iraqis from Baghdad," he said. "Forget the bombs, just make them listen to this goddamn radio station."

April 9, 2003
Princeton, New Jersey

The smaller the airport the more horrible the security staff; take Madison, Wisconsin. I arrived yesterday morning and checked in to find the dreaded four Ss stamped along the bottom of my ticket. The agent said it was random, but I'm always singled out by American Airlines, most likely because of all the one-way tickets. A gray-haired man asked for my suitcase and after giving it to him I stepped outside for a cigarette. On returning I saw the guy and his associate pawing through my stuff. The German translation of *Me Talk Pretty* was pulled out and they flipped through the pages, scowling, as if they had discovered a secret document detailing tank positions. It was strange to stand unnoticed and watch people going through my things. They emptied my shaving kit and unwrapped the tin I'd gotten Ronnie as a housewarming gift. When they started inspecting my cigarettes I approached the two and asked them what they were doing. "We're going through your suitcase," the gray-haired man said. And then he continued.

April 12, 2003
Wilmington, North Carolina

Before leaving Austin I heard a radio report on an Englishman who's giving out awards for stupid security measures. First prize goes to an airport scanner who forced a female passenger to drink from three bottles of her own breast milk. She'd pumped it before boarding, and they wanted to make sure it wasn't poison. This explains why sperm donors are traveling Greyhound.

April 29, 2003
Paris

On Sunday Hugh attended a Mets game with his old friend Jeff Raven. He called yesterday to announce that he now loves baseball and tried to sound all butch about it. "Jeff's son had a soccer match so we had to leave in the sixth inning," he said. "I watched the rest of it on TV and then read the review in this morning's paper."

Review?

May 29, 2003
La Bagotière, France
While touring in the United States I'd said time and time again that the French had a beef with George Bush but were able to distinguish between the American people and the American government. The audience would applaud, and I'd stand there thinking, *If only it were true.* Even Manuela has dropped the George Bush references and begun directing her criticism toward Americans in general. "I can't help it," she says. "It's just easier."

At Montparnasse yesterday morning I saw a poster for *A Man Apart,* the new Vin Diesel movie. Across the actor's face someone had written *US go your fucking home.*

June 5, 2003
Paris
Last night I watched a bit of the Miss Universe pageant. An American production, it was presented in English and translated into French by an off-screen couple, who made ruthless fun of the show's vacuous hosts. Five finalists stepped forward in their evening gowns, and poor Miss Serbia and Montenegro was asked the question "If given the choice, which would you rather be, fire or water?"

"That should solve the world's problems," the male translator said. The camera cut to Donald Trump, sitting in the audience with his hands to his chin.

"He's monstrous," the Frenchwoman said. "An ogre!"

Miss Serbia and Montenegro stared at the microphone for a moment, no doubt wondering if she'd misunderstood the question. "I am a human," she said. "A girl with feelings, so I do not understand what it is like to be an element that has nothing. I cannot make a choice like that, so I will prefer to stay myself."

She did not win.

June 11, 2003
Paris

I went to dinner last night with an Iranian woman named Marjane, who told the following joke:

A woman carries a large suitcase into the Bank of France and tells the president that she would like to deposit ten million euros. He looks at the money, impressed, and asks what she does for a living.

"Oh," she says. "I make bets with people. For instance, I'd be willing to bet a hundred thousand euros that your testicles are cube-shaped, like dice, but a little bigger."

The bank president agrees to the bet, and after the two shake hands, he lowers his pants, revealing that his testicles are not cube-shaped, but oval, like eggs.

"All right, you win," the woman says. "But if it's all right I'd like to wait and pay you tomorrow. My lawyer will come with me, and after he's verified that I've officially lost the bet, I'll give you your money."

The following afternoon the woman returns in the company of her lawyer. "If you don't mind," she says to the bank president, "I'd like you to show me your testicles one more time, just so my lawyer can see for himself."

The bank president lowers his pants.

"And if it's not asking too *too* much," she continues, "I would like to touch them, just to be absolutely sure they're not in any way cube-like."

"Fine," he says.

The woman bends forward, and just as she touches the man's testicles, her lawyer starts banging his head against the wall.

"What's up with him?" the president asks.

"Oh," the woman says. "I just bet him a million euros I could touch the balls of the president of the Bank of France."

June 24, 2003
Paris

Hugh and I had dinner with two visiting Americans and a friend of theirs who is also American and has been in Paris for twenty years. Deborah lives in what used to be a factory for making police uniforms, a small, three-story building hidden in a courtyard. She has the first and second floors and has turned the roof into a garden. A Frenchwoman lives on the ground level and was understandably upset when someone broke in and burgled her. Deborah promised to keep an eye out for anything suspicious and leaped into action when, a week or two later, she heard her neighbor shouting, "Stop, stop, I beg you."

It sounded like the woman was being raped, so Deborah ran down and pounded on her door. No one answered, so she went back upstairs and called the police, who said that the neighbor was probably just having sex.

Deborah explained that the woman had conjugated the verb *to stop* in a tense employed when speaking to more than one person, and the officer said, "So . . . she's probably having sex with two men." He then brought up Deborah's American accent and suggested that she had a lot to learn about Frenchwomen.

"And you," Deborah said, "have a lot to learn about American women." She asked for his name and badge number and when it looked like she might cause trouble, the officer sent a couple of policemen, who pounded on the door and discovered the Frenchwoman having sex with two men.

August 8, 2003
La Bagotière

It was 100 degrees by the time we reached Villedieu, half-way between here and Granville. The town was packed with vacationers, all of them walking on the shady side of the street. It was too hot to eat, too hot to spend time in the un-air-conditioned copper shops the area is known for, so people congregated at the market, where they stood around talking about the heat wave.

We'd parked on the outskirts of town and were returning to the car when we were passed by trucks equipped with loudspeakers announcing the coming engagement of a small circus. The trucks hauled cages inhabited by overheated animals. In the first were miniature ponies, two llamas, and a kneeling camel. "Look, a camel!" everyone said. In the second was a panting tigress and two cubs. Their tongues practically touched the ground, and you got the idea that, if freed, the worst they would do was drool on you. Still, though, it's not every day you see a tiger.

Our hotel in Granville was by the sea, between the casino and a rehab center for stroke and accident victims. Some of the residents were in wheelchairs but most walked with either canes or crutches, which left holes in the sand. It was an odd place to collect disabled people. The sea made sense, but the building was set into a cliff and getting up and down involved climbing hundreds of stairs, a trip that would take some time if you had casts on both legs.

The center had constructed a swimming pool in the sea. For half the day it was underwater, but when the tide went out, it reappeared and was used with great pleasure. You'd think that a rehab center might equip their pool with steps or maybe a ramp, but no. Handicapped people dove in, then clung to the murky sides, struggling to get out.

I went to bed at three and shortly afterward Hugh woke up, and we talked for a while. He'd dreamed that he was walking past a house and saw a man on the front porch reading a book called *Dress Your Family in Corduroy and Denim.*

I got up and wrote the name in my notebook. If it's not too late, his dream will be a prophecy. *Dress Your Family in Corduroy and Denim.* I think that's a great title for my new book.

October 10, 2003
Savannah, Georgia

Lisa and I woke up to heavy fog, which slowed us down but not much. It took two hours to drive from Boone to Greensboro and along the way we listened to Dr. Laura. The first caller had met a man over the internet and wondered if she should make arrangements to see him in person. "Are you *crazy?*" Dr. Laura asked. She insisted that the man was a pedophile and that the woman had no business dating until her children were grown and out of the house. "They don't need to see their mother chasing after men," she said. "You're a *mom,* not a big sister."

"What a bitch," Lisa said, and I agreed.

October 17, 2003
Memphis, Tennessee

I asked the concierge at the Peabody hotel where I might get a trim and she sent me to a black barbershop. What's strange is that haircutting is the most segregated service I can think of. You never see white people in a black barbershop or vice versa, the thinking being that a person can specialize in only one texture of hair. It's ridiculous, really, but there you have it.

The place I was sent to was on a desolate street five blocks from the hotel, and when I walked in a worried-looking black man asked me what I wanted. I told him, and the barber looked at his customer, saying that if I wanted a haircut, he guessed I could go upstairs.

Upstairs was the women's department, a salon. A stylist stood sewing extensions onto a client's head as a young man sat in the adjacent chair, looking on and talking about biscuits. Like the barber, the stylist asked what I wanted and seemed surprised when I asked for a haircut. "I'm sort of busy," she said. "You could come back tomorrow or...no, I guess...can you give me a few minutes?"

It looked as though she were stitching something directly into her customer's scalp. The needle went in and out and as I waited I leafed through a copy of *Black Hairstyles*. It was a celebrity issue, the cover featuring Lil' Kim, who wore a blue bob sprayed with the Chanel logo. I thought of asking for the same thing, but more than that I thought about leaving. I didn't worry the woman would give me a bad haircut—with me there's nothing to lose—rather, I worried the experience would be too awkward. It was clear that I didn't belong, but the stylist, who introduced herself as Shelly, went out of her way to make me feel comfortable. She finished sewing the back of the woman's head, and then she ushered me into the chair, asking me which razor length I preferred. I didn't know, so she attached something to the shaver and started in. "The trouble I have is to blend," she said. "Sometimes I do the bottom too much and then the top be looking heavy."

As she cut my hair, she resumed the conversation she'd been having with the previous customer and the young man in the chair. The comedian Bernie Mac was discussed, and then the topic moved to old people. "My grandmother is crazy," the woman with the new hair said. "Like all the old ladies, she always be putting powder in her underpants before leaving the house."

The hairdresser nodded and I wanted to say, *She what?* Then the woman told of the time she'd attended a funeral and left the bathroom with her dress tucked into her pantyhose. "I mean my ass was hanging *out*," she said, and the young man and the hairdresser doubled over laughing.

Though I was invited to join the conversation, my contributions failed to make much of an impact. The women pretended to be amused, but the young man acted as though I were taking something from him. Every now and then he'd look me in the eye and harden his face until I turned away. While touring in the United States, I'm reminded of the needling tension that exists between white and black people, the almost constant sense of competition. *They're funnier than we are,* I think. *Quick, say something casual and amusing.*

After my haircut, I returned to the hotel and noticed that the player piano had a tip jar on it.

October 19, 2003
Chicago, Illinois

Lisa sent me an *Atlantic* magazine article concerning a condition called apotemnophilia, an attraction to the idea of being an amputee. Trans people often say they feel trapped in the wrong body, and so too does this lot, sort of. It's the right body, there's just too much of it. One woman spoke of looking in the mirror and seeing herself as she was meant to be—armless. I thought this was a typo and that she'd really meant *harmless,* but later in the paragraph she got more specific and expressed her lifelong dream of matching three-inch stumps. Another woman had a similar feeling, but lower. "I don't understand why," she said, "but I always knew that I didn't want my legs."

The author of the article met most of her subjects through a chat room. No reputable doctor will amputate a healthy limb, so the apotemnophiliacs share information concerning hospitals in South America and Eastern Europe and little tips for those desperate enough to take matters into their own hands (at least while they still have them). One man gave himself a local anesthetic and stuck his unwanted leg in a woodchipper. It was all planned out in advance, the drive to the hospital and everything. Another man tore into his leg with a chain saw and was devastated when he woke up in the recovery room hearing, "Good news, Mr. Yardley. We think we can sew it back on." They couldn't, though, and so the story serves as one of those medical miracles, only in reverse.

I like to think I can wrap my mind around just about anything, but this really throws me, especially the woman who wants both her arms amputated. Does she not understand what this means? (I picture her on a street corner in New York. *"Taxi!"*) She'll never again tie her shoes or swat a mosquito, and I don't know how she thinks she'll get back into that chat room she's so fond of. To me it sounds crazy, but those who had rid themselves of unwanted limbs claimed to have no regrets. The man with the woodchipper, for instance; he wouldn't have it any other way.

I read the article on the plane to Chicago, and en route to the hotel my cab passed a minor accident between a car and a minivan. Both drivers were leaning against their vehicles talking into cell phones as a small crowd gathered to watch. I saw a boy of around twelve, a man in a black turban, and then, on the sidewalk, a woman with no legs tooling up in an electric wheelchair. Normally I would have felt sorry for her— not that she wanted my pity, not that it does anyone any good, but still, I'd have wished that things could have been different. Now, though, I looked at her thinking, *You made your bed, sister, now lie in it.*

November 7, 2003
Paris
According to an article in *USA Today,* American hunters are now baiting bears with candy. Factories sell their castoffs in

huge blocks—a fifty-pound lump of Snickers or Baby Ruth bars. The sugar is ruining the bears' teeth and one was pictured, her mouth open to display the decayed incisors. What does an animal do when it has a toothache? Does it bang its face against a rock, hoping to knock the tooth out, or does it just dumbly suffer?

They made a mistake on the plane and brought me a Bloody Mary rather than the Bloody Mary mix I had requested. The same thing happened exactly two years ago. I accidentally took a sip and then sent it back, wishing my sip had been much larger. It's the third time this year I've tasted alcohol. Last spring at Amy's I mistook white wine for water. Then at the wedding, Manuela's mom stuck her champagne-soaked finger in my mouth. I wish I could accidentally mistake a joint for a cigarette.

December 3, 2003
Paris

Last Christmas I gave Paul a lemon-size plastic monkey I'd bought at a flea market in Budapest. Wind him up, and instead of eating the banana he's holding, he uses the other hand and masturbates. Surprise! Lisa saw the monkey while visiting last month, and after she said how disgusting it was, Paul hid it in her bag of decaffeinated espresso. He figured she'd find it the following morning, but the following morning Lisa drank regular espresso. Then she drove to Winston-Salem, picked up Bob, and proceeded to the mountains to visit her in-laws, who were preparing to move into a retirement community. Mr. Evans has Alzheimer's but is still able to complete simple tasks—making coffee, for instance. He got into Lisa's bag of espresso, and you just have to wonder what conclusion he drew, this retired Baptist minister who found a masturbating monkey hidden in his daughter-in-law's coffee.

December 7, 2003
Paris

It was cold and cloudy yesterday and I stayed inside until three. The neighborhood was crowded with Christmas shoppers, and I milled around for a while, wandering the narrow streets between the rue du Four and the indoor market. At a store on the rue Princesse I bought a little vase, and then I walked to Sèvres-Babylone, passing one fancy shop after another. It's almost embarrassing, this neighborhood. Here's the place that sells cashmere oven mitts; here's the one specializing in hand-embroidered sponges. I walked as far as the rue de Rennes, where tens of thousands of unemployed people were marching for their annual Christmas bonus.

The demonstration was sponsored by the French Communist Party, and every now and then you'd see one of their red banners calling for solidarity. In America you'd expect the Communists to be either college students or crackpots, but here they looked much like anyone else: the middle-aged man in the smart coat, the blond grandmother with a quilted handbag. They weren't decrying the silly shops lining the neighboring streets, just demanding their place before the cash registers.

December 22, 2003
Paris

I turned on the TV last night and watched part of a program in which a group of Englishmen had to run around London collecting women's pubic hair. A few samples were plucked willy-nilly off toilet seats, but for the most part the men were straightforward and simply asked for what they wanted. "Excuse me," they'd say, pulling a pair of scissors from their back pockets, "I'm involved in a sort of contest and was wondering if you could possibly..."

They obviously didn't go to just *anyone;* rather, they sought the sorts of women who'd consider their proposition and think, *Well, it's not like I'm doing anything with it.*

At an appointed hour the men regrouped to see who had the greatest harvest. It was no surprise to see that the handsomest guy had the most pubic hair, but still it struck me as a little unfair. *You just got by on your looks,* I thought.

He had a pillowcase practically full of it, while the clear loser had little more than a tuft. As a punishment, he was forced to eat a pizza topped with what he'd collected. The others reminded him that there was cheese on it too, but come on, which topping are you really going to remember?

2004

January 15, 2004
San Francisco, California

Paul's new way of making people uncomfortable is to answer the phone as if he's in the middle of a fight with his wife. I called last night, and he picked up, shouting, "Goddamn you, Kathy!"

February 3, 2004
Paris

At dinner last night I attempted to tell Manuela about an autopsy I'd witnessed. She doesn't speak English, but I did all right until the wrap-up.

"All in all it was pretty ... pretty ..."

And I realized that I'd forgotten the word for "unforgettable."

February 11, 2004
London

While ironing shirts I listened to a talk-radio program, conscious of how different it was from one you'd hear in America. Unlike Rush Limbaugh, who is smug, and Bob Grant, who is even smugger, this host was fairly mild. Stories surprised him, but he never took the opportunity to judge or bully. This made him sort of dull, actually. A talk show needs a central character, and if the host won't step up to the plate, the responsibility falls to the callers, who aren't on air long enough to really establish themselves. Yesterday's topic was an eighteen-year-old university student who'd sold her virginity on the internet. The highest bidder was a forty-year-old man who paid eighty-four hundred pounds. It could have kept an American talk show going for weeks, but here no one seemed to care. "Well, I suppose it's her right," the callers said. "And university fees *have* gone up, haven't they?"

Even an old woman failed to muster any outrage. "I'm in the process of redoing my bathroom," she told the host, "and am having a devil of a time locating the right-sized washbasin." When the man steered her back toward the topic at hand she said only, "It *is* a good amount of money, eighty-four hundred pounds."

February 22, 2004
London

Early this week Tiffany called. Hugh and I were eating dinner, so I let the machine get it, thinking I'd phone her back the next evening. The following night I had an interview and so I put it off for another day, and another day after that. I was tying my shoes yesterday afternoon when Paul called, warning me that Tiffany wanted money. "She doesn't want to ask Dad for it, so she figured she'd go to you," he said.

I just sent her five hundred dollars, but it's not nearly enough to get her out of the hole she's in. A few weeks back she had her foot operated on. The check Dad sent her for Christmas is long gone and now she's out of work and three months behind on her rent. I could afford to send her more, but no amount would fix the mess she's made of her life. "She needs to go back to the fucking womb," Paul said, and that pretty much sums it up.

Nothing makes sense with Tiffany. She's on medication for

her feet and just filed a police report, claiming that while she was sleeping, someone broke in and stole twenty of her painkillers. It is significant that whoever it was did not steal *all* of her painkillers and that, before leaving, he or she took the time to do her dishes. I'm guessing she sold the pills and needed a police report in order to get a new prescription, but you never know with Tiffany. She's told me herself that when she gets money, she spends it wildly: "That's what we poor people *do*."

In her stories she doles out cash to those less fortunate than herself. She pays her landlady extra. She tosses twenties to the homeless. But I'm not sure I believe that either. Self-employment is not working for her, but to hear her tell it, she is physically unable to use her baking skills. "Don't you understand? I can't use my hands. I *can't*." They work just fine when it comes to cementing broken crockery to sheets of plywood but are apparently incapable of turning on a mixer.

Before the foot operation, Tiffany injured her hand, and before that she needed money for a root canal. She's had a bad year but seems to think that things like this will never happen again. Your teeth only need fixing once. Your left foot gets fucked up and then you can just cross it off the list. The older she gets, the more often she will break, yet she would never put aside money for an emergency. Tiffany prides herself on her poverty, speaks as though it were an accomplishment. She's of the belief that the best thing you can do for the poor is become poor yourself—that way you can talk to the homeless and "really connect" with them.

"If I were you, I'd tell her to call your father," Hugh says, not realizing that no matter who she calls, Tiffany is still my problem. When Dad dies, she will go through her inheritance and wind up exactly where she is now. Nothing will change.

"I keep telling her she needs to set a goal," Dad says. "I tell her she needs to get into voice-over work." He talks as if giving her advice amounts to something, as if she's going to run with it and thank him one day for being right. It doesn't take a genius to get out of debt. If you want money you have to work, but she seems incapable of holding down a job.

February 23, 2004
London

After wandering through bookstores yesterday, I went to the British Museum for a piece of cake. Beside me sat an English family with three children, the youngest of whom was in a wheelchair. The boy looked happy enough, but surely it was momentary. A pleasant half hour in the café and then it was back to a lifetime of being patronized and stared at. I was just admiring his bravery when his mother rolled him away from the table, and I saw that his leg was in a cast. Then I noted that the chair was a rental and put it together that he wasn't crippled, just laid up for a few weeks. This sort of thing has happened before, and it always leaves me feeling betrayed— as if the child had intentionally aroused my pity.

February 24, 2004
London

I called Tiffany last night and listened to her talk for two straight hours. The monologue began with a question, the only one she managed to ask: "Do you know who Homunculus was?"

To hear it from Paul, she's a complete madwoman, but when telling a story on her own, Tiffany can sound quite reasonable. Then she tells the story a second and third time, and things start to fall apart. At one point during her recent hospital stay, one of the doctors asked if she might be more comfortable in the psychiatric wing. "And I told him, 'This isn't about me being crazy, this is about you providing health care. The first line of the Hippocratic oath reads, "Do no harm," and you did

29

harm, man. *That's* what this is about, and you know what? If I'd seen you treat someone else the way you treated me, I would have written your ass up, because it isn't right.' I said, 'You'd better give me a pass to go outside and smoke because, you know what, sitting in this room and *not* having a cigarette is not a fucking option. It's just not.'"

Before going to the hospital Tiffany had arranged to read to the blind. It was volunteer work and her one day on the job has given her a new platform. "If everybody cared about their fellow man, we wouldn't have these fucking problems. The woman up the street hits her daughter and I don't call the cops. Instead, I go up to her and say, 'Hey, let me watch your fucking kid for a while.' And you know, David, if everybody did that, people wouldn't have to grow up the way we did."

Paul had warned me that Tiffany would ask for money, but she didn't. "Dad sent me a thousand dollars and you know what I did? I fucking gave it to this guy I know who has cancer, because that's what you do."

March 25, 2004
London

Up the street from us, on a corner not far from the park, is a mansion surrounded by a high brick wall. The owner recently had his yard spread with manure, and you can smell it from blocks away. Hugh and I passed last night on our way home from dinner and have taken to calling it "The House at Poo Corner."

March 28, 2004
London

There's a double-decker bus that goes from London to Oxford every thirty minutes or so and even has a toilet. The ride lasts around an hour depending on traffic, which wasn't bad yesterday. Hugh and I paid our fare and took seats on the upper level, across the aisle from a Chinese woman who loudly talked on her cell phone from the moment she boarded until she got off in some small town twenty minutes outside Oxford. She was an unattractive person with a lumpy nose and oversize teeth. Her feet were small, and she wore white sneakers with round toes.

After half an hour, Hugh threatened to take her phone and throw it out the window. He didn't say it to her, of course, just to me. Still, I worried he might do it, and that made me anxious. I assumed from the woman's laugh that she was talking to a friend, but what if I was wrong? She could have been speaking to a dying parent hooked up to machines in a Chinese hospital. Most likely my first guess was correct. It was a friend, and the woman either didn't know or didn't care that it was considered rude to talk so long and so loudly in an enclosed space. When we reached her stop and she descended the stairs, I started applauding and was joined by everyone on the upper deck. Everyone but Hugh, who hissed that I was being rude.

We spent our time in Oxford wandering around the Ashmolean Museum, and at five, we walked to Queen's Lane to catch our bus back to London. While standing there waiting, I noticed a fellow in his mid-thirties smoking a hand-rolled cigarette. His hair was shoulder-length, braided into furry white person's dreadlocks, and he wore a leather jacket over a patterned sweater. The guy said he needed twenty p. to catch the bus home, and after getting a no from Hugh and the four people who were standing in front of him, he turned to me. I was looking up at the sky, distracted, and said, "I'm sorry, but no."

"You don't sound like you're sorry," the guy said. "You're sorry what? You're sorry because you're ugly?"

He hadn't been hostile toward anyone else, but something about me seemed to set him off, and vice versa.

"Just leave me alone," I said.

"Well, *you* started it." We glared at each other and for a moment I almost wished that he would push me or throw a punch. Most likely I'd have lost the fight, but I felt willing to at least try, which is unlike me. How had *I* started anything? Was I the one who had approached a total stranger? Was I the one who asked for money?

Hugh would like to go back in time and attend Oxford in the year 1910. I'd like to go back in time and wait on the opposite side of the street. The bus would arrive, and I'd catch it at the last possible second—thus avoiding the guy with the dreadlocks. It's an egregious waste of time travel, but the incident left a horrible taste in my mouth, and I've been thinking of it obsessively. "Do you have twenty p.?" Well, of course I did. So did everyone else. We just didn't have it for *him*.

On the bus home I thought about how ugly I am and wished that things were otherwise. After arriving in London, I bought a newspaper and searched it for people who were less attractive than me, wondering if they'd have given the beggar twenty p. Finally, I thought of how I'd applauded when the Chinese woman got off the bus, and I decided that the incident with the dreadlocked beggar had been my punishment. Of course, things don't really work that way. Do they?

April 7, 2004
London
Yesterday afternoon I had my meeting with Age Concern, a charitable organization devoted to the needs of the Westminster elderly. I arrived at the office a few minutes early and gave my name to the secretary, who transcribed it as *Sid Harris*.

"All right, then, Sid," she said. "You just have a seat and I'll let you know when Mr. Walsh is off the phone."

I wanted to say that it was all one word, *Sedaris,* but worried that I might embarrass her, so I sat down, no longer myself but a Sidney, shortened to Sid. After a few minutes the secretary picked up the phone and dialed a number. "Still busy," she told me. A minute later she tried again. "Mr. Walsh, I've got a Sid Harris to see you."

He said something into his end of the receiver, and she smiled at me, saying, "He's on his way, love."

Harry Walsh turned out to be Irish, and I guessed him to be in his early forties, on the small side, with a full head of copper-colored hair. He led me upstairs to an empty room and we sat at the conference table, where he looked over my application for volunteer work.

For the first half hour the interview moved right along. I told him that I was hoping to visit elderly shut-ins and perform whatever small tasks needed doing. I'd prefer to clean, but if someone needed their shopping done or wanted to be wheeled to the park, I'd be happy to do it. I said I was available Monday through Friday from now until May 13, when I leave to go to Australia and then the United States.

"What you want is something we call 'a befriending position,'" Harry said, "but given your availability, I'm afraid it's impossible. Befriending is something that continues for years and won't work if you're leaving the country a month from tomorrow."

"Well, it doesn't *have* to be a problem," I said. "Don't you have anyone who's going to die on or about May thirteenth?"

Harry sat forward in his chair and folded his hands together. "Ours is not a death culture," he explained. "This

33

organization is not about dying but about celebrating the time that these people have left."

"All right," I said. "I'm sure that some of these befrienders must go on vacation. Can't I be a substitute and step in for a few days or weeks at a time?"

He started in about a training program and I said that I already knew how to clean toilets and wash windows.

"I imagine you do," he said. "I'm talking about sensitivity training. Dealing with the emotional concerns of our clients." This is just such bullshit in my opinion. These are people who survived the Second World War. Do they really need anyone asking how they feel about missing the toilet? "Does it make you sad when that happens? Do you want to talk about it?"

No. They just want the turd off the floor, and if I'm willing to do it for no money, then what's the problem?

May 5, 2004
London

It was cold and raining yesterday. Thunderstorms arrived in the afternoon, just as I was leaving Miss Babington's second-floor apartment. She lives in Maida Vale, and Age Concern sent me to help her unpack some of her belongings. "Oh, no, you don't," she said as I reached for my umbrella. "There's no way I'm letting you out in this weather." And so I stayed. In her kitchen are half a dozen large plastic tote bags, the kind Hugh and I use as laundry hampers. They're full of things she'd taken from her previous apartment, and I carried them into the living room so she could go through them and throw away whatever was unnecessary. The first included a clunky cassette player. "Now, this," she said, "I've been looking for this."

She set it on a rickety table next to the couch and then put it back into the bag, saying she'd sort it out later. The second bag was full of wrapped, unopened Christmas presents. "People send me these." She sighed. "I don't know why. But they do." In the end, each bag was sent back to the kitchen. "I'll sort it out later, but right now it's too exhausting. Have some coffee, why don't you?"

May 6, 2004
London

The English edition of *Dress Your Family* was released today, and I began my week of publicity by sitting for a half dozen regional BBC interviews, all of which were conducted long distance and sent down the wire from the main broadcasting house in London. None of the hosts had read the book, so to keep things moving I asked them what their town was like and listened as they ticked off the various splendors of Leeds or Brighton. The one exception was the host of Radio Jersey, who described the island as "an offshore pile of money with alcoholics clinging to it."

May 10, 2004
Dublin, Ireland

In the exotic-gift section of the Brown Thomas department store I came upon a small packet of tea leaves, the label reading, RARE CHINESE OOLONG HAND-PICKED BY SPECIALLY TRAINED MONKEYS.

I thought of the price—twenty dollars per gram—and then I imagined a group of unemployed peasants: "Goddamn monkeys coming over here and taking our jobs."

May 16, 2004
Bangkok, Thailand

In Bangkok it is not unusual to see half a dozen boiled duck heads heaped up on a curb. You also come across plastic bags that were used as takeout cups, the coconut milk fermenting in the 98-degree heat. You see sidewalks strewn with newspapers and tin cans, and yet I got fined for throwing a cigarette butt into the street.

They got me near the national museum as Hugh and I were walking toward the Grand Palace. The officer was dressed in a dark green uniform—the pant legs tucked into boots—and, after saying something in Thai, he led me across the street and into a tent where a dozen other officers sat at long picnic tables. I was ordered to write my name and address on a form, and when I asked what this was all about, the guy pointed to a sign announcing a thousand-baht fine for spitting or littering. It was written in two languages, but I'm guessing the ones on the street were only in Thai and that this was a way of squeezing money from unsuspecting tourists. Though it sounds like a lot, a thousand baht is only twenty-five dollars, not the end of the world, but still it bothered me.

Hugh, on the other hand, could not have been happier. "That's what you get," he said, and "Maybe it'll teach you a lesson." I swore that it did not, but for the rest of the day I crushed my cigarettes on the ground and carried the butts in my fist until I came across a garbage can. So maybe it did teach me a lesson.

Our driver to the airport this evening asked us to refer to him as Sammy III. He was in his early fifties, a farmer making ends meet until his rice crop was ready for harvest. At first, he seemed pious and long-suffering. "In Bangkok no money, no nothing," he said. We paid a toll to travel on an elevated highway and as the cab rose toward the horizon, the expression changed to "No money, no honey." By the time we reached the airport he was saying, "No money, no pussy," and telling us that a young whore costs much more than a tired old one. "The old one all stretched out," he said. "I with a lady last week and she say, 'Hey, take your ring off!'"

"Then I say, 'That not my ring, that my watch.' Get it? She think it my finger but it my fist up there! Get it?" It's hard to tell a joke in a foreign language and harder still when your passengers have never stuck so much as a tongue depressor into a member of the opposite sex. Sammy got a kick out of it, though. "Get it?" he kept saying. "Get it?"

June 2, 2004
New York City
I went by the office yesterday and met with Don, who seems completely lost now. "I've been thinking about sending those things that all the people are doing now just to keep up," he said. "You need to do things like that for business, so I think I'll get on the trusty thing there and give it a try."

"That's good," Cristina said, and then she handed me a stack of contracts and an Hermès watch in a beautiful orange box.

June 7, 2004
Pittsburgh, Pennsylvania
Ronald Reagan died on Saturday at the age of ninety-three, and I didn't find out about it until yesterday afternoon. My escort tacked it onto a story about her cat, Rusty, and though I don't remember exactly how she did it, I do recall being impressed that she could join two such dissimilar bits of information. Susie K. is sixty-two, with dyed red hair and a passion for male animals. "All my pets are boys," she said. "Even the fish. I like being the only woman in the house."

When I asked where she was from, Susie crushed her ciga-rette into the ashtray. "God gave the world an asshole, David, and it's called Johnstown, Pennsylvania."

Before my first radio interview we were supposed to go to a small independent store for a drop-in signing. "The owner is an old queen," she said. "I'm not putting him down, but, David, that's just what he is—a queen." The traffic was bad, though, and so she had to call him and reschedule. "If I canceled, he'd break down and cry," she told me. "I mean, he's got baklava and everything!"

Susie then told me that the Big Mac was invented in Pittsburgh, as was the Egg McMuffin. "I've got a brochure in here somewhere," she said and handed me a pamphlet titled "Pittsburgh First." Aside from the Egg McMuffin, Pennsylvanians came up with the recumbent chair, bifocals, flashcubes, and the idea of attaching an eraser to the end of a pencil. "You laugh, but it's true," she said.

Susie on politics: "I'll tell you, David, that I'm a Republican, lifelong, and I've never missed an election, not even for school boards and crap like that. My husband and I like to go to rallies and so forth, and I've gotten to where I can look at a woman and tell you how she votes. Now, David, I'm not saying that Democratic women are ugly, but they are fat—big as houses most of them. If you see a big woman with bad shoes and no makeup, I'll guarantee you she's no Republican."

She looked into the rearview mirror and patted her hair. "Aside from their looks, Democratic women lack...well, vaginal tenacity. That's what I call it. The female equivalent of balls. Now tell me I'm wrong."

June 8, 2004
Philadelphia, Pennsylvania
On the way to the airport this morning, Susie told me about an author who arrived at the baggage claim wearing socks with sandals. "No makeup, hair like a rat's nest. She'd written a book on macramé and was convinced it was going to be the next big thing." We missed our turn and she headed around the

block. "Now, if she wasn't a Democrat, I don't know who is." Then she told a story about visiting an Italian funeral home and watching someone spit in the face of a deceased bookie.

The Pittsburgh departure gates are reached by a train that leaves from a station just beyond the security check. I had just boarded when an elderly woman in a nylon tracksuit bolted through the closing door and held it open with her arms. "Phil!" she called. "Phil, you're missing the damn train!" Along with her tracksuit, she wore puffy white sneakers and athletic socks. A recorded voice announced that we were being held up by a passenger who'd interfered with the doors, and as Phil rushed in, I saw the woman's face flush to scarlet. "You damned dummy," she shouted. "Now look what you did!"

June 17, 2004
Houston, Texas

The host of last night's show had problems reading his notes and announced in his introduction that I'd gotten my start with the National Public Rodeo.

June 22, 2004
Santa Fe, New Mexico

The other day in San Francisco someone gave me a medical catalog called "Health Edu" (short for *education*). It's full of devices and visual aids, such as the "empathy belly pregnancy simulator" and "the shaken-baby model." You can buy rolls of fat that apparently feel like the real thing, and diabetic foot substitutes that come with four separate types of ulcers. I leafed through the catalog while the plane was boarding and felt my fellow passengers looking over my shoulder. I hoped they assumed I was a doctor but more likely they tagged me as a pervert, especially after I fell asleep to a full page of dilated rubber vaginas. Pocket pussies, my brother calls them.

July 10, 2004
London

Allison sent an envelope from Little, Brown UK marked *For Hugh. Don't read, David.* I opened it and saw a review of *Dress Your Family.* "When American humorists do it well, there's nobody better," the first line read. "Think Thurber or Parker." I put it back and resealed the envelope, imagining a second line reading, *But when they do it badly—think Sedaris—there's nobody worse.*

Is it a good quality or a bad quality that I imagine all my reviews to be terrible? Is one more narcissistic than the other?

July 13, 2004
London

Before going to bed I watched part of a show called *101 Things Removed from the Body.* The host was young and jovial and would frequently say things like "Ouch!" or "Talk about a pain in the neck!" Among the items extracted from a head were a steak knife, a nail, and a drill. A man was walking and when he tripped, the bit was driven up into his nose. Another man tripped while carrying a chopstick, which speared his eye like a cocktail onion. A third person was working on a construction site and fell face-first onto a steel rebar.

"Dwayne had an eye for the ladies," the host said. "Unfortunately, it was skewered by a metal rod and is now lying at the bottom of a hospital bin!" There was a javelin through the neck, a tornado-driven two-by-four buried in a woman's face, and on and on until I couldn't take it anymore.

July 23, 2004
La Bagotière

Mary Beth and Christophe came to dinner with their three rowdy children and by the end of the evening I felt as if I'd been violently mugged. Every sense was jangled, every bit of flesh sore from having been yanked or mauled. They arrived at eight, and thirty seconds later Nicolas and three-year-old Rose were in my office, screaming into the electric fan, which distorted their voices in a way they found amusing. I'd had the sense to hide my computer, but if I hadn't, it would be broken by now, not just on the blink, but in pieces. Everything in the house was touched with juice-covered hands: the freshly cleaned windowpanes, the curtains, the spiderwebs. At the end of the evening, we noticed footprints in the bathtub, and I saw that the basement curtains had been torn from their rings.

Dinner was complete bedlam. Rose announced after four cartons of juice that she had no intention of eating, so instead she stood beside the table and jumped up and down, laughing when the plates and silverware, the lamps and candlesticks jumped with her. Nicolas stormed over to the front stairs and pouted, furious that there was a potato on his plate, while his brother ate half a sausage and ran into the yard to terrorize the people next door. "What are you going to do?" Mary Beth said, resigned to it all.

She'd brought a friend with her, a Hawaiian woman named Marcie who sat across the table with her well-behaved ten-year-old-son. An only child, the boy said *please* and answered questions. He joined the fray after dinner, but you could tell that his heart wasn't in it and that he'd rather have curled up on the daybed with a good book.

Mary Beth and Christophe don't ask their kids to lower their voices. Rather, they just shout to be heard over the din.

"So, have you seen the Foxes lately?" Mary Beth screamed. She was referring to the American couple who live in Ségrie-Fontaine. *"They said I can come see them, but I have to come alone, without the children. Can you believe that?"*

Well, yes, I thought.

After they left, Hugh walked barefoot through the house, noticing the sticky spots on my freshly waxed floors. I'd been cleaning in advance of Jeff and Annie, and today I'll have to start all over.

August 5, 2004
Erquy, France
On our first full day of vacation Hugh and I sat for haircuts in the only French barbershop I've ever seen. There was no pole, but it was for men only and reminded me of the kind of place you might find in England or the States—not dirty, but slightly untidy, with out-of-date magazines on a coffee table and flyers pinned to the walls. The barber was warm and talkative. "Your French is excellent," he said, and I knew that had Hugh gone first, he would not have offered me the compliment. When not discussing the weather, we listened to the radio, which was tuned to a talk station. One moment the caller was discussing jam and the next he was carrying on about parakeets. "How did he get from one subject to the other?" I asked, and the barber shook his head, saying, *"N'importe quoi,"* which translates to either "Whatever" or "Anything goes."

I worried it would be hard to diet on vacation, but I've lost more weight at the hotel than I would have by staying put and riding my bike twenty miles a day. Our meals are included, and though they give the illusion of bounty, each course is smaller than the one before. Last night started with a thin slice of pâté followed by an *araignée*—a crab that looks like a spider. It was large, but, unlike a lobster, with its weighty claws and tail, there was really no meat to be had—a table-spoon, maybe, and this after laboring half an hour with a shell cracker and a thin, two-pronged fork.

"This is just busywork," I complained to Hugh. "They might as well have given us a stack of Popsicle sticks and told us to make a lampshade."

Whatever calories the crab provided were burned off trying to secure them, and so I'm not counting it as part of dinner. Then came a small lump of fish accompanied by a taste of ratatouille, a thimble of rice, three mushrooms, and a boiled potato the size of a molar. I skipped dessert and went instead to a stand near the fishery, where I got a scoop of ice cream.

September 21, 2004
Vienna, Austria

Before going to bed I appeared on a local television show. *Treffpunkt Kultur* was hosted by a woman named Barbara, whose English was good but slightly less than perfect. Her minor mistakes embarrassed her, and so the interview was conducted in German, the translated questions delivered to me by way of an earpiece. In addition to her culture show, Barbara cohosts the evening news. I asked if she wears a different outfit every night, and she said no, that she tries to be as much like her viewers as possible. "They are in their homes saying, 'Oh, I see that Barbara is wearing that same blouse from Thursday.'"

There was a ruckus at my post office in Paris yesterday, a man with an accent shouting at someone behind the counter. "You can't aggress people like that," my clerk said. "Lower your voice, sir. Behave yourself!"

The man continued, and after he'd left, I asked where he was from. "Eastern Europe," the clerk sniffed. "The *new* Europe. Take a good look, because that's what we're becoming."

The woman behind me agreed 100 percent. "Every time you get on the bus, there they are," she said. "Savages!"

September 25, 2004
London

A young woman approached my signing table a few months back in Boston, and after asking her name, I hit her with the most ridiculous question I could think of. "Tell me, Jennifer, how long has it been since you last...touched a monkey?"

I expected "Never" or "It's been years," but instead she took a small step back, saying, "Oh, can you smell it on me?"

It turns out that she works for Helping Hands, an organization that trains monkeys to work as slaves for paralyzed people—which was odd, as I'd just read an article about them. It was in the *New York Times* and showed a shriveled-looking capuchin loading a disc into a CD player. The Helping Hands people would probably object to my use of the word *slave,* but there was something unsettling about the photograph, a weariness in the monkey's eyes as he turned to face his paralyzed master. Then again, I suppose it beats picking tea leaves in China.

The Helping Hands woman was very nice and sent me a booklet on her organization, which was waiting for me when I returned from my tour. Included was a photograph of a monkey named Kukla, who sat turning the pages of a book, studying them as if she were actually reading. I showed it to Hugh, who pointed out that it was *my* book the monkey was reading. And I don't know if it was pride or what, but I sent off a check for two thousand dollars and have been invited to tour the center next fall.

October 2, 2004
Hamburg, Germany

In the bathroom of last night's bookstore I saw an odd sticker applied to the wall above the toilet. On it were two drawings. The first showed a man in the act of peeing. He stood looking straight ahead, his penis in his hand. Normal. This drawing was overlaid with a slashed red circle, the international symbol for "No." The second drawing showed the same man sitting with his pants around his ankles. It wasn't elaborately detailed, but you could sense that he was happier here, content that his actions, however inconvenient, were making the world a better place.

According to the bookstore manager, the sticker had been applied by a female employee, who hoped it might lead to serious reform. It's the most futile campaign ever waged, as every man feels blessed when it comes time to pee. The world could be falling apart, his personal life in shambles, but still he thinks, *Look at me! I can do this standing up!* Long lines outside the women's bathroom make us feel even luckier, and I'm afraid there's no way on earth we're going to give that up.

October 3, 2004
Munich, Germany

I had two interviews yesterday, the first with *Playboy* and another with a youth magazine called *Neon*. The second reporter wanted to talk about Christmas—the stresses and strains of, mainly—and so we spoke for an hour or so. When we came to the subject of shopping, he told me about Verdi, a German labor union that's pressing for new reforms. They're not against carols per se, but if a store plays more than eight in a row, the union is insisting they either give their employees a raise or let them break for at least five minutes per hour. "Studies show that this kind of music is very anxiety-provoking and can lead to serious mental-health problems," the reporter said.

The October 1 *F.A.Z. Weekly*—a supplement to the *International Herald Tribune*—featured an article on the WC Ghost, a talking device that attaches to the underside of a toilet seat and warns the user to sit down. "Peeing while standing up is not allowed here and will be punished with fines," one of them says. The ghost can be ordered with the voice of either Chancellor Schröder or his predecessor, Helmut Kohl, and the manufacturer sells two million a year. I guess the Germans are really serious about this.

October 8, 2004
Frankfurt, Germany
Sign hung beside the coatrack of last night's restaurant: WE DO NOT TAKE ANY RESPONSIBILITY FOR YOUR WARDROBE. THANK YOU.

October 10, 2004
Paris
The train from Göttingen was practically empty, and the conductor, a broad, cheerful woman in a too-tight uniform, doubled as a waitress. After punching our tickets, she brought us three coffees, which we consumed with a butter cake Hugh had bought the previous day in Frankfurt. It was the best moment of the entire trip. A cold fog had settled in, and at times we could see nothing, then a cluster of trees on a mountaintop, then a field of cows or a red-roofed village. We passed a burning house with a family gathered around it in their bathrobes, a boy holding a cat in his arms.

"Oh," Doris, my German publicist, cried, "I can't look!" As she leaned closer to the window, I realized she'd used the wrong word and had meant to say *I can't see!*

October 11, 2004
Paris

Behind us on our train back to Frankfurt yesterday sat a couple with two children, and as they talked, I thought of similar journeys: Hugh reading some crusty old novel and me lamely guessing what the people around me are talking about. I try to give them the benefit of the doubt, but most often I find myself relying on stereotypes. Passengers in Switzerland are discussing the time, while those in Italy are exchanging recipes. In the Netherlands the topic is dikes, the building and maintenance thereof, and in Germany it's all about peeing while sitting down.

October 14, 2004
New York

A group of Americans at de Gaulle this morning. Soldiers? The men are loud, drinking great steins of beer. Most of them are in jeans and slogan T-shirts, some wearing shorts, and all with baseball caps. The women wear the same thing, their caps turned back to front, making them look like umpires, freaks compared to the Frenchwomen in their carefully chosen travel clothes.

CNN reports on a bake-off between the presidential candidates' wives. First Lady Laura Bush's cookies are oatmeal chocolate chunk, a clear winner, preferred by 67 percent in a random taste test. Teresa Heinz Kerry submits a recipe for pumpkin spice cookies and later disavows it, saying she hates pumpkin. This, it is implied, speaks poorly of her character. We see people on a city street accepting cookies from a reporter. "Not bad," a woman says. On learning it is Laura Bush's, she spits it onto the curb. I laugh, and when a man does the same thing with Teresa Kerry's cookie, I think, *That's not funny.*

October 29, 2004
Pittsburgh

It's always a pleasure spending time with Sally Carpenter, who flits from one topic to the next. "My husband and I are going to Maine for Thanksgiving," she said. "And did you know that in order to break even, Starbucks needs to serve sixty customers an hour? I don't know how they do it, and oh, those stories about voter fraud in Ohio, doesn't it just make your blood boil? I said to my husband, 'I don't know what we'll do for Christmas. We could stay home, or'—say, have you read any good books about India?"

November 3, 2004
Chicago

At midnight Bush was ahead by forty points and now, seven hours later, it's all come down to Ohio, where it could take ten days to count the provisional ballots. That's what the radio says anyway. Bush is up by 130,000 votes, but I'm continuing to hope. This was the best turnout in something like forty years, but still only 63 percent of registered voters went to the polls.

Man on the el grousing about a pair of young women claiming to be college students: "They think rabbits lay eggs and a monkey jumped over the got-damn moon. Stupid bitches don't know shit. Rabbits don't lay no eggs. Go-rilla can't shoot no dice."

November 4, 2004
Saint Paul, Minnesota

Just before I boarded the plane to Minneapolis, CNN announced that Kerry was conceding. There weren't enough provisional ballots to cover the margin, and he didn't want to file for a recount and have the election decided by the courts.

There were maybe two dozen people in the waiting area, and aside from myself, none of them groaned or shook their heads muttering, "Fuck."

Some weren't even watching the TV—the woman behind me, for instance, who sat scolding her three children. "All right, Madison, time out," she said.

The flight attendant greeted us as we boarded the plane. "How are you doing today?" she asked, and I decided that everyone who said "Great" was a Republican and worthy of my contempt. I later decided that anyone who stood still on the moving walkway was a Republican, as was anyone who went through the security line carrying an open beverage. Anyone who does anything even remotely irritating is, from this point on, a Republican.

November 16, 2004
Maui, Hawaii

Hugh and I had dinner with his old friend Alan, who lives on Maui and does some sort of computer-type job at the island's one remaining sugarcane plantation. While eating, the two of them reminisced about their childhoods in Ethiopia. "Hey," Alan said as the dessert menus were handed out, "remember the time our guard and his buddy dragged that man from behind a horse?"

Hugh squinted into space, saying, "Hmmm."

"They tied his feet together and dragged him, oh, it must have been a good quarter of a mile," Alan continued. "Then they jumped up and down on his body. I was only ten but I remember hearing the guy's bones crack."

Hugh was a little fuzzy on the event, which surprised me, as that seems the type of thing a person might recall. "*Why* were they doing that?"

Alan set down his menu. "He'd stolen a jacket and then

tried feeding it to a horse, if you can believe it! The guy was mentally ill, I guess."

"And so they dragged him a quarter of a mile over sharp stones?" I asked.

Preoccupied with their menus, Alan and Hugh nodded as if to say *Of course* or *How much more of a reason do you need?* I thought for the umpteenth time that evening how different my upbringing was from theirs, and then I ordered the pineapple.

November 28, 2004
London

I was in one of the antiques stores on Church Street, looking around and half listening in on the owner and her male friend, who were lounging on leather chairs, a dog on each one's lap. "I don't know what it is," the woman lazily began, "but I always know when I'm reading a book by a Canadian."

"Hmm," the man said.

"I'll go along, giving it a try, and then on page seven or so there's always some mention of Toronto."

"Well, yes. That's one of their cities."

"Horrible writers, the Canadians," the woman said, yawning. "Can't finish their books to save my life."

December 16, 2004
Paris

I walked to the Madeleine late yesterday afternoon to see the crèche, which this year has a Native American theme. Figures wear headdresses and are draped in furs and buckskins. Jesus is barefoot, but everyone else is in moccasins. There's a taxidermied black bear ambling beside the wise men and a wolverine poking its muzzle out from behind the manger. Heads and antlers are mounted on the wall, and a pile of dried corn is offered as a gift. I never knew that this was acceptable—that you just choose a population and cast them. Odder still is that these particular people knew nothing about Jesus until we told them, and even then it was pretty late in the game. I read in yesterday's *Tribune* that the crèche at Madame Tussauds in London has been attacked. That one features David Beckham and Posh Spice as Joseph and Mary, with George Bush as one of the wise men.

December 17, 2004
Paris

On Wednesday Little, Brown made a generous offer for three books. Don called to give me the news and reminisce. "When I first came to this town I got a job for twelve bucks," he said, not specifying if it was twelve bucks a week or twelve a month. This was in 1934, so maybe it was even twelve bucks a year. He ended by saying he'd give me a call in a few weeks, "after the so-called stuff that we call it today," by which he meant the holidays.

2005

January 11, 2005
London

The *Guardian* ran a story on Gerald Allen, an Alabama state representative who wants to ban books with homosexual characters. They can still sell them in shops, but he wants them out of schools and publicly funded institutions, like libraries and state universities. If the book presents a tragic homosexual, the type who suffers and then commits suicide, that's okay. He just doesn't want the happy kind, the ones who, in his words, "promote homosexuality as a healthy and accepted lifestyle." *Which one am I?* I wonder.

January 12, 2005
Paris

The trial has started for Specialist Charles Graner, the alleged ringleader of the Abu Ghraib prisoner-abuse scandal, the one photographed behind a pyramid of naked Iraqis giving the thumbs-up. His lawyer is a man named Guy Womack, and he began his opening argument by asking, "Don't cheerleaders all over America form pyramids six to eight times a year? Is *that* torture?" Aside from the fact that cheerleaders *choose* to form pyramids—and do it fully clothed—I'm struck by his numbers, "six to eight times a year."

Where did he get that from?

January 31, 2005
London

At the banquet dinner the other night in Dublin, I sat between a woman named Geraldine and a man named Tom, who is gay and travels the world to have sex with people. "Take Syria," he said. "Police state, but the men are lovely. It's the same in Egypt. The people have nothing but would offer it in a second. They've a real sense of hospitality, not this stingy, uptight version we've got in the West."

Tom said that the rudest peoples in the world are the South Africans and the Israelis, and then he talked about the European move to ban the swastika, which he pronounced "swaz-teek-ah." "There used be a cleaners, the most popular in Dublin, with that name. Swastika Cleaners, remember them, Jerry?" And the man across the table nodded his head.

February 4, 2005
London

I walked to the Strand yesterday afternoon and was at the intersection of Regent and Oxford when I saw that one of the sidewalks was closed off. A crowd had gathered, and I looked up to see a black man standing on a high scaffold and staring down into traffic. "He's going to top himself," someone said. A minute or so later a policeman stepped out and approached the man, who moved closer to the edge. By this point I was near the tube station, standing beside two young women who were both smoking cigarettes.

"Imagine that he jumps, yeah," one of them said, and the other girl nodded. "And imagine that he lands on one of those poles, yeah. So then imagine that he ends up paralyzed and can't move nothing but his head."

The two of them laughed and another woman turned to them, saying, "Now, that's evil."

"Yeah," the first girl said.

March 13, 2005
La Bagotière

Since company arrived, Hugh and I have been sleeping in the attic, which is ice-cold and crawling with mice. Last night before going to bed he checked the traps he'd recently set and found in one a bit of nose speared with whiskers. "The rest of it seems to have gotten away," he said, and I wondered if this mouse was possibly still alive. *I don't smell anything,* I imagined him remarking to his friends. *Someone's making toast? Really?*

The traps were reset with peanut butter, and Hugh awoke this morning to find a new victim. "Poor thing," he said, as if the mouse had died by accident and not by his hand.

March 24, 2005
Paris

"Chapeau!" Dr. Guig's assistant said in reference to my gums, which are apparently a lot firmer than they were last October. I went yesterday afternoon for my biannual appointment and then met with Dad in front of the Madeleine. Lisa had suggested we visit the Musée Jacquemart-André, so we slowly walked over to the boulevard Haussmann. The museum was holding a Napoleon exhibit and displayed the emperor's toothbrush in a glass case alongside his comb and a few shirt buttons. There were other artifacts as well, but neither of us was terribly interested in them. After a half hour or so we headed to the café and were passed by two children who were running from one room to the next. *"Excusez-moi,"* they called, and when

they circled around and came back our way, Dad stood in the door frame and shouted, "*No!* No running! Got it?" They were French but understood perfectly. "Jesus," he said as we walked away. "Kids running every damn place."

In the café he endorsed Bush's Social Security plan and then moved on to the topic of abortion. "The problem is that you've got guys like Ted Kennedy politicizing it!" This is something he's picked up from Rush Limbaugh. Republicans don't politicize, Democrats do, especially Ted Kennedy. "The Supreme Court had no business getting involved with that," he said. "Their job is to interpret the Constitution, and that's all." He took a sip of his Schweppes and looked out the window. "Your mother was in favor of abortion, but me, I guess I haven't made my mind up."

Before dinner we sat in the living room, and Dad asked how much I had paid for the painting over the fireplace. "You've got to be kidding me," he said when I told him. "Boy, they sure saw you coming, didn't they? I wouldn't give fifty dollars for that thing." I pointed out that it was almost three hundred years old and asked why it shouldn't have cost that much.

"Because it's ugly," he said. "I wouldn't spend two minutes looking at something like that. My Brodersons, on the other hand, every night I sit in the living room and stare at them. My Alice Proctors too. *Cracked Man*—now, *that's* a work of art and I didn't pay more than five hundred dollars for it!"

Over dinner he discussed his diet. "I eat a lot of beans," he said. "A helluva lot of beans, and now I'm into green lentils. You ever try those? What I do is ... " He is fit, though. No one could believe he was eighty-one years old.

March 30, 2005
New York

I met with my accountant yesterday morning, then went to Don's and signed off on some permission requests. Cristina and I were almost finished when he walked in, fresh off the tennis courts. "I see you're talking to our fine young lady," Don said, and I saw that he'd forgotten Cristina's name.

We sat in his office for a while and when Susan stuck her head in the door, he asked me if I'd ever met her. "I'm going to have to get what's-his-name on the phone," he said. "I keep promising him a lunch to thank him for that thing he does. Well, you do it too, of course. It's that thing we all do in this crazy business."

April 12, 2005
Fayetteville, Arkansas

Black female security officer at the Charlotte airport: How you doing, sweetheart?

Me: That's so nice of you to call me sweetheart.

Her: All right, baby. Keep it safe.

April 22, 2005
Spokane, Washington

My hotel overlooks the Spokane River, which traverses a good-size park. I was walking through it yesterday afternoon when I came upon two raggedly dressed men who stood tossing bread scraps to what looked like a colony of groundhogs.

"What are those things?" I asked.

One of the men covered his mouth. "Marmots."

"Come again?" I said.

He repeated himself—"Marmots"—adding that he'd just had a tooth pulled.

A woman then approached carrying a full head of lettuce, and the animals dropped the bread they were eating and waddled over in her direction. The longer I watched, the more marmots I saw, not just on the lawn but farther down the slope, in the big rocks lining the riverbank. The park was beautifully laid out, and walking through it I came upon a carousel and, later, a pond crowded with seagulls. The downtown, too, was very pleasant, and on passing a barbershop I decided to get a trim.

My hair was cut by a man named Randall who was in his midsixties and had a tattoo on his forearm, a blue/black smudge he must have gotten ages ago. "What do marmots eat?" I asked, and he thought for a moment. "Well, marshmallows, mostly."

"No," I said. "I mean, what do they eat in the wild?"

He called to the woman cutting hair on the other side of the room, "Beverly, what do marmots eat in the wild?"

She, too, thought for a moment. "Bread, I guess," she eventually said. "Bread and, you know, anything, really."

I liked the way my barber talked. "I'll go to the riverbank with a bag of marshmallows, and sometimes I'll just linger," he said. "Feed the marmots, feed the seagulls. It's a lot nicer here than out where I live." He named a nearby town that's supposedly noted for its crime. "Lots of drugs and so forth, but I've been pretty lucky, knock on wood." We talked about one thing and another and I told him that in Idaho a barber had once vacuumed my head. "Oh, we do that here too," he said. "Mine's in the shop, though, so today we'll just use Beverly's." Then he ushered me to another chair and pulled out the hose. "Nothing feels better than having your head vacuumed," he said, and while I didn't want to contradict him, I could think of a thousand things that feel better, the first being *not* having your head vacuumed.

May 23, 2005
La Bagotière
Mice got into the chest of drawers and ate the relaxing eye mask that Joan gave Hugh for Christmas. It was a little fabric sack filled with lavender-soaked seeds, and now it's just a rag. They also ate a pair of my underpants.

June 1, 2005
Boston, Massachusetts
Before my reading at the Harvard Book Store I sat down with the event's coordinator, who had a few questions. "First of all, will your monkey be signing or just watching *you* sign?"

"Just watching," I said, though it turned out that she was actually pretty good at signing books—not her name, of course, but she could draw lines and seemed to really enjoy it. She also liked testing the mike, rearranging the shelves, and stealing focus. The store manager had set up a tabletop lectern, and at one point I looked beside me and saw that the monkey had crawled beneath her blanket and was weaving back and forth like a ghost.

During the question-and-answer, she pulled apart a press kit and began licking an envelope. If you've never seen a thing like that, or even if you have, it just melts your heart. "She thinks she's a secretary," the trainer from Helping Hands said, and everyone went, "Awwww."

The monkey arrived before the reading and stayed through the question-and-answer session, at which point she was ready for bed. As Judy took the last question, my little focus stealer curled up on the lectern with her stuffed animal, which looked almost exactly like her. The event was, by all accounts, a great success, and I wish that I could take her everywhere. Unfortunately, most of the stores on my tour have cafés, which means health regulations, which means no monkeys.

*   *   *

There was no sign of Tiffany last night. "She's so much like my sister Lark," Sally said. "She was dumpster-diving before there was even a name for it. Once her false teeth fell down a sewer, and she had to call my mother to help her fish them out. And she did, too—got them with a wad of gum tied to a stick. Can you believe it!"

June 5, 2005
Chicago

My bank card stopped working, so now, instead of cash, I get a little apology printed on a slip of paper. I tried four ATMs and each time it was the same: No, no, no, no. The funds are there, but for some reason they're being withheld. Cindy can fix things on Monday morning, but I needed money for the weekend, so I decided last night to simply ask for it. A few years back I put a tip jar on my signing table, but this is different. A tip is a reward for services rendered, while this was just begging. And it worked wonders. I was in Naperville last night and walked away with 243 dollars, nearly twice what I normally made with a tip jar. In addition to the cash, I also got two cigarettes, half a sandwich, and four unopened sticks of Blistex.

At the end of the night, I decided that maybe I wouldn't call Cindy on Monday morning. Instead I'd just keep begging and see what I wound up with at the end of my tour. What's odd is that I was probably the wealthiest person in the room. A pauper standing outside the bookstore might have earned three dollars in change, but for some reason people love giving money to someone who already has it, at least in theory. "Here's a five," they'd say. It became a weird kind of joke.

One of the women I met at the signing once worked for Target. "Do a lot of people defecate in your store?" I asked.

"Yes," she said. "But how did you know that?" When Hugh worked at the Gap in high school, people used to shit in the dressing rooms, but at Target anywhere is fair game. "A lot of customers use the children's department," the woman said. "And of course, housewares are pretty popular."

June 10, 2005
San Francisco

Ten minutes into last night's reading I realized that my fly was down. In a theater it wouldn't have been so bad. The podium would have hidden me. The audience would have been far away. But here there was just a music stand, and the audience was literally at my feet, eye level with my crotch. I zipped myself up as casually as possible, but everyone saw what was going on, and I could literally feel their embarrassment, which came forth in great waves and stayed with me for the rest of the evening. I thought I could maybe use it to rustle up some extra money, but people were reluctant to give, and I made only $127, this in addition to the $43 I'd gotten earlier at Cover to Cover.

For the first few days my begging was funny, a joke shared by everyone, but now it's gotten strange and I think I need to give it a rest, at least until I get to Alaska. Or Santa Cruz.

I asked a young woman what she did for a living and she pushed her hair away from her face, saying, "You know Koko the gorilla? Well, I used to answer her fan mail."

June 13, 2005
Anchorage, Alaska

Sometimes things happen and I don't know what to do with my face. Take Laura. I met with her a year ago in Australia and learned over dinner that she and her husband had just taken part in the world's largest tractor pull.

"There were over a thousand of us in an unplowed field, and you could see the dust from space!" she said.

I sat there with my mouth open, wondering how I was supposed to react. Do you say, *Great!* or *Big deal* or *I was in space and I didn't see any dust*? Do you laugh or cry or pass out on the floor? I honestly had no idea.

A similar thing happened during last night's book signing. A man approached my table with a couple of paperbacks and told me I should visit this bar. It's in the Yukon and serves something called a Sour Toe cocktail, which supposedly comes with a frostbitten toe lying like an olive in the bottom of the glass. "Now, what do you think of *that*?" he said.

And again, what do you say? "Can you order a virgin Sour Toe?" I asked.

"A what?"

"Say you don't drink alcohol," I said. "Could they make it with ginger ale or something?"

The man looked exasperated. "I guess so."

Then I said, "Oh. All right."

June 14, 2005
Anchorage

The room service at this hotel is incredibly fast, at least at four a.m. I ordered a pot of coffee and by the time I'd opened my blackout curtains it had arrived. I like the Captain Cook and am willing to bet that Ronnie and I are the youngest guests here. When we were walking through the lobby at eleven p.m., the place felt dead and depressing. Then I remembered that it was nighttime and gave it a break. The constant daylight is unsettling. After dinner we took a walk, convinced that it was six o'clock. All the stores seemed to be open, though they were just the ones catering to visitors: Grizzly's Gifts, the Gold Rush, that type of thing. They're a big business, and several of them literally sell shit—petrified moose turds collected in jars or glued to plastic swizzle sticks.

The highlight of my one day off was driving down the Seward Highway with Ronnie while listening to Dr. Laura on the car radio. A couple called saying they had a question, though of course they'd already answered it themselves and were just looking for confirmation. "Here's the situation," the woman began. "I'm the mother of three small children, and my father-in-law is a convicted pedophile."

"Tell me he's in prison where he belongs," Dr. Laura said, and the woman explained that he was on parole and was currently living back home with his wife.

"She took him *back*?" Dr. Laura asked.

"Well, the thing is—"

Dr. Laura interrupted. "I can't believe what I'm hearing! The woman is sick—you got it. She tore up her mother card and now I'm guessing she wants you and the kids to visit. Am I right?"

"Eagle," Ronnie whispered. As we pulled off the road, she pointed to the riverbank, where an impossibly large and angry-looking bird stood on the shore.

"I'd move to Venus before I brought my children into that environment," Dr. Laura said. "You drop by for even a minute and you're as sick as your mother-in-law is. Her and that husband, a man who *preys upon children*!"

"Get your camera," Ronnie said, and as we snapped our respective pictures the eagle took to the air and headed toward the treetops on the opposite bank.

"We don't make deals with predators," Dr. Laura thundered. Then she moved on to her next call.

June 15, 2005
Las Vegas, Nevada

No one in Alaska seems to be in any kind of a hurry. Not the tourists wandering downtown Anchorage, not the desk clerks at the hotel I stayed at, and definitely not the cabdriver, who picked me up at 5:15 yesterday morning and dropped me at the airport a half an hour later. It doesn't sound like much, but this was a really long thirty minutes, the kind that felt like hours. The driver was a woman in her early fifties with a round face and wavy hair that fell to the middle of her back. "Do you know anything about this state?" she asked after putting my bag in the trunk.

I made the mistake of saying no.

"All right," she said, clearing her throat as she pulled away from the curb. The woman spoke very slowly, as if she were being interviewed, and she took care to enunciate every word. "It is often said that Alaska is two and a half times the size of Texas. Now, let me ask you, sir, do you or do you not believe that this is true?"

I hate it when people ask trick questions and decided it was best to just get it over with. "Sure."

She stopped the cab then and turned in her seat to address me. "I had the state surveyor in here," she said. "He was sitting right where you are, and the truth is that we have no idea how big this place is. Oh, they *say* it's two and a half times larger than Texas, but that's just an easy guess. What percentage of Alaska do you think has actually been surveyed?"

And I was like, *Fuck!* Because I don't really care how big her state is. And I certainly didn't want her to stop the car in order to tell me. The woman identified herself as a libertarian. She made several unfavorable references to taxes and complained that politicians in the Lower 48 were trying to turn her home into a national park.

"The caribou population has almost doubled in the last twenty years and do you know why?"

I made a little whimpering sound.

"They started calving at the base of the pipeline. It's a little warmer there and they like the heat." When she asked what I had seen during my visit I made my second mistake and told her I'd gone searching for a bear. She looked at me in the rearview mirror and picked up her dispatch radio, which she held in her left hand. Something was wrong with her right one. It was swollen like a rubber glove filled with water, and she'd treated it with some kind of ointment, which left it slick and painful-looking. "Phyllis to base. Phyllis to base," she said.

I heard a scratchy voice coming from the other end. "Yes," she continued. "What time does Sears open?"

The voice said something I didn't understand, and she made a U-turn and headed back in the direction we had come from. "Do you know how big our bears are?" she asked.

When I told her I'd seen pictures, she laughed and shook her head. "I am going to show you a full-grown grizzly. *Then* we'll see if you *really* want to come across one in the woods."

"I sort of need to get to the airport," I told her, and again she laughed.

"Did you know that every private plane must, by law, be stocked with a gun?" she asked. "It's for protection, in case you have to make an emergency landing and run into one of your deadly friends."

Now the bears were my fault.

"You'll see," she said. The grizzly she drove me to was stuffed and stood in the front window of Sears.

"Get out of the car and stand next to it," she said.

"I can see it from here."

"No. I want you to get out and stand there for a minute.

64

Then tell me that you really want to run into a full-size bear in the middle of the woods."

I got out of the cab and wondered if she was maybe going to drive away and leave me. I would have lost my luggage, but I ultimately wound up losing it anyway. After showing me the bear, she took me the back way to the airport, a sort of long-cut that allowed her to pause and deliver her prepared lecture on private planes. "How much do you think one of those pontoons costs? Not the Cessna, but just the pontoon?"

"Twelve dollars?"

"Try ten thousand," she said. By the time we reached the airport she'd moved on to the state college system. "How much do you think it costs me to send my son to school?" Through the window of the cab I could see a great crowd gathered in front of the Alaska Airlines desk. Men with nets and fishing rods got out of a Humvee, and I watched them walk through the door, taking the space that should have rightfully been mine.

"I told my sons that they were free to do whatever they wanted. 'But first,' I said, 'first, I want that diploma hanging on my wall.' And what do you think they said to me?"

Answers swam through my head as I tossed her two twenties, grabbed my suitcase from the back of the cab, and ran for the door like someone being chased, possibly by bears.

July 3, 2005
Winston-Salem, North Carolina

On the way back to the house last night, Lisa and I passed a place called Digits. "That's where I get my nails done," she said. Then she told me about Paula Abdul, who reportedly got an infection while undergoing a manicure and almost lost a finger.

This was after we saw *War of the Worlds*. The theater was

crowded, and Lisa sat beside a woman in shorts with legs as thick as tree trunks. "I liked that lady," she later said. "The way she jumped up during the suspenseful parts, you could just tell she was a good person."

From the theater we drove to an Italian restaurant, a chain place done up to look like a Tuscan villa. Our waitress was named Iris and used a crayon to write her name on our paper tablecloth.

"Have you had a busy night?" Lisa asked.

Iris told us that the Jehovah's Witnesses were in town for their annual convention.

"Guess the bar was pretty slow, then." I love how easily Lisa connects with people. We later ran into the drugstore for some packing tape and were at the counter for five minutes, talking to the cashier. "When I worked in photo my name tag said only 'Terry,' but now that I'm in management it's got to read 'Terry Anderson,'" the guy said.

"Do people write down your name and call you at home?" Lisa asked.

Terry rang up my packing tape. "All the time."

"Well, you need to take that up with your supervisor," Lisa suggested.

"I tried to, but he says that it's policy and that if I don't want folks calling me, then I should get an unlisted number."

"That's not right," Lisa said.

Terry shrugged. "Tell that to my boss!"

We talked to gas-station attendants, bag boys, anyone who came our way, and then we moved on and talked to more people.

On the drive from Asheville we listened to Joni Mitchell and then to Marvin Gaye. Both records came out in 1976, when I was at Kent State and Lisa was at Mary Baldwin. She has a

CD player in her car, and after dropping off our things at the house, we switched to *Wave,* by Antonio Carlos Jobim, which came out even earlier. "Is this what old people do?" I asked.

Lisa said, "Yes, but who cares."

Now we're just sitting around before leaving for Raleigh. I'm at a table on the back porch, and she's lying on the sofa with her parrot, Henry. It's mating season and several times a week he rubs himself against her hand and leaves behind a droplet of sperm. "I just wash it off," Lisa says.

July 5, 2005
New York

I got thrown out of Don's lobby yesterday. I'd been standing there reading a document when the doorman told me to beat it. Number one on the *New York Times* bestseller list, and it was out on the street for me. The old heave-ho.

July 7, 2005
Paris

For the second time this year I was stopped by French customs officers and fined three hundred and fifty euros for the eleven cartons of cigarettes they found in my suitcase. As usual, everyone was super-polite, and very, very slow. Everything had to be done by hand, the forms painstakingly filled out and then stamped. At one point I caught the guy using a ruler to neatly x out the spaces that did not pertain to me.

This took a great deal of time, as did the arrival of the second shift, which had to be properly greeted. This meant four kisses for the women and handshakes for the men.

My plane landed at six a.m., and by the time I got outside it was after seven. Rush-hour traffic was in full swing, and it took an hour and a half to reach the apartment. Before leaving

New York, I'd heard that the 2012 Olympic Games had gone to London, so I asked my cabdriver how he felt about it.

"I fuck the Olympics," he said in French, shoving his fist into the air. "I fuck the Tour de France, and the World Cup, everything but the Grand Prix, which is openly corrupt and admits to it quite happily."

His beef wasn't with the English but with the French, who'd thought they could win their bid by acting like gentlemen. "Tony Blair, he went to all those little countries with his checkbook in his hand, and he bought their votes, just like Athens and Atlanta did. It's a business, and he acted like a businessman. France acted like it was the nineteenth century, so of course we lost. Fuck it."

There were moments when my cabdriver lost me, and others when I could understand him perfectly but couldn't quite believe what I was hearing. The man was maybe sixty, with graying hair that fell to his shoulders. "I was in Nevada with the Hells Angels, and I had an affair with someone who was as big as Madonna. She was my fantasy, and we made love for a week—not in Vegas, but just outside of it. Don't ask me who it was, because I am not the kind of man who tells."

"Cher?"

"No," he said, "Whitney Houston. She was young then, and nice to be with. This was before the sharks moved in and she got mean and addicted to drugs."

Hmmm, I thought.

The driver had a fleet of eight cabs and refused to hire Muslims as they sometimes pasted Koran verses onto the back of the driver's seat. "In Iraq, fine, but this is Paris!" he said. Last year he was sued for discrimination but won the case when he produced a signed document in which the Muslim had promised not to carry any religious materials except in the glove compartment.

July 8, 2005
Paris

Bombs went off in London yesterday and by this morning thirty-seven people were confirmed dead, with another seven hundred wounded. Ma Hamrick called to tell me about it and after hanging up, I turned on the BBC, which was broadcasting a cricket game. Then I turned on the TV and saw someone sobbing. I thought it was the news, but then I noticed that the woman was wearing an evening gown and realized I was watching a soap opera. The news was on the next channel but showed only a fleet of police cars and ambulances gathered round the Edgware Road tube station. The bombs went off underground, and as a French news presenter congratulated the British on their reluctance to panic (*"Quel calme!"*), the field reporter reminded her that we had yet to see any dead bodies. Hugh and I go to London next Tuesday and will be there for a week.

July 14, 2005
London

Police have identified three of the bombers, and they're kids, really. One of them was just eighteen years old and was pictured, smiling, on the front page of yesterday's paper. I thought of him when we were on Oxford Street yesterday. It was hot and everyone was out, walking, riding the buses. I don't know what it was like last Wednesday, but now everything seems to have returned to normal, at least aboveground. I'm impressed with the speed of the investigation. Every hour there's a new report.

July 29, 2005
La Bagotière

Yesterday's *Guardian* included an article on an artist named Mark McGowan whose most recent piece consisted of a sink faucet left to run in a London gallery. It was meant to draw attention to waste, and as of yesterday, when the utility company shut him down, he had run through 800,000 liters of water. It seems contradictory to call attention to waste by wasting, but then again, they never said he was a *good* artist.

Another article I read was about a parrot named Barney who lives at the Warwickshire Animal Sanctuary and recently told both the mayor and a vicar to fuck off. Now, like the erotic drawings at the British Museum, he can only be seen by special permission.

August 25, 2005
La Bagotière

Don sent me a manuscript of his book *How to Be an Agent*. They're stories about his clients, most of them good-natured. On the last page he talks about Sinclair Lewis, who in 1939 was sent to Wesleyan College to give a lecture. "How many of you want to write?" he asked. Most of the students raised their hands, and he said, "Good. Go home and write." Then he left the stage.

October 10, 2005
Paris

Hoping to lose a couple of pounds, Ronnie started going to Weight Watchers. The group operates on something called the Discover Plan, which assesses a food's caloric content and then assigns it points. Equally important are the weekly get-togethers, at which the members motivate and support one another. *I did it, and so can you* is the idea.

Ronnie found the meetings helpful, if maybe a little dull, until last week, when the group was addressed by a woman named Patty who'd lost sixty pounds and felt certain that she was speaking for everyone. "Ladies," she said, "don't tell me you haven't gotten out of bed in the middle of the night and put away an entire quart of half-and-half."

A quart of what? Ronnie thought. *No!*

"The same goes for Halloween candy," Patty continued. "You can deny it up and down, but there's not a one of you who hasn't filled her car with five sacks of Hershey bars, then pulled off the road on the way home and eaten every last one of them."

I haven't had a Hershey bar since I was ten, Ronnie wanted to say. *I'm telling you, this is* not *my story.*

We laughed about it on the phone last night, and after hanging up, I wrote a few similar testimonials, things, I'm thinking, that Ronnie can say when it's eventually her turn to speak.

All right, ladies, a show of hands. How many of you have gotten pregnant and had children just so you can drink your own breast milk? And how many *use* that breast milk to make butter? Now, how many mix that butter with fudge, form it into a ball, and press caramel corn into it?

What signifies spring more than Easter and daffodils? That's right, girls, the ice cream truck. And don't we all run at the sound of the bell and drop a king's ransom on Klondike Bars. There's the soft-serve, the brownie sandwiches, and just as we order our fifth Strawberry Swirlwind, the jackass driver will say, "Hey, lady, how about saving something for the kids."

Then am I the *only one* who reaches up, cups the smart aleck's face in her hands, and pushes in his eyes? Is it just me who presses until her thumbs are buried to the knuckles and she feels something burst inside his head? You're saying that out of everyone in this room, I'm the *only* one who then sticks those thumbs into her mouth, just to see what the ice cream man's ruptured eyes taste like? 'Cause, girls, if you expect me to believe that, you're not just big and fat, you're big fat liars to boot.

November 9, 2005
London
We had dinner at the Overseas Club, guests of Peter and Sally Palmer, whom Hugh first met in Somalia. Peter is Welsh and in his seventies. He has a white, wraparound mustache and drank eight cups of coffee with his meal. Sally, his wife, is American and fun-loving. "Tell David the story about our cook in Mogadishu," she'd say. "Tell him about the time our drama club did *Blithe Spirit*."

There were ten of us at the table, and I sat next to Lillian, a Scottish woman who's a government expert on Africa. Next week she leaves for Angola and I asked if she needed to bring a present. "To, you know, the king or whatever." I have no idea who's in charge in Angola—a chief? There was no way to hide my ignorance.

Lillian said that because she's a woman, the gifts are usually bestowed on her. I asked what kinds of things she's been given, and she thought for a moment before saying, "Well, the strangest present I ever received was a live crocodile."

I don't remember what country she was in, but she called the man who'd given it to her and asked what she was supposed to do now.

"Eat it," he said. And so her cook took over.

"What do you eat with a crocodile?" I asked.

She reached for her drink. "Anything, really. Potatoes, rice, whatever you've got."

"Could you have it with spaghetti?"

"I suppose." According to Lillian, it tasted like chicken but had the texture of a dense whitefish.

November 10, 2005
Paris

If you didn't read the newspapers, you'd never know that people are rioting on the outskirts of Paris. I got home at eight last night and looked out the window of my office. Across the street a man sat down to his piano. Couples ducked into restaurants. An elderly woman walked her dog. According to yesterday's *Guardian,* six thousand cars have been burned. A young man named Abdul was interviewed and said that the best method was to make a Molotov cocktail and throw it into the front seat. "When the gas tank goes it's really great," he said.

November 21, 2005
Paris

Hugh wants a human skeleton for Christmas, and I found one yesterday at the flea market. "It's very old and was in a famous movie," the stall owner told me.

I said, "Let me think about it."

I passed another one last night on rue Monsieur le Prince and thought that this was a pretty good town if you could see two skeletons in one day. The first is going for two thousand euros, and I'm not sure about the second. Money's not a factor so much as my general reluctance to buy a human, even a dead one. My objection's not moral so much as practical—how do you wrap it?

December 11, 2005
London

At an antiques store on Church Street I saw what is called a campaign bookcase, a trunk lined with shelves. Hugh and

I have been looking for something to hide the TV in, and when I lazily suggested that this might do the trick, the store owner butted in, saying, "Absolutely not." He had a high-class accent and wore a tweed jacket with velvet lapels. "If I knew that's what you wanted it for, I wouldn't sell it to you," he said. "Ruining the integrity of a piece like this, it would be a sin."

"What if it was a tiny TV?" I asked, and I held out my fingers to indicate a size of two inches.

The shop owner tugged at the hem of his jacket. "I am doing my best to keep it together," he said. "But don't push me."

December 19, 2005
Antwerp, Belgium

The best moment of our trip so far was on Saturday evening, when Hugh, his mom, and I were walking past the cathedral, looking for a place to have coffee. Snow was falling, carols were being played on a tuba, and the church bells rang. It was a triple punch of Christmas, and I stopped for a moment to take it all in. Unlike Brussels, which looks like Flers, Antwerp felt foreign. It's not as beautiful as Bruges or Amsterdam, but the old part of town is well preserved and functional without seeming embalmed.

My only disappointment was the shopping. There were things to be had, I just kept missing them, turning left when I should have gone straight. "It's nice what they've done with the lighting," Joan said, passing a massage parlor. "Do you think it's just for Christmas or a year-round decoration?"

At meals we lucked out, probably because I wasn't in charge. Friday night we ate at Vincent's in Brussels, a big, lively place not far from the Grand Place. Here we had dinner at a former stable called De Peerdestal. Our reservation was for nine o'clock, but there were no tables available, so we spent forty-five minutes at the bar, Hugh and his mom drinking free champagne. "This is just so nice with all the young people," she said. "You can just see how hard they work, all of them happy and trying to look their best."

I started with the eel in green sauce, and then I had the horse fillet. Hugh had horse as well, and it was incredibly tender. The restaurant was loud and crowded, and we sat on the second floor beside a table of twenty. All were men in their early thirties, and Joan admired them as we waited for our second course. "In America a group like that would be cursing or talking about women, but here they just have fun," she said. The men were speaking Dutch and could have been cursing up a storm for all she knew. They could have been members of a national rape team, but in Joan's eyes they were kind and innocent, a fellowship of boys discussing their plans for Christmas.

Everything was wonderful to her, even the Hotel Rubens, which I thought of as cheesy. The guidebook gave it three stars, but even before we headed upstairs, I'd demoted it to two on account of the life-size concrete Negro who stood between the front desk and the elevator. The hotel wasn't a dump, but neither was it worth 180 euros a night. I looked at my room and saw only the flaws: a floral bedspread made of what seemed like vinyl, the wall-mounted TV, anti-theft hangers, the lack of washcloths. Joan looked at hers and saw the free candies ("They're delicious!"). She later marveled at the turn-down service. "Someone came and took away the bedspread. Wasn't that nice? Then they left a chocolate on my pillow, just like a little fairy!"

Had we stayed in a tent or slept on a pile of coats at the bus station, she still would have found something to admire, and that's what makes her such a good traveling companion.

2006

January 27, 2006
Paris

Sales are still going on so I took Hugh to Crockett and Jones to look for a pair of dress shoes. Their Paris store is near the Madeleine, and yesterday it was staffed by a stern-looking woman in her early forties. Hugh tried on a pair of oxblood derbies, and she asked which was more comfortable, the left or the right. "No one's feet are exactly the same," she said. "One is always longer or wider than the other."

Hugh told her about the lump on his left foot, and when I added something, the woman corrected my pronunciation. Then I said something else and she curled her upper lip, saying that French was a very difficult language.

The shoes were a birthday present, and I didn't want to buy them with Hugh watching. After trying them on, he rummaged through his knapsack, and I took the opportunity to approach the saleswoman and tell her I'd return in fifteen minutes to pay for them.

When I came back, the woman was waiting on another customer. It would have been easy for her to excuse herself and ring me up. *I'll just be a moment,* she could have said. The man was pacing the floor in a new pair of brogues, trying to determine if they felt right. I was standing in front of the cash register, and the woman told me to sit down. "You should have bought your shoes when you had the chance," she snapped. "Now you'll just have to wait."

After the man decided he would take the brogues and after he finished paying for them, the woman made a personal phone call. She was at it for maybe three minutes, and when I left my seat and returned to the register, she covered the receiver, saying, "*J'arrive, J'arrive,* J'arrive" ("I'm coming, I'm coming, *I'm coming*").

After that she spoke to me in English, which was maybe the biggest insult of all. Had the shoes been for me I'd have been unable to wear them, as every time I looked at my feet I would think of her and want to kick something.

March 13, 2006
Paris

Don called last night and I have no idea what we talked about. "Of course, if you should like to change the thing you do, it could be done, possibly. The fellow there who used to be the big cheese, I'm sure you know who I'm talking about, he mentioned it once or twice and I know you were giving it some thought at that particular time."

March 17, 2006
Paris

I went to Printemps yesterday and could hear students chanting outside on the streets. It was hard to make out, but I caught the words *work* and, of course, *no*. On the way home I passed closed-off boulevards and battalions of policemen in riot gear. For the most part, though, things were pretty quiet until last night, when all hell broke loose. At around nine o'clock masses of students marched down rue Monsieur le Prince, and an hour later a pack of them passed outside my window.

One of the young men had a heavy stick and used it to beat

a minivan parked in front of the hair salon. His friends egged him on, and after the stick broke, they moved a few doors up and tried to overturn a car parked directly across the street from me. They were on the curb side and were just giving it the heave-ho when the woman on the third floor opened her window and threw a bucket of water on them.

It was a funny sight, but not to the young men, who were enraged. "Hey," they shouted. "You can't do that!" They picked up the remnants of their splintered stick and threw them at the woman with the bucket, missing her and breaking a window in the first-floor apartment. Just as they started looking for something better to throw, a troop of policemen rounded the corner, and the group scattered.

March 26, 2006
New York

Yesterday's *Times* included an article on Winston Moseley, the man who killed Kitty Genovese. He's been in prison for forty-three years and met with the parole board a few days ago. It was his umpteenth hearing, and once again he was denied. "You know," he said, "it's just not fair. For the victim or whatever the adventure lasts for a minute or two, but for the guy who done it, it goes on for years."

Well, yes, I thought. *Isn't that the point of punishment?*

March 28, 2006
New York

A few months ago I developed a slight rash on the side of my mouth. Genevieve suggested I try some cortisone cream, and when that didn't work, I asked Amy if she'd arrange for me to see her dermatologist when I came to New York. She made appointments for the both of us, and yesterday afternoon, we went. The office was on Fifth Avenue, in a converted loft with the air of a spa, or maybe a modeling agency. The reception desk was staffed with impossibly beautiful women who handed me a form and directed us to the waiting area, which offered both magazines *and* laptop computers. I'd never visited a dermatologist in my life, but the forms I was given seemed fishy to me. "Are you interested in Botox? Liposuction? Chemical peeling?" The medical-history section included questions about rhinoplasty and asked if I was allergic to collagen. Three pages, and at the end my arm ached from checking *no, no, no* over and over again.

The doctor we saw was maybe thirty-two and wore a tattered long-sleeved Comme des Garçons T-shirt under his lab coat. He knew Amy from previous visits, and after he'd hugged her, he settled me into the chair and looked at my rash.

"I'm no detective," I told him, "but I'm wondering if this isn't some kind of an allergic reaction to nickel. I'm always drinking out of the faucet, see, and the rash is on the side of my mouth that touches it."

The doctor put on a pair of rubber gloves. "I guess it *could* be an allergy."

"I'd normally ignore it, but I'm going on this lecture tour, and I don't want people thinking I have herpes."

"I don't *believe* it's herpes," he said. And that's when I lost all confidence in him.

"Unless herpes has a sixteen-year latent period, I think we can definitely rule it out," I told him. "Plus it's not a sore, it's a rash, and it never weeps."

"Right," he said. "I think we can give you something to clear it up, but you might not want to shave for a while. Maybe you should grow a Vandyke."

I didn't say that I'd rather have herpes, as the doctor had a Vandyke himself. It looked like he'd taken a big gulp from a mugful of hair. "If the spot doesn't clear in a few weeks, just take a picture with your high-resolution camera and email it to me."

A camera, a Vandyke, email—he was definitely talking to the wrong person.

"We can treat the rash, but I think you really need to do something about all this dead skin," he said, gesturing to my face in general. "Let's see if we can't fix you up with Kimberly."

The doctor stuck his head into the hall and called for a young woman, who led me into a windowless room and asked me to sign a waiver. "The laser skin peel is something we've come up with on our own," she said, "and we don't want you suing us if your face burns up. Ha, just kidding! Now, I want you to lie down while I put these shields over your eyes."

I don't know exactly what happened next but it took about fifteen minutes and involved a meteor shower of laser beams, a coat of acid, and then something that smelled like an avocado salad. "All right, then," she said. "You are good to go."

On my way out I returned to the reception desk, where the woman behind the counter gave me a tube of facial cream that was originally designed for burn victims and included the cells of fetal lambs. "Your skin is going to love this."

I asked for the bill, and she said, "Oh, no charge."

"But for the appointment."

"No charge!"

"Well, let me ask you this," I said. "The 'doctor' who gave me the face peel. Was I supposed to tip her?"

"Most people do," the receptionist whispered.

"And how much do most people tip?" I whispered back.

"Whatever you're comfortable with."

I took two twenties out of my wallet and put them in an

envelope. "How much would the peel have cost if I had paid for it?" I asked.

"Five hundred," she said, and I pulled out another twenty, which was all I had.

Then I was out on the street, walking to my next appointment because I'd spent all my cash tipping a dermatologist for something I didn't want in the first place.

March 29, 2006
Philadelphia

A Frenchwoman attended last night's reading and we talked about France's CPE (first employment contract) as I signed her book. "It is outrageous," she said. "To fire a young person without a stated reason, that is slavery."

Actually, no, I wanted to say. *Slavery is being put into shackles and forced to toil for no money in the blistering heat. Working with the possibility of being fired is just called "working."*

March 30, 2006
Philadelphia

At last night's signing I was approached by two men in their early forties. Both were gay, but the one who really stood out was bald and had no eyelashes. His face was slightly moon-shaped, and I got the idea that he was undergoing radiation treatment—for cancer, I thought.

"I just had my own book published," he said, and after shaking his hand, I asked what it was about.

The man leaned forward and lowered his voice to a whisper. "Ummm... fisting?"

I wiped my palms on my pants and said, "That's great! And what's it called?"

The incredible thing is that I've forgotten his answer.

David Sedaris

April 3, 2006
Syracuse, New York

At a fast-food restaurant in LaGuardia Airport, I ordered a sandwich, then stood behind a man who'd gotten two salads, one for himself and another for his wife. The cashier rang them up, and the guy noted a discrepancy on the bill. "You should have told me that the fourth and fifth toppings would be extra."

The woman, who was Indian, explained that the first three toppings were free and that the second three were seventy-five cents each.

"What?" the man barked. "I can't understand you. Speak English."

The woman had an accent, but I could understand her with no problem. The guy was just being a dick.

"Let me talk to your manager," he said. "The man in charge or whatever."

The fellow who had prepared the salads stepped forward, and the customer repeated his grievance. "You should have told me these toppings would be extra," he said. "What you did was sneaky, do you understand what that means? Deceitful."

I hoped that might be the end of it, but the guy refused to let it go. "You should have a sign telling people that the fourth topping costs seventy-five cents."

"We do have a sign," the manager said. He pointed it out and the customer complained that it wasn't big enough.

Eventually the manager shaved a dollar off the man's bill, but even then he refused to quit. I imagine he continued to talk about it on the plane and was still at it when he arrived home, wherever that is.

April 10, 2006
Austin, Texas

At last night's book signing I met a woman whose father had eaten her placenta. "He was a hippie, and he ate my sister's too," she told me. "When we each got our first haircut, he ate a few strands of our hair."

"Goodness," I said. "I hope he wasn't around when you got your first period."

April 11, 2006
Austin

Tim drove me to the Louisville airport and on the way there we talked about his father, who is dying of lung cancer. "What did he do for a living?" I asked.

"Owned a titty bar."

Tim's mother had nine children, and four of them died. I asked if that was traumatic, and he said no, at least not for him and his brothers. "The crib went up, the crib came down. It was more of a furniture issue."

April 12, 2006
Charleston, South Carolina

Early yesterday morning I rode in a town car driven by a man named Samir. He was relatively young, in his early forties, maybe, and used to work as a civil engineer. "This is much better, money-wise," he said. "Plus I've got some rental properties and a few good investments."

"I have a rental property as well," I said.

He asked me how much I had paid for it, and after I told him, he asked what I charged for rent. "Is that a lot for Paris? What's your mortgage rate?"

The guy dropped me off at the Delta terminal, and after

checking in, I heard my name announced over the speakers, followed by a request to pick up a white courtesy phone. I figured there was something wrong with my ticket or, worse, that someone had died, but instead it was Samir. "Yes," he said, "I was thinking about what you said and was wondering if you'd like to sell me that rental property."

I didn't know what to say.

"There's no rush," he told me. "It doesn't have to be *today* but, you know, maybe a few years down the line."

"Umm. Okay."

He invited me to call him, adding that he wasn't going to drive a limo forever.

"Super," I said, as if we had a deal.

As he recited his number, I stared off into space. "Got it," I told him after he had finished.

"Now read it back to me," he said.

Then I was busted. "Gosh, let's see...my handwriting's so bad. What do you say you give it to me again."

April 18, 2006
Wichita, Kansas

Whoever said that Christians are under attack has never been to Wichita. The FM band is solid God, so rather than listening to *All Things Considered* I bathed to a sermon and shaved to a call-in show. "I normally tithe a tenth of my earnings to the church, but my husband isn't saved and wants us to put that money toward an RV. What do I do?"

"That's a toughie," the host said. "On the one hand you want to honor your church, and on the other, you need to submit to your man's wishes. So, let's talk about this. Let's kick it around."

Later someone called to denounce Islam and criticize a new

law passed by the Algiers. The host used the same term, and I finished my exercises thinking, *That's "Algerians."*

On another station, the announcer reminded us that, as far as TV was concerned, Fox was the only news network that told it like it was. "They don't pretend that Islam is a true religion," he said. "They say, because it's true, that it's wicked."

April 20, 2006
Fargo, North Dakota

At last night's signing I met a woman who had tried to revive her dying cat. "I thought the heat might be good for her, but the oven seemed too harsh, and so I used a blow-dryer," she said.

A while later, I met a man who works at the local university and has been trying to catch the joker who shit in the student union ventilation duct. "Likely it's the same person who's been defecating in the urinals and then shat in a microwave and turned it on," he said.

It was a good crowd last night, and I liked the way that people spoke. "I borrowed this book to my brother and he never gave it back," a young woman told me. I later heard a similar thing from someone else. "I borrowed him money for my ticket."

Toward the end of the evening, I met a young woman who was wearing a face mask. It was the kind you might see on a dentist, only instead of plain white, it was printed with flowers. I asked about it and learned it was precautionary—a safety measure in advance of her upcoming bone-marrow donation.

I asked who she was giving the bone marrow to and she said she wasn't sure exactly. "I think it might be a woman, but that's all I know."

"So you're donating your bone marrow to a complete stranger out of the goodness of your heart?"

"I guess you could say that," she said, and the area surrounding the mask shaded to a light pink.

She was very modest about it, but I think what she's doing is extraordinary and should qualify her for a tax break. "Can you write off your bone marrow?" I asked, and she said no, which I don't think is fair at all. You get a break if you have children or buy an SUV, but save the life of a complete stranger and you can't even deduct the cost of your face masks.

April 25, 2006
Seattle, Washington

I was taken to the Orange County airport yesterday morning by a sedan driver named John who called my room and told me he was waiting down in the library. I wasn't quite ready to go, and when I asked him what time it was, he hesitated a moment, and then said, "Fifteen minutes to nine thirty."

Is that, like, a quarter past nine? I wanted to say.

I arrived in Seattle at three and went to a Mail Boxes Etc. located around the corner from my hotel. The place was small and shabby-looking, staffed by a young woman with green hair and multiple lip piercings. As I entered, she was talking to a man, and it took me a moment to realize that he had an iguana on his shoulder. It was the size of a cat, wearing a harness, and after staring at it for a minute or two, I noticed it was missing one of its feet. The front right one led to a gnarled paw, but the other ended at the wrist and was nothing more than a rounded stump. "So, right," the man said. "What's your name again?"

The woman told him and he petted his iguana. "I'm pretty sure I've seen you around the neighborhood."

All three of them nodded, including the iguana, and then

the man left, turning once on his way out to look at her. He was maybe in his late twenties and had his hair pulled into a samurai knot. "So, later," he said.

"I think that guy was trying to pick you up," I told the young woman.

"Really?" she said, sounding genuinely surprised. "I'm married and can never tell when guys are hitting on me."

"Would you sleep with someone who has an iguana?" I asked.

She handed me a shipping form and said, "If I wasn't married, sure. I like reptiles. One thing I always wanted was an albino python. Those are so cool-looking."

April 29, 2006
San Francisco

My plane from Arcata was delayed due to fog, and after waiting in the small terminal, I stepped outside to have a cigarette and met a man who drove a courtesy van for a local Red Roof Inn. I'd put him in his late fifties, unremarkable as far as looks were concerned, but clearly gregarious, the type you wouldn't mind standing behind in a grocery line but would hate to sit next to on a long flight. As I approached the ashtray, he handed me his lighter and remarked that my shoes looked comfortable.

"That's their reward for being ugly," I told him.

He lit a cigarette of his own, saying, "If you want ugly, you should see my wife."

I laughed because I thought I was supposed to, and he said, "Really, though, she's not so bad. I mean, she *is* ugly, but then again, it happens to all of us when we get older. My second wife, she was a real beauty, but on the inside, she was a monster. You know what I mean?"

I nodded.

"I had this young gal up in my van this morning, and she was just like her—a stuck-up bitch, through and through. So I told her, I said, 'You remind me of my second wife. She was a gorgeous woman and the sex was great—top-notch all the way—but she needed to work on her inner self.'"

The man looked at the glowing end of his cigarette. "I'm telling you, this girl I had this morning, she was a real bitch."

I wanted to ask if he often discussed sex with his female passengers or if he'd noticed the effect it had on his tips. It's one thing to talk that way with another guy, but with a woman, it's a whole different kind of creepy, especially if she's trapped in the back seat of your van. On top of that, who was he to dole out character evaluations? Three marriages is not a great track record, and telling complete strangers that your wife is ugly is a weird way to begin a conversation. This is to say that, all in all, I found the man enchanting.

May 2, 2006
Denver, Colorado
I left Ronnie's at 9:00 a.m. and was driven to the airport by a big black fellow named Dale who used to play football and has two children in the military. His daughter, a go-getter, loves jumping out of airplanes, but his son spends most of his time hanging out in Oakland with his friends. "A chuckle-head," Dale called him. "Going to get hisself killed in some senseless drive-by or some such thing. I said to him, 'You think you're a soldier, but you ain't nothing but a fool.'" Dale has six children altogether and often fantasizes that he could put on his old uniform and plow them down on a football field. "I'd hit 'em so hard they'd have blood bubbles coming out of they mouths."

May 5, 2006
Boston

Anne Stein picked me up at eleven and took me to Helping Hands, where I spent a pleasant hour feeding monkeys. "Which one is the ugliest?" I asked, and Jennifer, the trainer, politely mentioned that we don't use words like that. Then she whispered, "I think it's Cassie."

When Cassie joined us a few minutes later, I decided that Jennifer was right. This was one ugly monkey, friendly as all get-out, but not much to look at. I think my favorite was Becky, who's twenty-five years old and is thought of as the house matriarch. She worked for years, but then her quadriplegic died, and she returned to the center to await reassignment. In my memory, the monkeys were called things like Kee-Kaw and Thunderbolt, but yesterday's names were pretty straightforward: Stuart, Jimmy, Big Dave, Sandy. Someone named Blake had just been assigned a quadriplegic, and someone else, a female named Jill, was in heat and spent her break time making googly eyes at a trainer named Brian. It was so over the top, the sort of overt flirting you'd see in a silent movie.

While I was watching her, Jimmy came over and tied my shoes, this after they'd been untied by Kukla. Then he stole my pen and pounded it on the floor for a few minutes until I asked for it back. "I really need that," I said, and when he handed it to me, the trainers broke out in applause.

"The monkeys steal, but then they feel horrible about it," Jennifer explained. After returning my property, Jimmy threw himself at my feet and begged for forgiveness. "It's all right," I told him. "Really."

It was fun holding monkeys, but I felt like the grandfather you have to entertain because he gave you a big birthday check.

May 7, 2006
Delray Beach, Florida
On April Fool's Day, Paul called Dad and told him that Amy could be found topless in this month's *Playboy*.

"Really!" Dad said.

Paul couldn't tell if he was pleased or horrified.

May 10, 2006
Paris
In my absence Hugh has grown a beard and now looks like a sea captain. It's come in gray, with streaks of white along the chin, and before I arrived, he went to a barber and had the edges trimmed. After our dinner I sat on the couch and looked through the Lonely Planet guide to the Philippines. There's a Tagalog dictionary in the back of the book, and I learned that stamps are bought at the *pos opis*. I can send letters the normal way or I can post them *ermeyl*. It's like English on quaaludes.

More words:

Hospital: *Ospital*

Christmas tree: *Krismas tri*

May 12, 2006
Paris
Dad called before I left on tour and told me that the *News and Observer* was doing a story on Monet. The reporter would be coming to Paris in May and was wondering if she could interview me. "It would mean a lot to her," he said.

The reporter, whose name is Ellen, phoned yesterday and gave me the real story. "Your father keeps calling the paper and leaving anonymous messages," she said. "Whenever you have an essay in *The New Yorker,* he tells us we need to write an article about you."

"Oh, no," I said.

"He keeps insisting that you're famous and that Raleigh should be proud to claim you."

"Oh, no!"

May 18, 2006
La Bagotière

Dick Moose told a funny joke over dinner last night. It was a long one, involving a group of waiters who carry spoons in the top pockets of their jackets. "I heard that from Cy," he said, meaning Cyrus Vance, whom he worked with during the Carter administration. Before that he worked for Henry Kissinger ("A relationship that was not meant to last"). The joke led to a reminiscence on the Iranian hostage crisis, and then, because I asked, to a story about Charles Taylor, whom Dick met in Liberia in the late eighties, before he butchered tens of thousands of his countrymen.

Dick Moose is one of those people who really should write a book, as opposed to the thousands of people who say they should write a book but shouldn't. His wife, Maggie, wasn't feeling well, so they made an early night of it and cut out shortly after the calvados was served. Next to Mary Zimmerman, they're the most interesting houseguests we've ever had.

May 19, 2006
La Bagotière

We had an incident with a mouse yesterday. In my defense, I only screamed a little, and that was because I thought it was a rat. It certainly was big enough. I saw it on the stairway between the bedroom and the milking parlor and called for Hugh, who was standing in the kitchen with his dad and Nancy. "Oh, shut up," he said. "What are you making such a fuss about?"

Whenever I get upset, Hugh claims that I'm begging for attention. Like with that tax audit. "You just want people to feel sorry for you," he says, and I think, *Do I?* He treated the mouse as if it were an escaped hamster and tried to capture it with his hands. Then his father got involved and attempted to crush it beneath his boot. "Dad!" Hugh shouted as the mouse ran between the suitcases and disappeared behind the armoire. "Now see what you did!"

That was the end of it until an hour later, when I found the mouse cowering behind the washing machine. This time I didn't scream but calmly notified Hugh, who was putting the finishing touches on a tub of mashed potatoes. "Do I have to do *everything*?" he said, and then he chased the mouse into a T-shirt and carried it outside to the stone wall separating our yard from the Bacons'. "His tail is nicked, the poor thing. Did you do that?"

"How could I?" I said.

"Well, *someone* did it."

The mouse ran off, and we returned to the house to celebrate Maggie's seventy-fifth birthday. Hugh served a chicken and then a walnut cake made without flour. The Mooses were subdued last night and reflected upon the past week and the lovely time they'd had in Normandy. "It was perfect," Maggie said.

"Oh, better than perfect," Nancy said.

"The food was outstanding."

"Better than outstanding. It was marvelous."

I'd have liked it if Dick had revisited the subject of spy school, which he attended as a young man. "One of the things they tell you right off is that, if possible, you should always take the other guy's chair," he said. "That disorients him and makes him more likely to tell you things." He'd said this after taking my chair.

June 27, 2006
La Bagotière

While at the superstore mall, waiting on a replacement part for our refrigerator, Hugh and I went to a fast-food place for a coffee. A retired couple sat at the table next to us, and I was struck by how American they looked. The woman had on sweatpants, and her husband wore a baseball cap coupled with jeans, sneakers, and a pair of white socks with words stitched into them. This is where the French always get it wrong. Instead of reading *Knicks* or *Yankees*—the name of a specific team—their athletic gear bears words like *Basketball* or, as with this man's socks, simply *Sport*. Other times they just pick an English word, liking the sound but not really knowing what it means. Manuela and her thirteen-year-old daughter visited us in London last year, and when it came time to go out to dinner, Louise walked in wearing a T-shirt with PUSSY stitched across the front.

"I don't think that's such a great idea," Hugh told her.

July 1, 2006
London

I arrived in London last night at eight and got to the apartment an hour later. There were ten messages on the machine: some hang-ups, a reminder from the people at the Edinburgh Festival, and a strange call from an American who'd read my Princeton graduation speech in *The New Yorker*. "Pages thirty-eight and thirty-nine," he said, as if I'd written another speech that was located farther back in the magazine. It wasn't that he hated it. Rather, he found it offensive. "First of all, you didn't even *go* to Princeton," he said. "It's just more of the typical anti-H-and-Y propaganda found in *The New Yorker*."

It took me a moment to realize that *H* and *Y* stood for

Harvard and Yale. "Does Princeton have you on its payroll?" he asked. "Is that why you're doing this?" He then said that the speech was more of my same old thing and that I needed to find something new to write about. In the meantime, he and his friends were watching me. "And we say, 'Poop on you.'"

July 3, 2006
London

Printed in yesterday's *Independent* magazine was this parody of the current Mastercard ad:

One tube of Vaseline: 3 dollars

One box of condoms: 6 dollars

Three gay porn magazines: 24 dollars

Making your parents think your brother is gay: Priceless.

July 4, 2006
London

I saw a house for sale on Holland Street and spent a few days imagining that it was ours. It's silly to think that a little more space would solve all my problems, but Hugh had encouraged me to look at places, and this one seemed nearly perfect. The sale's being handled by an agency on Kensington Church Street, so yesterday I went by to find out the price and was shocked that it's roughly five million dollars. One of the interior photos showed the kitchen, which featured a tremendous stove fronted by a built-in island. Appliances gleamed, and on the wall, above a table, hung a portrait of Che Guevara.

July 18, 2006
La Bagotière

On Sunday afternoon we went with Joan to Ouistreham. It was hot and the tide was out, leaving a wide and crowded beach. Hugh swam while his mom and I sat in folding chairs, her dressed in jeans and one of my shirts. "Now, look at that girl!" she'd say. "She's so pretty with her blond hair and I guess that's her boyfriend with her. It looks like he's going to push her into the water, but he wouldn't do that. Look, he's got a tattoo! Oh, and that sunburn."

I hadn't thought of it before then, but Joan would be excellent company for the blind.

July 24, 2006
Hong Kong

I saw in the *Tribune* that starting September 1, all Marriott hotels will go completely nonsmoking, meaning that I will never again stay at a Marriott. Also in the news is the continued bombing of Lebanon. Fifty children were killed on Saturday and because there's no wood for coffins, wild dogs are eating their bodies.

I read that and thought, *Really, all Marriotts will be non-smoking?*

July 25, 2006
Hong Kong

It rained yesterday afternoon, and for the remainder of the day the air felt like steam. If it cooled down any, it was only by a degree or two, and by the time we left for dinner it must have been in the high eighties. Kara from the bookstore had suggested some restaurants in our neighborhood, and before choosing one, we went to an optician's office to pick up Hugh's new glasses. The streets were busy, and for the first time since arriving, I began to grow tired of being hawked at. In the beginning it was just the tailors, but now it was masseurs and, as the night progressed, prostitutes. They must have to play things down as far as their dress is concerned, as most of the women looked like either office workers or college students. "Do you want some company?" the first one asked me. She was in her early twenties and wore jeans and a white T-shirt. I was carrying three shopping bags and held them up as a way of saying that she was barking up the wrong tree. Then she asked again, and I said that I was a homosexual.

"What did you tell her that for?" Hugh asked. "All you have to do is say no."

That, though, might have hurt her feelings. I didn't want to suggest that she wasn't pretty or that I lacked confidence in her ability to bring pleasure. My answer was no, but I wanted her to understand that it wasn't *her* fault.

The next prostitute asked if I wanted a beautiful lady, and the one after that wondered where I was going. I told her, and she offered to walk me to my hotel and stay with me for as long as I wanted. "That's okay," I told her. "I'm a homosexual." I don't think her English was too good, as this only caused her to ask again. "I don't do things with ladies," I said.

I'm not often solicited by prostitutes and found it over-whelming to be approached by three in a single five-minute period. They didn't proposition Hugh, I noticed, but then again, he was walking really fast, and they'd have had to run to catch up with him. Could this be personal? I wondered. Would they have approached any Western male, or did I look more desperate than most? *Ask him, he's bound to be single.* Or maybe I looked like an adulterer, the type who left his family for a week of business and slept with a different woman every night.

Most likely, I'm thinking about it too much, the way I always do when someone picks me out of a crowd. "Shoeshine?" he'll ask, and I'll look at the feet of the person ahead of me.

July 26, 2006
Manila, Philippines

When people in Manila say they live close to the airport, they really mean it. Hugh and I looked out the window as the plane just missed a shantytown of tin-roofed shacks set on muddy unpaved roads. Farther along, at the "good end" of the runway, the houses were a bit more upscale and had doors and windows and wooden fences separating them from the tarmac.

Joonee, Minotte, and Lureen were waiting for us on the other side of the baggage claim, and I was surprised by how young and enthusiastic they were. Like college students. The Shangri-La had sent a van, and on the way from the airport to the hotel we passed dozens of people standing in the middle of the busy highway, most of them trying to sell things to stalled drivers. Batteries, fruit, cigarettes. Hugh saw a group of naked adolescent boys playing in a muddy ditch, and I saw a blind man being led by the elbow through a deep puddle.

This is autumn in the Philippines, meaning it's a few degrees cooler, and it rains all the time. Alongside the van were umpteen jitneys, scooters, and people on bikes. The buildings ran from unremarkable to horrible, each one connected to its neighbor by a thick garland of telephone and electrical wires that sagged in places and were propped up by boards. Nothing was remotely beautiful or comfortable-looking until we reached the hotel. Like everywhere else I've been to in Manila, entering involved a security check: the trunk searched, the bags scanned or looked into or sniffed at by muzzled dogs. Every business seems to employ a security guard, and according to Joonee, they have no idea what they're looking for. "I mean, trouble, sure, but there's no one form that really stands out."

The Peninsula in Hong Kong was very grand. They didn't want you to wear shorts in the lobby, and I'm sure they might follow you if you looked suspicious. It gave the illusion of welcoming everyone, and on checking into the Shangri-La, you could see the value of that illusion. Here the class distinctions are much more profound. There are the people inside the grand hotel, and then there are the people selling plastic bags of corn kernels in the middle of the road. The two groups watch each other constantly, and it's so overt you can't help but feel nervous and depressed.

Joonee offered to show us around town, and because I needed a pair of trousers, we wound up at the Greenbelt Mall. It's just across the street, but rather than walking, we took a hired car. At the door we were screened by security. Then we went to the second floor and had lunch at Jollibee. I had a champ with fries, and Hugh ordered the deep-fried fish back, which was served with rice. I like the Jollibee attitude—all smiles and warm greetings. Big happy bees stood guard at the doors, and their twins beamed from the single-ply paper napkins. It was the highlight of the afternoon.

From the Greenbelt we traveled by cab to the Makati Cinema Square. I think of it as a mall with cancer. The theaters it was named for are gone, and in their place are crowded stalls selling pirated movies. There might be a dozen vendors in the same subdivided store, each selling the same thing and each calling out to you as you enter, "Hello, sir, DVDs? I have all kinds." Then there was a shop in which everything cost eighty pesos, the equivalent of a dollar fifty. None of it was anything you wanted to buy: a pen with a feather glued to it, a pair of aqua-colored shorts, a cigarette lighter shaped like a bullet. The store had three employees and no customers.

Out in the hall the paint was peeling from the walls.

Sheets of wet cardboard were laid on the linoleum, and one of the staircases had been removed, the hole covered with plywood. On the next floor down, there were more DVD shops, many of them sandwiched between gun stores with Uzis in the windows. The better assault rifles were shrink-wrapped in plastic and bolted to the shelves with cables. One weapons store was located next to a ballet school that also sold powdered vitamin drinks, the kind used by bodybuilders. In the window were tutus, enormous cans of whey protein, and pictures of tanned, overdeveloped men who grimaced and looked, in Hugh's words, as if they were being roasted alive in a hot oven.

The Makati Cinema Square made no attempt whatsoever to seem cheerful. There was no music, no fountain of dancing waters, no promise that the merchandise would improve your life in any way. One stand sold stuffed waffles, another sold paper shopping bags with pictures of smiling Chinese people on them. I was just thinking that it couldn't get any sadder when we heard a voice calling out numbers and wandered into a bingo parlor. A young woman with no teeth looked up as we entered, and her fellow players followed suit.

If this was the mall that had cancer, the bingo room was its malignant tumor. Sorrow flowed from it and infected the entire building, which got sicker the farther down we went. In the basement they sold motorcycles and pets. The fish were pretty bad off, but it was the dogs you really felt for. I don't know if they were drugged or if they'd simply given up. None of them barked or jumped around. Poor Lisa would have broken down and wept.

We ended the evening at the Hobbit House, a bar completely staffed by dwarves and midgets. They wore jeans or skirts and blouses and behaved like bar workers the world over. After a few minutes you forgot that they were smaller than the average person, and you began to notice the sorts of things that would stand out anywhere: this drunk American woman, for instance, whose blond hair fell almost to her knees. She danced alone before a pair of blues musicians who were playing as we entered and who were replaced, in time, by a singer named Marc Velasco, who had a stunning voice and reminded me a bit of José Feliciano.

According to Joonee, everyone in the Philippines can sing. I'm normally not much for live music, but this guy was really something, and I wanted to bawl at his rendition of "Walk On By." I was running the song through my mind when we left, and a scruffy, beat-up-looking dwarf demanded twenty pesos for watching our car, which was occupied by our driver and needed no extra watching.

Names of stores at the Greenbelt Mall:
  The Badminton Hub
  All Flip Flops

At other malls:
  Sentimental Lane
  Ice Monster
  Alterations Plus
  Bread Talk

Names of people I either spoke to or signed a book for:
  Chester
  Milton
  Girlie
  Kitten
  Bam-Bam
  Bonnet
  Sassy

Twinkie
Charms
Pet
Genesis

July 27, 2006
Manila

After dinner we watched part of a documentary on Imelda Marcos, who was quoted in one of the Hong Kong papers the other day. The reporter began the interview saying, "You're known as one of the richest women in the world, so tell me, please, just how much money do you have?"

Her answer was bodacious but sounds even more so now that I'm here and have seen some of the poverty. "Honey," she said, "if you know how much money you have, you're not really rich."

I read in my guidebook that the Philippines has the world's fourth-highest child-prostitution rate, the top three slots going to Thailand, India, and the United States.

August 16, 2006
La Bagotière

The Dramatists Play Service is including a part of *The Book of Liz* in an anthology of monologues that work well for women. Cristina called to tell me about it, and then she put Don on the phone. The last time we spoke was a few months ago, and since then he's lost a good deal of his vocabulary. The word *rain* is gone, as are *week* and *day*. I asked about the weather and he said, "Well, you know how it is. The hours, the minutes, they pass along the way they do but before that we had a lot of water going up and down the way it occasionally does."

What he hasn't lost is his tone of authority. Certain words

are emphasized, and while the sentences themselves make no sense, they sound as if they are well thought out. "I wouldn't say that it's necessarily *hot,* but we've got around nine o'clock, generally speaking, which is *basically* the stuff that I like, or at least I can live with."

He mentioned the South Pacific at one point but forgot the word *war,* so we talked about the stuff that happened there, vis-à-vis the people. As always, he wrapped up by saying, "All right, then. I don't want to bore you with that now. It's been good chewing the fat."

October 5, 2006
Baltimore, Maryland

From last night's signing:

Me: What do you do?

Handsome man: I'm a lawyer, a litigator. I keep the world safe for rich people.

Me: What do you do?

Lesbian with stains on her shirt: I sell meat off the back of a truck.

I also met a couple who'd stepped outside to smoke. I told them of my tentative plans to quit, and the woman looked at me as if I were deserting her. "They say that cigarettes take ten years off your life, but they're the last ten years, so who wants them anyway?"

October 12, 2006
Portland, Maine

While I was waiting for Rob to pick me up at my Buffalo hotel yesterday morning, an African man approached and asked if

I would photograph him posing before the fountain. I don't know what country he was from, but he seemed very pleasant and enthusiastic. The camera he offered was one of those digital jobs that recalled the picture at the push of the button. After I took it, the man looked it over. "I wanted the whole me," he said. "My legs and everything."

My second attempt was too dark, so he offered some tips and showed me a few of the pictures he'd had taken the day before just to give me an idea of what he wanted, I guess. The first shot showed him standing in front of a grand building, the old post office, maybe. In the next, I saw him smiling beside the hotel's concierge desk, and in the third he was sitting on his bed, wearing nothing but his underpants, a pair of lemon-yellow micro-briefs. "Okay," I said. "I get it now."

October 28, 2006
San Diego, California
I talked about the Max Brooks book onstage last night, and then, while signing, I asked people how they felt about zombies. "What are they exactly?" one young woman wanted to know.

I told her that they were reanimated corpses that ate human flesh.

"Well, I wouldn't do that," she said. "I'm a vegetarian."

"But you wouldn't be if you were a zombie," I told her.

"Yes, I would," she said. "I'd never eat meat, especially another human."

"But you would be a zombie," I told her. "Moral decisions would be beyond your capabilities."

"Not mine," she said, and then I just gave up on her, for how can anyone be so stupid?

November 27, 2006
Paris

Joan was always a Francophile, but the past few months have fortified her position, that being that the French can do no wrong. I listen to her sometimes and realize that I sound the same way about the Japanese, whom I know almost nothing about. A purse is snatched, a girl props her feet up on a bus seat, a young man cuts in the taxi line, and I say, "That would never happen in Tokyo." This after spending three days there. I really need to start watching myself.

December 4, 2006
Paris

A woman called late last night and left a rambling message on the machine. "You sound very homosexual, so this must be the right number." She paused, possibly to take a drink. "I was looking for the David Sedaris who wrote that book called... oh, you know the one."

The woman was clearly drunk and said she had just moved to Paris. After offering to give me her number, she was unable to remember it, so she promised to call back. "I'll be here for three years, so we have plenty of time to get together and make friends," she said.

December 5, 2006
Paris

The woman who phoned on Sunday called back again last night. It was around ten fifteen, and I was making dinner. "Yes," she said. "Are you the one who wrote that book *I Talk Pretty*?"

I told her I was, and after saying that she had enjoyed it, she explained that she was new in town. "I know French people, but I don't know any Americans."

"I see."

"I think I called the other night," she said.

"You did. At one thirty in the morning."

There was a silence and she broke it by saying, "Now I feel embarrassed."

"Well, thanks for calling."

"Is that . . . oh."

"All right, thanks again."

I later felt guilty, but even ten fifteen is late to be calling someone you don't know.

December 15, 2006
Paris

The drunk girl called back last night at ten and got Hugh on the phone. I guess she thought that he was me, as she started by saying that she felt bad about our last conversation. What bothered her, I think, was that she didn't get more of a chance to talk. During their brief chat, Hugh identified himself and said that I wasn't home. Then he said that he was busy, and she accused him of hating women. I mulled this all over while lying in bed and wondered where this person was phoning from. What's her apartment like? How did she get the idea that it's all right to get drunk and then call strangers?

December 17, 2006
Paris

On our way home from Manuela's at one a.m., Hugh was bitten by a Jack Russell terrier. His master, a man in his late fifties, was walking it without a leash, and as we approached, the dog barked and charged. Meanwhile, the man did nothing. He was no taller than I am, balding and with a trim gray mustache. His trench coat made him look like a detective.

"He bit me!" Hugh said, raising his pant leg.

The man called his dog. He put him on his leash but did not scold him. Neither did he seem particularly concerned with Hugh, who looked at him and said in French, "He bit me and drew blood." The attitude in Paris is that when your dog is off the leash, he's not really yours. That's his time to belong to nature, and during it he can bark and bite and shit on your neighbor's doorstep all he wants.

Hugh took a few steps toward home, and when he raised his pant leg again and pointed out the depth of the wound, the man offered a weak apology.

"The little shit of a dog," Hugh said, and the man put his hands in his pockets and turned away. I always think of these things too late, but we should have pulled out my iPod and pretended that it was a telephone. *Get me the police,* we should have said. It wouldn't have healed the bleeding wound, but at least we'd have had the pleasure of watching this man run.

December 20, 2006
London

I met a woman in Sacramento last month who presented me with a manual typewriter. It was an old Royal, I believe, and it must have weighed twenty pounds. She knew it was too much for me to carry around on tour, and so she arranged to ship it to Steven, who would then forward it to France. After returning from my tour I wrote her a letter and told her that the typewriter was very special to me. "I'd be using it this minute, only it's back in Paris," I said.

I'd forgotten the whole thing until yesterday morning, when I arrived in London to find an envelope on the floor. It was from this woman, Linda, and she'd written to say that she'd received my letter. The embarrassing thing was that she hadn't yet sent the typewriter to Steven. So here I was, caught in a lie.

Amy suggests I write her back, saying, "If *you* didn't send me that typewriter, who did?"

December 28, 2006
Paris

I got defeated the other day when Rakoff called and I tried to run a few Japanese words past him. "Do you mean *keno*?" he asked. "Are you saying *nomumono*?" It was clear from talking to him that I need to pay more attention to my pronunciation. I've finally moved on to part 2 of my Learn Japanese program and if I manage my time properly, I should get another five lessons under my belt before we leave for Tokyo. A week from now we'll be in our apartment and I will not be smoking a cigarette. As time passes, the strangeness of that overshadows the anticipation of being in a new place, and I've come to think of Japan as a kind of rehab center.

2007

Last night, while I was walking down the boulevard Montparnasse with my headphones on, a young woman stopped me and asked for a cigarette. She was maybe twenty-five, tall, and wearing a stylish pair of glasses. I'm often asked for cigarettes in Paris, and it always puts me in a bad mood. Sometimes I keep walking and other times—last night, for instance—I stop and fish through my pockets. My expression was harsh, and if I had been this young woman, I would have said, *You know what? Why don't we just forget it.* No one ever says this, though, so I give them what they've asked for, and then get mad at myself for not saying no.

I've been at this for thirty years and don't ever recall asking a stranger for a cigarette. I think of myself as a prepared smoker, and now I'll have to think of myself as a prepared nonsmoker—the guy you turn to when you need a patch or a spare lozenge. When I handed the cigarette to the young woman on the boulevard Montparnasse, it was with the hope that this would never happen again. I can't recall the first stranger who ever hit me up, but with luck, I will be able to recall the last.

January 5, 2007
Tokyo, Japan

It's been thirty-eight hours since I had my last cigarette, and while smoking it, I made a point to call it my last. "All right," I said to Hugh after I tamped it out. "I'm finished now." He noted that there were still four more left in the pack, and I said that it didn't matter how many were left, I was done. And ever since then, it's been a lot easier than I thought it would be. I guess I'd expected a full-blown nervous breakdown—crying, teeth-gnashing, the whole bit—but so far I seem to be doing all right. This might be due to the patch I applied midway through hour five. I bought enough to last me two months but am thinking I'll use no more than just this one. As for the lozenges, I haven't even opened them.

At this time one hundred yen equals a dollar, thus one thousand yen equals ten dollars, and ten thousand yen equals one hundred dollars.

It costs thirty dollars apiece to ride the express train from Narita to Tokyo.

A bag of Lavazza espresso costs eight dollars.

A stick of butter is eight dollars.

A whole chicken is forty-four dollars.

Fifteen strawberries costs forty-two dollars.

January 14, 2007
Tokyo

At the grocery store last night I came across a can of tuna, its label reading LET'S ENJOY COOKING WITH SEA CHICKEN! The other writing was in katakana, which I haven't learned yet. I decided this was a hiragana weekend, and though I can't yet breeze through the alphabet, at least I'm making progress.

Last night, for example, I read the word for "bus." It maybe helped that the word was written above a drawing of a bus and that the sign was at a bus stop, but still, if a can of tuna can read LET'S ENJOY COOKING WITH SEA CHICKEN!, a sign at a bus stop could say anything at all.

January 17, 2007
Tokyo

Yesterday afternoon Hugh and I visited the Meguro Parasitological Museum. Among its many displays is a thirty-five-foot-long tapeworm pulled from the stomach of a middle-aged man. Folded into its jar of formaldehyde, the thing is hard to make sense of, so beside it they have a corresponding length of ribbon that you can unwind and marvel at. The deal with tapeworms is that they don't really look like anything, at least not anything living. Yes, you've got a creature inside you, one that's hogging all your food, but at least it doesn't have a recognizable face. None of the parasites did. Take the flukes, for instance. I wouldn't necessarily want one, but that doesn't make them as scary-looking as, say, a grass snake. With few exceptions, most of the display information was in Japanese.

Hugh and I could read the hiragana, but making out the words and knowing what they mean are two different things. One of the displays showed a human body. Arrows pointed to the head, the heart, the intestines, and so forth, and on the outskirts were little jars filled with dead creatures. Hugh saw a small crab, bite-size, the kind the Italians sometimes throw into spaghetti sauce. "They found this in a human body," he said.

"No, they didn't."

"But it's on the display along with these other things. Look, they found it in someone's heart."

I thought he was joking, but it seemed that he actually believed it. "Things with legs and eyes do not live inside of us," I said.

"Well, this crab did."

"No, it didn't."

"It's on the chart," he said.

I reminded him that I'd spent ten days at the Maricopa County Medical Examiner's Office and that out of all the cadavers I had seen, not a one of them had a live crab in its chest cavity.

"Well, maybe..."

"No," I said. "It's not possible."

"But what if..."

"No."

"Who made *you* a doctor?"

"No," I repeated. "No, no, no."

I'd hoped that the parasite museum might have a gift shop, and fortunately it did. I bought some postcards and as I paid, I asked the clerk if crabs could live inside a human body. "Not microscopic ones, but bite-size," I said.

"A what?"

"Crab," I said, and then I remembered the word in Japanese. *"Kani."*

"Oh, no," the man said.

I turned to Hugh. "See?"

"Are you a doctor?" Hugh asked, and when the clerk said no, he gave me that little look meaning *Bite-size crabs can* too *live inside of people.*

March 3, 2007
Tokyo

I'm really starting to wonder about Hugh. He always seemed so smart but lately says things I can only describe as moronic, such as last night's "Leeks are good for your back."

"What, do you rub them into your skin or something?" I asked.

"No, stupid, you just eat them."

He was calling *me* stupid? "How can a vegetable be good for your back?"

"I don't know," he said. "They just *are.*"

March 11, 2007
Sensui-Jima, Japan
According to one piece of paper, the place where we're staying is called the Benefit Hotel, and according to another it's the Kokumin Shukusha. Then there are the bath towels, which read HOTEL HOTEL.

It's an odd place, this. Certain rooms look onto the sea, and the management is almost apologetic about them, as if the sight of the distant islands or the sound of lapping waves might be a drawback. It isn't awful, just different. The hotel has six heated pools. Some are men-only, some are women-only, and one is designated as a family tub. Across from the check-in desk is a gift shop selling dried sardines, sea salt, and a narrow range of resort wear—vests, mainly, that tie in strange ways.

The dining room is on the second floor, and we took our table at seven, discovering too late that everyone but us was dressed in traditional robes. I'd seen them hanging in our closet, but it hadn't occurred to me that, as in a *ryokan*, we were expected to wear them for meals. If all the guests are dressed alike, it's easy to believe you're at a cult gathering or a rehab center rather than a hotel. It also makes it that much harder to gossip. *See that guy in the brown robe...*

It's more difficult still when everyone has black hair, and everyone's eating the same thing. The meal was lovely if you like fish heads. That was one of two main courses, and Hugh was crazy for it. "Look at you," he scolded. "There's a good third of a chin left here and you hardly touched your forehead." The other main course was a hearty fish-and-vegetable boil. The waitress brought the fixings on a platter, and we cooked them ourselves in a gas-powered kettle named, I noticed, "the Captain Stag." This was written in English, and so it jumped out at me, as did the word on the tea dispenser, which was called "Snuggly."

Hugh and I were the only Westerners at the hotel, and as far as I could tell we were also the only homosexuals, at least the only homosexual couple. Some sort of business had booked a dozen or more rooms, and the workers, who were all men and all dressed in traditional robes, ate their dinner at a raised banquet table. They were rowdy even before they sat down, and by the end of the evening, more than a few of them were drunk. At around eleven Hugh and I stepped outside to look at the water and when we came back in we were cornered by a fellow who had just gotten out of the first-floor bath. He seemed merry enough, but we couldn't understand a word he was saying. The solution, he decided, was to talk louder and lightly hit us on the shoulder before putting a thumb in the air.

"American, eh!" he said, and I noticed a little steam drifting off him, the way it might were he the devil. "Eh! America, eh?" This went on and on and on, until we just walked away.

I like that the hotel provides eyeglasses for what the girl behind the counter referred to as "old people." This was so they could read their bills and sign in the appropriate area. The glasses were placed on a little cushion and were right there on the check-in desk, beside the brass bell.

March 17, 2007
Tokyo

After lunch we took the train to Shinjuku Park. It's easily the most beautiful spot in town, and staring across the rolling lawns with their ponds and abstract, goofy trees, you wonder why more of Tokyo can't look this way. The bridges, the little buildings, even the crows seemed to have been specifically placed. "Caw," they said, "caw, caw," as if they were reading the words off a script. Due to the exceptionally warm winter, the cherry trees have started blooming a few weeks early. One we saw was in full blossom, and around it, crouched in various positions, were seven photographers. All had tripods and serious, complicated cameras; one in particular had so many lenses it looked like the Hubble Space Telescope. Then there were the reflecting umbrellas and the big black satchels filled with batteries and extra film. It was like the tree was a star.

March 22, 2007
Paris

Joan started physical therapy for her broken shoulder, and last night over dinner she questioned whether or not it was working. "I haven't been in pain like this since that horse bit me on the breast!" she said.

"What horse?" I asked. "Where?"

"Oh, it was years ago, in Ethiopia," she told me. "He didn't mean to do it, though. I think he was just hungry."

"For what?" I asked. "Milk?"

She said she'd had a sugar cube in her shirt pocket and insisted again that it was an accident. "Satan would never have intentionally hurt me."

"That was the horse's name?" I asked. *"Satan?"*

She nodded.

"Satan bit you on the breast and it surprised you?"

She nodded again and picked up her fork. "From our other horse, Charlie Brown, I'd have expected it."

March 24, 2007
London

I took the bus home from Regent Street and just as we reached the corner of Green Park, the man behind me pulled out his cell phone and proceeded to make a call. I didn't see his face until I got off fifteen minutes later, but his voice belonged to a person in his sixties, and I noted a slight Irish accent. "Yes," he said without introducing himself or offering a hello. "About that thing we talked about, I forgot to tell you that you know who invited me back to Russia." A pause. "That's what I said. I mean, can you really see that happening? The KGB has a file on me that's as thick as, well, I don't know what. Anyway, I meant to tell you that."

The man hung up and remained silent until the Royal Albert Hall, where he placed another call and again plunged in without introducing himself. "You know that cow with a desk up front, the one with the fat ass? I'm going to need her phone records. Find out who she's been talking to. I also want to look at her computer. This means you'll have to get rid of her for a few hours. Take her to lunch, shag her, I don't give a fiddler's fart, but I'll need her to be gone until at least three, the stupid cow. All right, then."

The man seated beside me had listened to the conversation as well. We didn't talk about it or even exchange looks, but I could sense that he had overheard and thought, just as I did, that this fellow was some sort of an asshole spy. It's bad enough to go through a woman's phone and computer records, but do you have to call her a cow on top of it?

Both me and the fellow I was sitting beside disembarked at the Kensington High Street station. We'd been on the upper deck, and as we headed down the stairs we both looked at the secret agent. I don't know about the other guy, but I was really

David Sedaris

disappointed: gray skin, gray hair, a lumpy black ski cap pulled low on his forehead. The man needed a shave and though I didn't see him from the chest down, he was clearly in no position to call anyone fat. It's silly, but I always expect spies to look like James Bond. This, I guess, is why we're all so easy to spy on. Then too, the guy might just have been crazy.

April 4, 2007
Paris
In need of jokes beginning with "A man walks into a bar," I looked on the internet and found the following:
—A ham sandwich walks into a bar and orders a drink. "Sorry," says the bartender, "we don't serve food here."
—A guy with dyslexia walks into a bra.
—A pair of battery jumper cables walk into a bar. The bartender says, "You can come in here, but you better not start anything!"
—A baby seal walks into a bar. "What can I get you?" asks the bartender. And the seal answers, "Anything but a Canadian Club."

April 7, 2007
Charlottesville, Virginia
A super-crazy woman came to the reading last night and asked a question during the Q and A. "Yes," she called from the fourth row. "How come you never give free readings in hospitals and prisons?"

"Gosh," I said. "I never thought about that."

Later that evening she approached the signing table and gave me, among other things, a fifty-dollar bill and an old magazine article on Daniel Pearl. The money had been drawn on with red ink. "I turned President Grant into a zombie," she

116

said. But he looked more like a werewolf to me: fangs, hair on his face, the whole nine yards.

"Thanks so much, but I can't take your money," I said, and when I pushed it toward her, she put her hand over mine and pushed it back.

"It's not money, it's a drawing," she insisted. In the end she gave me her address, and we agreed that I would mail the bill back to her after I had scanned it. Once this was settled, she leaned forward and, lowering her voice, told me, "Hey, I went off all my meds, cold turkey, two months ago. Now I'm going to open a school and teach this whole astral-projection thing."

"Wow."

"I know it," she said. "It's going to be the first of its kind, and really big. Maybe you can come sometime and give a reading. Can you do that?"

And I promised I would try.

During yesterday's drive we passed a Wendy's with one of those signboards out front. One side read CHRIST IS RISEN and the other read TRY OUR NEW FOUR ALARM SPICY CHICKEN SANDWICH.

April 24, 2007
Austin

Last week the Virginia Tech coverage was relentless. Every tear and hug was captured on camera, as were the prayer vigils held at other universities across the country. Classes resumed yesterday, and though they asked that the press stay away, the news teams were there in full force, including representatives of NPR. I understand that leaving and being asked to leave are two different things—I'm sure the White House would love it if the papers stopped covering the Gonzales hearings—but in the case of Virginia Tech, there's nothing else to report and there hasn't been for some time. *All Things Considered,* just like everyone else, is engaged in bone-picking. "And now the school table tennis team will find a way to move on. One day at a time."

May 4, 2007
New York

I spent close to nine hours on airplanes yesterday. The flight from Anchorage left an hour late and while we were waiting to learn why, the person beside me struck up a conversation. I'd guessed she was in her mid-sixties, a big, partially blond woman with a lapful of yarn and a crochet needle in her hand. After introducing herself, she told me that she was a geologist and had been in Alaska for fifty years. The college where she taught was on break, so she was going to Washington to visit one of her daughters, not the one who was also a geologist, but the other one.

I don't know how we got onto the subject of being shot at. It sounds like something I might have brought up, but I think that actually it was her. Everyone in Alaska has a gun and when they get drunk and bored they like to wave it around. "Had my windows shot out twice," she said. "Then another time, someone put a bullet into my truck. Been shot in the arm, and just missed getting shot in the leg. Course, I was younger then."

According to this woman's father, her ancestors were Hugue-nots, born and raised in Normandy. "Never been there myself and never wanted to," she said. "Found a book once that was written in French and gave it to a priest who understood the language and said that it was pretty good."

When I told her that I lived in France, the woman asked about the upcoming elections. "Sounds to me like they should take those Arabs and just send them back home," she said. "That'd be the easiest solution." She later said that Europe was too old for its own good. "They need to get with the program, start using computers and iPods and stuff like that."

"Right," I said.

May 30, 2007
London
A performance artist and animal rights activist is promising to eat a dog live on the radio, this to protest the royal family's treatment of foxes. He's chosen a corgi because that's the queen's favorite breed, and although he will be eating it, his press release underlines that he won't be killing it. The dog had already died, supposedly of natural causes, and I'm guessing they put it on ice or something on the off chance that someone might want to do a stunt with it, a publicity hound. Crazy, to me, is that he's eating it on the radio, where, for all listeners know, it's really just a steak or a pork chop. It's not like dog meat makes its own particular sound.

Also in the news is a German woman, a real estate agent, who wants to have the biggest breasts in Europe. She's now up to a "massive 42 H" and is quoted in the *London News* saying, "I am happy every morning when I look at my super breasts and my clients also think they're great."

In an unrelated article a woman named Denise Van Outen is quoted saying, "I do like my breasts. They're great, so much fun. You can do what you like with them."

June 3, 2007
London
Lying in bed this morning, I wondered if it cost thirty pounds to see *The Three Tenors.*

According to yesterday's *Guardian,* Mark McGowan did eat a corgi live on the radio. The dog was minced, served with apples and onion, and he described the taste as "disgusting." This is the same person who, last year, left a tap running to protest water waste. Before that he put a turkey on his head and walked backward for several miles as a comment on obesity.

June 4, 2007
London

I was sitting at my desk yesterday morning when someone knocked. It was a woman wearing a yellow sundress, and the first thing I noticed was her extraordinary beauty. It wasn't the kind you'd see in a fashion magazine, but something a bit curvier and more genuine. Her eyes were the main attraction, huge, and as black as her hair. The woman was carefully made up, and whatever she was wearing, whatever perfume it was, acted like a tonic and bewitched me.

"Have I been making too much noise?" she asked, and when I said nothing she explained that she lived on the other side of the courtyard. "Apartment fifty-five A, on the third floor. I can point it out if... well, may I come in?"

"Of course," I said. We walked into the kitchen, and as the woman pointed out the window, I realized that she was my neighbor. It seems I'd been seeing her for almost five years, but never close up.

She pushed back her hair. "The management told me that someone on the sixth floor has been complaining."

Just as I said, "It wasn't me," I remembered talking about her to one of the porters. The problem wasn't the woman, but her son. He's not so bad now, but a few years back he used to stick his head out the window and shriek, sounding like a baby dinosaur.

"I might have said something years ago, but not recently," I told her. "The boy is how old now?"

"I have two," she said. "The youngest is five, and the other is seven."

I asked if I ever made too much noise and she said no. Then we just stood there for a minute. "Are you the writer?" she asked. "What kinds of things do you write?"

I started to answer and realized that she was still talking. "Because I need to speak with someone, a psychiatrist maybe, but, oh, I don't know. You must think I'm crazy."

"Oh, no," I said. "Not yet, anyway."

"It's just that my husband, well..." And it was here that she started to cry.

"Maybe you should sit down," I said. "Can I get you something to drink?"

"Just a tissue." She lowered her face toward the table and gently touched the lower lids of her eyes. Tears ran down her index fingers and just as they reached her hands, I found the Kleenex. I'd only seen someone cry like this once, and it was in the movies: Emma Thompson in *Love Actually*. It's the way you cry when you don't want to ruin your makeup or swell your eyes with rubbing.

"My husband," the woman continued. "Oh God, my husband."

"Is he hurting you?" I asked. "Are you in danger?"

"Who do you write for?" the woman asked.

There was a *New Yorker* lying on the table, and as I placed it in front of her, she laid a hand on the cover, as if she had powers, almost, and this was how she soaked up information.

"I am Iranian, from Iran," she told me, and then she introduced herself.

"Do you speak Farsi?"

"Of course," she said, and as she looked out the window, I thought of how strange it must be to see her apartment from this angle, to realize that her kitchen is a sort of stage.

"My husband, he is forcing me...forcing me to..." And then she broke off.

"He's forcing you to do what?"

121

"It would not be safe for you to know this," she said. "I mean that it would be a responsibility you do not need. Maybe it is best if we are just friends."

"Whatever you think."

On her way out she admired the wood-graining Hugh had done in the living room, and the next time I saw her—some five minutes later—she was back in her kitchen, standing at the sink. I felt like I should wave or make some sort of signal— *Mum's the word* or whatnot—but I didn't want to compound her troubles. Strange was how cinematic it all seemed: the knock on the door, the beautiful stranger, the burning secret. In the movie version she can play herself, but the writer will definitely have to be recast. I'm thinking Russell Crowe but with glasses.

June 7, 2007
London

I returned to the library yesterday afternoon and rooted through the CDs alongside a black fellow I've been seeing around lately. He's maybe in his late twenties, nice-looking, and always riding a bike. The two earlier times I'd seen him, he had been talking to himself, just as he was yesterday at the library. The guy was in the soundtrack section when I arrived, and after a few minutes in jazz, he approached the checkout desk and held up a CD. "How do you call this?" he asked.

The man behind the counter asked him to repeat the question.

"I know it says 'Lightnin' Hopkins,'" the black guy continued, "but is that a person or a thing?"

No one seemed to know, so I stepped forward and said it was a person. "He's a blues singer and guitar player."

"Is it old? Is it old-fashioned? Is it old?" the black guy asked.

I said that it definitely wasn't new, and, after thanking me, he finished checking out. I thought he left the building, but a few minutes later I heard him talking to himself. "Does it matter?" he asked. "Does it matter? Does it? Does it matter?" He said *matter* like this: "maa-tah."

After asking himself a dozen or so times, he returned to the desk and asked the librarian. "Does it matter?"

"Definitely not," the librarian said.

June 17, 2007
La Bagotière

Olivier's father died last month and he's having a hard time with it. The man was young, only sixty-two. He was helping a neighbor bring in his horses and out of nowhere he had a fatal heart attack. When Olivier dropped by last week to talk about it, he started bawling. "I didn't know what to do," Hugh told me.

"Well, did you put your hand on his shoulder?"

"No."

"I'm pretty sure that's step number one," I said. "Then you're supposed to hug him."

"Really?"

"Then, if he gets the wrong idea and starts kissing you, you're supposed to gently push him away saying, 'Whoa,' like you would to a pony."

"I'll remember that," Hugh said.

June 23, 2007
La Bagotière

Due to strikes, the five o'clock train to Briouze was canceled. This meant that everyone had to fit on the 7:38, which had been added to, but not enough. The seats were long gone by the time that Hugh and I arrived, so we stood in the car that houses the restroom and snack machine. It was shoulder to shoulder, and then a man turned toward the door and shouted, "That's enough! No more people in here!" He wasn't an official, just a passenger. It seemed that once he had gotten on, it was time to pull up the plank.

"What a jerk," Hugh said.

I stood for over two hours, and the surprise was that more people weren't assholes. Hardly anyone bickered or talked on their cell phones. An attractive couple ate a smelly fast-food dinner, but they took the boxes and bags with them when they left. While on board, I read about the mating habits of mites, specifically the kind that live in the ears of nectar-eating moths. Every so often, I'd look up and watch a young woman standing pressed against the door. She had a rat with her, a brownish-gray one. I don't know if it was fully grown or not, but it looked pretty big to me, as long as a sweet potato, double that if you add the tail, which was hairless and putty-colored and difficult to look at. For a while the rat ate lettuce. Then the young woman stuck it under her stocking cap, and it took a little nap on her head.

Before taking the train, I cleaned the apartment and listened once again to *Pretending to Be Me,* Tom Courtenay's one-man show on the life of Philip Larkin. This is him on the subject of strikes: "When I was young, if you wanted more money, you worked harder. Nowadays, you simply stop working."

July 18, 2007
Paris

While waiting for the subway at the Odéon station, I looked into a display case full of six-inch figurines. The turbaned man, the woman with shorn hair, the children carting baskets: they were not just dark, but black. Slaves are what they were, and each had been turned into something else: a lamp, for instance, or a candy dish. *We are at your service,* they seemed to say. *Here, let me take that business card. It's okay, that's what I'm here for! You can leave your change as well, I won't steal it, really, I've been trained.*

The figurines were from a shop called Espace Higgins, and if you mentioned that you'd come by subway, you'd get an automatic 10 percent discount according to a sign one of the slaves was holding.

July 29, 2007
London

I'd been swimming for half an hour when the lifeguard stopped me. It seemed that there was poo in the water, and they needed to clean it up.

"There's *what* in the water?" I asked.

The young man was Russian, and his accent was very slight. "Poo."

"You mean to tell me that someone shit in here?"

He nodded. "It's the third time today."

Walking toward the changing room I saw an assembly of turds, each the size of a cat's hairball, lying in a sunbeam near an inflatable vest. I wanted to be angry and disgusted, but I was actually grateful for an excuse to leave. Saturday afternoons are a free-for-all, and I kept having to shoo people out of my way. The lap swimmers' lanes are clearly marked, but no one seems to notice or care. At one point a boy of ten and a girl who was either his sister or his tragically young mother blocked my way and proceeded to throw a pair of goggles back and forth. "I'm sorry," I said to the girl, "but these are lanes for people who want to swim from one end to the other." I pointed to the opposite side of the pool. "You want to be over there," I said.

The boy said he was sorry and as he started to move away,

125

the girl called him back. "We don't have to go anywhere," she told him. "He doesn't know what he's talking about."

"But—" I said.

She looked away, as if I were invisible. It was then that I thought she was likely the mother rather than the sister. Her hair was dyed almost white and she had one of those silver balls, the kind that looks like a cupcake decoration, stuck through the flesh beneath her lower lip. There were tattoos as well and instead of a swimsuit, she wore what looked like boxer shorts and a tank top. This would never happen at the other pool I go to, but then again, no one there would have shit in the water either. I was so mad at this girl. Each time I swam a length I'd have to avoid her, and when I saw her getting out of the pool, I was jubilant. *Good,* I thought, *she's going.* I guess I didn't notice that everyone else was going with her. There were turds in the water, and I wound up being the last one out.

August 1, 2007
London

I went to the Kensington Leisure Centre at three o'clock yesterday afternoon, and for the first half hour it was close to perfect. For a while I shared a lane with a young woman in a bikini. She was neither fast nor slow and I thought that we made a pretty good team. Everything was great until these three boys arrived. They were maybe fifteen years old, and their effect was immediate. It was as if they'd released sharks into the pool, that's how destructive they were. The group definitely had a leader, and whenever he did something particularly vicious, the other two would look at him and voice their approval. The main kid was not particularly tall, but he was very handsome and athletically built. One moment he'd be running to the other side of the pool, and the next he'd be holding a chubby girl underwater or pushing someone in. He was everywhere at once, and you couldn't not look at him, that's how charismatic and fascinating he was.

The lifeguards did nothing, not even when he went upstairs and started jumping off the balcony. It was the mother of a child taking a swimming lesson who eventually called the police. They arrived just as I was leaving, and I wish that I had stayed and witnessed the outcome. After leaving the pool I took a bus to Oxford Street, thinking all the while about those boys. It's as if I were fifteen myself, that's how bullied and awestruck they left me.

August 10, 2007
La Bagotière
While cutting an onion for yesterday's salad I lost my grip and sliced off the tip of my thumb. Then I guess I ate it. Had it been the tip of someone else's thumb I might have some worrying to do, but I think it's all right to eat your own, especially if it's mixed with other ingredients. The sickening part was the bleeding, which went on and on until I started feeling faint. Thursday is when I go to the post office, and while riding my bike was no different than it ever was, folding the letters and putting them into envelopes took twice the time, this on account of all the tape and toilet paper I'd used to bandage myself. It looked like I had a lemon growing out of my hand. After the post office I went to the supermarket in Athis, where the cashier looked at me, saying, "What did you do this time?"

Every week it's something new: the infected middle finger, the nail I slammed in the car door, and now this. She asked to see the wound and as I pulled off the lemon, and the people behind me in line gasped, the cashier leaned in closer. Then she thought for a moment and suggested that I sleep with my thumb in my mouth. "Like a baby," she said.

Her last two home remedies worked wonders, but come bedtime I stuck with the lemon because my sheets are too beautiful to stain with blood.

August 27, 2007
London

In order to get what's called "indefinite leave to remain," Hugh and I have to take a citizenship test. The preparation book is called *Life in the UK,* and it explains, among other things, the difference between the House of Lords and the House of Commons. I've learned that British women won the right to divorce their husbands in 1857, that children aged fourteen and under are not allowed to deliver milk, and that there are 1.7 million people living in Northern Ireland. After studying for two weeks, I bought a book of multiple-choice sample questions that includes the following:

Q: How might you stop young people from playing tricks on you at Halloween?

A. Call the police
B. Give them some money
C. Give them sweets or chocolates
D. Hide from them

Q: Why did large numbers of Jewish people come to Britain during 1880–1910?

A. To escape famine
B. To escape racist attacks
C. To work in textile factories
D. To invade and seize land

September 14, 2007
London

We took Hugh's nephew to Oxford and returned to London by bus at five. On the way there, the three of us sat up top, not far from a woman who talked on her cell phone for all but two minutes. I never caught her name, but she and her boyfriend, Tom, had just moved in together. There's a spare room in their flat but it still needs decorating. The young woman eats her lunch every day at one. She doesn't like going home before meeting her mates at the pub because that's just a waste of time. And speaking of waste, she just lost the heel on her favorite shoes. Brand-new, practically, and they want thirty quid to repair it! The woman would call a friend, talk for fifteen minutes, and then call someone else. Her favorite phrases were "That's weird, isn't it" and "How annoying."

We went for dinner at Wagamama and were waited on by a young woman from Thailand. I asked if she'd by any chance taken her *Life in the UK* test and after wiping the spooked expression off her face, she said that she was taking it tomorrow at ten. "How did you know?" she asked.

The waitress is taking her test in Hammersmith but ours is in Kensington, at the library. I made perfect scores on two of my last three practice tests but that doesn't mean I'll ace the real one. All I really care about is getting a higher score than Hugh.

September 15, 2007
London

At four o'clock yesterday afternoon, a woman handed me a certificate and offered her congratulations. I know that I passed my *Life in the UK* test, but I don't know by what

129

margin. Out of twenty-four questions, the only iffy one concerned eye exams for people over sixty. Are they free? I said yes, and later learned that I was correct. Other questions included:

—What percentage of religious people are Catholic? (10 percent)
—How old must you be to buy cigarettes? (sixteen, but it goes up to eighteen on October 1)
—Do parents pay for school uniforms? (yes)
—What is England's largest minority group? (Indians)
—Can Scottish money be used in England and Wales? (yes)

I'd prepared by memorizing dates and statistics, but most of my questions were practical. What do you do if you can't get along with your neighbor? Who do you turn to if you have health and safety concerns at work?

There were ten of us taking the test. We were given forty-five minutes, but by half past everyone had finished. I started studying three weeks ago, and now I don't know quite what to do with myself.

September 25, 2007
Paris
To honor the death of Marcel Marceau I observed a minute of silence.

September 26, 2007
Paris
The Lion King is in previews now and while the French seem happy enough with the production, the Americans are saying "Never again." Especially the costume woman. For his part,

Hugh was doing okay until yesterday, when, for the umpteenth time since last Friday, somebody moved his paint. What had been in the basement was now in the courtyard, getting rained on, and when he asked that it be covered with plastic, the guy in charge of such things said, "What for? The cans have lids, don't they?"

They call this fellow La Friteuse (the vat of hot oil for frying things) because his hair is so greasy. He started to walk away after their conversation and Hugh called him *un espèce de con.* This is to say "a type of asshole."

"I guess it could also translate to 'a species of asshole,'" Hugh told me. I asked why he didn't just call him an asshole period and he shrugged. "I don't know. That's just how people do it down at the theater."

October 4, 2007
Buffalo, New York

Walking from the elevator to my room at 2:15 in the morning, I passed a naked man wearing a T-shirt. This sounds like a contradiction in terms—how can he be naked if he was wearing something? I understand the question, but still I'd stick with my description, perhaps because he looked so vulnerable. The T-shirt was a few sizes too small for him, and he was pulling it as far down as it would go, which wasn't quite far enough. Maybe when he was younger it would have hidden everything but now his balls were droopy and hung slightly beneath the hem, like the clapper of a bell.

Late fifties, I'd say he was, bald on top of his head. I thought for a moment that he'd been locked out—perhaps he was putting his room-service tray in the hall and the door had closed behind him—but looking back, I'm pretty sure it was something else. I'm now thinking he was thrown out of someone's room. How else to explain the tiny shirt and his strange silence? If I were him, I would have asked me for a towel. Then I'd say, *I don't want to put you out, but do you think you could call the front desk for me?*

This fellow didn't have a key in his hand, and I don't know what eventually happened to him. If he had spoken to me I would have talked back, but instead we passed in silence, each entertaining his own wild thoughts.

While waiting for my ride to the theater I saw a kid in a T-shirt that read LOSER. (N.) ANY PERSON WHO WOULD TAKE THE TIME TO READ AN ENTIRE MESSAGE WRITTEN ON A T-SHIRT.

October 7, 2007
Washington, DC

I was told last night that earlier in the week, my name was mentioned on *Ugly Betty*. The show apparently centers around *Mode,* a fake fashion magazine, where one of the editors called a friend to recount his miserable day. "Then I had to tell David Sedaris that we were cutting his article down to five hundred words," he said, later implying that I had a fit and screamed at him. If this were really my reputation it might bug me, but I can't remember ever raising my voice to an editor. Instead, with dignity, I quietly slander them behind their backs.

October 9, 2007
Charleston

I was very cranky yesterday, and it scared me. It started in the morning, when I boarded my flight and found a man in my seat. He was perhaps in his late thirties and wore shorts and a button-down shirt. "Do you mind if we swap?" he asked, and as he stood to let me in, he pointed to the seat beside him.

"So I'll be sitting in the middle?" I asked.

"That would be great," he said. "It's either that or be with my kids." His two boys, Skyler and Chase, were sitting across the aisle with his wife. I sighed, deeply, and capped it off with a little groan.

"I appreciate it," he said.

A few minutes later the man with the window seat came by. We stood to let him in, but just then he saw a vacant space in the back and decided to sit there instead. "Well, that worked well," the father in the shorts said. "Now we can stretch out."

I moved to the window seat, angry that I was no longer being inconvenienced. *How dare you take my seat in the first place,* I thought, aware of how petty I was being.

Yesterday's *Times* carried an article on a group of men called the Rastas who live in the forests of the Congo, dress in LA Lakers shirts, and are notorious for burning babies, raping kidnapped villagers, and chopping people up with machetes. Pictured were a half a dozen of their victims, women who'd been forced into sex and then gouged with bats and tree branches. I read this on the plane and then felt even worse for being grumpy.

October 15, 2007
Canton, Michigan

I met a flight attendant at last night's book signing, and during our brief talk she taught me a new term. "You know how a plastic bottle of water will get all crinkly during a flight?" she asked. "Well, it happens to people, too, to our insides. That's why we get all gassy."

"All right," I said.

"So, what me and the other gals will sometimes do is fart while we walk up and down the aisle. No one can hear it on account of the engine noise, but anyway, that's what we call 'crop dusting.'"

October 25, 2007
Tucson, Arizona

Last night's signing lasted for four hours and it was twelve thirty by the time I left the theater. All the decent places were closed, so Ken Shorr and I went to a McDonald's drive-through and ate at one of the outdoor tables. The patio lamps were off, but there was enough light to see our food by. We could also see a woman two tables away. She looked to be Mexican or maybe Pima, and she sat before an open notebook with a gallon bottle of Dr Pepper. Ken and I were talking about short stories when the woman interrupted and asked if she could pose a question. "I have to go before CPS tomorrow, right? I was in rehab and then I relapsed for a while. Now I'm trying to get my kids back and the judge wants me to write everything down on paper. The thing is: Do I write everything going way back into the histories and everything, or do I just write about the incident?"

I suggested she recall the incident but impregnate it with history. "You could say, for example, 'My daughter's knife wounds hadn't healed so she was a little cranky,'" I offered.

"It's a son, not a daughter," the woman said. Ken then offered some advice and on the way back to the hotel, we reflected upon the many similar encounters we've had over the years. There's something about our combination that attracts intriguing people.

October 30, 2007
Seattle

The airport in Bend, Oregon, is very small, and while waiting in the security line I examined an ad for a golf resort called Pronghorn. On another wall was a mammoth screen touting the Ranch of the Canyons, a housing development. I made note of the places with the best names, but there were plenty more where these came from. On each poster, mountains were silhouetted against a cloudless blue sky. A hawk or elk gazed with approval at a new multimillion-dollar home while someone with a golf club shielded his eyes against the perfection of the green. So caught up was I in the advertisements that I lost track of the real world. All of a sudden I was at the front of the line, and a security screener was asking for my ticket and ID. She was a bored-looking woman in her late twenties, and noticing the badge pinned to her shirt pocket, I was struck by how false and real estate–y her name was. "Are you *really* Misty Roebuck?" I asked, and then, for good measure, "*The* Misty Roebuck?"

November 11, 2007
London
Lisa and her supervising second-grade teacher were caught cursing last Friday. They thought they were alone, but just as Lisa said, "Fuck," she looked down and saw a little girl staring up at her.

"That's right, Mrs. Evans, we're going to have *fun*," the teacher said. "A whole lot of *fun*."

"That's what you do when you get caught," Lisa explained. "Deny, deny, deny."

November 15, 2007
London
Harrods has opened a Krispy Kreme counter and before sitting down to a doughnut and a cup of coffee, I went to use the restroom. There was a young man beside me at the urinal, and after he had finished and walked to the sink to wash his hands, the attendant asked him if he'd flushed.

"Uhh . . . yes," the young man said.

"No, you didn't," the attendant insisted.

The young man returned and as he pulled the handle, we exchanged that particular glance meaning *The washroom attendant is crazy.* His was the sort of behavior you'd expect at a public toilet in Paris, not in a department store, especially such a fancy one.

The attendant was black and looked to be in his sixties. His accent suggested that he was from the West Indies and his expression said, in no uncertain terms, that he hated these toilets and everyone who used them. When my turn came I made a great show of the flushing, glaring at the urinal and its contents as if to say *Be gone, you!* Then I washed my hands. There were towels folded beside the sink but using one might have angered the attendant, so instead I wiped my hands on my trousers. This seemed to please him, and I left the restroom thinking, *He likes me!*

November 24, 2007
London

Listed in the *Guardian* under "Books with Terrible Titles," Hugh noted *Cooking with Pooh,* as in Winnie-the-.

December 8, 2007
London

I always know when it's Anne Crosby on the phone. "Is this Hugh? No? Well, let me speak to him, please." It's as if I'm the housekeeper. "He's out? Well, take a message, then."

December 18, 2007
Paris

I got a notice regarding a Chronopost package so yesterday afternoon, carrying my passport, a book that needed mailing, and Ken Shorr's manuscript, I went to the post office. The line stretched to the door and for the first ten minutes it seemed not to move at all. The reason, in part, is that people bank there. Look at the slowest-moving counter and you're bound to see someone with a passbook. Then you see the clerk stamping forms the customer has just taken ten minutes to fill out.

Of yesterday's four counters, three were doing bank business. The customers left at roughly the same time, and just as I hoped we might be getting somewhere, two old people came out of nowhere, flashed their badges, and went to the front of the line. They can do that here. Armed with laminated cards saying, in effect, *I am ancient,* seniors can claim priority. Worse still is that they cut in line to bank. Meanwhile me and everyone else was thinking, *Why now? Why the week before Christmas at the busiest time of day?* Because it wasn't just *these* old people. Once they left, they were replaced by others, one of whom was wearing jeans.

If someone is wheeling an oxygen tank and walking with a cane, I can understand their need for priority, but otherwise I think the French government has got it backward. It's the young who should be allowed to cut—the people with jobs and stuff to do. These seniors go to the post office, jump to the front of the line, and that's it—their day. Nothing to do now but go back home and complain that the government's not doing enough for them.

It took me forty-five minutes to reach the front of the line, and by the time I arrived I had to pee so bad I couldn't stand it. It was starting to well up in the back of my throat when a perfectly normal-looking person, a man in his forties with no limp or glasses even, flashed his handicapped badge and cut in front of me. I gave him a doubtful look and he said, "What, do you want to *inspect my badge?*"

And the thing is that even if you *are* old or handicapped, it doesn't mean you *have* to cut in line. That takes a certain kind of person, someone whose laminated card might better read ASSHOLE.

Just as he stepped in front of me, a new station opened. The clerk asked if anyone had a package to collect and after a brief second of gloating, I stepped in front of the so-called handicapped person and went to her window. The package I received was sent by Amy, and I think there might be a pony inside it—that's how huge it is.

"I also have these padded envelopes to mail," I said to the clerk. She was a woman dressed, like all of them, in street clothes. This for her was an orange sweater and a pair of black corduroys. "Oh, I'm not equipped to do that," she said. "You'll have to get back in line."

There was no way I could do to others what I myself had spent the better part of an afternoon complaining about, so after running home to pee and drop off the enormous box, I went to another post office and did it all over again. This second one was near the Sorbonne. It was on a hill, and rather than tire themselves before cutting in line, the old people remained at sea level, and things moved much faster.

It sounds petty, but this is one of the reasons I'm moving to England. There you're old, you're handicapped, and you stand in line just like everybody else. Unfortunately, by the time I've finally made up my mind to move, I'm almost old and banged up enough to cut in line myself.

December 23, 2007
Paris

On the last day before Christmas vacation, one of Lisa's students showed up in a T-shirt reading I MAKE DIRT LOOK GOOD.

"Rhodesia," Lisa said, "I'm not sure I understand that."

December 31, 2007
La Bagotière

Hugh and I went swimming yesterday and returned to find Joan in front of the fire, reading a biography of Richard Yates. "I can't get over those mice," she said, and when she raised the book I got the idea there was a chapter I had missed.

"Mice?"

"Upstairs," she said, and we heard the unmistakable sound of something with its head in a trap.

"Just leave it," Hugh said. But how could I?

The mouse was in the center of the attic. The bar had come down on his neck and he was flipping both himself and the trap over on the floor.

"Just leave it," Hugh called from the kitchen. "I'll take care of it later." The last time I tried to free a mouse I got a pretty good story out of it, so I figured I'd try again. First, I put on the gloves Dad gave me eight years ago. Then I carried the trap onto the front porch. The last mouse had it much worse than this one did. His eyes had been bulging to such an extent I thought they might burst. This one's eyes were swollen, but not that badly. He looked, I thought, like he had been crying. What with the gloves it was much easier to raise the bar. The mouse freed himself on my first attempt and jumped off the porch into the hydrangeas. Maybe he died of a neck laceration moments afterward but I'm telling myself that he's still kicking. Maybe a little sore. Definitely crabby. But alive.

2008

January 5, 2008
Paris

Walking out the front door yesterday, I ran into our upstairs neighbor, Madame Sheppers. "Mr. Sedaris," she said, and she held out her hand. "May I offer thee my best wishes for the coming new year, not just for health, but happiness too?" She speaks French like a flowery vampire and is so unnervingly polite that all I can do is stand there. I'd wanted to complain about her barking dog but before I could begin, she pointed to the suitcase in my hand. "Are we losing you, dear neighbor? Are you going on a voyage?"

"This is for Mr. Hamrick's mother," I said. "She's leaving tomorrow for the United States."

"A short visit, I hope."

"Yes," I said. "Then the next day, I'm leaving as well."

"And Mr. Hamrick?"

"He's in London," I said.

"Then I hope it won't inconvenience you if I collect your mail. I'll just take it from the box and leave it inside your front door. That is, if it won't be a problem."

"No," I told her. "No problem at all." It really is amazing, this talent she has of doing me a favor and then asking if it puts me out. It's like she knows karate and has just chopped the pistol out of my hand. I want to blast her about her dog but there I am, completely disarmed.

February 2, 2008
Munich

When signing books for married couples in America I'll often ask if the two of them have any children. Then I'll wince as they answer, "Oh, our dogs are our children." As if teaching a springer spaniel to stay off the sofa is really the same as getting a teenager through high school in one piece.

In Germany, though, it's a different story. At last night's signing I asked a woman if she had a dog. Then I watched as she picked her book off the table, saying, "Oh, my children are my dogs."

February 5, 2008
Paris

A man knocked ten minutes after I got up yesterday morning and said that he was here for the skeleton. I wasn't expecting him until later and was embarrassed because I hadn't made the bed yet. "So you'll make a casket out of cardboard?" I asked, thinking of ten years ago, when I learned the word *cercueil*. Everyone told me I'd have no use for it, and now here I was, proving them wrong.

The second mover arrived a few minutes later and watched as his colleague lifted the skeleton off its mount. "Come on, big guy," he said. Then the two of them, or, rather, the three, headed down the stairs.

Five minutes later, just as I was making the bed, someone rang the buzzer. I picked up the intercom phone and heard, "Yes, hello. We'd like to talk about Jesus."

The last time this happened I made the mistake of letting them in. Then I was stuck with two Jehovah's Witnesses for what felt like hours.

"I do not care to discuss Him," I said into the phone. When the Witnesses asked why not, I said that I was not a believer.

"All the better," the man said, and it occurred to me that I should hang up. Other people do it all the time, so why couldn't I? On top of that, they're Jehovah's Witnesses. They're used to being hung up on, or at least they should be. I just couldn't, though, and wasted another two minutes standing near the door with a phone in my hand. After they left, I got a call from a salesman asking to speak to Monsieur Sedaris. "He's not here," I said.

"Is this *Madame* Sedaris?"

"Non," I said. *"Pas du tout. Je suis un homme."* (Not at all. I am a man.)

The salesman offered a laugh I translated to "You are a fag," and then he asked when Mr. Sedaris might be home.

"April," I said. "Late, late April."

March 13, 2008
Paris

I'd been up for half an hour when the bell rang. I opened the door, and there stood Madame Sheppers dressed in a mismatched tracksuit. "Ah, Mr. Sedaris," she said. "I wish thee the most pleasant of mornings." This is her in a nutshell. First, she drives you crazy with that barking dog of hers, and then she smothers you with formality. "I was wondering, sir, if you might be so kind as to sign the form that slipped your notice during last week's co-op meeting."

She didn't have a pen on her, and because it seemed rude to leave someone in the hall like that, I ushered her in. There were several pens in my office, and as I looked for one, she admired Hugh's wood-graining. "Ah, this must be the handiwork of the talented Mr. Hamrick! I have heard much about his artistic gifts and now I see that the talk was well founded."

I invited her to run her hand over the fake panels. Then I looked above my desk at the naive painting I'd just hung. It's two hundred years old and pictures an imp standing on the small of a woman's back, hoisting some sort of a needle. She, meanwhile, is hunched over a chamber pot, shit oozing from her exposed ass like a long ropy tail.

"Hugh painted the front door as well," I told Madame Sheppers. "Come and see!"

March 22, 2008
Paris

A huge deal is being made over Barack Obama's pastor, who was caught on tape talking about how shitty America is. His remarks are nothing, but Fox News has them on a tape loop. Obama delivered a speech on the subject and last night, after returning from my walk, I watched it. Then I read an article on John McCain's pastor, a man named John Hagee. He's quoted as saying that Hurricane Katrina was God's punishment for homosexuality but no one on the right seems too worked up about it. This leads me to believe that most people find the statement, if not true, then at least reasonable.

You'd think, though, that if God were to punish a city for its homosexuals, He would go after a place where homosexuals actually live—San Francisco, say, or New York. The New Orleans Garden District is pretty gay, but that was one of the few areas that came through Katrina relatively unscathed. Maybe the hurricane was God's way of punishing straight people in baseball caps and promotional T-shirts with mai tais in their hands—that's all I ever see when *I* go to New Orleans.

April 5, 2008
Athens, Greece

Yesterday afternoon, after checking into our hotel, Hugh and I walked to a park located near the parliament building. Yannis, the son of my Greek publisher, later explained that the government was letting its public spaces go, hoping they'd be privatized. That explains the state of the place. Coming from France, where the park maintenance can best be described as authoritarian—all trees and plants in military formation—the Greek park seemed positively wild. Oranges and newspapers littered the ground, aborted paths led off to nowhere—it looked like my dad was in charge of it.

Just when we thought it couldn't get any sadder, we wandered into an area housing a small children's zoo. There were four roofless pens there, each surrounded by a high wire fence. In the first one we came to, a smudged white rabbit sat panting in the dirt. With him were three grown goats and a kid, who climbed a waist-high stone wall separating one half of the pen from another. When the kid jumped back down, the rabbit marched across the dirt and bit him on the ankle.

"Boy, that's a bossy fucking rabbit," I said to Hugh, and he agreed. We turned the corner and found, in the next pen, two stray cats blinking into the weak sun. I guess there used to be something else there, and it died. The cats climbed in and whoever's in charge looked at them thinking, *They'll do.*

The third pen was home to two chickens, a rooster, a donkey, another stray cat, and another rabbit, this one brown and a lot less bossy. Really, though, it didn't matter what was in there. It could be a tiger or a hamster, and still I'll stand before it until my feet get tired, saying, "Awwww."

April 6, 2008
Athens, Greece

Talk to a Greek—any Greek—and it's just a matter of time before he mentions his parents. Maybe he'll say, "My mother doesn't like my new neighborhood" or "My father is hoping to get a dog," but it's always something, which is nice, I think.

*　　*　　*

Driving to the old port of Piraeus we passed a restaurant called the American House of Toast. The sign pictured a young woman dressed in a gown and a graduation cap. Behind her was an American flag and in front of her, coming right up to her chest, was a massive hamburger.

Yannis says that Athenian cabdrivers fall into two groups: those who talk about aliens and those who talk about sex. Of the former, it is often believed that the ancient Greeks came here from outer space, built the Acropolis and the temple at Delphi, and then went home.

April 12, 2008
Turin, Italy
"A man loses his soul when he has two houses or two women." This is an old Italian proverb and though I'd love to reject it, I suspect that truer words were never spoken. It was Stefania who quoted it to me, and after it had sunk in, I asked if a man might regain his soul by having three houses.

"I don't think it works that way," she said.

"Four?"

Yesterday at the cultural center I met a young woman who works at the front desk and comes from Lake Como. Her parents still live there, as does her grandfather, who is eighty-one and has spent the last fifty years making heads out of wax and occasionally selling them to museums. "Emotionally he was very distant, but he has every tooth my sister and I ever lost," the woman said.

Whoa, I thought.

"He also collected hair from our combs, and our fingernail

clippings," she told me, sounding very practical, like that's what all grandfathers do, peel off your scabs and put them in their special drawers.

April 28, 2008
Sherman, Connecticut

Hugh is working in Sherman this week and because I was relatively close by, I took the train up from New York. He and Manuela, who speaks maybe ten words of English, collected me at the station and then the three of us went to a park. My French sucked on Saturday, and on Sunday it wasn't much better. At one point we passed a vulture brooding on the side of the road. "He eats carrion," I announced, and Manuela marveled at my vocabulary.

"Where did you learn a word like that?" she asked, wondering, I imagine, how a person can know the word for decaying flesh yet not know the subjunctive of the verb *to go*.

April 29, 2008
Paris

On my last morning in New York it rained. I had promised to drop by Don's office and by the time I arrived, my wet trousers were sticking to the backs of my legs. There were a number of contracts to be signed and I was just reaching the halfway mark when Don wandered in. I hadn't seen him in a year and a half and was struck by how much older and thinner he seemed. Had Michael not been there to prompt him—"You remember your client David Sedaris, don't you, Dad?"—I don't think Don would have recognized me. They say that dementia brings out your true nature, that the things the functioning you kept hidden, the new, naked you can't help but expose. Don was always a kind, decent person, and dementia has only made him sweeter.

When I entered the office he smiled and held out his sweater. There was a suede patch on the elbow, and he stroked it with his fingers for a moment. "Isn't it marvelous," he said. "I took it to this very nice lady and she just...did what it is that she does so very well." A moment later he admired the yarn. The word resonated, so he stuck with it for the next few minutes. "Speaking of which, I was thinking of the last time we talked and I told you about these wonderful old yarns that read so well. You'd wanted me to do what I do with them and I recall that we discussed the possibility."

I had no idea what he was talking about, and it embarrassed me to fake it in front of Cristina and Michael. "Oh, right," I said. "I think we definitely talked about it."

"So many of those yarns, well, you remember, of course, how marvelous they were."

Michael stepped in then. "We'll talk about it later, Dad, when David has a bit more time."

"Well, of course," Don said.

Convinced that the skeleton on the cover of my new book is smoking a joint, officials at army bases are refusing to carry it.

May 8, 2008
London
I was on Kensington High Street, walking by the Tesco, when I passed two policemen being shouted at by a red-faced woman in a car. "Fuck off!" she said. "My sister lives round here and if she sees you, she'll tell you the same! So fuck off. Fuck you!"

Beside the woman was a girl who looked to be around eight years old. Everyone was staring and she looked like she wanted to crawl under the seat and die.

"Piss off, you! Fuck off!" the woman repeated and the police, like everyone else, laughed.

* * *

I went to the pool yesterday and listened as the child in the next cabin talked to her French nanny. *"C'est quoi ça?"* she asked.

"They're veins," the woman said. "Like...autoroutes for the blood."

There were more children in the bathroom. I had to pee and entered to find a boy standing before the locked door of a stall. "Roger," he said. "Roger, is that you?"

"Yes."

"What are you doing?"

"I'm wiping my bum."

"That's the worst part, isn't it?"

May 22, 2008
Paris

Walking through the Notting Hill tube stop yesterday morning, we passed a billboard picturing the head and shoulders of a remarkably unattractive woman. She looked to be in her fifties and had a big nose with noticeable pores, bloodshot eyes, and jowls. The caption beneath her read, *If you drink like a man, you might start looking like one.*

May 25, 2008
Paris

A few months back I started buying my coffee from a shop across from Saint-Sulpice. The man who owns it is polite and efficient and makes me think of my old coffee shop, the one on Thompson Street. There the employees had tattooed necks and played music that sounded as if it were made by steam shovels. They weren't rude, but they weren't polite either. As a customer, you had the feeling that you were bothering them.

The guy on Saint-Sulpice, by contrast, seems grateful for your business and goes so far as to remember your last order. Yesterday afternoon, as he ground my Colombian, I looked on his shelf and saw a canister of tea labeled FUKUYU.

I started on an animal fable and wound up watching Komodo dragons on YouTube. In one memorable video, the dragon ate a deer that was lying on the ground, wounded but still alive. As chunks of its back were torn away, the deer seemed to sigh, as if to say *I knew this would happen.*

June 1, 2008
Winston-Salem

Lisa bought a new refrigerator and when it started rattling, she called a repairman, who arrived sometime last week. He was in his early thirties, thin, with a goatee. I don't know what it was, exactly, but there was something about him that she didn't quite trust. "I didn't think that he was going to *kill* me," she said. "I just didn't want to leave him alone in my kitchen."

The repairman laid out his tools and as he worked, Lisa stood not far away and leafed through a magazine. Then she decided to check her messages. "I'd just picked my cell phone off the counter when the guy looked over and glared, like I was being rude or something," she told me. "I put the phone back down beside the toaster, but the longer I thought about it, the more it bothered me. Like I later said to Bob, 'Isn't this *our* house? Can't I do whatever I want?'"

After stewing for a few minutes, she decided once more to check her messages. The repairman glared at her again and because she knew that to look at the phone was to obsess over it, she put the thing in her pocket and turned back to her magazine.

"It took him maybe half an hour to fix the refrigerator," she told me. "Then he packed up his stuff, which took another few minutes. I walked him to the door and was just about to close it behind him when he said, 'I'm sorry, but can I have my phone back?'"

June 2, 2008
Winston-Salem

Late yesterday morning, after taking her African gray parrot, Henry, out of his cage and setting him on the kitchen table, Lisa and I retired to the living room. A minute later we heard the flapping of wings and then the sound of long toenails striking linoleum. "Don't look at him," Lisa whispered. This was clearly some game they play, but how could I resist looking?

What I saw was Henry at the crossroads. He was standing in the hallway, a sunbeam hitting him the way a spotlight would. To the left was the book-lined study and straight ahead was me in the living room. Our eyes met, and, after considering his options, Henry took a left and trudged into the study. Lisa and I continued our conversation and ten minutes later he arrived in the doorway.

"Henry!" Lisa said, and she scooped him up and put him on her shoulder. There he commenced to preen her eyebrows. He did the same to her lashes and was just moving on to her hair when she opened her mouth, saying, "Floss me."

He stuck his entire head in and must have found something— remnants of breakfast, I guess—stuck between her teeth. It was Henry who decided to stop. Having cleaned her teeth, he turned his attention back to her hair, separating the strands as if he planned on coloring them.

Later in the day Lisa and I visited her local YMCA. At the door to the locker rooms we separated, her to the treadmill and me to the pool, which was large and clean. Families splashed around in the horseplay lane and I dove in beside a fellow in his thirties. The two of us comfortably shared a lane and I had just finished my fifteenth lap when the lifeguard came up and announced that she was closing the pool.

"How come?" I asked, assuming, like always, that someone had shit in the water.

"Well," she said, "this other guy, Cliff? Was supposed to be here an hour ago? But he still hasn't showed up and I have to go to my parents' house."

I looked at her as if I hadn't heard.

"I have to go to my parents' house and do laundry," she said.

"The pool is closing, and all these people have to go home because you need to be at your *parents' house?*"

She didn't seem the least bit ashamed or embarrassed. "Yes," she said. "I have laundry to do."

And I wished for the umpteenth time that there was such a thing as a citizen's dismissal. It's like a citizen's arrest, only you get to fire people. *Oh, you're going home, all right,* I wanted to say. *You're going home and you're not coming back, because you are fucking fired. While I'm at it, I'm firing Cliff as well.*

God, it made me mad.

Bob, Lisa, and I went out for dinner and just as we returned home, Dad called. "Golly," he said. "Gee, how the hell are you doing?" We talked about feet and how I should soak mine in vinegar and hot water. We talked about seven-button shirts and then, finally, he got down to business. "Hey," he said. "The Holy Trinity is building an addition and I want you to give them ten thousand dollars."

"Why?"

"Because your mother would want you to."

"No, she wouldn't."

"Yes, she would." He then added that it was tax-deductible.

151

"I'm familiar with the concept of giving," I told him. "I just don't want to give to the church. I don't care about it."

"Yes, you do, and you're going to give them ten thousand dollars."

"No, I'm not."

"Yes, you are."

"No, I'm not."

"Yes, you are."

"How come *you* don't donate ten thousand to the church?" I asked.

"I haven't got that kind of money."

"Yes, you do."

"No, I don't."

"Yes, you do."

And on it went.

June 6, 2008
New York

I've started asking random men if, like me, they have a problem with leakage after they pee. One guy last night offered a two-point plan. "Number one is your rigorous shake," he said. "And I mean *rigorous*."

The problem here is one of perception. Shake too much and the stranger at the next urinal will likely think you're masturbating.

"Step two: be patient," the fellow said. And here, I think, is my real problem. I'm always in such a hurry to get on with things that I wind up wetting myself.

Another, older man answered my question with the following poem, something he'd once read on a restroom wall:

You can shake it all you want
and do a little dance

But the last three drops
are always in your pants.

June 9, 2008
Pittsburgh

I arrived in Pittsburgh just before noon and was met at the baggage carousel by my media escort Susie, who's thinner than I remember. The last time we met she was brightly dressed. This time she wore white slacks with a matching jacket. Her hair, which is dyed a sort of Bozo red, was teased out. I commented on the color and she patted it with her palm. "It's not natural, if that's what you're asking," she said. "This is to say that the cup doesn't match the saucer, if you catch my drift."

This is Susie all over. It doesn't work to hold a conversation, as she's more comfortable talking than listening. The best you can do is steer her onto this or that topic, then sit back and enjoy yourself. On the way into town, I asked about her son, the youngest one who works as a cop. He's only forty-five but recently retired on account of his osteoporosis. "Is that the disease where you stoop over?"

"God, no," Susie said. "You're thinking...oh, I can't remember what that one's called. What Bob has are brittle bones. He'll crack a rib just stepping out of the car, so of course police work is out of the question."

On the way from the hotel to the bookstore I learned that Susie's husband recently retired. "I want him dead," she said, adding that she should probably keep this to herself. "The poor thing will have a heart attack and people will say, 'Well, Susie told me...' Next thing you know I'm behind bars!"

From there we jumped to politics, specifically to what she called "the Muslim problem."

"Say what you want, but this is a Christian country. They

come over here wanting to change things and it's about time that somebody stands up."

Later she alluded to gay marriage, forgetting, I think, that I'm gay. "Next thing you know we'll have people marrying dogs and cats and I don't know what!"

When we got to the bookstore Susie disappeared. I started signing and saw her a few hours later. "Gee, can I get you a snack or something? Some chips?" A while after that, as the afternoon veered toward evening, I heard her complaining to a woman who was waiting for her son. "It's not fair," she said. I pricked up my ears and realized that she was talking about me. "With most authors it's in and out. Him, though, he takes too long. Listen to how he's talking to everyone, acting like there's no line at all!"

Later, of course, when she was talking to me, there was no mention of my taking too much time. We didn't discuss the store or the signing, just Ron Jeremy, whom she escorted a few months ago. "My son said, 'Ma, do you know who that is?'

"And me, of course, how the hell should I know? 'Your dad and I, we're too old for porn,' I told him. Johnny Holmes—or Johnny Wad, he was called—that's a name we know but this new generation, forget it."

Ron Jeremy's event was something else, according to Susie. "All these young girls wanting their you-know-whats signed. If they were my daughters I'd faint. Ron Jeremy, though, he's a pretty smart cookie. I'm talking investment-wise. 'Susie,' he said, 'if I felt like it, I could retire tomorrow.'"

This got her back on the subject of her husband. "Oh, I could just kill him," she said.

On the plane from Philadelphia, I sat in the last row, right across from the bathroom. An enormous man wedged in beside me, and just before takeoff he asked for a seat-belt extender. I spent the flight with my arms folded against my chest, listening to the woman in front of me, who was in her sixties and would not shut up about Toastmasters. I'd met a person from this group before and, like her, he proselytized. "Communication is what it's all about," she said. "I talk to you, you talk to me, but if we can't understand each other, what have we got?"

Her seatmate, a young woman of twenty, had just left her boyfriend for a summer internship in Pittsburgh. "Toastmasters won't make you miss him any less, but it *will* help," the woman said.

As we taxied to a landing she took her case across the aisle to a loud, friendly man who happened to be running for state treasurer. "You don't have to sell me," he told her. "Communication is my bread and butter."

"Well, of course it is, being a politician and all," the woman said. "Look at George Bush. His first two years in office, he was a terrible speaker."

"His first two years?" the candidate said.

"Then he got a lot better," the woman explained. "The difference is just amazing."

"Isn't it just," the politician said. Then he turned and introduced himself to the man in front of him, adding the word "Democrat" to "candidate for state treasurer."

July 10, 2008
Toronto, Canada

I spent a day flying from Rio to São Paulo to Miami and then on to Canada. The actual in-the-air time amounted to twelve and a half hours with another eleven hours spent waiting. The killer was my layover in Miami. I got there at six in the morning and took off at one thirty in the afternoon. Hugh was with me for a short while until his flight to New York left, but after that I was on my own. At around ten I called Lisa. She recently bought a pedometer and has taken to walking five miles a day—not on the street, but in her basement. "Pacing, I guess you could call it," she told me.

After that, we talked about Tiffany. She's just moved out of her apartment—*snuck out* is more accurate—and is now in Maine for a week. Her traveling companions reportedly have guns but where she met them and how she managed to tag along is a mystery.

"She's seriously sick now," Lisa told me, adding that Tiffany will call several times a day and just rant.

The Miami airport pumps lite jazz throughout its terminals. If that wasn't bad enough, I had to listen to the announcements: the one warning you not to smoke, the one welcoming you to Miami, and, dumbest of all, the one reminding you not to take packages from strangers. Over and over, I listened to these. Over and over and over.

July 21, 2008
London

Hugh and I walked to the Lido last night. The café there is open until nine in the summer, so we stopped and had a coffee. On our way back home we passed some cattails on the edge of a pond. Hugh remarked that they reminded him of Canada, and in that moment his eyes filled with tears.

"Are you thinking about your dad?" I asked. And he nodded.

Hugh cries like he falls asleep—instantly. I tend to forget that his father died only five months ago.

July 26, 2008
Paris

Yesterday's periodontal appointment was a real bloodbath. Dr. Barras concentrated on my top teeth, specifically the ones in the front, and before beginning she shot me full of Novocain.

The result made me feel as if I had a cleft palate and only half a nose. "Am I swollen?" I asked. I was shocked when she held up the mirror and I saw I was no different than ever.

When the appointment was over, she pulled out her prescription pad and asked me what I normally took for pain. I told her that I didn't usually have any, and as she scribbled away, I wondered how I'd act when faced with Percocet or Vicodin or whatever it was she was about to give me. Would I become addicted? When would I finally face up to it? Would it take a month? Years? After leaving I looked at the paper she'd handed me and saw that she'd written a prescription for Advil. "Is that *it*?" I asked, both grateful and disappointed.

August 12, 2008
London

There was a madwoman at the bus stop yesterday and after chasing everyone off the bench, she set to arranging and re-arranging the plastic bags in her knapsack. In profile she was, if not pretty, then at least well made. I liked the line of her nose, which was regal, almost. Her eyes appeared to be gray and just as I strained to see more of them, she turned to face me, and I gasped. The four teeth between her incisors were missing and her mouth was brown at the corners. Of course, her tongue wasn't forked, but it might as well have been, that's how angry and evil she seemed. "Get off me, fucking cock horse," she hissed, and as she turned back to her knapsack, I stood there thinking, *Cock horse?*

August 18, 2008
Sydney, Australia

Before dinner I found Hugh drinking from a bottle of Evian that had been sitting on the dresser in our hotel room. "How much did that cost?" I asked. When he shrugged, I looked at the little bib hanging around the neck and saw the price written in small, light-colored letters. "This water is nine dollars!"

"So," Hugh said.

"So, you should have opened one of the waters next to the bed, the ones with bibs reading *With our compliments.*" Those bottles weren't Evian but something called Mount Franklin, and their packaging amounted to the oldest trick in the book. "The hotel assumes you'll think that because *that* water is free, *this* is as well, and you fell right into their trap," I said.

Hugh refilled his glass. "So what?"

"So, we just paid nine dollars for a little bottle of water."

"We're not the ones paying," he said.

But this was not the point.

"Then what *is* the point?"

"The point is that you should have read the bib before opening the bottle." I hadn't meant for this to turn into a fight, but that's exactly what it did turn into, and by the time we left for dinner he was no longer speaking to me. Walking in silence to the restaurant, I wondered why I'd gotten so bent out of shape about it. Water is precious, you can't deny that. One day it will in fact cost nine dollars a bottle. But this is not that day. Except that it is.

September 10, 2008
London

In order to drive a cab in London you have to take a test called "the Knowledge." To pass it is to know every street by heart, and seeing that this is a vast, confusing city, it means you have to start studying when you're young. I mean, very young. Like, the minute your eyes commence to focus.

Because the test is so demanding, almost everyone who passes is a native-born Londoner. Radio-car chauffeurs, on the other hand, are often recent immigrants and tend to rely on a GPS.

This is all to introduce the driver I had yesterday afternoon. Zoe and I were going from the BBC to Victoria Station, where we would catch a train to Brighton. The radio car arrived on time, and behind its wheel was a small, brown-skinned man I guessed to be in his late thirties. His eyes were a few shades lighter, a beautiful copper color—but what I really noticed was his hair, which was black and pinned into the biggest, gnarliest bun I had ever seen. At first I mistook it for a mohair cushion, that's how completely out of control it was.

The man was on the chatty side, so within a block I learned that he was from Sri Lanka and had been in London for three years. He spoke very quickly and with a heavy accent, so I had to really concentrate in order to understand him. "What?" I kept saying, and "Oh, gosh. Can you repeat that?"

We talked for a moment about the traffic, and then he confided that all of this was new to him. "The driving, sir, this is not what I'd wanted to do with my life. Not that it is bad, sir, not that I am complaining, but my original business, my real business, if I may say, is oil, sir."

I must have sounded so dumb. "You mean, like, to cook with?"

"No, sir. I mean petroleum. I had a business that was called Shell Oil but was not Shell Oil, if you know what I mean."

It seems to me that you're either Shell Oil or you're not, but in the interest of time I let it slide.

"Then, sir, this business of mine was taken away from me. I won't say that it was unfair, but I will say that it was wrong, sir. Terribly wrong. I was then bankrupt and left penniless. Penniless, sir. So now I am driving this car to raise money for a solicitor. I am taking my case to the highest court in the land and, God willing, I will win."

"Well, good for you," I said, struck by how severe and hard-hitting that word was: *penniless*. It made me think of Charles

159

Dickens, and as I looked out the window at the narrow Georgian buildings, it felt all the more real to me.

"In the meantime, sir, I plan to make it into the *Guinness Book of World Records*."

He seemed a shoo-in for the World's Biggest Bun, but still I figured that I should ask. "The world record for what?"

"I am trying, sir, to take the youngest baby to each of the seven continents." He looked at me in the rearview mirror and raised his dark eyebrows. "Yes, sir, you have heard me correctly. As it is, the youngest baby started at nine months and took three hundred days to finish his journey. My baby, sir, is two months old, and I hope to complete our mission no later than March first."

"Wait a minute," I said. "This is *your* baby?"

"Yes, sir."

"And you're trying to beat the current record holder?"

"Exactly," the driver told me. "Just last Tuesday we went to Turkey, where there is a bridge spanning Europe and Asia. That is two continents, sir. Next comes Australia."

"But that's a twenty-hour flight," I said. "What baby wants to spend that much time on an airplane?"

"Oh, this child loves flying, sir. She is very well behaved, but should she start crying, my wife will pull out a breast and feed her. She is shameless that way, sir."

I guess I'd forgotten that it takes two to make a baby. "So this wife of yours, she doesn't work?"

"Oh, she does, sir. She is a physician."

Then I thought, *Okay, what mother, especially one who went to medical school, would want her baby to fly to Australia for no reason? Jet lag is a serious problem for infants. That aside, how does the wife fit into the penniless business? If you're really that broke, how can you afford a pair of tickets to the other side of the world?*

"The only thing I worry about is Antarctica, sir. I think that I have found a boat that will carry us there from Argentina. I just worry that ice will box us in, and we will find ourselves trapped."

Again I looked out the window at the great crowds of people crossing the street.

"The baby may likely get frostbite or die from exposure," the driver continued. "She may not make it back alive, but nothing will keep me from trying!" It was here, I think, that I lost all faith in this supposed wife of his. *Twenty percent chance our only child will survive an uncalled-for trip to Antarctica? I'm in!* Doctor or not, what sort of parent would agree to that?

The strangest part of his story was the keenness to set a world record. The world's strongest woman, the man with the longest beard or greatest number of teeth—those are things that a person might be interested in. Taking the youngest baby to each of the seven continents, though, if that's not in the back of the book, I don't know what is.

September 16, 2008
Glasgow, Scotland
At last night's signing I met a Scotsman named Stuart, a social worker with short, slightly graying hair. "There was a great tragedy in our district recently and I went last Sunday to tell my mother about it," he told me. "This woman was on the second floor of her house, bathing her toddler in the sink. We don't know how long she'd been at it, but at some point, her doorbell rang. She must have thought the baby could be left alone for a minute, so she went to the stairs, tripped over the laundry basket, and broke her neck in the fall. Her child, meanwhile, slipped under the bathwater and drowned."

We shared a mournful pause.

161

"So, I told this to my mother," Stuart continued, "and when I'd finished she asked, 'So who was at the door?'"

October 12, 2008
Charlotte, North Carolina

At the Cleveland airport I passed a display near the security station. HERE ARE SOME OF THE ITEMS FOUND IN PEOPLE'S LUGGAGE, read the large sign. In a case beneath it was a hammer, a grenade, and two sticks of dynamite taped together. There were guns and knives too, of course, but it's the explosives that really capture the imagination. *I forgot it was in there,* I imagine someone saying, someone who, what, though—derails trains? Captures villages?

October 30, 2008
Boulder, Colorado

So many Democrats are having their campaign posters stolen that the Obama people have printed a new one. YOU CAN TAKE MY SIGN, BUT YOU'LL NEVER TAKE MY VOTE, it reads.

Paul's having a similar problem, only with his Halloween decorations. After the third one was taken from his yard, he set up a video camera and caught someone's T-shirted back as he ran off with a ghost. "You, too, could use a sign," I told him. "A good one might read, 'You can take my rubber hobo hanging by the neck from a pine tree, but you can never take my dignity.'"

December 14, 2008
Binghamton, New York

I arrived at cousin Joan's at around one, and Dad got here a few hours later. "This gal on the plane started a conversation and I literally jumped," he said as I helped him out of his coat. "Talk about ugly, she had a mouthful of absolute spikes. I'm talking stalagmites and stalactites—just the worse damn teeth you ever saw."

Joan's son-in-law Dan hunts, and over dinner he talked about a deer he'd shot earlier this fall. "Ever think of going hunting with a camera?" Dad asked, and the table fell silent.

"And eat what, the film?" I asked.

Dan then noted the various things he and Becky make from their frozen deer meat. "There are burgers, roasts, stews, sloppy Joes…"

"Actually, that would be sloppy *does*," I said, and for the rest of the night I chuckled at my little joke.

December 24, 2008
London

It was early afternoon, the sky a flat gray color, like wet cement, and Amy and I were walking through Kensington Gardens. "Tiffany told Dad last week that she wants to be a cop," she said.

"A what?"

"She said she wants to go to the academy and become a policewoman."

"But she can't even drive."

"I know it, but…"

Later, at a gallery, Amy bought some cups and saucers. The woman who makes them is in her nineties and spends half the year in Italy. This I learned last summer, when I bought some cups and saucers of my own. The person who sold them to me was sadly not there yesterday. In her place was what Amy called "a dummy," a tall, slender woman who couldn't keep the prices straight. Then she ran Amy's card through the machine and told her that it didn't work.

"It might if you didn't insert it backward," the gallery assistant timidly suggested. And so the woman tried again.

As all of this was going on, the gallery owner's husband was pointing out an earthenware bird. It was done by the same woman who made the pottery, and I couldn't think of a single thing to say about it. Instead, I turned to a plastic box on the floor. "And what's this?" I asked.

It was, apparently, a worm farm.

"And how does it work?"

Amy came out and together we watched as the lid was raised, and the gallery owner's husband revealed a banana peel resting on a bit of rotting newsprint. That was when the Australian woman stepped out of the office and gestured at Amy's pottery. "Is it all right like this?" she asked. "I'm afraid we haven't got any bubble wrap or bags."

"So we should carry the cups and saucers home in our arms?" I asked.

"Well, yes," the woman said.

All we could do was stare.

December 28, 2008
London

On Christmas Day a man in Philadelphia went to the movies and found himself seated near a couple of chatterboxes, a father and son, according to the report. The two were asked several times to be quiet, and when they continued their conversation, the man who had shushed them pulled out a gun and shot the father in the arm.

Reading this, I thought, *Well, finally.* Everyone knows that calling the manager doesn't do any good, and why have liberal gun laws if we're not going to take advantage of them? If someone won't shut up during a movie, they *should* be shot, and as often as possible. My only amendment would be that the shooter use a silencer; that way the rest of us won't be distracted.

2009

January 15, 2009
Paris

Today's paper includes the story of three-year-old Adolf Hitler Campbell. That would be the brother of one-year-old Joyce Lyn Aryan Nation Campbell and another girl who's kind of named after Heinrich Himmler. The trouble started when a local ShopRite refused to put Hitler's name on a birthday cake. This prompted the father to say, "I think people need to take their heads out of the cloud they've been in and start focusing on the future and not on the past. There's a new president and if he says it's time for a change, well, then, it's time for a change."

One longs to ask if he voted for the president he's so fond of quoting, but the answer is pretty obvious.

The story made me think of the time I was in the Denver airport and heard Adolf Hitler paged over the intercom. I was on the moving walkway, hurrying to catch a flight, and it stopped me for a moment. *Hitler!* I thought. *Now, where could he be going?*

January 19, 2009
London

Eighty buses across the UK are now carrying signs encouraging people to "come out" as atheists. THERE IS PROBABLY NO GOD, they read. NOW STOP WORRYING AND ENJOY YOUR LIFE.

David Sedaris

It is impossible to imagine such a campaign in the United States, but more than that, I'm struck by the rather lame wording. If there is *probably* no God, then there is *possibly* a heaven and *maybe* a hell where you *just might* burn for an eternity. Thus, we're back to square one.

On Italian buses the posters reportedly read THE BAD NEWS IS THAT GOD DOES NOT EXIST. THE GOOD NEWS IS YOU DO NOT NEED HIM.

January 25, 2009
London

Just before yesterday's lunch I started feeling queasy and by midafternoon my forehead was hot. By the time it got dark there was no denying that I was sick. Everything ached, and unless I was either directly in front of the fire or buried beneath three blankets, I trembled violently from the cold. While eating dinner I watched the last episode of *Cranford,* in which one character had a leg amputated and died during the surgery. Afterwards I read that Mariana Bridi, a Miss World Brazil runner-up, recently lost her hands and feet due to complications of a urinary tract infection. There was a picture of her in happier times, leaning back against a boulder, and I studied it for several minutes. Her beauty made the whole thing just that much more tragic, but why? I wondered. Homely people need hands and feet too, maybe even more.

At three o'clock I went to bed. I must have slept, but my dream was so thick and important-seeming that it felt like I was awake. This was one of those complex, problem-solving dreams. *Don't let me forget this,* I thought. *I could win a Nobel Prize. Don't let me...for...get...*

The problem, as I now recall it, had to do with doctors never knowing whose legs to cut off. And the solution was to say either "I'm sure I have gangrene" or "I feel fine, thank you."

166

It's so stupid, but in my sleep it was a real breakthrough. I didn't wake up until almost noon and learned not long afterwards that, following her surgery, the Miss World Brazil runner-up had died.

February 2, 2009
London

Tyler arrived at Pam's house a year ago yesterday. To mark the anniversary of the event, Hugh and I met the two of them at Whole Foods and celebrated with coffee and cupcakes. Our coffee was real while Tyler, who is four and a half now, drank a babyccino—steamed milk with some chocolate sprinkled on top. He was in a good mood and without quite meaning to, I tested it. "Oh," I said, gesturing to the toy brontosaurus in his hand, "you're playing with my dinosaur."

"No," he corrected me. "It's mine."

"Afraid not, sport. This morning your mother sold me all your stuff—the TV, the DVD player, your fish, your toys. She sold it all for three pounds."

"No, she didn't."

"Did too. She even sold me your bedroom. And even your name. From now on, Tyler Golden—that's me. Not you."

It was this more than anything that seemed to bother him, so of course I drove it into the ground, stopping only when Hugh stepped in.

"He's kidding," he said to Tyler. "Your mom would never sell your things."

I was like, "Thanks a lot."

Hugh was like, "*He's four*, okay?"

By the time we left it was late afternoon, and snowing. TV productions of *A Christmas Carol* lead you to believe that this happens all the time in London, but it's really very rare. Tyler went wild and took to prancing.

"Now that it's snowing, do you think Father Christmas will come back?" I asked.

The look Pam gave me sent two clear messages. The first was that we have been friends for twenty-five years. The second was that twenty-five years is a long, long—sometimes a terribly long—time.

February 4, 2009
London

Lisa called Dad and read him a poem written by one of her students.

"That's beautiful," he told her. "I hadn't realized it, but you have a chance to make a real difference in people's lives."

Lisa was touched. "That I do."

"Just make sure you don't blow it," Dad said.

February 7, 2009
London

We finished season three of *The Wire,* a program in which not a single character has ever used a trash can. Cops, union officials, junkies, drug dealers, lawyers, each and every one of them is a litterbug. I'll be in someone's corner, behind him 100 percent, but the moment he pitches an empty bottle onto a railroad track I think, *Okay, you can die now.* I'm not counting cigarette butts as litter, but I am counting bullet casings. This is what turned me against Omar, who until last night was my favorite person on the show.

I walked to Home Base for two sacks of firewood and was dragging them home on my collapsible trolley when a man stopped and asked me the time. His hair was roughly cut, as if with a steak knife, and his teeth were brown. In his arms was a large cardboard box, unfolded, and I sensed he was going to use it as a begging carpet. A drug addict, I figured he was, on his way to the prime spot outside Waitrose.

I had my iPod on and was dragging the firewood behind me, thus it was an inconvenience to stop and pull the plugs from my ears. Then I let go of my load and turned up my sleeve. "It's five fifteen," I told the guy. And instead of thanking me, he threw up his hands, saying, "Is that *all*?"

March 14, 2009
London

A *New Yorker* fact checker phoned Bob Evans and asked if he'd really taken me to Costco at the start of my book tour. "And you were looking for light bulbs? And you bought strawberries?"

Bob verified the story, and then the guy called Costco and learned that they do not sell five-pound boxes of strawberries. "You'll have to change that to a *four*-pound box," I was told.

I'd written that I bought a gross of condoms, meaning, to me, a big boxful. I don't know how many were in there, but according to the fact checker a gross is a dozen dozen, or 144. I can't say *gross* unless it was an actual gross, so I'm changing it to "a mess," which makes it sound like the condoms were already used.

March 30, 2009
New York

On Friday night in Paris I went to bed and discovered a lump the size and feel of a deviled egg bulging from my right side, just beneath the rib cage. *What's located there?* I wondered. *Is it my gallbladder? Did my intestine rip? Is this a hernia? Is it cancer?*

I completely understand the guy who walks into the doctor's office with a growth the size of a pumpkin resting like a second head upon his shoulder. "Do you think you can take a look at this thing?" And when the doctor asks when he first noticed it, the man answers, "What year is this?" Like him, I tell myself that things will go away. I'll wake up tomorrow and it'll be gone. Meanwhile I'm stuck with a growing dread. *Cancer. I have cancer.*

I told Hugh about the lump and he asked if I wanted to see a doctor.

"That's okay," I told him. This means *If I am going to live, you'll have to take care of everything.*

It was Saturday morning, almost noon, when he phoned Docteur Medioni, who has an office a couple of blocks away, on the boulevard Saint-Michel. Ten minutes later I was on his examining table, and I had my shirt raised. The doctor felt the lump, then instructed me to lie sideways. Another few moments of fondling, and he announced that I had a lipoma.

"So, cancer?" I said.

"Oh, no," he told me. "It's just some fatty tissue is all. Ninety-eight percent of the time these things are completely benign, but you should have an echograph just to make sure."

"Will my fatty tumor get bigger?"

"A little," the doctor said.

"Why won't it get a *lot* bigger?" I asked.

Docteur Medioni shrugged. "Why don't trees reach the sky? Things can only get as big as they're supposed to." He then looked at his watch and charged me thirty euros, which today is about forty dollars, a small price for such considerable peace of mind.

April 2, 2009
Pittsburgh

On Wednesday afternoon I was met at the airport by the dean of students, Felicity, and her departmental colleague, a fellow in his late forties named Conner. The guy wore a sports coat with a forest-green sweater, and, for no reason in particular and every reason in general, I immediately identified him as gay. On the ride into town he mentioned a remodeling project. "We've just had hardwood floors put into the living room," he said, "and now we've started expanding the kitchen."

The following morning Felicity came by herself and drove me back to the airport. Conner, she explained, had taken the day off and was meeting with a contractor. She mentioned the headache of his renovation project, and I asked how long he and his boyfriend had owned their house.

"His what?"

"He said, '*We* had new floors put in,' so I just assumed he meant him and his boyfriend. But, what, does he live with his parents or something?"

"Conner's married," Felicity told me.

"To a woman?"

"Well, of course," she said. "Not only that, but they have two kids."

There are times I've been wrong about this sort of thing, but as far as Conner's concerned, there's really no debate. "He's gay," I told her.

"Impossible," Felicity said. "His family aside, when would he have the time?"

She said this as if being a homosexual took hours of practice, not just at the start but every day of your life. Keeping your walk up, maintaining your little outfits—people think it's easy, but it's not.

"On top of the event planning, Conner works with the drama department," Felicity told me. "Then he's got the glee club and another chorus he sings with on weekends."

To her, this made sense, the perfect defense of his heterosexuality. To me it was like saying, *How can he be a vampire when he's shut up in that coffin all day?*

April 3, 2009
Mount Kisco, New York

Toward the end of last night's signing a woman asked me where I was staying. I said I was at the Holiday Inn, and when she asked if it was a good one, I told her that there was no such thing. This one, for instance, has no elevator. It's not that it's out of order; it just doesn't exist. But then, a hotel—guests with babies, people toting heavy suitcases from one floor to the next—why would you need one, right?

I left my Holiday Inn at six o'clock and was brought back seven hours later, at around one a.m. It was shortly afterward that I turned on the TV and was knocked off my feet by a violent stabbing sensation in my lower left side. It was as if someone had knifed me and was now twisting the handle. Because I've gone through this before, I knew exactly what it was—a kidney stone. Aside from the location, the giveaway was the pain. It doesn't begin as a mild ache and build to something stronger; rather, it just appears, full force, like an overhead light that's suddenly been switched on. You tell yourself that if you lie down or bend to the right it won't hurt as much, but it always does. There is no position of comfort, and knowing this, you seek it anyway, always moving, moaning, rolling your eyes into your head.

I must have looked monstrous as I descended the staircase and presented myself to the young woman behind the check-in desk. A college student, I figured she was, sitting on a stool and reading a paperback novel.

"Could you please call me a...taxi to the...hospital," I asked. The lobby was empty except for us two, and as she dialed, I doubled over and cursed myself for being so pathetic.

The first cab company didn't answer, and the second said they could be there in an hour. All this might have taken four minutes, but it felt like forever. "Let me try another place," the desk clerk said, and when they, too, failed to answer, she hung up the phone and thought for a second. Then she put up a sign reading BACK IN FIFTEEN MINUTES and drove me to the hospital herself, this lovely young woman, this complete stranger at the Holiday Inn.

And her car was filthy.

April 23, 2009
Saint Louis, Missouri

When I arrived at my hotel yesterday it was not quite two in the afternoon. I went down the street for a sandwich and while eating, I decided to try the light-rail system. There's a station not far away, and for $4.50 I took a train to downtown and back. The plan was to go swimming, but the Y was in a weird neighborhood, and I arrived to find a man passed out on the stairs. He was sprawled there spread-eagle, his pants yanked down beneath his hips.

The Saint Louis Y charges $15 for day passes, and the pool closes every few hours to give the lifeguards a break. Entering meant I wouldn't make it back to the hotel until late, so I skipped the swim and went to Macy's, which was empty. "Can I help you?" the shoe salesman asked.

I told him I was looking for laces.

"Oh," he said. "We don't sell those." This as if I had asked for something outlandish, like a lion cub.

"Can I help you?" In the sock department I said I was looking for something in gray.

"How about these?" the saleswoman asked, and she held up a pair that were a light tan color.

Only the candy department had what I wanted. Then I got

back on the train, which was clean and comfortable. I chose a seat near the window and was just settling in when the woman behind me got on the phone. "Hi, baby," she said. "It's me!" She told the man she was calling that she loved him and then he must have denied it. "Oh, but I do!" she said. "You know I do."

It seemed she had come from a successful job interview. "I start tomorrow and guess what? If I work from Thursday morning at nine to Friday morning at nine, I can make a hundred dollars!"

This works out to four bucks an hour, a figure that sounded good to her. "Can you believe it, baby? I can work five days and make—are you ready—five hundred dollars!"

She was a white woman with a hushed, almost husky voice. "The girl I'm replacing, her boyfriend is black too. I showed her your picture and she said, 'Well, he's big, isn't he!' And I said, 'Big in every way!'" She laughed. "I think she knew what I was talking about."

As the train advanced, I learned that she worked as a nurse's aide. The person she'd be tending to was an old woman with Alzheimer's, the mother of a local politician. "She can't hardly speak or make sense but she put her hand on my cheek and said...guess what? 'You are so beautiful.' Can you believe it? She called me beautiful!"

I envisioned this person taking the train five days a week and working twenty-four-hour shifts. How boring it would be, I thought, and what a toll it would take on her relationship. It's rude to visit someone else's town and get depressed, but to pass this bleakness every day, to hang out with a demented old person and know that her fate might be your own, would be more than I could bear.

When the train reached my stop, I went to the door, then turned so I could see who had been talking. She was blond, her skin pocked with acne scars, perhaps in her mid-thirties, with a thin, almost pretty face. "We're entering a tunnel," she said into her phone. "I don't want to lose you but if I do, just know that I love you."

April 30, 2009
Los Angeles, California

The surprising thing about Phyllis Diller was that she was so...Phyllis Diller, just like the one on TV, but older. She's ninety-one now, and her eyes leaked steady tears. Every twenty seconds she had to blot them with Kleenex, and as she did so I'd notice how thin and veiny her hands were, like talons. Otherwise, she looked fantastic. "I had all my plastic surgery done forty years ago," she said. "Since then—nothing."

Accompanying Phyllis Diller was a friend of hers, a playwright. The two arrived at the Bel-Air hotel shortly after noon, Jeanie on foot and Phyllis—or Miss Diller, as I was instructed to call her—in a wheelchair. The hotel is magnificent, or at least the grounds are. I pulled up a few minutes early and walked around for a bit. "The booth behind us is Nancy Reagan's," Miss Diller pointed out. "She and Betsy Bloomingdale camp out here. She's younger than me but in much worse shape."

After settling in, I was presented with pepper. "It's my passion," Miss Diller said, and she squinted at the label. "This is mixed with lavender, and it's fantastic. Pepper! I love it!"

She also loves vinegar and had arrived with her own, a small vial she kept in her purse. "Sometimes I'll put it on spinach or something, but if you ask the waiter he'll bring a whole pitcher of the stuff. I'll use a few drops, and then they'll take it back to the kitchen and throw it away."

"That's so wasteful," Jeanie said.

"Well, the thing is that it takes something like thirty years to make," Miss Diller said. "The Italian farmers age it in oak casks or some damn thing and I just hate to think of all their hard work going down the drain. It's crazy, I know, but stuff like this—waste—really bugs me!"

I liked how kind Miss Diller was to the waiters. Before ordering food, she asked for a drink, a cocktail of rum and whipped egg whites. "You have to at least have a sip," she said. I told her I didn't drink but I think she forgot, as when it arrived, she told me again to try some.

"All right," I said, because what can you do? This wasn't some stranger at a dinner party; this was Phyllis Diller insisting that I drink from her glass.

I had maybe half a thimbleful. It tasted like medicine.

Before ordering we talked about drugs and hospitals. "God, I love morphine," Miss Diller said. "That's the best, but they don't give it to you for nothing." Her last hospital visit was for a broken neck. "I fell out of bed, a real danger for people my age." I noticed that when turning to look at something, she had to pivot her entire body.

"Does it hurt?" I asked.

She made a tsking noise. "Not so much."

Miss Diller cowrote her autobiography. It came out in 2005, and she'd brought copies for me, Hugh, Lisa, Amy, and Gretchen. In the book I learned that she never smoked. The cigarette in her act was just for show, a wooden prop used much like a conductor's baton. "When you want a cab, what do you do? Raise your hand! That's what I used my cigarette holder for: to stop and start the audience."

For fifty years she toured the country. "Loved every minute of it, and never once had to use an iron. The secret to packing is tissue paper—well, that and neatness." She was never much for room service, partly because she's Phyllis Diller. "I'd call down for a sandwich and four people would arrive to set up the table." Instead, she'd get suites with kitchens and do her own cooking.

Our lunch lasted for a little over two hours. It's hard for Miss Diller to sit for long stretches, so she spends a good deal of time in bed, watching reruns of *Frasier*. "Call me," she said after she'd been wheeled to her car. "I mean it, pick up the goddamn phone and give me a ring." She'd carefully read my books and remembered things I'd long ago forgotten. "You're a stand-up only you don't know it," she told me.

May 13, 2009
Paris
I was interviewed by a Frenchwoman yesterday, a writer for *Elle* named Sophie who had recently spent time with Penelope Cruz. "An incredibly nice person," she reported. "And beautiful too, with flawless skin and the eyes of a donkey."

I couldn't help but laugh at that and when Sophie looked confused, I tried to explain. "In English we'd say she had eyes like a doe, this because a deer is generally better-looking than a donkey."

And Sophie said, "Oh, okay."

We sat for a moment in a puddle of awkwardness, the kind that comes when you correct someone.

"Though donkeys have nice eyes too," I told her.

May 28, 2009
Paris
Hugh's been putting pictures in his photo albums. I find see-through corners stuck to the sofa cushions and look over his shoulder at his sister Ann leading a horse through a verdant field. There's his brother Sam at twelve. I found some pictures of my own family and they made me want to cry, especially a shot of us standing in the yard with Jeff Jenkins. I must be about twenty, and Paul is still a kid. We all look great, so I

don't know what there is to cry about, or, rather, I guess I do. "Isn't it so unfair that people have to get old," I said to Joan. She'd come for dinner and stayed to sew some buttons on my shirt.

Hugh made lamb meatballs served with rice and scolded his mother for cutting the cheese wrong.

"It's just a block of cheddar, my goodness!"

"Well, you're going to hurt yourself," he said. "More people lose fingers cutting cheese than...any other way." It's unlike him to make things up, but I seriously doubt that this is true. "I don't want you ending up in the hospital is all," he said to his mother when I pressed him on it.

It wasn't a special night but still it felt special for some reason, perhaps because Joan and I are both leaving soon.

June 15, 2009
San Francisco

I was driven from Capitola this afternoon by a woman who used to work at a sleep-disorder clinic. "It was mainly filing and data entry but because I suffer from that stuff myself— from, like, insomnia, only worse—it was interesting," she told me. "There are nights, I'm serious, last Tuesday, for example, when I just want to kill myself!"

I don't know how we got from there to the subject of horseback riding, but we did. "I learned as a kid when we would visit our relatives in Mexico," she told me. "One of my uncles had a ranch and a son who got his arms chewed off by pigs."

"Whoa," I said. "Arms chewed off by what?"

"Pigs," she repeated. "They have really mean ones down there, and they got to him when he was just a baby—chewed both his arms off right to the nub. He's smart, though, and learned to do everything normal people do, only with his feet. Like, one time, I saw him sew a button on his shirt. Now he's a hotshot lawyer—so see? Anything can happen when you put your mind to it!"

If I had my arms chewed off by a pig, I could probably push a door open and turn the bathwater off. I could pick a pair of underpants up off the floor and kick a pillow back onto the bed, but that's stuff I do with my feet already. I'm pretty sure I'm too old to compensate, but maybe I'm not giving myself enough credit. I thought about this for a minute or two, and when I came out of my reverie, the driver was talking about another cousin of hers, a trans woman who recently had fat injected into her butt. "She thinks it looks good, and I had to tell her, 'Honey, it might be big but it's got no shape to it. No shape at all.'"

Oh, how I hated getting out of that car.

July 6, 2009
London

On our last afternoon in Capri, I sat for an interview with one of the big Italian dailies. Then I had my picture taken. The photographer was an unshaven, potbellied guy, maybe a few years younger than me. "The article is supposed to run in October, so we need it to look like fall instead of summer," he said. "This is too bad, as I'd wanted you to stand in the pool with your clothes on."

"I don't believe I would have done that," I told him.

"Well, then, I would have pushed you," he said.

"Then I would have thrown your camera in the water."

"Then I would have charged a new one to the magazine," the photographer said.

I can't remember the last time I so immediately disliked someone. Normally I'd have tried to hide it, but on this occasion, I was openly hostile, and it felt great. "You're so predictable, you famous people," he said. "You want the world to give you attention, and then you get mad when we take your pictures."

Tattooed on the man's wrist was a Chinese symbol meaning, he said, "artist." This alone marked him as an asshole. "After this, I'm going back to fashion," he spat. "You tell a model what to do, and she does it. The photographer is in charge, not some...what do you do?"

"I write."

"Not some writer."

I pulled out my notebook and wrote *Asshole*.

"Do that again," he said. "I'll take a picture of you writing."

"That would be fake."

"So what?" he said. "You think everything's not fake? You think that Robert Capa picture of the soldier falling backward is real? Even Iwo Jima is fake. You, though, I guess you need it to be *real*."

"It's something I did because I felt like it," I said. "Now I don't feel like it anymore."

My next note reads *Pussy*, though I can't exactly remember why. It must have had something to do with him, as for the first time in my life, I completely stood up for myself, not caring that someone would dislike me.

"How about this," he said. "You write in your notebook what you are thinking and afterward, you can send it to me. Then I'll send you the picture."

"I'm not giving you anything," I said. "And I don't want to see your picture. Not in the magazine, not ever."

"Then I don't want to read your book."

"Great, then don't."

The man snapped a few photos. "You have a nice face," he said. "Not charismatic, but okay."

"Thanks."

A few more shots, then he said, with disgust, "I've had enough," and started gathering his equipment.

August 12, 2009
La Bagotière

Throughout America, members of Congress are holding town-hall forums. The subject is health care, which seems to have whipped the conservatives into a frenzy. Egged on by talk-show hosts, old people in shorts and baseball caps are storming the meetings and shouting until the forums are adjourned. When Democrats shouted down Bush, I was delighted, but these people are just plain unbalanced, especially the ones equating Obama with Nazism. "His health-care plan is straight from Hitler's playbook," Limbaugh said on his show last week.

Now you see signs with swastikas on them and posters of the president with a little mustache. I watch the news on the computer, and each time I'm amazed at how poorly the protesters are dressed. On CNN Chris Matthews interviewed a guy who brought a gun to a presidential event. There were pictures of him waving a sign, the pistol holstered against his bare leg. For the interview, he changed his T-shirt and even removed his baseball cap. "Why did I bring a gun?" he said. "Why not?"

August 13, 2009
La Bagotière

Over dinner last night, Pam talked about her childhood orthodontist, a man who was later jailed for child abuse. After his wife left him, he pulled his children's teeth as a way of getting her back.

"So, wait," I said. "Where does the abuse come in?"

Tyler's lost some teeth recently, and it looks like someone hit him with a pole. He has to chew on the sides of his mouth, but it hasn't slowed him down much. We took him to the aquatic center in Condé yesterday, Aron and I taking shifts. While he watched Tyler shoot down the water slide, I swam laps, and vice versa. I'd never spent time in the children's pool, hadn't realized it's where the lifeguards focus all their attention. I got two separate scoldings, and though both were gentle, I still felt like crying afterward.

Following our swim we went to Intermarché. There I came to understand why parents might shop online and have the groceries delivered to their house. "I want that," Tyler would say, grabbing at a jump rope or a crayon set or a Kleenex box with Wall-E on it. The best stuff was displayed low enough for him to reach it, and though he handled the rejection with grace, I saw how tiresome it would be to do this on a regular basis.

August 18, 2009
London
A woman I don't know wrote me a letter saying that a friend of hers discovered a wounded beaver and literally nursed it back to health. On paper I didn't doubt it, but when recounting the story to Ronnie, I couldn't believe what was coming out of my mouth.

"A real live beaver?" she said.

"A baby one," I told her.

"So she breastfed a baby beaver."

"That's what she told me." Then I pictured a pair of buckteeth clamping down on a human nipple, and doubt set in.

September 11, 2009
Reykjavík, Iceland

Our final stop on yesterday's literary-festival outing was the home of Iceland's best-known writer, a prolific novelist and playwright who died in 1998. His house was half an hour outside of Reykjavík, and the tour of it was sort of pathetic. Each of us was given a headset that led us from one room to the next: "On the wall behind the piano is the tapestry that Auður had made after her beloved husband won the Nobel Prize."

"He liked blue, so I used that for the background," a woman's voice added.

The house was not particularly grand, and the things inside it were not significant except in their relation to the writer. Here was the fifties coffee table; here was the easy chair only he was allowed to sit in. The great man's belongings, everything from his desk to his tie rack, screamed *I am an asshole!* My favorite thing was a crocheted turtle lying on his wife's bed. The two had separate rooms, both of which were filled with his books.

"Do you think a tour of your house would be any better?" Hugh asked, and after wondering what he meant by "your house," I supposed that he was right.

October 2, 2009
Buffalo

I met a woman at last night's signing whose friend spent a summer working at their local country club. She was in the dining room one afternoon when a well-dressed, middle-aged woman beckoned her to her table. "Hold out your hand," the woman demanded. And when the employee did, the diner spat a wad of chewed food into her palm. "There's a bone in my chicken salad," she said.

I started collecting rudeness stories a few days back, and this was by far the best.

October 13, 2009
Tulsa, Oklahoma

The plane from Little Rock to Dallas was small and not very crowded. I had a row to myself and sat across the aisle from a young man—maybe nineteen or so—wearing jeans and a hooded sweatshirt. A few minutes after he'd settled in, a woman in her late sixties boarded and pointed to the window seat beside him. "I believe that's me," she said.

The fellow stood to let her in, and after buckling up, the woman started a conversation: Was the young man a student? No? In the army? Well, that was nice! Did he have a girlfriend?

Though I imagine she was boring him, the soldier was patient and polite. "Yes, ma'am," he'd say, and "No, ma'am, no girlfriend."

When the woman's phone rang she answered it and said to the person on the other end that in her rush to get to the airport, she'd had to skip breakfast. Then she said, "Don't tell me that!" After hanging up she turned to the soldier. "Of all the nerve! Here I am, famished half to death, and my gosh-darn daughter calls me from the Golden Corral!"

The soldier nodded sympathetically and then leaned back and closed his eyes. Upon our landing in Dallas, he opened the overhead bin and was approached by the fellow in front of him who was around the same age but had bad skin and was wearing a baseball cap.

"I just want to thank you for your service," he said. "I was going to join up myself but had some family issues. My girlfriend, actually. She wants to get married."

"I hear you," the soldier said, and he fixed his eyes ahead of him, on the flight attendant standing beside the door. Put on a military uniform, and you become a magnet for a certain type of person. I often see these kids getting approached in airports. "You're in my prayers, son," someone will say, and "I just want you to know how much we appreciate your keeping us safe." Often the speakers' eyes will tear up. Their voices will crack, and I always wonder what the soldiers make of them.

I was on a plane last spring and the flight attendant announced that there were some Marines on board. "I want you all to give them a big round of applause," she instructed, and as the people around me went at it, I sort of rubbed one hand against the other as if I were applying lotion. It's the equivalent of moving your lips during the Pledge of Allegiance or keeping your eyes open while those around you say grace. What bothered me was the command—someone *telling* me to applaud the soldiers. The flight attendant was, either by accident or intention, making this about herself rather than them. But what if she'd made a different announcement? A few days earlier, the comedian Wanda Sykes was on my plane. Had someone asked us to give *her* a hand, would I have hesitated? Of course not.

So what we were really doing was voting. *Those of you in favor of the war, put your hands together. Those of you against it, sit there and feel conflicted and self-conscious.*

October 17, 2009
Champaign, Illinois

I was driven to Champaign by Bill Mooney, a short, red-faced man who wore a vest and told me the following joke:

A Jewish fellow named Saul Epstein owns a nail company, very successful, and when he retires he hands it over to his son-in-law. Then he moves to Florida and is there one day, reading the *New York Times,* when he comes upon a full-page

185

ad. It's a picture of Jesus hanging on the cross, and below Him are the words *They Used Epstein Nails*.

Furious, Epstein calls his son-in-law. "Are you out of your mind? That's no way to sell our product!"

The young man promises to fix everything and a week later, Epstein opens his *Times* to find another full-page ad. This one shows a cross standing empty on a hilltop. In front of it, lying with His face in the dust, is Jesus Christ, and on either side, looking down at Him, are two Roman soldiers, along with the words *They* <u>Didn't</u> *Use Epstein Nails*.

October 31, 2009
Boise, Idaho

At five a.m. in the lobby of the La Valencia Hotel, two employees were discussing parental advice. "I tell my sons they should always hold the door open for a woman," said the desk clerk. He was a Latino man, portly, with a lot of silver in his mouth. A second man stood not far away, putting newspapers into bags, and he nodded in agreement. "I tell them it doesn't matter who the lady is. It could be a fat chick, but on the other side of the room a pretty one might look over and notice, so even then it's not wasted."

November 16, 2009
London

I was walking alongside Kensington Gardens, heading toward Queensway, when I came upon an altercation between a cyclist and a driver. I missed the accident, or, more likely, *near* accident, but arrived in time for the shouting match. "Get the fuck away from here," yelled the driver, a Middle Eastern man who looked to be in his late forties.

His opponent was ten years younger, and English. He put

his fists in front of his face, and before anyone could stop them, the two were going at it, not with grace, the way men fight in movies, but awkwardly. The pair stumbled against the hood of a car and then the Middle Eastern man grabbed the bike and tried to throw it into the passing traffic. It was here that a third fellow entered the scene. A moment later he was joined by a fourth, and the two pulled the fighting men apart. "Bitch," yelled the Middle Easterner. "I am going to fuck your mouth, you bitch!"

"Learn to drive!" responded the Englishman.

A guy walked by with two soccer balls in a mesh bag and raised his eyebrows as if to say, *What did I miss?*

It was dusk, so I could barely make out the cyclist as he remounted and the driver as he climbed back into his car. Interesting, to me, was that the Middle Easterner's first tactic was to attack the Englishman's manhood, calling him a bitch. I'd have thought the cyclist's response would be *Go back where you came from* and was sort of impressed when it wasn't.

Dad called me in New York the other day just as I was checking out of my hotel. "Hey," he said. "What's your jacket size?"

I phoned him back last night and told him, politely, that I didn't need another sports coat.

"Aw, baloney. I'm going to get you one for Christmas."

"I won't wear it."

"Sure you will. It's wrinkle-free, just what you need."

Toward the end of our conversation he asked me again to give $10,000 to the Greek church.

"No, thank you."

"Do it for your mother," he said.

"That's okay."

"Aw, baloney."

December 3, 2009
Paris

Michael Congdon called to tell me that his father has died. Don was ninety-one and he passed away in his sleep on Monday night. I know I should be sad but I'm not. To live a long, remarkable life and die peacefully in your own bed—isn't that what everyone wants? It couldn't have happened to a more deserving person, as far as I'm concerned.

When I think of Don I'll remember the many hours spent sitting in his office, him talking about William Manchester, whom he referred to as "Manchester." He'd also talk about Salinger and Bradbury, Lillian Hellman, Bill Styron, Thomas Berger. *When are we going to talk about me?* I'd wonder. It was probably for the best that we didn't, though.

While sitting in the office, listening to long stories from the past, I'd ask myself what other people's agents were like, though it never occurred to me to jump ship. Don was perfect, the last of the New York gentlemen. I loved his Pucci ties and his little white mustache like the man on the Monopoly board's.

December 21, 2009
London

I was wrapping gifts the other night when I heard what I at first thought was a record. It was a choral arrangement, one of those Christmas songs I never know the name of, with lots of *fa-la-la*s. The voices were beautiful, and I looked out the window to see they belonged to carolers, actual live people who were making their way up the street. "Hugh," I called. "Come up here and listen."

"Close those shutters," he shouted. "And get the ones in the living room while you're at it."

He was afraid that the carolers would come to our house and we'd have to stand at the door with those awful frozen smiles on our faces, wondering whether or not we should tip and, if so, how much. I understood that, but their voices were so enchanting. Like Sirens, they were. Through the slats of my office shutters I watched them progress down the street, and noted that one of the four—a tall man in a down jacket—had a backpack on.

December 25, 2009
London

Amy and I were a block from Queensway when a stranger who spoke very little English stopped us and asked if we knew where a particular street was. Actually, she didn't say a word, just pointed to a printout she'd gotten from a website. With the woman were three teenage girls, each lugging a thigh-high suitcase.

I pulled out my map, but the longer I looked at it, the more hopeless I started to feel. It was around this time that a cheerful-looking British woman approached. She was stocky and well dressed and as she got close, I could see that she had a lot of hair on her face. "Excuse me," I said, "but do you know where we might find this street?"

"Lost, are we?" she chirped. "Oh, why must this always happen at Christmas! Don't worry, though, we'll get you on the right path." She was the spirit of Christmas, right there in the flesh, all two hundred pounds of her. The map was hard to read, and she accepted my plastic magnifier, saying, "Brilliant!"

The Englishwoman found the place where the visitors needed to go. "It's parallel to you, so what you must do is walk up two streets, taking not the road but the narrow lane just beyond it." The visitors nodded in that way that you do when you're pretending to understand, and after we'd all thanked the Spirit of Christmas, Amy and I led the little group to their destination. The mother made a noise meaning, *You don't need to do this,* but we did need to. We were happy to. On top of that, it was complicated.

When we reached the hotel, the mother employed her daughter to say, "Have a nice holiday." And then we were off, buoyed.

Walking down Connaught Street a short while later, Amy and I were approached by a man in his mid-sixties. "Get the fuck out of my way or I'll punch you," he said, the Anti–Spirit of Christmas.

December 28, 2009
London
A twenty-three-year-old Nigerian named Umar Farouk Abdulmutallab tried to blow up a Northwest Airlines flight from Amsterdam to Detroit and might have succeeded were he not stopped by a fellow passenger. As a result, the airlines are limiting carry-ons to one per passenger. The items in the bag must be related to your flight, thus no more breakable gifts, at least for the time being.

Amy returned to New York yesterday and reports that during the last hour of the flight, she wasn't allowed to have anything on her lap, not even a book.

We had drinks last night with our neighbor, who said, in reference to a schoolmate who had gone on to amass a great fortune, "When a friend succeeds, a little part of us dies, doesn't it?"

2010

January 17, 2010
Sydney

It's interesting doing shows in countries where I'm not on the radio. After last night's reading, a man approached, saying, "Midway through your first story a light came on, and I realized, 'This guy sounds just like a Muppet.'"

January 20, 2010
Perth, Australia

I walked to the center of town yesterday and approached an information desk staffed by cheerful volunteers. "Can you tell me how to get to the art museum?" I asked.

As I pulled out my notebook to jot down directions, a woman with white hair pointed to a pedestrian overpass. "What you want to do is walk the overhead path into the train station," she said. "Keep going straight, and then take a right on the other side of the river."

"Overhead...straight...right," I repeated.

"After the right you'll turn left," the woman continued. "Then you'll turn right again but I'm afraid the museum is closed today. It always is on Tuesday."

Why didn't you start with that? I wondered.

January 25, 2010
London

The 49 to King's Road stopped at the South Kensington station and the driver announced that this was it—he would not be going any further. We all got off and when the next bus arrived some five minutes later, I naturally assumed that it would be free. "Either use your transport card or pay the two pounds," the driver said.

"But that's not fair."

"Either use your card or pay the two pounds."

I used my card and moved down the aisle, certain that the incident would stay with me for the rest of my life. *As long as I live, I will never get over this,* I thought. It's not that expensive in the great scheme of things, but why should the trip cost me four pounds instead of two?

It was still on my mind when we arrived at Town Hall for the antiques fair. I'd picked up a flyer at the flea market the other day and noted that it didn't mention an entry fee. The location, yes, the hours, the dates of future antiques fairs, and even a phone number; that was all. The omission seemed sneaky, and so I asked about it when I arrived at the front desk and was told to pay two pounds. "Really?" I said. "It doesn't say anything about that on the flyer."

The man I was speaking to had obviously gotten this question before, and it was clear that it irritated him. He was dark-haired with a high, shiny forehead and arched eyebrows. "Well, it's a flyer, isn't it," he said. "A miniature poster, you could say."

"Sure," I agreed.

"So it's just got the pertinent information on it."

"Isn't an admission fee pertinent?"

He sighed. "Have you ever seen the ticket price listed on a film poster?"

"Well, that's not really the same thing," I said. It wasn't my goal to be obnoxious, but it really *isn't* the same, as you *expect* to pay for a movie. Part of me wanted to turn around and leave, but Jane and Hugh had already gone in, so I surrendered my money and entered, muttering under my breath. Coming on top of the bus rip-off, I was now out four pounds, which is roughly seven dollars, money I could have given to Haitian earthquake victims. Money I *would have* given to poor Haitian earthquake victims had this godforsaken country not swindled it out of me.

Then I found the most darling cushion, and once again, England was forgiven.

January 28, 2010
London

I went to the supermarket yesterday afternoon and fell into line behind a Middle Eastern woman who wore a black scarf on her head. "What is this?" she asked, and she handed me a plastic-wrapped Styrofoam tray. Inside it were two breaded fillets and a tag reading LIGHTLY DUSTED RIVER COBBLER.

"What is that, a river cobbler?" she said. "You think it is fish?"

"Well, it has the word *river* in it, so I'd say yes," I told her.

The cashier, who was Eastern European, looked up from her scanner. "Snakes live in the river also," she caroled. "So it could be that."

I looked at her like, *Who hired you?*

"Well, I'm afraid of snakes," said the Middle Eastern woman. "I do not like them, and I do not want to be eating them."

"I'm pretty sure it's fish," I said. "In fact, I'm *certain* it is. Tesco wouldn't sell snake meat. There's no market for it."

The cashier, who was no help whatsoever, shrugged, and the woman abandoned her river cobbler, tossing it to the dumping ground on the other side of the conveyor belt. It landed facedown beside a spotted banana, and I thought of another Tesco, the giant one not far from our old apartment, where, on my first visit, I found something in the luncheon-meat section called Crumbled Ham Dummy. The combination of words struck me as ridiculous and just as I'd finished copying them down, a store detective approached and told me in heavily accented, almost indecipherable English that it was against the rules to take photographs in the store.

"Oh, I'm not," I said, and I held up my notebook, which was slim and pocket-size and could, I supposed, easily be mistaken for a camera. "As long as you're here, though, can you tell me what a Crumbled Ham Dummy is?"

"No taking picture in store," he repeated.

"I'll make sure I don't," I said. "But about this Crumbled Ham Dummy…"

"No taking picture in store."

And I realized that, like a talking doll, he was equipped with only a handful of phrases. As an immigrant myself, I can hardly cast stones. It's just by accident of birth that I'm fluent in English, but listen, Tesco: If you're going to pull words at random out of the dictionary and give things names like Lightly Dusted River Cobbler and Crumbled Ham Dummy, is it too much to ask that you hire people capable of explaining them?

January 29, 2010
London

For the past twenty years or so Nancy (my cousin) has served as the principal of a troubled elementary school in Florida. I recently asked how things are going, and yesterday she emailed me pictures of a miniature horse, a live one, who wears sneakers over his hooves and comes in twice a month to be read out loud to by second- and third-graders.

"But why in sneakers?" I wondered.

"So he won't slip on the floors," she wrote.

My next question concerned his purpose. "Why read out loud to an animal, something that can't correct you or even recognize your mistakes?"

"Well," Nancy explained, "this is a certified therapy horse."

That's how we educate in the United States. A child has trouble reading, so we put sneakers on a horse, give him a certificate, and send him in to fix things.

February 21, 2010
London

Yesterday was our neighbor's ninety-eighth birthday. Hugh baked a cake, and shortly after one o'clock we went next door for the party. Most of the other guests were relatives in their seventies and eighties. There were a lot of canes in use and after everyone had hobbled to the buffet table, Eleanor was wheeled in, looking remarkable for someone her age. A cake was presented, and someone called, "Make a wish."

"I wish," Eleanor said, her face aglow in candlelight, "I wish I could walk again."

Aside from being so sad you could just hardly stand it, I was impressed that she so readily knew what she wanted. On my birthdays I tend to hem and haw, ending up with something sloppy, like world peace.

Eleanor got some help blowing out the candles, and then one of her nurses handed her a knife, which she took in her trembling, clawlike hand and hovered unsteadily over the cake. "Make a wish," someone called, and when I said that she already had, the person told me that in England you get two wishes, one when you blow out the candles and another more powerful one—"A wish shared only to the wind"— when you cut the cake.

"No one ever told me that," I said, and I thought of the fifty-three powerful wishes I never got a shot at. "I could *be* somebody by now," I whispered to the person beside me.

He was seventy-five but looked younger due, he said, to "a lazy thyroid." The mullet helped too, I thought. The man was Eleanor's nephew Michael, and he'd come with his wife, a woman named Mary. Both were using canes, her due to a recent hip replacement.

"I was in hospital for two weeks over Christmas," she explained. Mary wore a purple floor-length dress. Her hair was dyed brown, and her hands were spotted, like leopard paws. As with her husband, I found her delightful.

"Do you do things on the computer?" I asked.

"Well," she said, "I'm having a go at the email, but him, he lives on it."

"I like a game called Civilization Four. Have you tried it?" Michael asked. "It's jolly good fun."

Before retiring, Michael taught math at a boarding school in Oxford, where he and Mary still live. His mother died four years ago at the age of one hundred. Toward the end she could still hear, but speaking was out of the question. "She was a bit paralyzed as well," he said, and he drew in his arms and balled up his fists in imitation of a mummy—his mummy. "We used to massage her." He told me that her father changed his name and ran off to Australia when she was young. "Mother lived in Surrey, had a little sister with a humpback who later became a nun."

I could have listened to them all day.

March 17, 2010
London
This afternoon's Radio 4 quiz show included the line "One in three Americans weighs as much as the other two."

March 27, 2010
Paris

Walking through Les Halles to the movie theater yesterday, I couldn't help but notice the poster-size photos hanging from the ceilings. They were of naked men embracing, and as I passed a fellow of twenty in the arms of a fifty-year-old, I thought, *Good for you, France.* No American mall would ever celebrate homosexual love, especially when there's such an age discrepancy. In the next picture, one man was in his forties and the other had white hair and liver spots. In the one after that, the younger man was twelve at most, and just as I thought, *Yikes,* I saw a sign reading FATHERS AND SONS: A PHOTO EXPOSITION.

Okay, I thought, *but no American mall would ever picture them naked.*

April 1, 2010
Paris

I peed fourteen times yesterday. Then I typed *overactive bladder* into Google and found that one of the symptoms is peeing seven times per day. So I have it twice.

April 10, 2010
Kingston, New York

The other day Adam gave me a Claritin-D, promising it would clear my head and dry up my extra mucus. It did indeed, so after lunch I went to the Target in search of more. A clever person can cook his allergy medication and turn it into methamphetamine, so though these particular pills are sold over the counter, you need an ID in order to buy them, and they'll only sell you so much.

I'd been told that this would happen, so I brought my passport with me to the pharmacy. There were three young women working, and as I approached, I overheard one of them on the phone. "I'm just saying that we're swamped, and it's going to take at least three hours," she said.

"They got to send us some help because this just ain't right," griped another of the young women. A third seemed too angry to speak, and it was she who turned to help me. "You got to have an ID in order to buy that," she said.

I handed her my passport and she looked at it, frowning. "No," she said, speaking as if I didn't quite understand English. "An *ID*. You have to have an *ID*."

"This works just fine at the airport," I told her.

"Well," she said, "this is not an airport."

Oh no! I wanted to say. *You mean I can't get a flight to Los Angeles from the cold-remedies section?* What surprised me was the lip. *Can cashiers in America talk to you like that?* I wondered. It might be different if I were being difficult but my only crime, as far as I could see, was that I'd never learned to drive and thus didn't have a license. "I'm sorry," said the cashier, "but without a state ID, I can't help you."

Just then her associate got off the phone and stepped over.

"It's okay if he doesn't have a license," she said. "Instead of scanning, you just have to type in his information."

My cashier sighed and asked for my address. I gave it to her, and then she said, "England? What state is that in?"

I tried to break it to her gently. "It's actually a country."

She moaned and called out to her associate, who said over her shoulder, "Just write in *New York, New York*. That usually works."

May 6, 2010
Los Angeles
Joey and I drove from Riverside to Los Angeles, and before going to my luncheon we stopped at a florist, where I bought

a bouquet. Phyllis lives on Rockingham Avenue in a yellow house positioned behind a gate. It looks fairly modest but is actually ten thousand square feet. "Four furnaces!" she told me. "Five and a half baths. Ha!" I arrived to find the door open and the music of Bill Evans pouring out of it. Karla, the assistant, met me in the foyer. "Let me get Madame for you," she said.

A short while later Phyllis teetered around the corner. She wore white slacks with patent leather shoes and took little baby steps. As she approached, I noticed the roses on the entryway table. There were more on the console and more still in the distant living room. Dozens and dozens and dozens of them.

"Get him a drink," Phyllis said, and she turned, asking, "What'll you have?"

"How about water."

"Vodka and water?"

"Oh, just water."

"With a splash of vodka in it?"

"Just water."

"Karla, David will have a vodka and water and I'll have a martini in a little glass."

We took our drinks out on the patio, which meant traversing the Bob Hope room. There was a large portrait of him propped up on an easel, which was near a grand piano topped with photos: Phyllis with Hope, Phyllis with Crosby, Phyllis with Gerald Ford. The room was regal but at the same time gaudy, with reproduction furniture and gewgaw cases. It had been decorated for her, in the seventies, most likely.

The terrace overlooked the backyard, which was vast and beautifully landscaped. Three pigeons marched beside the birdbath, and Phyllis identified them as a married couple and the husband's mistress. "All they do is fuck," she said, and she threw back her head. "Ha!"

When lunch was ready, we walked through the kitchen to the smaller and less formal of the two dining rooms. Photos hung on the red walls, one of Phyllis's first husband and another of her father. A massive oak lighting fixture hung over the table, this dark, heavy, wheel-like thing with fruit carved on it. Phyllis rang the bell and Karla delivered little salads with cottage cheese on the side. "You can use your knife to push stuff around with," Phyllis said. "That's what I do."

Following the salad was some dried-out rice topped with what must have been Chun King canned chow mein. Then came ice cream. "I've got a joke," Phyllis said, and she held out her hand. "A priest and a rabbi are walking down the street. The priest says, 'Let's find some little Catholic boys and screw 'em.'

"And the rabbi goes, 'Out of what?' Ha!"

She told another. "Man goes to the doctor, who says, 'You've got to stop masturbating.'

"The man asks, 'Why?'

"And the doctor says, 'So I can examine you.' Ha!"

I worried during our lunch that I was boring Phyllis. Upon entering the house I'd put my name in the guest book and noticed I was following Elliott Gould and Richard Lewis. *What sort of company were they?* I wondered.

After lunch, Karla led me upstairs to "the gallery." This was a long hallway hung floor to ceiling with paintings her employer had done. Each was framed, and each had a price tag on it. None of them were terribly good, but Phyllis seemed to recognize this and reflect it in her price list. Small portraits went for two to three hundred dollars, while the larger ones in her studio—paintings the size of doors—went for five to six thousand. I bought a bucolic print of cows in a pasture, possibly a restaurant place mat. On it, Phyllis had dabbed some paint, added a few birds, and written what amounts to her mantra: *On this happy day I am thankful for my blessings. And I pray for renewed belief in myself and others and hope this bond of love will expand to envelop the entire universe.* The writing is spidery and crooked, so it's actually quite nice.

The price tag read $400, but I got a discount. After I had chosen it, Karla presented me with a bill and instructed me to make my check out to Phil Dil Productions.

By the time I left, the music had degenerated, and instead of Bill Evans it was maybe Mitch Miller. Joey was scheduled to pick me up at three, and while waiting for him to arrive, we somehow fell into the subject of religion. "A bunch of garbage," Phyllis called it.

"So you're an atheist?"

"Hell yes."

She told me that she has trouble sleeping and that often, while she was lying awake, her mind would turn things over. "Like, Jesus, okay," she said. "If *BC* stands for 'Before Christ,' and *AD* is 'After Death,' what happened to those missing thirty-three years? I mean, shouldn't this be 2043?"

Just before Joey arrived, Phyllis's grandson called. "I've got to get this, sweetie," she said. We shook hands and then, the painting under my arm, I left.

July 6, 2010
London

After our weekend in Sutton with Viv and his wife, Gretchen Anderson, Hugh and I went to a real estate website and began looking at properties in West Sussex. Each house we came across had a name, and of course the one I want is called

Faggot Stacks. I said to Hugh, "Can't you just see the return-address stamp?"

He's pushing for the more soberly named Swan Cottage and made an appointment for us to look at it. *Are we really doing this?* I wonder. How crazy to buy a place based on one night— not even an entire weekend—spent at a friend's house. We have no idea what the area is like in the winter or how much the renovations might be. And where would I swim?

July 10, 2010
London

Shortly after noon, Hugh and I started off for West Sussex. Someone told me that yesterday was the hottest day of the year so far, which is easy to believe. After waiting ten minutes for a bus, we walked, sweating, to the tube, and I took it as a bad sign when a roosting pigeon shit all over Hugh's jacket. It got on his shirt too, these great clinging gobs. He cleaned it off as best he could with a napkin and had just discovered a patch on his trousers when the train arrived. We got off at Victoria and bought round-trip tickets on the 1:05 to Bognor Regis. There's a station in Amberley, but no cab service, so we got off in Pulborough.

The house—a cottage—is located on the curve of a shady lane. There's no building across from it, and the neighbors are hidden from view. The weathered brick, the sloped roof, the windows with their panes no larger than playing cards—it's grade II listed, which means you can't change anything, not that we'd want to.

There are, in total, five buildings on the property: The main house, which has four bedrooms; the slightly smaller house— a former stable—which has two bedrooms; and a third, much smaller structure that was converted to a catering kitchen but has a separate bathroom. The fourth building looks like you'd slaughter animals in it, and the fifth is a wooden garage.

Every room in every house was filthy, with stuff piled everywhere: a guitar, a sleeping bag, a machine with sharp blades, a bucket. All the nice touches—the inlaid nooks above the fireplaces, the Dutch doors, the built-in corner cabinets—were made un-nice by having beer cans in them or stickers affixed to them. Hugh can look at a wreck like this and see potential while I just tend to see the junk.

Outside it was beautiful, though. I like the lawn beside the main house and the shady orchard beyond the garage. I like that the house is only an hour and twenty minutes from London, but still I hesitated. "You know what—fine!" Hugh spat. "Forget it, but I don't want to hear another word about a place in the country." He always goes so quickly from cajoling to threatening.

July 13, 2010
Paris

It's the strangest sensation, feeling a screwdriver in your mouth, this after having four teeth extracted, and exploring the now-empty space with your tongue. The incisors Dr. Guig pulled yesterday morning were on the bottom row. I'd had umpteen shots of Novocain by then, so though I saw the pliers dripping with blood, I felt no pain. It was like having work done on the apartment one floor down. *What could they be doing with that router?* you think, and *Do I smell sewage?*

Hearing my four teeth hit the bottom of a shallow metal tray was devastating—the sound of failure. *Is this my fault?* I wanted to ask, but there were hands and instruments in my mouth, so talking was out of the question. It's pretty clear that my periodontal disease was caused by smoking. Dr. Guig was the only French person who ever advised me to quit. He said, in fact, that he wouldn't do the implant surgery until after I'd stopped and stayed stopped for two years—something about the mouth not being able to heal properly.

But what if it *was* caused by smoking? Was the sound of four teeth hitting a metal tray so horrible that I'd take it all back if I could? *Well, yes,* I thought, as, unlike hard work or practice, smoking doesn't lead to anything, at least not anything productive.

It's a moot point anyway, as I can't take smoking back any more than I can travel to the 1950s in a time machine and buy a dozen Philip Guston paintings. If the teeth in the tray were not the fault of smoking, they were the fault of my negligence. In 1989 Dr. Svarnias told me I had gum disease and my response was to put my fingers in my ears and not see a dentist again for another twelve years, until I was in such discomfort I had Hugh call and make me an appointment.

Dr. Guig said yesterday that after our first session, he envisioned himself pulling every tooth in my head. "Your turnaround has been remarkable," he said, and I felt that singular blush of pride that comes with being complimented by a health-care professional. *"Il est génial"* (He's terrific), he said of me to the man who'll be fabricating my replacement teeth. Then he put his hand on my shoulder. "How long have we known each other, Mr. Sedaris?"

It was hard to talk with a mouthful of wadding but I managed a weak *"Depuis* Toy Story Deux." (Since *Toy Story 2.*)

Because I'd expected to be disoriented after my procedure, Hugh came with me and sat in the waiting room. I thought I'd need to take a cab home, but though the Novocain was starting to wear off, I felt fine taking the bus. I didn't want Hugh to see me without my four teeth, though, so whenever I talked I covered my mouth.

"Speak up!" he kept saying.

On our way home I learned that our offer on the house in West Sussex had been rejected. Hugh gave me the bit about the seller really loving the property, and though I suspected there was no other interest and that the guy would come around in a month or two, I told him he could go ahead and submit the asking price. The agent was phoned and shortly after returning to the apartment, we got a call and learned that our offer was accepted.

Hugh was delighted, yet three hours later he was seated at his desk, crying. *I'd* had four teeth pulled and *he* was crying. It seemed he'd emailed his mom about West Sussex. Now she'd written back to say that while she was happy for us, she was sad for the place in La Bagotière—and that's what set him off. "It's exactly the way *I* feel," he said between sobs. "That poor house."

I said that this was going to be a change but that as long as we had each other, any change was bearable. This is the sort of hokeyness one engages in after buying a new property. We dance about, we pinch ourselves, we scheme.

July 17, 2010
La Bagotière
Hugh started proofreading *Squirrel Seeks Chipmunk* this morning. "What are you laughing at?" I called from the bed.

"The Migrating Warblers," he said.

Then I heard nothing. "Why aren't you laughing?" I called.

His one note, thus far, is that I've overused the word *acorn*.

"Is that it?" I said. "I mean, *that's* your note?"

August 19, 2010
La Bagotière
I rode my bike to Flers yesterday and was just cresting the hill at the edge of the city when I saw something on the road

that at first I thought was a mouse. On closer inspection, I noticed that it had a long snout and hardly anything in the way of ears. The creature was walking in a circle the size of a manhole cover, and as I bent forward to get a closer look, a car approached. The driver was a woman in her seventies, at least, and as she neared, I got off my bike and held up my palms—the international sign for "Please don't kill my important scientific discovery." She politely braked and I wrapped whatever this thing was in the bandanna I use to wipe sweat off my forehead. Then I tied the ends together, threw it into my basket, and rode to a supermarket, where I bought a box of hamster food and a bag of what looks like mattress ticking my creature might want to nest in.

Back at the house I dug out my terrarium, dumped in the food and the ticking, then introduced Hugh to Valentine. It was the name of the cashier at the grocery store I'd stopped at.

"What is it?" Hugh asked. He normally gets mad when I bring something home. "Oh, the poor thing," he'll say. "You're being cruel. Let it go." It's usually just a toad or a doomed mouse with teeth marks in its back, but this time he didn't nag me to release it. "Huh," he said. "What on earth..."

It wasn't a vole. I learned that soon enough. It was what our nature book identified as a shrew. On further reading I learned that they don't go for seeds and bits of dried corn but insects and slugs. I also learned that, like their associates the moles, they can't go long without eating or they'll die. It was getting too late to collect the sorts of things he likes, so, with a heavy heart, I released Valentine into the garden. He made a squeaking sound, like a rusty wheel in a hamster cage, and Hugh told him to keep it down lest he attract a fox or an owl.

Our shrew ran under the raspberry bushes and for the rest of the night I worried about him. "Oh, Valentine," I'd sigh, wondering if he still remembered me. "I saved his life, you know."

To this Hugh would respond, in that comforting way of his, "I know you did. I know."

August 24, 2010
La Bagotière

I left the dressing room and had just approached the lip of the pool yesterday afternoon when the lifeguard pulled me aside. "Your bathing suit's on inside out," he whispered.

"I beg your pardon?"

"Your bathing suit," he repeated. "You are wearing it inside out."

I followed his eyes and saw my swimsuit liner, looking like a pair of white mesh bikini briefs senselessly slipped over a slightly larger and uglier pair of underpants. I saw my pockets drooping like ragged ears from my sides, and then I covered my face and ran like a crazy person back to the dressing room.

September 7, 2010
London

I told Zoe that before buying our cottage in West Sussex, we considered one called Faggot Stacks that was located between the villages of Balls Cross and Titty Hill. Americans die laughing at those names but Zoe, who is British, remained straight-faced and told me that as a child she'd spent her summers in Slack Bottom, which is in Yorkshire midway between Slack Top and Big Dike.

September 15, 2010
Makkum, the Netherlands

Amy got a cell phone and shortly after we boarded the Thalys to Amsterdam, she pulled it out of her bag. "Just calling to tell you that we made the train," she brayed. "We're leaving a few minutes late but I want you to know that I got...yes, I've got the prisoners. Okay. I love you." People scowled in her direction, the way they do when someone's creating a disturbance, and then they noticed that her phone was fake, a child's plush toy. She called again when we arrived, and then she phoned from our rental car to make a dinner reservation. "That will be three for eight o'clock, then. All right, goodbye. Yep, I love you too."

We ate dinner at a restaurant in what used to be the post office. Amy paid and while eating I learned that there'd been another child between her and Gretchen, a miscarriage. "You didn't know that?" she asked.

"Wow," I said. "So there should have been seven of us."

"Not necessarily," Hugh said. "I mean, she probably just wouldn't have had Paul." He said this as if after six children my mother's body would have naturally maxed out. It was nice to sit in the little restaurant. Outside it was raining, and yellow leaves were falling from the trees. It's autumn here.

October 8, 2010
Atlanta, Georgia
Message on a T-shirt worn by a big-breasted woman at last night's show: I WISH THESE WERE BRAINS.

October 14, 2010
Columbia, Missouri
On the way to last night's theater, the producer and I stopped at a drugstore, where I bought a jug of liquid laundry detergent. On leaving I passed a woman who was walking very slowly to a car she had parked in the handicapped space. She must have been in her nineties, as thin as her cane, and with white hair. *What a sweetheart,* I remember thinking. That was

before I noticed her bumper sticker. MARRIAGE = 1 MAN + 1 WOMAN, it read.

As I watched the brittle old hag struggle with her door handle, it occurred to me that people who get the handicapped space should not be allowed to voice political opinions. You got the best spot, so just shut up already.

October 17, 2010
Philadelphia

The producer of tonight's show was supposed to pick me up in Philadelphia but his plane was running late and so he sent a car service. The driver was black and perhaps in his late sixties, a tall chunky fellow who wore a dark suit and a flat-topped cap. While waiting for my luggage, he complained that people have lost their sense of civility. "Take this lady on my way here this morning. I'm behind her in my car and when the light changes, she just sits there, texting. I think, *Well, she'll finish in a second.* Then when she doesn't, I tap my horn, just lightly, and she gives me the finger!" He shook his head. "People and their phones, don't even get me started."

When I told him I didn't have one he said, "You've got to be kidding me!"

"Nope," I said. "Never owned a cell phone. Never driven a car either!"

"Well, good for you," he said. "When those cell phones first came out, people used them for emergencies. Now, though, they've just gotten lazy and use them for everything, especially while driving, and over the stupidest, most useless things you can imagine. I'm telling you, we were better off without them."

When my luggage arrived, we headed toward the parking deck, talking along the way about the many changes we've seen in our lifetimes. Computers were mentioned, and then the new TVs. "I got one of them high-definition models and I'm telling you it isn't always kind," the man said. "Take this lady who comes on at one o'clock in the afternoon, you know who I'm talking about. She's on channel ten. NBC."

"I don't live in Philadelphia," I told him.

"It's a national show," he went on. "Oh, come on, it's a blond lady, talks about the news."

"Diane Sawyer?"

The man's tone grew irritable. "She's not on in the day-time," he told me. "Come on, now, think! You know who I'm talking about."

When we reached his town car, he dumped my luggage into the deep trunk, muttering, "Now, damn it, what is her name?" A few minutes later, at the exit of the parking deck, he handed his ticket and twenty dollars to the attendant. "This is just stupid," he grumbled. "A blond lady I've been seeing every day for ten years."

After we'd reached the highway, he pulled out his phone and started dialing. "Lucille," he said to the person who answered, "what's that lady's name what comes on the TV at one in the afternoon?"

I heard a faint voice on the other end.

"No, not Oprah, the white news lady with the blond hair?" Lucille offered a few more possibilities and the man cut her off. "Put your mother on the phone," he demanded. A car veered over from the other lane, and as he swerved in response, my tote bag fell onto the floor. "What do you mean she's not home?" the driver said. "Where'd she go?"

He hung up in a bad mood and tried to think of other people he could ask. "Goddamn it to hell," he said. "I will not rest till I get that lady's name."

October 30, 2010
Tacoma, Washington
A joke I heard last night:

A guy finds a genie who grants him three wishes, adding that everything the man gets, his wife will get doubly. "Great," the guy says, and he wishes for a big house. Then he wishes for a car. Finally, he says, "Okay, now I want you to beat me half to death."

October 31, 2010
San Francisco
An excellent joke I heard at last night's signing:

It's late at night and a man is getting ready to go to bed when he hears a knock on his door. He opens it and looks down to see a snail. "Yes," it says. "I'd like to talk to you about buying some magazine subscriptions."

Furious at being disturbed, the man rears back, kicks the snail as hard as he can, and storms off to bed.

Two years later there comes another knock. The man answers and again he finds the snail, who looks up at him and says, "What the fuck was that all about?"

November 1, 2010
San Francisco
I'm in a hotel room with two beds, one of which has Ronnie in it, asleep. We got back from last night's show at around two. It's a ninety-minute drive from Santa Rosa and we slept through most of it, waking shortly after we'd crossed the bridge into San Francisco, which was rowdy with Halloween and World Series revelers. The streets were crowded with young people, most of whom were dressed in costume.

"What's she supposed to be, a whore?" Ronnie asked,

pointing out the tinted window to a girl in thigh-high boots. "We had someone like her walk into the shoe store the other day, said she was looking for orange knee socks. 'I'm going to be a chicken for Halloween,' she told me.

"And I said, 'I'm sorry. But if you're not going to be something scary, forget it.'" She wiped some sleep from her eye and turned back to watching the crowd on the corner. "And you just knew she was going to be a sexy chicken."

November 15, 2010
Birmingham, Alabama

A joke from last night's signing:

Q. What's the worst part about having sex with Jesus?

A. He's always wanting to come into your heart.

November 16, 2010
East Lansing, Michigan

Last night's event was at Schuler's in East Lansing. The store gave out numbers and after I'd been signing for four hours, the room went strangely silent, and I could hear a woman talking on the phone. She was in her late sixties, quite large, with a lime-green scarf around her neck. "He's talking to every goddamn person who comes along," she said. "They're telling him jokes and it's taking forever." I looked at her and she looked back. Then she said, "I've got to go," and covered her face with her hands.

Everyone heard what she'd said, and they all watched quietly as I had the manager bring the woman to the front of the line, where she was really quite charming, all "I'm so embarrassed" and "You're my daughter's favorite writer."

After she'd left, I learned that she'd been complaining for hours. "I heard her say that she was going to kick your ass," a young woman told me. Another said that when I asked for a joke, the woman planned to say, *I been waiting for five hours. How's that for funny, asshole?*

November 25, 2010
Halifax, Nova Scotia
Jokes from last night's signing:

> Q. How do you stop your husband from stumbling
> around in the front yard?
> A. Shoot him again.

A bear and a pony go to a karaoke bar. "Why don't you sing?" asks the bear, and the pony explains that he's a little horse.

November 28, 2010
Salt Lake City, Utah
Jokes from last night's signing:

A man and a woman board the elevator at a medical donation center. "What are you selling?" the woman asks.

The guy answers, "Sperm. They pay fifty bucks per visit."

"How is that fair?" asks the woman. "I'm giving plasma and only getting *five* dollars!"

A month later they again meet on the elevator. "Back to give more plasma?" asks the man.

And the woman, her mouth obviously full, says, "Uh-uh."

A group of middle-aged Jewish women are eating in a restaurant when the waiter walks up and asks, "Is anything okay?"

December 2, 2010
Phoenix, Arizona
A joke from last night's show:

> Q. What's the difference between a whore and a bitch?

A. A whore will sleep with anybody. A bitch will sleep
   with anybody but you.

December 10, 2010
London
Our train left Paris forty-five minutes late. I had an aisle seat,
across from a teenage girl and a person I took to be her
grandmother—both Americans. The woman had her pewter-
colored hair pulled into a ponytail and from the side she
resembled a man—General Custer, I decided. The impression
was bolstered by her outfit—heavy corduroy pants and a
suede, tan-colored vest. Around her wrist was a gold charm
bracelet and she often had her hand on her knee, massaging it.
I took the pair in, and then I turned to my magazine.

An hour had passed when, on my left, I noticed a flurry
of activity and saw the grandmother hitting the teenager
with a book. "You. Are. A. Very. Self-centered. Child!" she
barked, pausing after each word for emphasis. "Lazy. And.
Self-centered. And. Awful!" The girl started crying and her
grandmother hit her again. "Don't you do that!" she scolded.
"Don't you dare, you lazy lump, expecting me to do everything
for you. I told you to go through the guidebook and pick out
things you wanted to do in London but instead you're expecting
me to do it all!" She said that the girl's sister hadn't acted that
way on *her* trip to Europe and she'd been only ten. "Five years
younger than you are now and with twice the gumption!"

It was a good lesson in exposition—a dialogue that told
you everything you needed to know about their relationship
but never seemed forced.

"If this is the way you're going to behave I'll put you on the
first plane home," the grandmother hissed. "And don't think
I won't!"

The girl complained that she was always being criticized,

and the woman answered, "Stop giving me things to criticize and it won't be a problem!"

She shoved a guidebook into her granddaughter's hands and then crossed her arms, the golden charm bracelet jangling as she did so. Twenty minutes later, the girl presented her with a list. "The Tate Museum." The grandmother moaned. "That takes hours and I've already been. If that's what you want to do, then I'll just drop you off." She wasn't impressed with the British Library either or any of the other sites on her granddaughter's surprisingly mature list. After handing it back she told the girl to look out the window. "You haven't even noticed the scenery! God, you're so incurious I can't stand it."

The girl turned to the window and her grandmother gave her another slap on the shoulder. "You're not looking. You're just pretending to look."

My instinct was to lean across the aisle and say, *Excuse me, but do you have to be such a complete asshole?* The hope was that the woman would come to her senses, would say, in essence, *I don't know what's gotten into me!* Far more likely she would have told me to mind my own business and would have treated the girl even worse, so I said nothing and hoped that the teenager kept a notebook tucked away or, better yet, a diary. Her grandmother was a gold mine dressed like a gold miner, and looking at the girl, instead of feeling pity, I felt jealousy.

December 18, 2010
London

I noticed an extreme amount of trash yesterday morning on my walk into Amberley, so on my return trip I collected it. Empty crisp bags, tall cans of stout and ale, flattened plastic water bottles; none of what I found was interesting or in any way traceable. For a while I felt put upon, but in truth I like picking up litter. I even like crawling into the bushes for it.

On a bike, forget it, but while walking and listening to an audiobook, it's the perfect little activity.

Later in the day we traveled to London. The train we'd intended to take was canceled, and the one that followed it was trashed. Hugh cleared a table of sandwich wrappers and empty cans, and we'd been sitting for fifteen minutes when the conductor announced that due to some problem or other, Horsham would be our final stop. "Oh, bloody hell," said the woman across the aisle. "This fucking country is a joke is what it is."

She pulled out her cell phone and called the person who was expecting her. "Can you fucking believe it?" she asked. "One bloody inch of snow and this joke of a country shuts down." She picked at the trash heaped on her table. "I've lived in Sweden, I have, and you'd better believe *they* don't bloody shut down." The woman speculated that there'd be no more trains until tomorrow and that she'd be forced to find a room in Horsham. "I used to fucking live here. Can you believe it?" she said.

A short while later we pulled into the station. Hugh and I switched tracks and within minutes were on our way to London. This train too was filthy. I saw a middle-aged, normal-looking woman eating potato chips and drinking tea and when her stop came, she took her bag and disembarked, leaving the mess behind. I'd have loved to have stopped her and asked what she thought she was doing, but of course I didn't.

I guess it's a trade-off. The French are tidy but take up as many seats as possible, while the English take only the space that they need and then trash it.

December 24, 2010
London

For the first time in my life, a young man offered me his seat on the tube. I assumed he'd be getting off at the next stop, St. Paul's, but he didn't. He didn't get off at Chancery Lane or

Oxford Circus either, and the longer he stood there, the worse I felt. *Did you offer this to me because I'm old or because I have a lot of packages?* I wanted to ask.

On the one hand, I was grateful to be sitting down, but on the other, I found I was unable to appreciate it. *Does he think I'm in my seventies?* I wondered. Then, too, it could just be a Christmas thing. Maybe he had the spirit and decided to do someone a favor. But why me?

December 25, 2010
London

Hugh planned to make my family's traditional avgolemono soup for Christmas Eve dinner and when he realized at the last minute that the chicken was spoiled, I ran around the corner to see if Tesco was still open. It was, so I bought a replacement. The store was crowded, and I got into the express lane behind a Laotian woman in a wig. She had more than ten items and was carrying a paint roller on a long pole she'd bought a few doors down at the hardware store. *Is it a gift,* I wondered, *or is she going to go home and paint her ceiling?* After the woman was rung up, she slowly pulled out her purse. Then she pointed behind the counter and asked for a few lottery tickets. *On Christmas Eve?* I thought.

After returning home I called Dad. He was going to Paul's for dinner but for the first time in years was skipping church. It seems the priest was given six weeks to pack up and move to Atlanta. His replacement arrived last Monday, and, in protest, Dad is boycotting the Christmas service. He has no plans for today and though I am sorry for him, it's sort of his own fault. If he was at all Christmassy, one of us would have invited him—not that he would have come. *I have to work on my taxes,* he'd probably say or, likelier still, *I don't want anyone breaking into the house while I'm away.*

2011

January 2, 2011
Rackham, England

The last time I was here I picked up all the trash between our house and the village shop. Walking to the pub yesterday afternoon I noticed that someone had replaced it all, and then some. *Who does this?* I wondered.

"It's awful, isn't it?" our neighbor Thelma said.

After lunch I got on my bike and headed for parts unknown. There's a forest beyond the bend and it might be magnificent were it not for the trash, which is distracting once you start to notice it. Was France like this? Wouldn't I have noticed if it were?

I rode to Greatham and had turned onto the two-lane road to Pulborough when I came upon a man picking up bottles and stuffing them into a massive plastic bag. He looked to be my age and was wearing a black stocking cap. "Excuse me," I said, "but are you paid to clean up?"

He said that he was not. "I live up the road and do this twice a year—have filled seven bags since leaving my drive."

"Who does this?" I asked.

"Everyone," he said. "They wait till nobody's looking and chuck it out the car window. I find a lot of McDonald's waste, sandwich wrappers, that kind of thing."

"Well—" And I said the queerest thing. "You're an out-standing citizen." After returning home, I grabbed a bag and

218

joined Hugh on a short walk. It took no time at all to fill it, mainly with bottles and cans. We hadn't gone very far when the sun began to set. Returning the way we'd come made sense but Hugh saw a footpath and so we trudged through a forest and crossed a field of cow shit. Then it was through the mud and over a barbed-wire fence. "Lift your leg!" he yelled, and I explained that I *was*.

"The problem is that I'm short and haven't got as much leg to lift," I told him.

January 4, 2011
London

I can't get over the amount of rubbish there is in West Sussex. Had I noticed it last July I never would have bought the house, but from talking to people I get the idea that it's like this all over the UK. Yesterday I took a walk with a plastic bag and before I reached the neighbor's place I'd filled it with Lucozade bottles and empty beer cans. There are paper cups, candy wrappers, and lots of plastic drink lids pierced with straws.

This morning I headed in the opposite direction and filled four much larger bags. I'm not finding a lot of discarded opera tickets, but still I don't think of this as a class thing. In a survey I read, one in every four English people admitted to throwing rubbish out their car windows—and those are just the ones who admitted to it. *What are they thinking?* I wonder. Aside from the general litter, I found a microwave oven and a toaster, both dumped onto the forest floor as if they'd be happier there.

Hugh, meanwhile, has made an appointment to get his English license. He has to take a driving test, and I'm predicting that at the end he'll have to back out of a parking space while tossing a bottle out the window.

January 27, 2011
Beijing, China

At the breathtaking Beijing airport, I handed over my passport and looked down at four buttons. MY SERVICE WAS: EXCELLENT. GOOD. FAIR. DISAPPOINTING.

"This is my first time in China," I said to the young woman behind the counter.

She leafed through my passport and said in carefully enunciated English, "I can see that."

I rated her excellent.

In the arrival area we were met by Kadi Hughes, whose Chinese name translates to "Unicorn" but who is usually addressed as "Miss Unicorn." She's young and pretty, dark-haired, perhaps in her late twenties, and moved here from Boston two years ago. There was an elevator to the parking level and as we boarded, I felt myself being shoved from behind. *But that can't be,* I thought. *Not in Asia. Perhaps someone fainted and what I feel is his body falling against mine.*

That happened a lot yesterday. Coming from France, I wouldn't have noticed so much, but coming from Japan it was shocking. The honking horns were another big change, as was the sight of pedestrians storming into traffic.

"Rules and regulations are thought of as bourgeois concepts," Kadi explained, and we watched as two boys on a bike cut in front of a car that had run a red light. Other differences became noticeable later on. In Japanese shops, the sales assistants stand quietly with their hands behind their backs until a customer arrives, at which point they welcome him. Here, the employees gather in knots, talking amongst themselves. At the supermarket my cashier yelled what I imagine amounted to *Hey, Brenda, you got any quarters?*

The girl she was talking to threw a heavy roll of change in our direction—threw it hard, like a baseball—and I'm just lucky it didn't hit me in the face.

January 28, 2011
Beijing

Yesterday's high was 25 degrees and because my coat is made of corduroy with cotton lining, Hugh and I started the day with a walk to Yashow Market. The place was recommended by Duncan, who told us that we had to bargain. "They'll give you a price, and the first thing you do is reduce it by seventy percent," he said.

"Right."

I don't like the puffiness of down but seeing as it's so horribly cold and nobody cares what I look like, it made sense. Yashow is a multistory building crowded with competing stalls. On the ground floor there were coats and clothing and, below that, designer-knockoff bags, shoes, and accessories. Look at anything for more than a nanosecond and you're immediately set upon. "You want?" said the saleswoman when I glanced too long at a T-shirt picturing Obama dressed like Chairman Mao. I tried explaining that only an asshole would wear it, but she didn't seem to understand, and so I walked away, her calling after me, "Hey! Hey!"

The girl I dealt with next was perhaps in her mid-twenties and had long hair cut bluntly at her shoulders. She showed me a brown down jacket with a small logo of a fox over the left breast, and though I don't care for hoods, I tried it on. "How much?" I asked.

"For you, two hundred fifty rmb," she said.

That's the equivalent of $35 and it seemed fair to me.

"I'll give you one hundred," Hugh said.

"Who you kidding?" the woman countered. She frowned

and suddenly looked twenty years older. "This coat is good. You ask anybody."

She glanced at me. "Who he? You brother?" Hugh and I do not resemble one another in any way. He doesn't even look like he could be my friend.

"Come on, David," he said and he helped me out of the hooded coat.

I told the woman that we would be back, and she said, "Yeah, right. Nobody ever come back. Why you even say that you come back?"

I walked away feeling hated and wandered down other corridors where equally young women called out after me, "You want coat?" "You want shirt?" "Look at price I have for you!"

In the basement I stopped to consider a hat and within a moment a woman was upon me. "That good hat. You need hat?" This was one of those fake fur–lined hunter's caps with flaps that come over the ears. "One hundred fifty rmb," the woman said, and she set it, crown-like, upon my head.

"I'll give you eighty," Hugh told her.

The woman turned and offered a frown. "Who he? Your brother?" I was getting the idea that Caucasians look pretty similar to the Chinese.

"They can't tell our ages either," Kadi later told me. "They'll say, 'What are you, twenty-three? Fifty?' "

Hugh said that if the salesgirl wouldn't take eighty we'd go somewhere else.

"Where you from?" she asked. "Where you live at?"

I told her we were based in London and she asked if we had any London money. "Give me some for souvenir."

I leafed through my wallet but had none on me. "This is really a nice hat, you know," she said. "You need to give me fair price."

Hugh offered 100 rmb and she hit him on the shoulder. In the end I got it for 120, which is around 17 dollars.

Back upstairs we revisited the coat lady. She, too, wound up hitting Hugh. "You not fair to Chinese people," she said. "Specially now at New Year." We walked away, Hugh feeling fine about it but me feeling conflicted. "The woman most likely lives in a crate," I told him. "She wants an extra dollar fifty for something I'd pay more for in a London charity shop, and I'm *not* going to give it to her?"

I returned to buy the coat and the young woman gestured toward Hugh, who was looking at T-shirts across the way. "He so mean. I no like him, but you, you okay."

That was the start of a day the likes of which I hadn't experienced since Bangkok. Everywhere we went, we were yanked on and hawked to. "You want rickshaw ride?" "You want tour?" "You need gloves?"

Outside the Forbidden City a man on crutches hobbled up beside me and pointed to his foot, which might more accurately be called a hoof. It looked like something you'd find on a goat but was skin-colored and had a little socklet dangling from the end of it. The man pointed to his hoof and then to his stomach.

I continued walking and as the man kept pace beside me, I wanted more than anything to remove my shoe and reveal an even smaller hoof. Of course, that wasn't possible, so in the end I gave him money.

Another shock coming from Japan is the subway behavior. I've never seen anyone talk on their cell phone in the Tokyo metro but yesterday I saw a woman who was not only talking but eating corn on the cob at the same time. Eating corn on the cob on the subway!

I'm also startled by the constant spitting. Even women do

it. You hear the sound of someone culling mucus, seemingly from the depths of his or her soul. Then out it comes. On the train I heard the dredging noise and saw a man hawk phlegm into a plastic bag. "That was decent of him," Kadi said when I told her about it later. "Usually they do it right there on the floor."

After buying my coat yesterday, we walked through a shantytown. This was what I'd thought of when I thought of China: the rickety houses with sleeping bags for doors, the grim communal toilets with turds in them. Boy, did I see a lot of those yesterday. Hugh led us to a lake that was supposed to be quite beautiful—Lake Turdly, I called it. The water was frozen a foot thick, and on it were human feces. In one spot people had broken the ice with hammers. I saw a man and a boy carrying shards of it in plastic bags and then I saw a pair of swimmers. The two had just come out of the water and stood on the freezing banks, drying themselves with hand towels.

Another of the things I saw yesterday was a man in curlers standing outside a shanty and smoking. This was somewhere between Lake Turdly and the Forbidden City. The latter hadn't interested me much, but I wound up liking it. What intrigued me were the great numbers of Chinese tourists, many with a child in tow. "Hello," the kid would say. "Good afternoon to you." One of the little boys stopped us to shake our hands. Others marched by in school groups.

Last night's book signing lasted until 11:30 and afterward Kadi led us to a Sichuan place not far from the bookstore. Dave Eggers joined us, as did a British woman named Helen and her friend, Ed, who works in the music industry. Both spoke Chinese, as does Kadi, but still they gave us English menus—

or, well, sort of English menus. Aside from Water Seepage Bullfrog, the restaurant offered:

Unwanted Effort However Mutton

Saliva Green Wool Stomach

Steams the Valuable Fish

Old Vinegar Flower King Spinach

The Cabbage Mixes the Hibernation of Insects
   Head

The Cucumber Dips the Sauce

The Bamboo's Fragrant Hand Rips the Chicken

Burns Kale in Vein

I liked listening as our hosts told stories about their lives here. Helen moved to China knowing no Mandarin but seemed to have picked it up in no time, as had Kadi. "This guy shoved me on the subway the other day and I called him a dirt dumpling," she said, adding that when it comes to insults, them's fighting words.

We stayed at the restaurant until 1:45 a.m., when, in order to clear us out, the waitress opened the door. It was cruelly, bitterly cold and even in my hooded down coat, I shivered all the way back to the hotel.

January 30, 2011
Beijing

Over dinner Alex mentioned that China has a zero-tolerance policy when it comes to drinking and driving. "One drop and if you get behind the wheel, you're arrested," she said.

I pointed out the window at the unbelievable chaos taking place on the other side of the parking lot. "You mean those people are *sober*?"

If there are rules here, I certainly can't guess what they are. People run red lights with impunity and make U-turns anywhere they like. "It's a nation of new drivers," Alex explained, adding that five years ago, hardly anyone had a car.

March 7, 2011
London

For dinner Hugh cooked the venison he'd bought yesterday at the farmers' market. The label read LOCALLY STALKED, which is not like saying "locally raised," but "locally spied on," "locally plotted against."

March 23, 2011
Paris

The furnace repairman came yesterday afternoon. Once a year he conducts a checkup and as he dug around in the kitchen, I sat at my desk and fumed. "Do you hear that dog?" I asked after twenty or so minutes. "Can you believe how much he barks?" The man didn't understand what I was talking about, so I pointed to the ceiling. "My neighbor's dog," I said. "All he does is bark."

The repairman nodded and told me what *he* does to barking dogs. It sounded delicious but he talked super-quickly, so he lost me after "slip it under the door"...

"I think all the time about killing him," I said, and it's true. I'm too chicken to do it on my own, so in the fantasy I hire a hit man. Madame Sheppers goes every morning to the supermarket around the corner. The dog is left tied to a post out front so all this person would have to do is toss him some poisoned meat. The problem is that hired killers always come back to blackmail you. At least in movies and on TV shows.

"It's not normal to bark like that," I said to the repairman. "And it goes on all day, I'm telling you."

The man nodded the way polite people do when they want to be left alone. He picked up a tool and as he returned to his work, I went back to my office and thought of the last conversation I'd had with Madame Sheppers, who must be in her early eighties and has lived in our building since 1950-something.

"Do you not notice it?" I'd asked.

She told me that her dog was barking because it was lunchtime. "He sees the rest of us sitting at the table and feels left out!" As if I'd asked *why* the dog was barking.

Robinson, his name is, a miniature collie. Strange, but I don't know a single French dog with a French name. It's always Jim or Eddie or Hudson. The Gerbennes' black Lab is named Barry. "After Barry Goldwater?" I asked. "After Barry White? Berry Gordy?" They didn't know who any of those people were. They just liked the sound of it—Barry.

Robinson's only ten. Worst-case scenario is that he'll last another six or seven years. But then they'll likely run out and get another, the same type probably, and it'll start all over. Because they never tell the dog to shut up. Instead it's all "Well, yes, Robinson, it *is* a beautiful day."

It's supposed to be very cute but it drives me out of my mind. Normally when I'm in the house I wear headphones, the big noise-canceling ones they dole out in factories. People ask, "How come you never pick up when I call?"

I say, "You called?"

The mailman rings with a package but I don't hear the bell and so I have to go to the post office, where I wait in a long line and think every moment of how much I hate that dog.

I don't know if Madame Sheppers picks up after him or not. It's the law, but that doesn't mean she follows it. She's taped all these notices to her mailbox: NO JUNK FLYERS. Then it turns out she earns extra money by going from building to building and stuffing other people's mailboxes with them.

I don't know what he found while he was checking out our

furnace, but the repairman was in there for a little over an hour. "Now I hear it," he said as he was packing up. "It took a while but once you notice it, you can't stop noticing it."

"Thank you," I said. Because sometimes I worry—and who wouldn't, really—that I've finally, officially, been driven crazy.

April 7, 2011
Chicago

Last night's reading was in Waukegan, Illinois, and by the time we left the theater and headed back to Chicago it was after midnight. The producer, Steve, had rented a car with satellite radio, and he tuned it to a station that broadcasts nothing but show tunes. "Now *this*," he said. "This is outstanding."

He's such an interesting mix of contradictions. "God, I love *The Pajama Game*," he told me, then, over Bernadette Peters's "Moonshine Lullaby," "Call me crazy, but I actually prefer this to the original Ethel Merman version!"

And he's straight! With three children. Straight with three children *and* he lives in Salt Lake City.

After twenty minutes of show tunes, Steve switched to the satellite porn channel, tuning in as two women interviewed an award-winning actress. The award was for Best Inter-racial Sex Scene of 2011, but still, she took it as quite the accomplishment. "Anything else you'd like to plug?" one of the interviewers asked, and the guest mentioned that her new line of sex toys could be viewed on her website.

"And I'd like to add that a certain percentage of the sales goes to charity!"

I fell asleep for a few minutes and when I awoke one of the women was asking, "And did he ever pee on you?"

"Only once, in the shower," the actress said.

Steve merged into the next lane. "I don't know that that really counts," he said. "What do you think?"

"What?"

"Peeing on someone in the shower," he said. "It's like, I don't know, talking dirty to them while they're asleep. How are they even supposed to know you're doing it?"

I said something noncommittal like "Good point," and then I drifted off again. By the time I woke up Steve had returned to the Broadway channel and was singing along to a song about secretaries. "What's this from?" I asked.

"You don't know *How to Succeed in Business?*" he asked. "Where have you been, son? This is from the 1994 revival!"

I blinked.

"With Matthew Broderick? For which he won a Tony Award? Ever hear of those?" He shook his head, disgusted.

"All right," I said. "Lay off." And we continued on to *Chicago,* which originally opened in 1975 and ran for 946 performances.

April 18, 2011
Gainesville, Florida

After lunch yesterday afternoon I walked to the strip mall down the road from the hotel. There, at the UF bookstore, I bought a decal and a notebook with an alligator on it. Then I went to a reptile shop to confront my worst fears. It was situated between two haircutting places, and I knew upon entering that I needed to return late at night with a group of brave men and burn it to the ground—all of it, the whole row of buildings, just in case anything escaped and was lurking in a stockroom or inside a computer at the store that just sold ink cartridges. Many of the snakes were babies, less than four inches long. "Cute," I heard someone say, referring to what looked like a week-old cobra. "Look how cute the baby is."

David Sedaris

Little snakes are cute the way that little guns are, which is to say not at all. *That person should be killed,* I thought.

After the snakes there were snakes with legs: iguanas, geckos, bearded dragons, and even a monitor lizard, a miniature dinosaur, essentially, that was maybe ten inches long and was clawing at the sides of its tank. Mice do this, and you think that they want to run away somewhere safe where they can raise their families in peace. Monitor lizards do it, and you get the idea that it's not safety they want, but you. *What kind of a person would buy these? Mustn't they be white supremacists?* I don't know why I leaped to this conclusion, but it's the same way I feel about alligator owners, pets whose loyalty factor is zero but that are great if you've got a body to dispose of.

A few of the leathery frogs were nice. I might save them before I burned the place down, but not the alligator snapping turtle, which was the size of a turkey platter and lurked at the bottom of a deep tank. Its mouth was open and on its tongue were two worm-like tentacles that twitched back and forth, luring unsuspecting fish. For two dollars you could feed it, and while part of me wanted to, another, stronger part successfully fought it, knowing that were I to throw it a mouse or a fish or whatever the horrible thing ate, I'd be no better than the sadists who post their feedings on YouTube. Next to the snapper was an equally large matamata turtle that looked as if its head had been stepped on. Sheets of flesh were peeling off its legs, and its eyes—or what I'm guessing were its eyes—were not much larger than pinpricks. WATCH ME ENGULF A SHINER—$2 read the sign taped to the front of its aquarium.

I was trying to make sense of the matamata turtle when I noticed a young woman beside the register who had dozens of hoops through her ears. There were more rings in her lips, and then there were the tattoos, a great number of them, on her arms and legs. The young woman's hair was cropped short. She was dressed in a T-shirt and cutoff jeans, and coiled around her wrist was a reddish snake, maybe a foot and a half long. It was the only one in the room that was not locked in a terrarium, and at the sight of it, I panicked and began to sweat.

Must-get-out-of-here, I thought, but I was too frightened to move. The young woman noticed me, and the expression on her face, fleeting but nevertheless there, suggested that I had just made her day. For isn't this what reptile owners are hoping to induce—fear? Why else bring your snake to the restaurant patio or the crowded street fair if not to watch people jerk and shudder?

At last night's signing I met a woman who owned an enormous iguana. "He was just small when I got him," she told me. "Then he grew larger and heavier and I moved him to a pen in the backyard. It was such a mistake, this iguana, four feet long, and my God, did he stink."

"Really?"

"To high heaven," she said. "In the end I brought him to a reptile shop and said, 'Take him, please. I don't need any money.'"

I asked if the iguana recognized her and she said no, lizards aren't that way. "They don't cuddle or any of that good stuff," she told me. "I think *pet* is the wrong word to describe them."

The girl with the snake wrapped around her wrist might have argued differently, but she was a sociopath who needed to be killed, just as the owner of the reptile shop needed to be killed along with everything he sold, except for the two leathery frogs, which were adorable.

April 23, 2011
Tempe, Arizona
A joke from last night's signing:

A woman leafs through the morning paper and looks up

at her husband. "It says here that women in Las Vegas get a hundred dollars every time they have sex. That sounds like a pretty good deal, so I'm going to move there."

"I'll go with you," her husband offers. "I want to see how you live on two hundred dollars a year."

May 24, 2011
Rome, Italy
On the flight from London, I looked through my books and learned to call Hugh *ciccino mio,* which translates to "my little fleshy thing." He listened to his Pimsleur lessons and before we knew it, we'd arrived and were standing at the baggage claim. They hadn't fed us on the plane, and on the long ride into town, my hunger tipped and became something else. "I believe you would call it fasting," Hugh said.

After checking into the hotel, we went to the rooftop. In the photos the pool looks to be Olympic-size but in real life, it's no more than five yards long. Likewise, on the website the bar is throbbing with action; in person it was not just empty but forsaken. Our room is not awful. I like the high ceiling but we're at the back of the building and overlook a parking lot. In the restaurant this morning I asked the waitress for more coffee, beginning with *"Scusi, signora."*

"You should have called me *signorina,*" the woman said. "That means I am not so old."

I noticed that the couple at the next table skipped the *signora/signorina* part altogether and never said "Thank you," not even in English. It's the best part of this hotel, the breakfast room. When we were on the elevator to the first floor, a man in a suit stared hard at Hugh's shirt. Then his eyes moved downward, and his mouth curled in disgust. "What did I do?" Hugh later asked.

May 25, 2011
Rome

Yesterday's schedule included two radio interviews. The first was for a weekly book program hosted by a woman named Laura who is my age and has three sons in their late teens. "Any pets?" I asked, and she told me she owns two Komodo dragons. "Just little," she said, and she held up her hands and adjusted them to a distance of six inches apart. When I shuddered, she laughed, claiming they're just like kittens.

I said, "Soft?"

"Well, no," she admitted.

"Playful?"

She said, "Not so much."

I repeated this to my translator on our way back to the hotel and she said, *"Mamma mia!"*

I went, "Wait a minute, you people actually *say* that?"

"Why, of course," she told me.

This made me think of my first trip to Normandy when I heard Hugh's friend Genevieve say, *"Oh là là,"* and I'd thought, *You've got to be kidding me.* Years later, in Tokyo, my Japanese teacher said, "Ah so," and I reacted the same way. Then our plumber in London said, "Blimey," and I lost it.

"What would you expect someone in the United States to say?" I'd asked him.

And he said, in his best American accent, "Oh my God."

I suppose that's common enough but it was long ago eclipsed by *awesome,* which is completely out of control.

May 28, 2011
London

Told to me last night at Cadogan Hall:

"I was at a bar with friends, all of us telling jokes, and I said, 'What do you do if an epileptic has a fit in your bathtub? Throw in your laundry.'

"Everyone laughed and then this guy behind me said, 'Hey— my *brother* was an epileptic. And he *died* in the bathtub.'

"I was like, *Fuck*. 'Did he drown?'

"And the guy said, 'No, he choked on a sock.'"

June 25, 2011
London

I read online that a nineteen-year-old Hawaiian kid has been fined \$100 for slapping a monk seal. Quite a few comments followed the article, most along the lines of "How dare he!" But if you were going to slap something, wouldn't a seal be at the top of your list? Not because they need to be punished, but because it would make such a satisfying sound, like clapping your hands together but wetter, meatier. Waves might drown it out, though, so when I slap my seal, I'm going to do it in a quiet room, an office, maybe, after everyone else has gone home.

July 12, 2011
London

In a television interview, Tim Pawlenty was asked whether homosexuality was innate or whether it was caused by outside forces, such as the way a person was raised. They always present the Republican candidates with this question. Then, my hand in the air, my brain moaning, *Over here! Call on me!*, they say either that it's a choice or, like Pawlenty, that "the science isn't in yet."

And I'm like, *Why don't you ever ask a gay person? Why should Sarah Palin's or Herman Cain's or Tim Pawlenty's responses carry any weight whatsoever?*

Well, I can imagine someone saying, *according to Michele*

Bachmann, it's a choice, so I guess that explains that. I must have been asleep when my options were presented. *Do you want to lust after the girl who will never know you're alive or the boy who will never know it but would round up his friends and set you on fire if he ever for one moment suspected you were interested in him?*

And I suppose I said, *I'll take the boy with the torch!* Though I sure can't remember it. What with the excitement of choosing my blood type, I guess I just blocked it out.

July 17, 2011
Rackham

Again last night I fell down a YouTube hole. All roads lead to people feeding live mice to snakes and snapping turtles, but this time I went beyond that and stumbled upon a woman named Donna who weighs six hundred pounds but would like to weigh a thousand. "I guess I'm sort of a reverse anorexic," she said. "I see myself in the mirror and feel that I'm too small."

There are a lot of Donna clips on YouTube but this particular one was from *The Tyra Banks Show.* Banks is a former model, so her response to all this was pretty much what you'd expect. "I'm sorry," she said, "but what about, like, your health?"

"Oh, I'm healthy enough," Donna said. They showed footage of her enjoying an average breakfast: a dozen scrambled eggs, an entire pack of bacon, eight slices of buttered toast.

"But you can hardly walk to your mailbox," Banks reminded her. "If you keep this up, you won't be able to move!"

The studio audience murmured their support—"Yeah, what about that. Ever think of *that?*"

Donna—bless her—answered that walking was overrated.

"I don't like movement," she said. "I like to lay in bed and watch TV, that's what I like to do."

It's like she was designed in a lab to outrage a slender talk-show host. "But..." Banks kept saying. "But...but..."

It's the "You're not healthy" business that gets to me. That's the same angle people take with smokers—assholism disguised as concern: "We don't know each other but I want you in good shape so I can tell you for longer how to live your life."

To this, Donna leaned back in her tiny-looking chair, saying, in so many other, politer words, *Fuck you.*

July 20, 2011
London

I walked into the kitchen as Hugh was listening to *I'm Sorry I Haven't a Clue.* It's a BBC radio quiz show, and the category was "Movie Titles That Would Be Greatly Changed with the Removal of One Letter."

"Think *The Count of Monte Cristo,*" said the host.

July 23, 2011
Rackham

Last month the city of Phoenix was overcome by a massive dust cloud the media referred to as a *haboob.* I loved how round and exotic that sounded and couldn't say it enough times—*haboob.* Some people, though, were not so pleased. A man wrote the *Arizona Republic* saying it wasn't fair to our troops. "They serve in Iraq and then come home to hear us using Middle Eastern words?"

The flap was written about in the *Times,* which pointed out that *algebra* is also an Arabic word, as are *khaki, pajamas,* and *zero.*

August 27, 2011
London

The other night after dinner, Jenny suggested that I download the Google app to my iPad. It has an audio option, so rather than typing the word for whatever it is you're looking for, you just speak.

"Try it," she said.

There are a trillion things I could have looked up, but suddenly, with everyone watching, I couldn't think of a single one. "Okay," I said. "All right." Closing my eyes, I thought of last week's vacation and, with my best Scottish accent, came out with "Cookery book."

The screen went dark for a moment, then up came *gay*.

September 2, 2011
Rackham

Yesterday afternoon I was interviewed by a woman named Nina Myskow for her Radio 4 show *Food for Thought*. We sat in my kitchen eating sushi, and just before ending she asked what I'd want for my last meal.

"Like if I was on death row or something?"

"Exactly," she said.

While deciding between my mother's manicotti and Hugh's roast chicken, I wondered if anyone ever requests something he's never had before. What mass murderer answers, "I wouldn't mind trying Micronesian food" or "What's the specialty in Tonga?" Wouldn't you want something you were familiar with? Something that reminded you of gentler times? What if you got the Micronesian food and hated it? Then what? You'd go to the electric chair with a bad taste in your mouth. Ick.

September 28, 2011
Paris

I've been reading about this new app. Is My Son Gay?, it's called, and it consists of twenty questions. Many have denounced it as lame, and while I agree that "Before he was born, did you wish he would be a girl?" and "Are you divorced?" are not particularly telling, there's probably something to "Does he like musical comedies?" Other questions include:

—Does he like to dress up nicely?
—Has he ever gotten into or participated in a fight?
—Does he have a best friend?
—Does he like diva singers?

The questions leave me feeling sad—not for gay teenagers but for straight ones. Is your son friendless? Does he fight? Does he listen to tuneless, abrasive music with lyrics about killing people? Congratulations, he's a heterosexual!

October 5, 2011
London

Dad called last night saying, like always, "David? David, is that you?" We started talking about Christmas and when I asked him what he wanted, he answered, "I want for you to get a goddamned colonoscopy."

"So for Christmas you want for someone to shove a pipe up my ass?"

"You're damn right I do."

When I told him I was leaving on tour and would not be back until December 13, he said, "Fine, make an appointment for when your tour is over. How about the fourteenth?"

"I want a light at the end of the tunnel, but not *that* tunnel," I told him.

"Well, you need to have a colonoscopy and you need to do it now."

Every time I changed the subject, he changed it back, until finally, exhausted, I told him I had to go. We hung up and two minutes later the phone rang.

"Or an iPhone," he said.

"I beg your pardon?"

"Or for Christmas you can get me an iPhone." Then, as if adding the word *goodbye* would substantially drive up his bill, he hung up on me.

October 7, 2011
Paris

I took the Métro to Dr. Guig's office and was halfway there when a street musician entered the car. The man had a karaoke machine strapped to a dolly and on top of it, secured with a bungee cord, was a banana.

Dr. Barras, the woman who deep cleans my teeth, was in a foul mood when I arrived, but still I enjoyed her company. "Has Mr. Sedaris done a good job brushing?" I asked.

She scolded me for referring to myself in the third person. "Who do you think you are, Alain Delon?"

Afterward I returned home and was eating lunch when I decided to look at *Gawker*. One of the articles concerned a young female screenwriter. The post wasn't about the new movie she has coming out; it was just a pointless rant against her in general, a who-does-she-think-she-is-being-successful sort of thing. At the end of it, like always, there were comments. The first person to write said that she, too, hated the screenwriter and often fantasized that she could meet her in person and tell her face to face how much she sucked.

The next comment was posted by someone named Unicorndog who said he had a similar fantasy but involving David Sedaris and with added violence.

I hadn't expected to see my name and spent the rest of the afternoon feeling depressed about it and hating myself for looking at *Gawker*. *What did I ever do to Unicorndog?* I wondered.

October 11, 2011
Syracuse
The man who drove me to the airport this morning asked what I did for a living.

"I write," I told him.

"Well, don't you ever give up," he said. "No matter what nobody tells you, don't you ever quit."

"Okay," I said.

"I mean it," he told me. "This is your dream and if you want to make it happen you got to work on it."

"Will do."

Later he asked if I was married and when I said no, he told me that I shouldn't be alone. "Maybe you can find a girl who likes to read," he told me. "Maybe you could let her read your writing and give you comments." He looked at me in the rearview mirror. "Hey, you never know!"

October 14, 2011
Bangor, Maine
My driver to the Newark airport was a sixty-three-year-old former investment analyst who lost his job two years ago. "At my age, who was going to hire me?" he asked. Driving a limo for ten- and twenty-dollar tips was not his first choice, but he has a child in college and a wife with cancer, so sitting at home is not an option. The man had thick white hair

neatly parted on the side. He'd played baseball for the army during the Vietnam War, so I asked for details. As he began to provide them, I looked out the window at a figure hanging by the neck from the third floor of an apartment building—someone's Halloween decoration. Across its chest was a sign reading THIS IS A NICE TIME OF YEAR.

October 20, 2011
Concord, New Hampshire

While waiting for Pete and Artie to arrive, I sat in the lobby of the Pittsfield Crowne Plaza and listened to the woman at the front desk. She was perhaps in her early sixties and if I had a business, regardless of what it was, I would return to that town and coax her into working for me. I liked that she never launched into corporate-hotel-speak; there was no "How was your trip in?" or "I'm sorry, but guaranteed check-in isn't until three o'clock." Her cheer seemed genuine, and I got the idea that she welcomed a challenge.

I'd been watching her for ten minutes or so when a teenager in a hooded sweatshirt skulked in and went to her position at the counter. "Yagadanny jobs?"

"I beg your pardon?"

"Jobs," the kid repeated. "I want a job. Dishwashing or...I don't care. Just something."

"I can certainly give you an application," the pleasant woman said, and she reached beneath the counter and handed him a sheet of paper.

"Pen," he muttered.

"Excuse me?"

The kid said, "*Pen?* I need a *pen?*"

Had he sat back and listened to her for a few minutes he could have returned home, put on a tie, and had a job by the end of the afternoon. As it was, though, pen-less and with his face obscured by the hood, there was no way. Everything about him said *I will work for three days and on all of them I will be late.*

I was bad at applying for jobs as well, but I think they could see that with me it was just nervousness, not contempt.

October 22, 2011
Erie, Pennsylvania

I read yesterday that when starved for food, the humpback cricket will chew off its own legs. If they regenerated this might be a half-decent idea, but they don't. So it eats its legs, and, unable to escape danger, it promptly gets eaten itself. That so seems like something I would do.

October 24, 2011
Columbus, Ohio

A car met me at the airport yesterday. The driver was around my age, and he began our conversation by asking me where I lived.

"England," I said, adding that I was on a long trip, going to a different city every day for six weeks.

The man whistled. "Wow," he said. "That's a lot of traveling. So where are you off to tomorrow?"

I told him I was going to Detroit, and he explained that here in America, that was known as the Motor City. "It's where our automobile industry was located."

It seemed weird that he was telling me that. Of course cars were made in Detroit; did he think I was an idiot? I realized then that when I'd said that I lived in England, he'd taken it to mean that I was born there and knew very little about the United States. It would have been easy enough to set him straight, but I didn't want to embarrass him. So I said, "Really?"

"It's also the home of Motown Records," he continued. "Ever hear of that?"

"I think...yeah," I said. "Yes, I have heard of it."

For the rest of the drive he told me things about the country I was born and raised in, and I pretended to be learning. "Gosh," I kept saying. "Really? How interesting."

At last night's signing I met a young woman whose father is a construction worker. He often sits around the house in torn boxer shorts, and when I asked, "Why torn?," she explained that port-a-johns rarely have toilet paper in them, so what the guys do is tear off the hems of their underwear and use the fabric to wipe their asses with. Fascinating.

October 26, 2011
Muskegon, Michigan

I was driven to Muskegon by three U of M students. Sam and Nick are brothers, and joining them was their friend Blake, who sat in the back seat with me. I don't know much about contemporary college life and was relieved to hear that kids still take acid and that they still go outdoors to do it. "Inside means corners," Sam said. "And I absolutely cannot handle them when I'm tripping."

"Right angles either," Nick added. "Those things flip me out."

The brothers were freaked out by corners but not, strangely, by reptiles. Sam owned a bearded dragon until it got an infection in its tail and died. And both Nick and Blake own snakes. "We need to go to your houses right now and kill them," I said.

The two thought I was joking. "Are you kidding? These snakes are sweet!"

Sam told me that a few years ago, on Saint Croix, he

saw a wild pig that would puncture a beer can with its teeth and empty the contents. "The original one that did it died of cirrhosis or whatever. This was his son and he only drank NA beer."

Kids today like to drink Sizzurps, a combination of codeine-based cough syrup, Sprite, and Jolly Ranchers.

"You mean the candy?" I asked.

"We mean the candy," Sam said. "It's a Lil Wayne thing, a drink he invented."

Four Loko was also popular. Then it got banned. "It was malt liquor with caffeine," Blake explained.

The three told me about no-pants parties, which are just what they sound like. "The last one I went to was thrown by my girlfriend's gay roommate," Sam said. "So I get there and all the guys are in briefs. I was the only one in boxers, can you believe it?"

Kids also go to ABC parties. That stands for "anything but clothes," I was told. "You can cover up your dick or whatever, you just can't do it with traditional clothing."

"Meaning?"

"You use a scarf or a notebook or something," Nick said.

"Or a hat," Sam added. "A hat would work."

October 31, 2011
Athens, Georgia

Thirty years ago a housepainter and I were eating lunch, and he told me that the previous evening he'd gotten a call from his father. "I really had to go to the bathroom but couldn't get him off the line," he said. "So what I did was shit in my hand."

He'd presented it as a problem-solving story, so while my inner self whispered, *Oh, no, you didn't,* my outer one acted like *Good thinking, you!*

At the time I guess it wasn't so outlandish. This was what

happened when phones had cords and were attached to the wall. Still, though, it's not like the president was on the other line. Couldn't you ask your dad to call you back?

I repeated the story on Saturday night to B., and when I had finished, instead of laughing or making a horrified face, she said, "Haven't *you* ever shit in your hand?" This in the tone I might use when saying, "Haven't *you* ever washed whites in cold water?" Like it's one of those things you maybe don't do all the time, but in a pinch—why not?

"I have never," I told her.

We were in her car and it was late. College students dressed for Halloween crowded the sidewalks on either side of us, some of them howling like wolves.

"I haven't done it a *lot*," B. said. "Maybe eight times. Or, okay, ten, no more than ten. And always in a public toilet. I don't want to make a splashing sound, see, so what I do is go in my hand and then gently lower it into the water."

I couldn't believe what I was hearing.

"You're trying to tell me that you've never done that?" she asked. "Well, I think most people have. They maybe don't talk about it but I'll bet you anything that it's really common." I looked at her hand on the gearshift, the slender bejeweled fingers ending in long, sculpted nails, and I gasped.

The good thing about being on tour is that you get to talk to strangers and in a way you can't to most people you don't know. "Excuse me," I said to a woman in last night's signing line. "I'm conducting a little survey and was wondering if you've ever shit in your hand?"

The woman was nicely dressed, and I liked what she'd done with her hair. "Have I ever *what*?" she asked.

I went into a bit more detail, and she told me that if it was a splashing sound my friend was worried about, she should first fill the bowl with a big wad of toilet paper. "That's what I do," she said. "It makes a sort of landing pad for my business to fall onto so there's really no splash to speak of."

What on earth, I thought. And later that night I met three other people who do the exact same thing, one of them a forty-year-old married man. This came as something of a surprise, as I'd always thought a straight guy would shit anywhere. Put an empty coffee can on the sidewalk in front of a department store and he'll pull down his pants, thinking, *Oh, why not. I won't get another chance until I reach that job interview.*

"Oh, no," said the married man when I mentioned this. "I'm terribly shy that way."

An hour later I met a guy who worked at a gym, and he told me it is not uncommon to find turds in the shower, eroded to lumps by the hot running water. So that's the last time I pick *my* gum up from out of the drain.

November 1, 2011
Athens, Georgia

On the flight from Orlando I was bumped up to first class and seated beside a fifty-seven-year-old Middle Eastern wholesale gold salesman. The man's aftershave left him smelling like a sanitary urinal cake, so for most of our ninety-minute flight I resented him. That changed when, shortly before landing, he cleared his throat, introduced himself as Mike, and asked in a heavy accent if I lived in Atlanta.

"Me?" I said. "Oh, gosh, no."

The man spoke quickly and during our short conversation I learned the following:

1. Mike starts most mornings with a shot glass of olive oil, not because it tastes good but because it's good for him. Did I drink it too? No? Well, I should.

2. Mike's birthday is January 17. Thus, like me, he is a Capricorn and has been blessed with good luck, which has helped him in his wholesale gold business.

3. Only twice has his luck run out. The first time was in London when he was robbed by two black men. The second time it was Mexicans.

4. Mike has five children. Four were by his first wife, who died in 2003 and who he had known since childhood. The youngest, a product of his second marriage, is a girl, aged five. He showed me her picture and she looked like a baby maid. It wasn't her skin tone that gave that impression but rather the way that she glared into the camera, her face a hard mix of exhaustion, defiance, and resignation. "Oh," I said. "She's adorable!"

5. Mike hoped to make $8,000 in Atlanta. That was his goal but if he didn't meet it, well, that was okay too. There's always next week. The important thing is spending time with our families. Speaking of which, where was mine? Did I have a wife? Did I have kids?

"Oh, look," I said, and I pointed out the window. "The leaves are changing!"

November 3, 2011
San Antonio, Texas

Before leaving Miami, Adam and I sat down to a horrible breakfast of fake eggs, mushy hash browns, and bacon strips that looked like bookmarks painted to sort of resemble bacon strips. Sitting there was pleasant, though, talking. From Miami we flew to Dallas, where we boarded our plane and were immediately asked to collect our belongings and return to the terminal. There was a problem with one of the switches or something and while waiting for a new departure time, I listened to a woman seated nearby as she talked about her cat. It was long-haired, apparently. Then one day she came home and found that he had been shaved.

"Well, in this heat, that's probably for the best," the man she was talking to said.

"Yes, but it wasn't *me* who shaved it," the woman said. "It was somebody else!"

"A stranger shaved your cat?"

"That's what I've been trying to tell you, yes!"

November 7, 2011
San Francisco

"I think we have the same father," said a fellow named Theo after last night's reading. His dad, like mine, is Greek and hoards food.

"And is your father cheap?" I asked.

"Is he ever!"

"Does he sit around in his underpants?"

"No," Theo told me. "He sits around in *mine*. I'll throw them away when they get ratty and he'll pick them out of the trash and wear them until they disintegrate."

"Oh my God," I said. "We really *do* have the same father."

November 12, 2011
Knoxville, Tennessee

On our way into town from the airport yesterday morning we passed a billboard reading WILD TURKEY: AMERICA'S HONEY.

"But doesn't America already have honey?" I said to the driver. "And isn't it called honey?"

November 25, 2011
Kailua, Hawaii

Here in Hawaii, every day is the same: sunny with a high of 82. Sometimes clouds gather but by the time you notice them, they start to disband, like truants. Yesterday, on Thanksgiving, it was normal. I was up by five, as was Gretchen, and after a few hours of work she changed into her new fudge-colored tankini, the one she bought on our first morning in Honolulu. Then we rode our rental bikes to the grocery store, a Safeway next to Pinky's Pupu Bar. It's not far—a mile and a half at most—and the ride couldn't be easier or less stressful.

We were almost at the shopping plaza when we saw a woman lying in the grass. She looked to be in her mid-forties, formerly pretty but now most likely a meth addict. Many of her upper teeth were missing; not the front ones, but the three or four to the left of them, and her skin was cured-looking, like a tobacco leaf. Beside her was a grocery cart heaped with clothing and small appliances, and beneath it, grazing on the close-cropped lawn, was a long-haired guinea pig, light tan–colored, with a filthy ass.

Like Lisa, Gretchen will talk to anyone. "What's its name?" she called.

The woman looked up and brushed her bangs away from her face. "I named him Skeeter," she said. "After, you know, the actor."

What actor? I thought.

"And he doesn't run away?" Gretchen asked.

"Naw," the woman said. "I traint him."

Everything about our morning was strange. The grocery store was bustling, people in shorts and tank tops buying ready-made pie crusts and tubs of Cool Whip. Like most women I know, Gretchen has no problem asking where things are. "Can you tell me where I might find pecans?" she asked an employee stocking the fruit section. "And how about coconuts?"

There's a military base not far away, so a lot of shoppers were young. Many of the women were pregnant, and the guys they were with were almost comically muscular. While waiting in line I listened to people on their cell phones. "Happy Thanksgiving, Grandma," they said, and "I love you, Daddy." Gretchen and I put our groceries into the knapsack we'd bought at Goodwill and took the scenic route home. The road we were on for most of the way was divided by a palm-lined median, and on it, picking things out of the grass, were dozens of geese. All of them had warty, turkey-like growths at the bases of their beaks. We also saw a lot of egrets. Gretchen stopped and looked at one that was following behind a man as he cut his grass. "He's hoping the mower will churn up some delicious insects," she said.

It's interesting going places with her, as the things she tends to focus on are so very different from the things most other people do. "What do you think this fern is called?" she'll ask, or "Whoa, look at this beetle!" Watching her cycle ahead of me, her long graying hair blowing in the wind, I thought of how impossibly old we'd seem to our younger selves, how different we are although we've hardly changed.

December 18, 2011
Rackham

Before leaving London, I went to Portobello Road to look for a gift for Amy. "Anything in particular?" asked the basement dealer who I often buy things from.

"Well," I said, "grotesque is a plus."

"I'm afraid I haven't got anything grotesque," he told me, "but you're free to look."

After examining the many things hanging on the dealer's

walls, I bent to look into his case. "What's that?" I asked, and I pointed to an oval wooden figure no larger than an egg.

"That," he said, "is an eighteenth-century snuffbox carved in the shape of a French hunchback shitting."

He handed it to me, and I noticed the knobbly little turd emerging from the figure's ass. "Well," I said, "if you *do* get anything grotesque, give me a call."

December 21, 2011
London

I called Dad last night and could hear Fox News playing in the background. It was seven p.m. Raleigh time, and after asking about my travel plans, he fixated on Kim Jong-un, son of the late Kim Jong-il. "I'd like to write that guy a letter and tell him he's on the threshold of greatness," Dad said. "I'd say, 'Set your people free and you'll be remembered forever because I'm telling you, you're on the threshold of greatness.'" He repeated the phrase five times, clearly pleased by the sound of it. "I mean, he's on the threshold of greatness!"

He also mentioned Paul's Christmas decorations. "That guy's the talk of the neighborhood," he told me. "Cars are lined up ten deep just to look at his yard. They even take pictures!" He did it up for Halloween as well, but Dad wasn't behind him on that one. "I said to him, 'Who wants to see crap like that?'"

"Like what?" I asked.

"Like a man in a tree who's had an accident with a chain saw," he said. "His damn bloody leg is lying on the ground and it's just terrible to look at. Then he's got a guy who's been run over by a lawn mower. There are body parts lying in the drive-way, brains in the grass. I told him, 'It scares the kids.'"

"But isn't that what Halloween is all about?"

"Aw, baloney," he said.

2012

January 11, 2012
Melbourne, Australia

At dinner last night a woman named Annie recalled a T-shirt she'd recently seen someone wearing. It read:

WHAT DO WE WANT?

A CURE FOR TOURETTE'S.

WHEN DO WE WANT IT?

CUNT.

January 17, 2012
Sydney

It was sunny when I left the hotel yesterday morning but ten minutes later the sky opened up. My umbrella protected most of me, but my feet got so wet you'd think I'd been pushed into a pool. After returning to the room, I took my socks off and put the red-hot iron on them. Then I found the blow-dryer and trained the nozzle on the insides of my shoes. A half an hour later everything was back to normal, but my room smelled like I'd set fire to a hobo.

January 27, 2012
Tokyo

Since our last visit, Simon and Reiko have left Kawasaki City and moved to Jiyugaoka, a lively neighborhood full of good shops. After they showed us their apartment, we went to a restaurant they like and ordered fifteen or so small dishes. While waiting for the first of them to arrive, I mentioned an advertisement I'd seen the day before yesterday. It was for McDonald's and pictured something called a Grand Canyon Burger.

"They have many new things such as that now," Reiko said in her careful, hesitant English. She pulled out her phone and showed me that McDonald's Japan is also offering the Brooklyn Burger, the Texas Burger, the Las Vegas Burger, the Broadway Burger, and the new Beverly Hills Burger. They were pictured on her phone's small screen, each one the size of a ladybug.

When the first dish arrived, some sort of tofu concoction, I mentioned that I'd recently found a rat in our house in Sussex.

"We had them at work," Reiko said. "Not at the job I have now, but when I was with Coca-Cola in Roppongi, rats would come from the subway, take the elevator to my floor, and eat the ladies' hand creams." She took a bite of her tofu. "Rats really like hand creams."

January 30, 2012
Tokyo
We joined Simon and Reiko for dinner at a place in Shibuya, a basement restaurant. It wasn't fancy, and we liked the tableful of merry people seated behind us. While eating, I learned that the Japanese have no word for "hate." "Only 'don't like,'" Reiko said. She told us that following last year's earthquake, a lot of people got married, but an equal number broke up, realizing that life was too short to spend with the wrong person.

I also learned that the word for grandmother, *obaasan*, is very similar to *obasan*, which means, according to Reiko, "over-the-hill lady."

February 4, 2012
Rackham

The woodshed is stacked high with old beams, most of them over five feet long. I'd hoped to cut them down to size with the chain saw, but Hugh won't allow me to use it. "You have two left hands," he said over dinner, a stew made with what turned out to be oxtails. "You're uncoordinated and you spook too easily."

"Yes, but I'm an adult."

"I don't care," he said. "You're not using the chain saw."

"But..."

"But nothing."

He's just like Dad that way. I mean, here I am, fifty-five years old. In another ten years the thing will be too heavy for me to lift.

"I let you drive once and that was enough," Hugh said.

I'd liked the stew when I didn't know what it was. Now, though, I thought of cows, their ropy tails smeared with shit, and I stuck with the turnips. "Who are you to tell me what I can and cannot do?"

"Last week I was using the chain saw and the chain flew off," Hugh said. "Do you *still* want to use it?"

Of course I didn't.

February 10, 2012
Paris

Hugh and I took the two o'clock train from London. Our car was crowded, and off and on throughout the trip I'd tune in to the women across the aisle from us. The younger one was French, and her seatmate, who looked to be in her late fifties, was English. "My son is in Paris," she told the younger woman, "so I'm going for a long weekend to see him."

Her French was pretty good, but every now and then she'd slip up. "He works as a...mushroom for British writers," she said.

The Frenchwoman leaned forward. "I beg your pardon?"

"A mushroom," the Englishwoman repeated. "My son is a mushroom for writers."

"I see," the Frenchwoman eventually said.

April 1, 2012
Rackham

Since we'd returned to England, every day had been the same: Warm and sunny. Shirtsleeve weather. But yesterday we reverted to winter and in the afternoon I rode to Storrington, where I noticed seniors doing good deeds. A woman in her eighties deadheaded the flowers in the planter in front of the post office. Another woman scraped gum off the sidewalk. I picked up all the rubbish I could find but there wasn't much to be had, so I'm guessing someone beat me to it.

After an hour at the leisure center, I went to the butcher shop and confused the guy behind the counter. "No one understands me when I talk," I said to Hugh when I returned home. "It's really no different here than it was in France."

"That's because you speak in non sequiturs," he said. And of course he's right. Yesterday afternoon, when the butcher asked how my day had been so far, I held up my hands, which were scratched and bleeding from reaching into blackberry bushes for stray bits of trash, and said, "Don't I look like I own a cheetah?"

I later said the same thing to my cashier at the grocery store but changed it to *tiger*. Not that it altered the reaction any. I just can't for the life of me figure out what to say to people. I never have been able to, no matter what the language.

April 5, 2012
Rackham

We met yesterday morning with Andrew Baldwin, a local councillor who lives in Horsham and is, by his own admission, "paranoid about litter." I think he means *obsessed,* as *paranoid* seems a word better suited to a litterer than a litter picker-upper. Andrew had attended a meeting earlier that morning. Now it was over, and he wondered if we'd like to join him for a couple hours of cleanup. "Would we!" Hugh and I said.

On our way to the road that leads from Pulborough to Storrington I pointed out the areas I'd already done. "Good on you," Andrew said, looking at the pristine verges and the trees with no plastic bags hanging from them. "Full marks!" It was great talking to someone who shared my interests.

"And the fly-tipping!" I said. "And the people who pick up after their dogs and then hang the bags of shit from branches!"

"I know! I know!" Andrew kept saying.

We parked at the nature reserve, and while Hugh and Andrew headed up toward Pulborough, I went in the opposite direction. The thornbushes were thick with candy wrappers and crisp bags, and I found that the grabber—which I'd normally pooh-pooh—was a real help. At one point, deep in a thicket, I came upon a couple of bones and then a leather pocketbook. It was stiff with age, and inside it, among the dirt and moss, was an auto club membership and a savings card for M and S, both of which had expired in 1993.

"Can I buy you lunch?" Andrew asked after we'd been at it for a few hours. We went to the Labouring Man, a cheerful pub in Coldwaltham. While eating, he discussed the high cost of prosecuting someone.

Then he told us a story about going to Italy. "I have two

daughters," he began. "My youngest girl gets carsick, and we're just heading to Naples when she has an attack. I handed her a plastic bag and after she vomited into it, I tied it shut, put it into a second bag, and put it in my rucksack, figuring I'd throw it away when we reached the airport. The bloke who's driving us, though, he keeps gesturing to me. 'Throw it out the window, throw it out the window,' he seems to be saying. But I can't. See, I'm paranoid about rubbish!" he repeated.

"Shall we do this again when you get back?" he asked after lunch, adding that we could keep the vests and gloves he'd given us. I'm really impressed that an elected official would actually go out and pick up garbage. "I like to put my money where my mouth is," he said. "Then, too, if it's lying on the grass in front of me, how can I *not* pick it up?"

April 24, 2012
Austin
At the check-in desk for yesterday's flight, my counter agent, who was middle-aged and wore glasses with dark rectangular frames, asked for my boarding pass. Then she stood there, frowning at it.

"Is there a problem?"

"Are you a comedian?" she asked.

"No," I told her. "Just a writer."

"Well, I could swear I've heard your name somewhere or other." She put a luggage tag on my suitcase. Then she said, "Hey, here's a joke you might find funny. I read in the paper that they pulled over Willie Nelson's tour bus last week and it"—she began to laugh—"it reeked of marijuana!"

If this was supposed to be a joke, she had clearly left something out. Still, though, out of politeness I pretended to laugh.

"I thought that would tickle you," she said, and as she stuck my luggage receipt to the back of my boarding pass, I told her that I, too, knew a good Willie Nelson joke. "I shouldn't tell it, though, because it contains some bad language."

"Oh, go on," she said. "I'm not squeamish."

"Okay," I said. "What's the last thing you want to hear when you're blowing Willie Nelson?"

She cocked her head.

" 'I'm not really Willie Nelson.' "

It's the funniest thing in the world but the woman didn't seem to get it. "See," I said, standing in the crowded terminal before a number of anxious passengers waiting to get their bags checked, "the only reason you'd blow someone who looks like that is because you think he's famous."

"Okay," she said.

"Then to find out he's not who you thought he was, that he's just some old guy with a bandanna and braids, it would be sort of devastating, wouldn't it?"

"If you say so," she said.

Rushing off toward the security line I wondered what my mother would say if she could see what had become of me. If her number-one rule was never to explain a joke, number two was never to introduce the subject of oral sex to a strange woman at the airport. I had violated both rules at once and was now wondering—and deservedly so—if it was possible to literally die of shame.

April 26, 2012
Saint Louis

It's a four-hour drive from Indianapolis to Saint Louis and we got a late start. By the time we hit the interstate, it was almost ten thirty. I'd sneezed eight times before leaving my room, so Tim offered to stop at a drugstore and get me some Claritin-D.

"I think I'll be okay," I told him.

"Well, you sound terrible," Adam said. He was in the front seat scrolling through messages on his iPhone and eliminating the ones that didn't interest him. It was a bright, warm day. Tim's SUV was the size of a Conestoga wagon, an association that made the land seem even flatter than it was.

"So how's your mother?" I asked Tim.

"Dead," he said. "She passed away, oh, about three weeks ago."

"That's a shame."

"She had emphysema pretty bad but died the morning after her colonoscopy. I'm wondering if they didn't fuck it up somehow, but what the hell, she didn't have much time left."

I leaned forward and stuck my head between the two front seats. "But to spend your last day having something shoved up your ass!"

"That feels like every day to me," Tim said, sighing.

Adam asked if there was an estate to settle and Tim said not much. "My sister's getting the house. My brother wants the car, so all that's left are the dolls. Did I tell you my mother had over three hundred Barbies? Not all of them are valuable but some of them should be."

"What kind of person owns three hundred Barbies?" Adam asked.

"A hoarder," Tim said. "You should have seen the way this woman lived. It was just like on the TV show."

I asked if she had always been that way and Tim said it started in the eighties with QVC. "She'd have two TVs going at the same time and would just sit there buying shit. Lawn sprinklers, curling irons, frying pans—didn't matter what it was. She just had to have it."

"Where'd she get the money?" I asked.

"Had three husbands and bled them all dry."

Tim's mother hadn't wanted a funeral, so they cremated

her and held a Mass in Kansas City. "Anyone hungry?" he asked as we neared Terre Haute. Adam wanted to stop at McDonald's, but I had never been to a Cracker Barrel, so we went there instead.

April 30, 2012
Seattle

"Would you like a muffin or maybe a Danish to go with that?" asked the counterwoman in the Boise airport when I ordered a coffee yesterday morning.

"Why do you do that?" I asked.

"Do what?" She was in her early sixties, thin and worn-out-looking, with shoulder-length hair.

"Ask if I want a muffin?"

"It's called 'upselling,'" she explained. "It's a sales tactic."

"Does your boss make you do it?"

"Actually," she told me, "I've been in retail so long it's just second nature. Why?"

"Because I hate it," I said. "I buy a paper and they ask if I want a soda. Like the two go together somehow and you shouldn't have one without the other. And if you're in airports a lot—like I am—you hear it a dozen times a day."

"If you don't like it so much, maybe you could write a letter," the woman said. She handed me my coffee and I walked away thinking, *A letter to whom? What are you talking about?*

May 2, 2012
Santa Barbara, California

Steve and I drove over from Salem, Oregon, yesterday morning, and after returning the rental car, I realized I was running short on time. On Alaska Air you check in by kiosk, then stand in a general line in order to get your bags tagged. With other airlines it moves fairly quickly—everyone's doing exactly what you are—but with Alaska, the person ahead of you might be booking tickets to India and back for a troop of Girl Scouts who are all returning on different flights. In any city it can be frustrating, but Portland is the worst. Both agents were occupied when I got in line with my boarding pass. There was a fellow in front of me, and, in time, four people behind me, but neither the agents nor the people they were talking to seemed to notice. "That's *my* philosophy," I heard one of them say to a blond woman whose bag she was ticketing. "And if my husband doesn't like it, I told him he can go ahead and lump it!"

The agent's colleague was ticketing a party of three. I don't know what they were talking about, but it amused them all greatly.

"I'm glad *someone's* having a good time," spat the fellow ahead of me. He had his boarding pass and his ID in his hand and was glaring, as was I, at the chatty ticket agents.

"I've been standing here for, I swear, ten minutes," he said.

"What on earth are they carrying on about?" I asked.

"Life," he groaned. "And how funny it is." I looked to the woman behind me, hoping she might get in on it too, but she was engaged with her phone.

"I hear it's lovely," said the counter agent to the blond woman. "Of course, everything is, compared to here!"

"Oh, but Portland's beautiful," caroled the would-be passenger I hoped might die in an accident.

"It is, it is, but you have to deal with the rain, which, honestly, I'm fine with. It just took a few years to get used to."

"Where are *you* from?" asked the whore with the blond hair.

And the agent, who was formed wholly of dried semen and human shit, said, "Originally Florida. But we left when I was young."

When it was eventually my turn I was greeted with a smile. Then a frown. "I don't know if your bag's going to meet the forty-minute cutoff time," the agent who was born of Satan and spent the whole of her life sucking his cock and diddling her fingers inside of his asshole said.

I wasn't rude. In fact, I said nothing. Just looked at her. "But maybe we'll be okay," she told me. After handing me back my boarding pass and luggage tag she asked, "Do you know how to get to your gate?"

"I'm sure I'll figure it out," I said, and then I hurried to the security line, where the agent in charge was looking at people's IDs and saying things like, "California, the Sunshine State!" The TSA agents were equally chatty and then I went to Starbucks, which was completely out of control. There were two counters open and at each was a chatterbox, one a man in his late forties and the other a plump woman. The guy was buying several of those thermos-type mugs, and the woman was saying that her niece had one and seemed to like it pretty well. Of course, she liked just about anything. She was a very positive person. It turned out that the guy was too. Nothing seemed to bother him, so when his credit card was rejected, instead of getting huffy, he just called his wife and asked if she'd had *her* card rejected lately.

"Oh, for the love of God," I said.

The people around me seemed oblivious, so I looked at one of the employees behind the counter—a college kid, I'm guessing—and when I twisted my eyes up in the international symbol for "That person is crazy," he gave me a sympathetic nod.

"Well," said the man after hanging up with his wife, "I guess you've got to do what you've got to do, but I have to say, it doesn't speak very well for your leadership qualities."

"Somebody shoot him," I said, not yelling but not exactly whispering either. I didn't know then what was in store for me: a plane that would be delayed, then delayed again, and again. My hour at the airport would eventually be six and a half, and when, at four o'clock, my flight was finally canceled, I'd retrieve my bag and take a van to a satellite terminal. From there I'd board a private jet, just me and two pilots who looked like men who'd play doctors on TV. On a private jet, the snack basket is laid out on a bar and you're invited to take whatever you want. Free coffee. Free candy. Free peanuts. And you *feel* so free. No need to turn off your devices for takeoff and landing. No one crabbing at you to wear your seat belt. The plane leaves whenever you want it to and takes you wherever you like. I'd later learn that my freedom had cost me twelve thousand dollars. At the time, though, as I was sitting back with a bag of peanuts in one hand and a copy of *People* magazine in the other, the world felt finally, perfectly, right to me.

May 3, 2012
Los Angeles

After my breakfast in Santa Barbara yesterday I went for a bike ride into Montecito and bought Phyllis a nice bottle of vodka. A car collected me at noon, and an hour and a half later I was in Los Angeles, talking to Shelly. "Karla just put on Madame's makeup and will bring her in now. Would you like to sign the guest book?" she asked.

The Phyllis who tottered in a few minutes later was markedly different from the one I saw last November. She's had a stroke since then and can no longer look down. Disorientation was a problem as well, and for most of our visit, I doubt she knew who I was. "I'm drinking beer," she announced after Karla and Shelly had settled her onto the sofa. "It's my new thing and it's delicious." When the glass was in her hand she was fine, but after setting it down she had a hard time relocating it. "Your drink is right in front of you, Madame," her helpers would say.

It's a good thing we had company. "My beau will be joining

us any minute now," Phyllis whispered, and a short while later, Bernie appeared. He might have been in his mid-seventies, a former trial lawyer who now collects Disney memorabilia and has a store. He was great with her, especially when she'd do something weird like put a potato chip in her mouth, crunch down on it, and let the shattered pieces fall into her lap. A couple of times she admitted to being confused. "I have no idea what's going on," she'd say, and then she'd give her trademark laugh and everything would be fine.

At two we went into the small dining room for a Mexican lunch: tacos and enchiladas ordered from a nearby restaurant. "Where are my Kleenex?" Phyllis asked after taking her place at the table.

"Right where they always are," Bernie said.

After locating them, Phyllis would touch a tissue to her watering eyes and then toss it on the floor. Whenever she seemed lost or crabby ("Stop whispering around me, I hate that," she said at one point to her helpers), Bernie would pull her out of it.

"Phyllis, tell David how your mother used to answer the phone."

She put her fist to her mouth. " 'State your business.' How's that for warmth. Ha!"

"Someone once said that the key to success is sincerity," Bernie said. "Once you can fake that, you've got it made."

"Ha...ha!" Phyllis brayed. "Ha-ha-ha."

She was lucid as well when the subject turned to prayer. "Isn't that the worst," she said. "I hate it even more when they want you to hold their fucking hand. Blech!"

When the ice cream was brought out, I had a bowlful and then another. Phyllis, meanwhile, became very concerned about her pickled eggs. She had Karla bring them in, and then, after using a special slicer, she decided that, on second thought, eggs didn't really go with ice cream. "Later," she said. "I'll have them later."

After a round of pictures, we said our goodbyes. Then Bernie brought me to my hotel. "She has her good days and her bad," he said, suggesting that this was one of the latter. "Just two months ago she did *The Bold and the Beautiful*. Then she called from the set. 'My makeup looks fabulous,' she said. 'Quick, take me out to dinner.'"

May 9, 2012
New York

At last night's signing I met a woman who took mushrooms and then went to the Anne Frank House. "And while you were there, did you have sex?" I asked, adding that it didn't really matter, as already she was doomed to spend an eternity in hell. "Mushrooms in the Anne Frank House," I kept repeating. "That is *so* bad."

May 13, 2012
Raleigh, North Carolina

"Do you have any idea what you look like?" Dad asked yesterday afternoon as we left Paul's and headed to Madelyn's dance recital. "The sneakers, the striped shirt, and that jacket—my God! Who's your haberdasher, Bozo the clown?"

"You don't like the jacket?"

"And those little glasses," he added. "God, you look awful."

"My glasses aren't little."

"Yes, they are."

It was the last comment that really bothered me, the little-glasses bit. When I think *little glasses* I think of, I don't know...of Santa's, of frames no larger than bottle caps.

"Do you think my glasses are little?" I later asked the check-in clerk at the Marriott.

"If you mean small for your face, no," she said. "Why do you ask?"

"My father says they're little," I told her. The woman continued with her paperwork. "He's old and mean," I added.

"I love your jacket," a young woman said on the elevator a few hours later, after Lisa and I had returned from dinner.

"Well, thank you," I said. "My father hates it."

"Really? It goes so good with your glasses."

I turned to Lisa, glad to have a witness. "You made my night," I said to the young woman.

Dad criticizing the way that I look is nothing new. The day he says that he likes what I'm wearing is the day I'll quit buying my own clothes and turn myself over to Paul. What really bugged me was his vote on Amendment 1. North Carolina already had a ban on gay marriage, so this was just a little something extra, the Republican state house and senate's way of saying, *We really, really mean it.* Amendment 1 bans not just gay marriage but gay civil unions, and my father voted in favor of it.

This I'd learned as we got into Dad's car. Paul insisted on driving and when he turned the key, Rush Limbaugh came on. It was like connecting a hose to the tailpipe and filling the interior with carbon monoxide. Dad spends his afternoons listening to this poison. Then he heads inside to watch Fox News. Then he goes to the polls. "Yes, I voted for that," he said after I'd asked Paul to cut off the radio.

"You *what*?" I said.

Dad crossed his arms. "You heard me. I voted for it."

"How could you?"

"It sends the wrong message," he said.

"And that would be?"

"It sends a message to kids that any kind of sex is all right," he said. "Man on man, woman on woman—"

I should have waited to see what was next on his list but instead I interrupted him. "So that kind of sex is *not* all right? So…what? Gay people should abstain? Or live in shame? I don't get it. Madelyn has a gay aunt who wants to marry her girlfriend. How would their wedding send the wrong message?"

"I don't have to explain myself to you," Dad said.

"Actually, I think you do," I told him.

"It sends the wrong damn message, and there's nothing else to say about it."

That was pretty much it for Dad and me talking. He took another swipe at my jacket once we reached the restaurant last night, but he and I were on different sides of the table. He was between Kathy and Marshall, separated from his children, none of whom wanted anything to do with him. Dad looks a lot older than he did the last time I saw him. He seems to have shrunk, and his jacket was too big on him.

May 14, 2012
Winston-Salem
There was a Starbucks across the road from our Raleigh hotel, so yesterday morning, after checking out, we went. "I love your earrings," Lisa said to the woman behind the counter. She was young and had a lot going on from the neck up.

"Which ones?" she answered. Her fingers moved from the studs gathered like ladybugs on her lobes to the two-inch silver bar that cut across the top of each helix like the international symbol for "no." "You mean these, the industrials?"

"Yes," Lisa said. "I love them. Not for me, of course, but they're really cute on you." She put her purse up on the counter. "What I don't like are those grommets you see on people nowadays."

As the two of them got into quarter-size holes I realized we were in the spot where Piccadilly Cafeteria used to be. The door to the rest of the mall was open, so I walked down the wide corridor, passing nothing I recognized. When I returned to Starbucks, the young woman behind the counter was telling Lisa about all the extra shifts she'd picked up. "Which of course I'm able to do now that school is over."

"Well, I just think that's great," Lisa said.

"So what was that about?" I asked when we got back into the car.

"Oh," Lisa said. "I asked her if Starbucks gave her health insurance and she told me they did, but you have to work a certain number of hours per quarter. She had to cut back a little on account of school, so now she's making up for lost time."

We were supposed to meet Dad at Paul's place but I wanted to see the house, so after getting coffees, we swung by. Since I last dropped in—ten years ago? more?—he's had the area in front of the trash cans laid with paving stones. "I think he's suing the person who did it," Lisa whispered as we got out of the car. "The guy did it wrong or not fast enough or something."

Another change was the Porsche in the carport. For thirty-five years it was covered with a tarp, and when you lifted it up you saw that it was coated in layers of pollen. Now it's shiny and new-looking, totally revamped.

I thought the inside of the house would resemble an episode of *Hoarders* but what I saw of it was no more cluttered than it had been when Mom was alive. Surprising too was the silence. I expected Fox News on at least two TVs, but everything was off. Dad was still dressed in his church clothes and he gave me a brittle hug. "Hey there!" It's like his mind is a slate and he wipes it clean before going to bed each night. He's not direct, just oddly forgiving, or at least elastic.

"I want you to take a look around and see if there's any artwork you'd like," he said. "After, you know, I'm deceased."

I walked into the living room and was reminded of something Gretchen had told me earlier that morning. Paul Dean is having an art exhibit somewhere and had written in his statement that his biggest influence was coming to our house as a teenager. It was the first time, apparently, that he'd seen paintings that weren't pretty. "How about this Broderson," Dad said.

"It's fine and everything," I told him. "But it's not for me."

He pointed out the painting Betty had given us in the seventies, of a man who'd been shot and was now lying on the ground, bleeding to death. When, again, I said it wasn't quite my taste, he started to lose patience. "Then what the hell *is* your taste?"

I admired the pastel portraits done of Lisa and Gretchen in New Orleans in the early 1970s, though in my opinion neither one looked like its subject.

"It's the artist's job to dig deep and get to their inner selves, and that's what this guy did," Dad said. I liked seeing the various paintings again and wondered what it might be like in the future when they weren't corralled into the same room. The artwork reminded me of my youth, of *our* youth as a family, but that wasn't reason enough to take anything.

"I can't figure out your taste," Dad said. "You liked that painting of the dog in England but for the life of me I don't know why. God, that thing was terrible."

He wasn't being critical, exactly, not like he'd been the previous evening. This was gentler, perhaps because he was in his own environment and was more relaxed. "Well, what *do* you want?" he asked. "Some furniture? The speakers?" It's rude to reject everything that's being offered, so I said I would like the Vip bar guide.

"The what?"

"A paperback book illustrated by a cartoonist," I said. "His

269

name was Virgil Partch, shortened to Vip, and you have it downstairs behind the bar. I'd like that."

Dad walked into the living room and returned with the battery-powered monkey I'd given him for his birthday once. Turn him on and after his eyes pop out, he clangs together the cymbals he's holding. "And I bet you'd like this."

"Okay."

"And how about *Cracked Man*?"

"That's something Tiffany wants."

"*Tiffany?* Where the hell is she going to put it? She hasn't got any space!"

He talked to Lisa about something or other and I went to the bathroom off the upstairs hallway. Since I last visited, it's been taken over by his shirts, which now hang off the curtain rod. There was a stuffed pelican in the sink, and as I peed, I examined the Klimt print that's hung on the wall since Mom had the room repapered in the early '80s. The doors to two of the three bedrooms were closed so I didn't open them. I did stick my head into Dad's room, though, and looked at the framed photos taken at the beach. In them, Paul looks to be around twelve years old, which would put me at twenty-three.

"Hey," Dad said when I returned to the kitchen. "I want to talk to you about something." He turned to Lisa. "Would you mind giving us a little time?"

She went somewhere in the car and the two of us took seats at the kitchen table, upon which were heaped many forms and scraps of paper. "I've redone my will," Dad said, rooting through a stack. "You're going to get a little cash now, but first I have some questions."

He asked what I planned to leave everyone in my will and then talked about a scholarship fund he wanted to start at the Greek church. "When I die, the Sedaris name dies with me," he said.

"Speak for yourself," I told him. "Mine is on, like, nine million books."

"You know what I mean," he said. "Unless Paul has a son, this is the end of the line, and I want to leave something, a legacy, I guess you could call it."

The scholarship fund he talked about sounds pretty paltry. "I want you to contribute twenty-five thousand," he said. "Will you do that for me?"

I said probably not, but if it meant that much to him, he could take it out of my inheritance. The fund he's hoping to establish will award grants of between one and two thousand dollars—chicken feed, really. "If you're going to do this, why not *really* do it," I said. "Why not actually send people to college?"

It was such a strange conversation, "the Big Talk," as it were. I wondered when I would be in the house again and under what circumstances.

When Lisa returned and led me to the car, I wondered if I might start crying. I'd told myself that when Dad eventually dies, I'd feel nothing. And that might have been the case if I left him on Saturday night and we never saw each other again. On Sunday, though, it was a whole different story, not because of the money, which I know I'll never get, but because he seemed so old and vulnerable. "What about my cassette tapes?" he said. "Can I leave you my tapes? I've collected some jazz off the radio that is just…man, oh, man!"

I told him I don't listen to tapes anymore and he brought out a handwritten list of songs and artists he's been keeping over the years. "Or I could give you this, and you could buy the CDs yourself!"

In the end, I said I would take both the cassettes and the list. "Well, good," he said. "At least I can leave you something."

On the way out he showed me a cardboard box. It was stacked

on two workbenches outside his door, and a bird had built a nest in it. "I have three babies in there," he said. "Isn't that the craziest thing. I just noticed it the other day. Baby birds!"

We saw Dad again a half an hour later, at Paul's place. He arrived there a few minutes after Lisa and I did, and we all stood around the backyard and looked at the galvanized tub half submerged in the backyard. At three o'clock Lisa and I said our goodbyes again and drove back to Winston, passing, along the way, a young black woman in a late-model car. She wore a do-rag on her head and painted on her door were the words *Luv Tay Tay*.

"Do you think she's Tay Tay?" I asked.

Lisa turned to look. "Oh, definitely."

After returning home I went for a walk in the rain. Now, fifteen hours later, it's still coming down.

May 29, 2012
Rackham

Gretchen Anderson is recovering from a hip replacement, so I took her some flowers yesterday morning. She was on her way down the stairs when I arrived, moving very slowly on two canes. Her London house is the size of ours, beautiful, and filled with great furniture. Even on two canes and with no stomach, she was cheerful and positive. "Why don't I see you in *The New Yorker* anymore?" she asked.

I told her I'd just submitted a story about a taxidermist in North London. I said I'd seen a Pygmy skeleton there, and Gretchen told me about the live ones she'd seen years ago at a fair. "They were tiny," she said. "Little people with great big buttocks, which everyone seemed to like."

She has a way of phrasing things that always makes me laugh. After sitting in her kitchen for a while, she picked up her crutches and together we went to the corner and back.

Then we sat in the front garden and talked for two hours until someone came to deliver lunch.

One day I'll wish I had a recording of Gretchen that I could play when I start feeling sorry for myself. I don't know that I've ever met a more enthusiastic person. Her key, I think, is that she's never stopped being interested in things. She's never decided that everything reminds her of something else, that everything worthwhile has been crossed off her list.

June 12, 2012
Rackham

On Sunday morning, while walking from the church to his car, Dad felt something crawl up his leg. "So what I did," he told me on the phone last night, "was undo my belt and take my pants down."

"With everyone watching?"

"What choice did I have?" he asked. "It was a bumblebee, I'm telling you. There I was, my trousers around my ankles, both hands inside my underwear, and I thought of you."

"But I've never had a bee in my pants," I said. "I've never had my pants down in church either."

"Well, anyway, you were on my mind," he said.

On Sunday afternoon, riding my bike back from Amberley in the driving rain, I fell behind two women on horseback. They were riding side by side, taking up the entire road, and as I got closer, one of the women shouted to a pedestrian who had left the pub and was rushing toward her parked car: "Excuse me, but would you put your umbrella down?"

The pedestrian said, "What?"

"My horse is afraid of umbrellas, so you'll have to fold yours up until we pass."

Who are you, the queen? I thought.

David Sedaris

July 1, 2012
Rackham

We went to Sutton for dinner last night. The last time I saw Gretchen Anderson, she was hobbling on two crutch-like canes. Now, miraculously, she is walking on her own and at her normal pace. Ewan made pork cutlets for dinner, and while serving them he mentioned an article he'd read about a guy who's surviving on roadkill. "The bloke ate a fox not long ago and claims that it tasted like petrol." Ewan put down the dish of carrots. "I'm just wondering, how does he know what *petrol* tastes like?" He later mentioned someone named Dominic Smithers.

"Oh, yes, Dominic!" Gretchen said. "How is he?" This got us onto the topic of names, and she mentioned a friend with a child called Parsley. "Only I can't remember now if it's a boy or a girl. That's the thing with names like Parsley, isn't it?"

I asked how things were going in the shop, and Ewan told me about a dealer down the street. "He wants to hang a sign in his window saying 'No Chinese Allowed,' but I don't think he *can,* can he?"

The Chinese, apparently, are pains in the ass. "At that cane shop across the road a group of them came in saying, 'I'll have that, that, that, and that.' The owner gave them a price and after he'd wrapped it all up, they wanted to pay half the amount they'd agreed to twenty minutes earlier. Can you beat that!"

After dinner we joined Gretchen in the living room, me thinking as I enjoyed myself how very much I'd miss these evenings in Sutton. No one beats Gretchen Anderson.

"Am I bourgeois?" I asked Hugh on the way home. Gretchen had said in the living room that an old acquaintance of hers was, and that had made me paranoid.

Hugh said that I was not bourgeois. "How can you be when you spend hours every day picking up trash?"

That, to me, is the essence of bourgeois, but it was a beautiful night and rather than beating myself up, I chose to look at the road ahead of me and take pride in how clean it was.

August 11, 2012
Rackham

David Rakoff died late Thursday night. He was in his apartment with his family, and, according to Ira, who heard it from his mom, his last words were "Thank you."

I got the news in the form of an email. First I heard from Marlena, then from David's sister, Ruth, then Steven, then Ted, then Ira and Adam.

The *Times* ran a nice long obituary, as did the *Paris Review,* and, as of now, some 350 other blogs and newspapers. People are writing comments in response. In one I read yesterday, a guy whom Rakoff barely knew fell into debt, and David wrote him a check for $2,500. There were quite a few stories about his generosity. One asshole wrote to the *New York Times,* saying that if this David Rakoff person had been conservative and not gay, he doubts his death would have made the papers, but everything else I've seen is thoughtful and heartfelt.

Amy called just before dinner and I think it was only the third time in my life that I heard her cry: once when Mom died, once when her rabbit Tattle Tail died, and yesterday.

Before getting the news I was at the castle in Arundel. I'd thought that Tyler would love it, but after the first stairway he seemed to lose interest. The dungeon perked him up a bit, but he didn't fully return to life until we hit the gift shop. He wanted a sword and shield and I told him that if he begged his mom, formally, on his knees, and if she agreed to it, I'd buy him one.

"On my *knees*?"

The sword I bought Tyler was hollow, and made of plastic,

but the one I got for myself is more substantial. The blade is beechwood and the hilt is pine. I had it tucked into my belt loop and was marching through the formal garden when I somehow missed a step and fell on the ground. A number of people were watching, including Pam, who ran to my side crying, "Oh my God, are you all right," and Hugh, who laughed and told me I got exactly what I deserved.

I can't remember ever being so embarrassed. After I picked myself up, we continued through the gardens, my face burning. There was a petting zoo near the greenhouses, so Tyler and I ducked inside and saw the baby meerkats. There were ferrets there as well, and guinea pigs with long hair. On seeing them, a pair of boys said, "Jesus, look at those. Jesus!"

"Don't say that," their mother scolded, and she looked my way. "Some people get offended."

August 13, 2012
Rackham
Hugh was leaving the village shop yesterday when he ran into the owner of the pub. The man was walking his elderly Jack Russell, a dog that he insists is suffering from Alzheimer's. "He gets very confused and often doesn't know where he is."

"Not even at the pub?" Hugh asked.

"Oh," said the man, "I can't take him in there anymore because he's an alcoholic. If someone lowers a glass level with his head, he'll empty it and beg for more."

"So your dog has Alzheimer's..." Hugh began.

"And he's an alcoholic."

August 29, 2012
Rackham
On the train from Sussex I listened as two women in their seventies discussed their youthful love lives. Rather, one

woman did. The other, a foreigner, just listened. "Ah, the Spaniard," the chatterbox said. "It was he who painted me in the nude."

"From life?" the foreign woman asked.

"I never thought I was marvelous, but yes," the woman said. "He wanted to marry me but his family wouldn't allow it. This was probably for the best because if we had married, you see, I'd never have met the Jew, who was the love of my life." The woman wore a necklace made of chunky beads. The one in the center was the size of a child's block, and she rubbed it as she spoke. "A lovely man, carried away by cancer."

September 12, 2012
Rackham

Last month Thelma's lawn had a half dozen mounds of dirt on it. Disheartened, she called the exterminator. Now her yard is back to normal, and when Hugh asked about it yesterday afternoon, she told him that she'd killed the moles herself. "With a fork," she said.

I was told this over dinner, and before Hugh ruined everything by explaining that by *fork* she meant "pitchfork," I pictured our eighty-year-old neighbor on her hands and knees randomly stabbing the earth with the silver she'd just eaten lunch with.

November 7, 2012
Chicago

I saw both sides of it yesterday. At a Coffee Beanery in the Detroit airport, the counter people, both of them young and black, were shouting, "Go, Team Obama!" I smiled but the fellow in front of me didn't. "What's *your* problem?" the girl who had waited on him asked.

The man began to give his Romney speech—Obama had had four years to fix the economy and now it was time to give someone else a chance—but the young woman cut him off. "Well, you is just going to *lose* today. That's all I can say."

The guy stormed off and I thought of how much trouble the counter girl would get into if someone were to tell on her. Hers was not a very good business move but she was young and impassioned, and besides, it's Election Day.

Hours later I was at the Ritz-Carlton in Chicago, where I'm willing to bet that, aside from the busboys and a woman at the table behind me reading a Junot Díaz book, I was the only Democrat in the lobby-level restaurant. Beside me was a table of twelve loud men. They looked like they were made out of steak, and when they got up to leave I saw that one of them was Dennis Miller, the former *Saturday Night Live* cast member who went on to host his own conservative talk show. He was shorter than I'd imagined, and unlike his tablemates, he was not wearing a suit. "Great meeting you," the others called out. "Here's hoping we pop some corks tonight."

One of the men said, "Get her done!" and again they all laughed.

They can't honestly believe that Romney will win, can they? I wondered. I guessed it was like me holding out hope for Kerry in 2004.

It pleases me that they did *not* pop any corks. I'd worried that, like in 2000, we'd have to wait before getting the final election results, but by eleven o'clock it was pretty much over. I watched the coverage on PBS and stayed tuned until shortly before midnight, when Romney delivered his gracious concession speech. In 2008 Obama supporters rallied in Bryant Park but this year it was at McCormick Place, which was two miles south of my hotel and was already so packed I probably wouldn't have gotten any closer than I already was. I did see Air Force One, though. It was parked at O'Hare and while our plane was taxiing to the gate, the man behind me, a pilot, pointed it out. During the flight he'd talked to the teacher across the aisle from him and I'd learned he was married to a Chinese woman and had an eight-year-old daughter.

It was a good day to travel. I don't know that I'd ever seen the Detroit airport so empty, and Chicago was slow as well.

My driver from O'Hare, a white guy in his early thirties, was of the opinion that voting did no good. "With me or without me, it's the corporations who are going to win," he said. I supposed this was true enough, but who wants to be the guy on Election Day who doesn't vote?

Walking to get my coffee this morning, I kept thinking, *We won!* All I did was vote and give money. Lisa and Dawn worked at the polls and gave rides to shut-ins. They're the ones who should really feel a sense of accomplishment.

November 11, 2012
Red Wing, Minnesota

It was a beautiful drive from Duluth to Minneapolis, especially the start of it, when we were farther north. The weather was perfect, misty with temperatures in the low thirties and a flat, steel-gray sky. The trees were silver birches mixed with pine and something else that was low and leafless. Disrupting the peaceful landscape were a great number of billboards, many of which had babies on them. I COULD SMILE BEFORE I WAS BORN read the first we came across. The print beneath the headline was harder to make out but I assumed it had something to do with abortion—specifically, not having one. BABIES: OUR HEARTS ARE BEATING EIGHTEEN DAYS AFTER CONCEPTION read another.

Next came an anti-Obama message: FED UP WITH SOCIAL- ISM? VOTE IT OUT IN NOVEMBER. After that we were back to abortion. LOOK, I'M THE FUTURE: BABY'S EYES ARE OPEN IN THE WOMB; GOD KNEW MY SOUL BEFORE I WAS BORN; GOD'S FINEST CREATION: A BABY.

Then we hit Minneapolis, where I saw, standing by the side of the road, a committee of twelve turkey vultures. It was the billboards, though, that really haunted me. "Did you know that fourteen days after conception, a fetus can hold a miniature tennis racket?" I said to someone in last night's signing line. "It can't return a serve—that comes later—but still, it's a remarkable achievement."

Next I told someone that at the gestational age of two months, an unborn baby can tune a guitar and braid a lanyard. "Did you know," I said to a woman named Barbara, "that three weeks after conception, an unborn baby can write a check?"

She looked startled. "No one uses checks anymore!"

And I said, as if that were the miracle, "I know!"

November 29, 2012
Santa Fe

It was chilly and bright yesterday, with temperatures in the low fifties. I took a walk in the late afternoon and passed a men's clothing store that seemed promising. After entering and realizing I was wrong about it, I agreed to try on a pair of trousers. They weren't really my thing but the salesman was insistent, and I felt bad that there weren't any other customers.

"How are they?" he called from the other side of the curtain as I stepped into them. I'd gotten a size 31, and rather than requesting something larger, for they were way too small—clearly a 29 *mistakenly labeled* a 31—I stepped back into my original trousers, which now felt tight as well. It was, I figured, the result of my lunch.

"Can I interest you in something else?" the salesman asked.

I said no, thank you, and walked out into the sunshine, buttoning my sports coat against the chill. The part of town I was in, the tourist area, seemed fairly empty. I passed one jewelry store after another, all of them selling Navajo squash blossoms and kachina dolls. At a shop called Native Jackets Etc. I bought a red and black Pendleton blanket woven in an old Navajo pattern. After arranging to have it shipped, I walked down to Water Street and found a few things for Maddy, which I also had shipped. Then I stopped by Starbucks, got a coffee to go, and returned to my hotel.

"Welcome back," said the doorman.

"Welcome back," called the woman at the check-in desk. I smiled and nodded, enjoying the role I've been playing these past few months: the distinguished gentleman in the fine hotel, the one whose robe and slippers are laid out every night and for whom no request is too outlandish, especially one pertaining to his comfort, for isn't that the world's goal, to attend to his every whim?

Back in the room I removed my jacket and discovered that all afternoon, or at least since leaving the clothing store, it had been crammed into my trousers. Not the entire thing, of course, just the back panel. It's the equivalent of a woman tucking her dress into her pantyhose, and no one had said a word about it, thinking, perhaps, that it might visit upon the distinguished gentleman some unwelcome embarrassment.

December 15, 2012
Paris

A young man in Newtown, Connecticut, opened fire on an elementary school yesterday morning, killing twenty six- and seven-year-olds and half a dozen adults. Not long afterward Larry Pratt, executive director of Gun Owners of America, said that gun-control supporters have the blood of innocent children on their hands. If it weren't for them, the teachers could have been armed and might have picked off the shooter after his first or second student.

By that argument, why not arm the kids? Who says a first-grader is too young to carry a loaded pistol?

Others blame what happened on the lack of prayer in school. On his radio show, Bryan Fischer said, "Here's the bottom line—God is not going to go where He is not wanted. We kicked God out of the public-school system. I think God would say to us, 'I would be glad to protect your children, but you've got to invite Me back into your world first. I'm not going to go where I'm not wanted. I am a gentleman.'"

So God, like a vampire, has to be invited in?

December 18, 2012
London

According to James Dobson, founder of Focus on the Family, the cause of last week's school shooting was not guns or mental illness but "Americans who have turned their back on God and embraced abortion and gay marriage." In short, it's all my fault.

They released pictures of the murdered children and I can't go an hour without thinking of their parents and how terrible their lives will be from now until they die. Six is such a lovely age, especially this time of year, when kids are so looking forward to Christmas. Obama spoke at a memorial over the weekend, and I listened to sections of his speech last night as I wrapped gifts in my office. Then I went online and looked at pictures I knew would upset me: mounds of teddy bears and, worse still, angels, lying in heaps beside plastic-wrapped flowers and handwritten notes. Since when did grief translate to a trash pile? And the angel business, please, don't get me started.

December 19, 2012
Rackham

My sister Gretchen arrived by cab early yesterday morning. She'd come from Paddington and when the driver told her that it would be eleven pounds, she asked how many euros it would cost.

"How many what, dear?"

I ran up to get my wallet, and after I paid the guy, Gretchen told us that upon landing at Heathrow, she'd gone to the currency exchange and asked for $500 worth of euros. "The girl said, 'Are you sure?'

"And I said, '*Positive*.'"

She had a cigarette out in the garden and recalled a time this past summer when she was giving a lecture to a group of visitors. "I'd been using a water bottle as my ashtray and without thinking I raised it to my mouth and took a big swallow of butt juice. In front of everyone!"

At midmorning, after stopping by Valerie's and the Lacquer Chest, we headed out to Kew Gardens. It was a cold, gray day but not at all unpleasant. Gretchen wanted to see the fungi exhibit at the Shirley Sherwood Gallery, and afterward we wandered through one of the greenhouses, noticing, among other things, the world's tallest indoor palm. Then it was lunch in the café, after which we headed back to the tube station. It was surrounded by nice-looking shops and I stopped at one and got my hair cut by a young Algerian man. "So what's with this madness in the United States?" he asked, referring to last week's shooting. It's so hard explaining American gun rights to foreigners. "But why does anyone need an assault rifle?" they ask.

Yesterday morning before leaving the house I saw an ad for the Bushmaster—the weapon used by the shooter in Connecticut a few days ago. It was a picture of the rifle and beneath it the words *Consider Your Man Card Re-Issued*. It's such a stunted, embarrassing notion of masculinity.

2013

January 4, 2013
Paris

Asya and I went over the second batch of copyedits for the new book. "On page twenty-six, I'd like to change *asshole* to *arsehole,* if that's okay," I said at one point. A while later I heard myself say, "That should be a comma after *cunt,* not a period."

Jesus, I thought. *What kind of a writer am I?*

January 16, 2013
Boston

At last night's book signing I met a Harvard professor. We got to talking and when I referred to someone or other as a barbarian, he asked if I knew what the word originally meant. "It's someone who can't speak Greek," he said. "Someone who makes a sound like *bar-bar-bar.* Funny, huh?"

Later in the evening I met a woman from Bucharest. "My publicist is Romanian," I told her. "Not full-blooded like you, but still, she can curse a little. Her favorite saying taught to her by her grandparents is 'I shit in . . .' God, what is that? 'Shit in . . .'"

"'I shit in your mother's mouth'?" the Romanian woman asked. "That's probably what it was. It's a very popular curse."

She walked away and I thought, *Well, I can see why.* I shit in your mother's mouth. Does it get any nastier than that?

284

February 6, 2013
Rackham

The following is a list of genuine guest complaints filed with Thomas Cook Holidays, a company that arranges vacations for British people.

— "On my holiday to Goa in India, I was disgusted to find that almost every restaurant served curry. I don't like spicy food at all."

— "The beach was too sandy."

— "No one told us there would be fish in the sea. The children were startled."

— "There are too many Spanish people. The receptionist speaks Spanish. The food is Spanish. Too many foreigners now live abroad."

— "We found the sand was not like the sand in the brochure. Your brochure shows the sand as yellow, but it was white."

— "I compared the size of our one-bedroom apartment to our friends' three-bedroom apartment and ours was significantly smaller."

And my favorite:

— "It took us nine hours to fly home from Jamaica to England. It only took the Americans three hours to get home."

March 1, 2013
Warsaw, Poland

Diet-wise, Poland is a real throwback. Last night's dinner, for example, started with bread and lard. We ate at a stuffy, oppressively decorated place not far from the hotel. In most restaurants nowadays your food is huddled in the center of the plate, but here it covered every centimeter of it. There was nowhere for your eye to rest, either on the table or on the walls, upon which hung dreary paintings and photos of men in uniform. Lace doilies sagged from the mantel, and the woodwork was the color of root beer. The music, too, was old-fashioned, scratchy-sounding, as if it were coming from a Victrola.

After the bread and lard, we were given borscht, then half a duck stuffed with prunes and apricots. It tasted like the restaurant: heavy and out-of-date. Listen to me, complaining because they gave me too much rich food. It was the first time in recent memory that I pushed my plate away. Then I said no to dessert.

Our waiter, a stocky, balding fellow, was very helpful and seemed to get a kick out of my baby Polish. That said, my act goes over much better with women than it does with men. I started at Heathrow, on a person beside me in the waiting area. "Excuse me," I said in Polish. "Are you a Polish woman?"

She looked at me warily. *"Tak."*

"Great," I said, in English now. "Can you tell me how to pronounce this?" I showed her the address of our hotel.

"Kosh-chell-nah," she said. *"Ooh-leet-tza Kosh-chell-nah."*

I keep forgetting the word for "Thank you," so I think I told her, "Please."

March 2, 2013
Warsaw

Hugh and I crossed a street and were headed to a bus stop when two female cops called out to us. Both were young and pretty, carrying notebooks and wearing warm hats. One of them started saying something and after listening for a few seconds, I reached into my two weeks of language study and told her that I did not understand. "Are you a Polish woman?" I asked. *"Che pany yest Polcomb?"*

She looked at her friend. *"Tak."*

"Well," I said, continuing in her language, "you speak Polish beautifully. I am an American, but I speak a little Polish. I understand a little too. Hello!"

The two had warmed up now and were laughing.

"Today I would like to buy something," I said. "What, I do not know, but I have a lot of Polish money. What are you doing?"

The answer was giving tickets. The woman tried to explain something, and I understood the words for "here" and "there."

"She caught us jaywalking," Hugh said.

I feigned horror. "I am so sorry," I said.

I think the cops said, "Don't worry about it." Then I think they asked how I learned Polish. I reached into my bag and pulled out my index cards. One of the women took them and the other leaned over to see. "Would you like to drink something with me this evening?" I asked.

The Polish police officers howled.

"At the hotel on Piekna Street."

They roared and handed me back my cards. After telling them goodbye, Hugh and I proceeded to the bus stop. The 180 came, and as we rode away, I looked out the window and saw that they had stopped another jaywalker, a Polish one, apparently, who could not charm them with his Pimsleur.

March 3, 2013
Warsaw

Yesterday afternoon, shortly after passing a hair salon called the Atelier Stylissimo, we saw a man dragging a galvanized metal bucket full of something heavy up a slight hill. He'd tied a rope around it and would take five steps, pause, then take another five. It's how people lived before the invention of the wheel, and you couldn't help but wonder where he was coming from and how much farther he had to go. We saw a lot of rough-looking people yesterday, especially in the morning, when we visited the flea market.

Many of the vendors were missing teeth and more than one was drunk. Their wares were equally sad: a lamp with no cord, a coffee cup full of nails.

Hugh and I bought postcards from a nice pair of men in their fifties who spoke to us in rapid Polish. Thanks to my Pimsleur program, I was able to ask how much things cost and was able to understand the answers as well. There were a lot of very bad paintings for sale and every time we passed one, I'd give it a title: *Kitten in a Sunbeam. Girl Smiling on Horseback.* Then I came to what could only be called *Greedy Old Jew Clutching a Coin.* It was hard to tell, but I didn't get the feeling it was sentimental. Rather, it was like seeing a picture of a black man eating a watermelon. The woman selling it was also offering a hair dryer from 1985, a suitcase with a missing wheel, and a tulip-shaped lampshade.

March 13, 2013
Rackham

I started my morning by listening to the White Network, a radio station for white supremacists. I'd found the link on *Salon,* which had included it in a post about Charles Krafft, a Seattle-area ceramicist. He was celebrated for his Nazi imagery until it turned out that he kind of meant it. Totally meant it, actually. Several articles appeared condemning him, and then he went on the White Network and spoke to Carolyn Yeager, host of *Saturday with Carolyn Yeager.*

"Now, it says here on your Wikipedia page, Charles, that you began by painting pictures on plates. Can you tell us a little something about that?"

Eventually they got to the "Holocaust myth," and Carolyn started sticking her oar in. "One of the things that gets me is that the word *Jew* is always capitalized while the word *white* isn't," she said. "Have you noticed that?"

How fucked up are these people that that's what's ruining their day? I wondered. Poor white supremacists. Without the capital *J* that comes with *Jew-hating*, they wouldn't get any respect at all.

March 23, 2013
London

Frank and Scott went to an Indian restaurant the other night and took a picture of the menu, which offered what it called "a carnival of snackery."

April 7, 2013
Stockbridge, Massachusetts

I signed a book for a woman with two daughters. One of them, the twenty-five-year-old, started by saying, "Oh God, Mom, just shut up. He's going to think you're insane."

The mother was perfectly charming. "I've loved you since the first book," she said.

"Mom, he's heard that, like, a million times, so why don't you just shut up."

"That's okay," I said to the daughter. "I really like your mother."

"See?" the mother said.

"He's just saying that," the daughter told her.

Later, back at the hotel, I came upon the mother and her two daughters in the lobby. "Hello again," I said. They looked up, surprised, and I saw that the difficult daughter was reading a book called *Living Sober*. "I'm doing my ninety days," she said.

"Keep your voice down," her mother hissed.

April 11, 2013
Harrisburg, Pennsylvania
"I want you to inscribe something shocking and offensive to my mother," said a nineteen-year-old at last night's book signing. He passed me a copy of *When You Are Engulfed in Flames,* and after thinking it over for a moment, I picked up my pen. *Dear Mary Lou,* I wrote. *Your son Jesse left teeth marks on my dick.*

I handed it back and realized by the look on his face that by *shocking and offensive* he'd meant "lightly disturbing."

April 26, 2013
Phoenix
After checking into my hotel yesterday I met Ted for lunch. While eating I asked about his father and stepmother. Both are in bad shape, and he's having to get them settled into nursing homes. We'd been on the outdoor patio for maybe an hour when the waiter brought the dessert menu. "Want to share a piece of coconut cream pie?" I asked.

Ted said sure, and when it was placed before us, we each grabbed a fork. On my second or third bite, I looked to the other side of the patio and saw two other men doing the same thing. They were in their fifties as well, a couple, I assumed, and watching them, I realized how gay we were being. "Would you ever share a dessert with another man?" I asked Abe when he arrived to take me to the theater.

"With a woman I would, but another guy...I'd have to say no," he told me.

I brought it up later at the book-signing table and understood that I was onto something. "I'd share a plate of buffalo wings with another man, but pie...that's crossing the line," one man told me. Another said he recently shared a dessert with his brother but made it a point to say to the waitress, "In case you're wondering, we're straight."

"You felt that self-conscious about it?" I asked.

Even a guy who shaved his chest wouldn't eat off another man's plate.

An interesting exception were the five or so straight men more concerned with dessert than with their masculinity. These guys were bulky for the most part and would likely eat pudding off another fellow's dick if that's what it was being served on.

"I had these friends in college who'd share a soda at the movies," one guy said. "They'd even drink from the same straw! It's something I think about to this day—and they were straight!"

I had a good crowd, so I also tested my theory that guys with beards have fathers who own guns. Granted, I'm in Arizona, where just about everyone is armed, but I pretty much batted a thousand last night. Toward the end of the evening, I met an Asian guy with a sketchy goatee. His father does not own a gun but *does* have a box of bullets. This is the person who taught me the acronym ABC, which stands for "American-born Chinese."

May 4, 2013
San Francisco

A joke from last night's signing:

A plane develops engine trouble and when the pilot announces that soon they will drop into the ocean, a female passenger takes the floor. "If I'm going to die, I want to die happy," she shouts. "Is anyone here man enough to make me feel like a woman?"

A fellow stands up a few rows away and takes off his shirt. Then he tosses it to her, saying, "Here, iron this."

May 6, 2013
San Francisco

A joke from last night's book signing:

A woman goes to her gynecologist, who settles her in and begins his exam, saying, "You've got the biggest vagina I've ever seen in my life. You've got the biggest vagina I've ever seen in my life."

"You don't have to say it twice," the woman scolds.

And her doctor says, "I didn't."

May 11, 2013
New York

Last night's Radio 4 news quiz included the following newspaper quote:

"A woman in Herefordshire was found guilty and fined for not paying for her Botox injections. She remained expressionless in the dock when the verdict was read out."

And, from the *Guardian* TV listing: "Movie: *There Will Be Blood*. Period Drama."

May 30, 2013
Baton Rouge, Louisiana

For some reason or other, the phone Adam gave me wasn't picking up a signal. It might have been on the fritz for a while, but I didn't notice until I arrived in Dallas yesterday afternoon and received an email from Marlena. "Call me when you land," it said, and because there was no jokey sign-off, I figured it was serious.

I have a calling card in my wallet, so I found a pay phone, punched in the numbers, and got a long message informing me that I may have won a cruise. I tried a second time, and when that didn't work either, I approached a man who was texting and asked if he knew why I couldn't get a signal. He was a bit younger than me and had a suit on. I think he suspected that I was going to ask to use *his* phone, so he said, "No idea," and turned away.

What an asshole, I thought.

Marlena later told me she'd tried calling me on the last pay phone I'd used and when that didn't work, she had me paged under her name. The white courtesy phone was next to my departure gate, but when I picked up the receiver, nothing happened. So I stopped a security person, who pushed in a series of numbers. This got me through to a woman who thought she could help me. The message that played when she put me on hold was about how great the Dallas–Fort Worth airport is, and I listened not wanting it to end, knowing that when I finally reached Marlena, she would tell me something that would change my life forever.

I thought something had happened to Maja Thomas, that she'd been killed or hurt while hiking through France. If something had happened to Dad, I figured that Amy or Lisa would have contacted me. I didn't think of Tiffany until Marlena said it. "I'm so sorry. Your sister was found dead." She told me that a patrolman had contacted her earlier in the day, asking if Tiffany had a history of drug use.

My connection was boarding, so after twenty seconds or so, I said goodbye and got in line. It took an hour to reach Baton Rouge and on the way, I decided that this was some kind of a joke, that it wasn't a cop but Tiffany's friend who'd called Marlena. I saw it as a bridge that would bring us back together—a mean joke, but clearly forgivable.

It turned out that my phone only needed rebooting. On landing in Baton Rouge I pushed two buttons simultaneously and when I saw that I had a signal I called Lisa, who answered on the second ring and told me that no, it wasn't a joke. Tiffany was really dead. It's like the door to the rest of my family's life has been opened, and I can see that everything on the other side of it is horrible.

Amy put it well in an email she sent:

I can't wrap my head around Tiffany being dead. Dead. Tiffany is dead. Tiffany died. My sister Tiffany died. My younger sister Tiffany died. The last time I saw my sister Tiffany was at my brother Paul's wedding.

Lisa, when I talked to her, said that she had spoken with the police. They think Tiffany might have died on Friday, that she had been dead for five days by the time they battered down her door. They're going to perform an autopsy and find out what drugs were in her system. Lisa feels fairly certain that it was a suicide. "I got a message from her last Friday while I was out." She said that the message was incoherent and rambling and that she'd been trying ever since to get a hold of her.

I'm at a dismal Marriott on the highway with a minifridge and a window overlooking a Hooters billboard. After arriving in Baton Rouge, I went to the Barnes and Noble and signed books for six hours. While reading I thought of Tiffany, and all during the Q and A. I thought of her as well while signing, but I don't think that anyone suspected. "You look fantastic in that tunic," I said, and "What's your take on sausage?," remembering the time Tiffany joined me at the Brookline Booksmith and told everyone who came through the line that they had beautiful eyes or the world's most perfect hands. She was wild that night and had her friends distribute cards that read TIFFANY SEDARIS, DAVID'S LOSER SISTER. MOSAIC ARTIST. I saw her only once after that.

"How you doing!" Dad asked. I called him on the way from the airport to the hotel and he sounded like Tiffany had died years ago. "That's the way the world turns," he said. "She's in a better place."

June 7, 2013
Asheville, North Carolina

According to an email Amy sent yesterday, Tiffany defined herself, privately, as hypomanic. "Look it up," she said. "It's Tiffany to a T."

According to what I read during lunch, hypomania falls under the umbrella of bipolar disorders. Bipolar II, it's sometimes called. Symptoms include:

—Excessive happiness, hopefulness, and excitement
—Sudden changes from being joyful to being irritable, angry, and hostile
—Restlessness, increased energy, and less need for sleep
—Rapid talk, talkativeness
—Distractibility
—Racing thoughts
—High sex drive
—Tendency to make grand and unattainable plans
—Tendency to show poor judgment, such as impulsively deciding to quit a job
—Inflated self-esteem or grandiosity; unrealistic beliefs in one's own abilities, intelligence, and powers. May be delusional.
—Increased reckless behaviors (such as lavish spending sprees, impulsive sexual indiscretions,

      abusive alcohol or drug use, or ill-advised busi-
      ness decisions)
—Some people with bipolar disorder become
      psychotic, hearing things that aren't there. They
      may hold on to false beliefs and cannot be
      swayed from them. In some instances, they see
      themselves as having superhuman skills and
      powers—even consider themselves to be godlike.

Another website's symptom list included overgenerosity. This is something Tiffany definitely suffered from, though *suffer* is an odd word to apply to something as positive as giving things away. It explains why she kept her money in other people's hands, afraid she would spend it all or give it away if she held on to it herself. Yet another website states that, as with standard bipolar disorder, "the person may deny that anything is wrong. Without proper treatment, however, hypomania can become severe mania in some people or can switch into depression."

June 9, 2013
Emerald Isle, North Carolina
"Look," Amy said as we drove from Raleigh to Emerald Isle in a rental car late yesterday afternoon, "strawberries!" Hugh pulled over at a stand by the side of the road. MISS MADISON'S read the cardboard sign. The woman behind it was perhaps in her early eighties. Her arms were thick and the skin on them was leathery, almost alligatored. Flanking her and holding playing cards with oversize numbers on them were two teenage girls. Both were extraordinarily beautiful and much more sophisticated-looking than their grandmother. "So where y'all from?" she asked.

    "Raleigh," Amy said.

    "Well, you come to the right place," Miss Madison told her. "I got strawberries fresh picked this morning by Mexicans. They taste like *real* strawberries and this is the last day of the season."

Hugh bought a big box along with four tomatoes. "Are these from your garden?"

"No," she said. "They's from a friend's place but they's good too and you have my word."

The woman had a fantastic accent. "Are you from here?" I asked.

"No," she answered. "I'm from Calypso. You ever heard of that place?"

I said to Amy when we got back into the car, "I felt like I should have paid with Confederate money."

June 14, 2013
Emerald Isle

Yesterday morning Hugh, Kathy, and I met with a real estate agent named Phyllis. "Y'all will just have to tell me to hush and walk away," she said. "I mean, I'm a real talker!" She might have been in her mid-forties, pretty and blond, wearing a white skirt and a blue V-neck T-shirt. Phyllis was born on the other side of the bridge and has lived in the area all her life. The house she showed us is oceanfront, two stories, and split down the middle, each side with three bedrooms and two baths. "Get it," Hugh whispered. "Make an offer."

"You make an offer," I whispered back. "Are there snakes?" I asked Phyllis.

"There are," she said. "But that's just a fact of life. Why? You scared of them?"

"Terrified."

"Me too," she said. "But they're better than cats."

"Are you afraid of cats?" I asked.

She winced and nodded. "Horrible things. Sneaky. Can't hear them coming."

June 15, 2013
Emerald Isle
The offer Hugh made was accepted. "Yippee," everyone said. "A beach house!"

July 5, 2013
Alba, Italy
A month ago in Philadelphia I met a young woman who was studying German and had recently been forced to memorize the question "What are you doing with that rope?"

It's such a curious thing to learn, especially in your first year. Then again, all I remember of my freshman Italian course is *Come si chiama questo ventaccio gelido?*—"What is the name of this harsh north wind?" The question lay dormant in my brain until yesterday afternoon, when Hugh and I landed in Turin. A volunteer from the literary festival picked us up at the airport and discussed the weather as she drove us to our hotel. "You just missed the really bad heat," she said. "Last week this place was an oven, but on Tuesday a cool breeze moved in."

"Ah," I said, and, tailoring my one Italian phrase for the summer, I shortened it to "What is the name of this wind?"

Prospects for "What are you doing with that rope?" aren't quite as sunny. The best the student of German can hope for is that the person will be hanging himself rather than tying her to a radiator, but still, it may eventually come in handy and maybe even earn her a compliment.

July 29, 2013
Rackham
"Why are there no pictures of Jesus smiling?" Vanessa asked over dinner last night. "You have to think twice about a religion that has no fun in it, don't you?"

It's a good point, so over dessert, we googled *Smiling Jesus*. Quite a few images came up, but they were all fairly recent—illustrations you'd find in a Sunday-school book rather than an art museum. For the most part, they're pictures of Christ hanging out, sometimes with a lamb in His arms and sometimes on a boat. In all of them He's trim and good-looking, with clear skin and all His teeth. In this respect, much like casting directors, the artists strike me as lazy. They want you to fall for their leading man, and so they make him attractive and muscular.

Buddha, on the other hand—there's a challenge. Unlike Jesus, who's traditionally grim, this guy can't keep a straight face. His smile speaks louder than his weight, even when he has his shirt off, but still I get snagged on his really long earlobes. They practically touch his shoulders, and whenever I see them, I recoil, thinking, oddly, *Jesus!*

August 23, 2013
Edinburgh, Scotland

Two months ago, toward the end of my American tour, I signed a book for a Louisiana woman who approached my table saying, "You got me to put my bra back on."

I set down my pen. "I beg your pardon?"

"I take it off the second I get home from work, and that usually means it's off for the night," she said. "It means I'm not going anywhere for any reason, but then a friend called and told me you were here, so I put it back on and dashed over to see you."

"Well...thank you," I said.

I repeated our exchange the following evening in Atlanta, thinking it might get a nice response. It did, but the laughs were ones of recognition rather than surprise. "Do you take *your* bra off the moment you return from work?" I asked the first woman in line. She was perhaps in her mid- to late fifties, and she laid her book upon the table saying, "Baby, I take it off *before* I get home."

"At the office?" I asked.

"No," she said. "In the car."

"You take your blouse off?"

"Ain't no need to do that," she said. "What you do is unhook it in the back and then pull it out your sleeve."

"And after it's off, is it off for the night?"

"You know it is," she said. "A friend could call drunk and wanting a ride and I'd say, 'Honey, I got my bra off. Get yourself a cab.'"

Next in line was a male college student. "I can always tell when my mom borrows my car because she leaves her bra in the glove compartment," he told me.

Over the next few weeks, I met hundreds of women, and just about all of them had something interesting to tell me. "I once took a *sports bra* off while driving," Julie in Columbus, Ohio, confided. "You have any idea how hard that was?"

I thought it was just an American phenomenon, but when I returned to England I learned that I was wrong. "Once this thing comes off, I'm in for the rest of the evening," women told me in London and Manchester and Liverpool. I got similar responses last night in Edinburgh. "So you remove it on your way home from work?" I asked a young woman who works as a nurse.

She nodded.

"In your car?"

"Oh, no," she told me. "I do it on the bus."

August 26, 2013
London

My train left Edinburgh on time yesterday. Everything was great until we reached Newcastle. From there to York the lines were down, so after sitting in the station for close to an hour, passengers were told to disembark and board the earlier train to London that had left a half an hour before ours and was parked on track number 3. I made the change as quickly as possible and was able to find a seat in first class.

It was at a single table, as was my earlier, reserved one, but it was marked PRIORITY, meaning it would have to be surrendered should someone old or disabled or pregnant come along. Of course, a gentleman would do this anyway, special sticker or no special sticker, only here, with this seat, my chivalry would count for nothing.

I'd have moved if I could but between the passengers who were already seated and the ones fleeing the train I'd been on earlier, there were no other options. I was just settling in when I noticed the two women sitting across the aisle. One was perhaps in her late forties and had an arm that seemed pretty useless from the elbow down. Across from her was her mother, who was stout and gray-haired and carried a cane.

"Excuse me," I said. "But do you think I could borrow that for a few minutes?"

The older woman looked confused.

"The cane," I said. "I don't need it now, but later, if someone who's old or handicapped comes along, I could use it to defend my right to this seat."

The daughter seemed put out, but her mother was fine with the idea. "You can take it," she said. "I won't be going anywhere until York." I later learned that she and her daughter had spent the weekend in Edinburgh, where they'd seen a few shows at the festival. "We don't usually go first class but thought we'd treat ourselves just this once," she explained. "You sure you don't want the cane now?"

I reached across the aisle and said, weakly, "Thank you."

September 20, 2013
Berlin, Germany
A few months back in the United States I asked the audience to give me T-shirt slogans. I was looking for the kind that really test the First Amendment, the kind you see and can't believe are legal — 50,000 BATTERED WOMEN A YEAR AND I'VE GOT TO EAT MINE PLAIN, for instance.

I thought it was a strictly American phenomenon until last night, when I mentioned it onstage.

"It's just as bad here as it is in the U.S.," a young woman told me when she came to get her book signed. She held up her phone and showed me a photo of a group of young men. They were drinking at a table and on the back of one guy's T-shirt was written, in German, BEER WITHOUT ALCOHOL IS LIKE EATING OUT YOUR SISTER. IT FEELS RIGHT, BUT IT'S WRONG.

In a slightly different vein, a woman named Francesca told me that her brother lives in Ghana. A lot of the clothing there is donated by American relief organizations, and he recently saw a man on the street wearing a T-shirt that said in big bold letters THIS IS WHAT A DYKE LOOKS LIKE.

October 6, 2013
Rackham
Hugh made a côte de boeuf for dinner and followed it with a pie made from apples off our trees. "I'm going to cry," Rebecca said, adding that she'd been doing that a lot lately. "We're having the perfect vacation," she told us. "The other day Jeff and I were buying bread in Paris, and when he turned around for the money, I had tears streaming down my face."

While we were eating Jeff recalled my family and what it was like to hang out at our house in the '70s. "You had jazz playing from those huge speakers," he said, "and all these people coming and going." He recalled Dad saying of his daughters, "These are the prettiest girls on this block." And they were. We seemed so golden then—not me so much, but at least by high school I was relatively happy. I had the drama club, and friends.

"I don't remember any good times with my father," I said.

Jeff seemed sad. "Really?"

"You will later, after he's dead," Rebecca promised. Her father, an alcoholic, died in a fire four years ago. She has two siblings she's close to and another, crazy one who is sixty and is just entering dementia.

"When crazy people get that or Alzheimer's, don't they just become like everyone else with dementia or Alzheimer's?" I asked. "Doesn't it just...even them out?"

"But wait," Jeff said. "You really can't remember anything good about your father?"

"With my mother I can't recall anything bad," I said. "But with him it's the other way round." I try to see Dad the way Jeff does, this jazz enthusiast in golf pants snapping his fingers to Hank Mobley, but in my memory, he's always yelling at me to shut the door or get off the phone. All I ever see when he looks at me is disappointment.

October 8, 2013
Rackham

The train we took to London yesterday was fuller than I'd expected, and I thought that perhaps a football match was taking place, or maybe a tattoo convention. The men in front of me were completely marked up and spoke like criminals in a Dickens novel. Things changed a bit at Gatwick when a great crowd of American teenagers boarded, herded by two teachers barking, "Quick, before the doors close!"

The kid who took the seat beside mine looked to be around thirteen. Because of the braces on his teeth, he tended to keep his mouth open, the lower jaw just sort of hanging, as if he were dumbfounded. The young people were very well behaved, and I liked hearing them talk. "If you could eat anything right now, what would it be?" one boy asked his two friends.

"Um, I'd have a beef and cheese burrito from that place near the mall or maybe something from Wendy's."

They discussed the favorite places they'd stayed on their trip—"Not the youth hostel in Milan"—and then one boy asked the others where they'd like to be right now. "I mean, if you could be anywhere on earth."

"You should want to be here," said the man seated on the other side of the table from him. He'd been on the train since I boarded and was drinking a tall beer from a can while reading the newspaper. "If you're unhappy where you are, you should resolve to stay and make it a better place."

Oh, shut up, I wanted to say. *They're behaving themselves, so just leave them alone.*

I'd been tempted to ask the kid beside me where he was from, but no one that age wants to be talked to by an old man.

Again, to their credit, the kids were polite. "I guess you're right," one of them said to the beer drinker. "I'll try to keep that in mind in the future."

Later, on the bus, Rebecca, a stylist, mentioned a few of the photo shoots she's worked on. In one she had to put three necklaces on a llama. "The art director wanted them spaced out, so I used tape," she said. "That was bad, but nowhere near as hard as tying ribbons on piglets, which I had to do for the same shoot."

October 25, 2013
Charlotte

Last night I signed a book for a man named Henry Snuggs and another named Lexy Nash. As far as names go, I thought they were pretty hard to beat. Then I met a Chinese-American named Rich Jew.

"You've got to be kidding," I said.

He held out his ID. And there it was: *Jew.* As for his first name, it's technically Richard. "But everyone shortens it," Rich Jew, who is neither rich nor Jewish, said.

October 26, 2013
Shreveport, Louisiana

"I've never been to Shreveport before," I said yesterday afternoon to the check-in clerk at my hotel. She was black and pleasant, with long hair.

"Shreveport," she said. "It's sort of little but hey, it's okay."

I later thought that that might make for a good motto: "Shreveport. It's okay." To me it's a bit less than okay, actually. The people are nice, but it's pretty hard to look at. I'm on the eighth floor with a view of the murky river and all the sad casinos on it. As in Las Vegas, their windows are tinted. "Who gambles here?" I asked a woman at last night's signing. She worked at the El Dorado and said that 40 percent of her customers are local. The woman she was with worked at the casino as well. Last night's show wasn't sold out, but the audience made up for it by being superrowdy. People shouted "Yeah!" when they heard something they liked.

Among those in attendance was the woman I met in 2008 who asked me to name her two donkeys and whom I later mentioned in an essay. "I 'bout died to see myself in your book!" she said, adding that the donkeys had turned out to be assholes. "They wouldn't come when I called them or even pose for pitchers with hats on." She spoke with a beautiful small-town accent I could have listened to all night. "In the end I just kinda let 'em wander off."

This sounds harsh but they only wandered to the property next door. The owner of it had eight donkeys of his own and welcomed a few more.

Dinner was catfish from a restaurant that also offered mozzarella cat tails and something they called "dill frickles."

"That's nasty," people said, frowning down at my paper plate. "They shoulda got you something from Russell's."

I later learned that Russell's had Styrofoam plates instead of paper ones, though I don't know if that makes it more fancy or less.

November 1, 2013
Chicago

A few months back, the School of the Art Institute asked if I could come and present an award to a faculty member. I said yes, and they asked if, while I was at it, I might also say a few words about my time as a student. The organizer suggested I speak off the cuff, but the idea made me uncomfortable, so I spent several days crafting a speech. Looking back, I wish I'd asked who was going to be in the audience. It's the single most important bit of information a person needs, and I can't believe I proceeded without it. If I could go back in time, I'd throw my written remarks away and improvise, no matter how sloppy it might have sounded. Instead, after walking into the room and finding fifty or so people, almost all of them in their mid-eighties, I went ahead as planned. The problem wasn't the speech so much as the joke I used to start it:

An old man looks out the rain-streaked window, saying, "If this weather keeps up, the roads are going to be a real nightmare."

His grandson rolls his eyes and sneers. "Tell me something I *don't* know."

The old man thinks for a moment, then says, "Okay. Your grandmother's ass can take my entire fist."

Nobody laughed. No one.

November 7, 2013
Bloomington, Illinois

Just before last night's show I met a young man with long, pointed fingernails. "I don't have a book," he said, "but was just wondering, have you ever entertained a rape fantasy?"

I know I don't have to answer every question that's presented to me, especially by a stranger. Rather than changing the subject, though, I said, "Well, sure, once or twice."

"Me too," he said. "I think everyone has. In mine I tie the guy down and cut away his clothes while he—"

"Wait a minute," I said. "In your fantasy *you're* the rapist?"

"Of course," he said. "Aren't you?"

"Not so much," I told him.

I later related the conversation to a woman in the postshow signing line. "Can you believe it?" I asked. "Who fantasizes about raping people?"

And she said—no surprise, really—"Um, rapists?"

November 13, 2013
Vancouver, Canada

The other night in Seattle, I met a young woman who wanted a special message written in her copy of *Let's Explore Diabetes.* "My husband and I have a boat in North Carolina, and I want you to tell him that we need to name it the *Sea Section,*" she said.

"But that's the name of my beach house," I told her. "You're stealing."

She blinked.

"You should name your boat . . . *Row v. Wave,*" I said.

She didn't seem all that impressed but I think it's perfect. I later mentioned it to Joyce, who suggested the captain shout "All abort!" when it came time to leave the dock.

Someone else said, "I hope it doesn't get overturned."

November 29, 2013
Emerald Isle

After lunch yesterday afternoon we gathered on the beach to scatter Mom's ashes, which were in an octagonal-shaped metal tin with a Christmas scene on top. "Did someone give you cookies in this?" I asked Dad.

He took it from my hands as if the weight would answer the question. "I believe so."

It was a beautiful afternoon. Sunny and clear with a high in the upper forties. Several groups of fishermen were out, and quite a few people were walking dogs. "What are we going to scoop out the ashes with?" Amy asked.

Gretchen handed her a shell that seemed to have been designed specifically for that purpose. Then she gave one to each of us and we opened the tin. In it was a plastic bag with a strong tie on it, the kind you need a special tool to undo. Because we had no special tool, I cut open the plastic with a steak knife. I mean, really. It's like putting a padlock on a paper house. The ashes were eggshell-colored with bits of coarse bone in them, and they were half of what the crematorium gave us. Dad has the other half and would like for them to go into his casket and be buried with him up in Cortland.

Twenty-two years ago when Mom died, we would have balked. "She doesn't *want* half her ashes in his casket—he was terrible to her."

But was he really? Wouldn't a man so happy to be rid of his wife have remarried by now, or at least have dated? With the exception of Lisa's, the relationships the rest of us had back in 1991 were in their infancies. I'd been with Hugh for all of nine months, and Gretchen and Marshall were still in the flirting stage. What did we know of the wear and tear, the slow bleed of a thirty-five-year marriage? Mom talked shit about Dad all the time—it's just the kind of person she was. What he said about her, by contrast, was minor. After she died, I saw how inarticulate he was, almost like someone who was just learning English and had memorized only a half dozen platitudes. "She was a wonderful woman," he'd say, giving no examples and leading us to doubt that he had any.

I also don't think we realized how young we were when she died. At thirty-four, I felt more middle-aged than I do now, but walking down the stairs to the beach, following Dad, who was ninety and was dressed in jeans and a flannel shirt buttoned up to the neck, the tweed cap I gave him in 1975 pulled down low on his forehead, I'd have given anything to be that young again. I think we all would.

"Should we say a few words?" someone asked.

"No," Gretchen said. "I think we should just be silent." She dug in her shell, and the rest of us did the same. Paul and Amy took their shoes off and walked into the surf, while I was more like one of those sandpipers that dash to the water's edge and then dash back. By my second scoop I was crying. So were the others, I'm pretty sure. We didn't look at each other until the tin was empty and we were standing in a row. Out on the horizon, a shrimping boat trawled, and hovering behind it were hundreds of seabirds. It made me think of Mom. "Jesus," she'd call from behind the locked bathroom door. "Can't I even go to the john without being followed!"

I hadn't expected so many things to come flooding back. I don't think anyone else had either. "I feel like we've set her free," Gretchen said. Our mother had been trapped, genie-like, in a plastic bag, and it was nice to think of her finally let loose after all these years. She loved the coast of North Carolina and would have loved having this beach house, especially in the early days, before her drinking got to be too much. Those last few years were sad ones and I'll always wonder if we couldn't have done something to make them better for her.

December 11, 2013
Rackham
After I got into bed last night Hugh turned to me, saying, "Your hands feel dirty."

"Sticky?"

"No," he said. "Just...dirty. Did you wash them?"

The room could not have been any darker, and when I asked how anyone's hands could "feel" dirty, he asked me what I'd been up to since doing the dinner dishes.

"Well," I said, and I thought for a moment. "I went to the shed to get the milk I'd left in my bike basket."

"You touched a *lock*?"

I admitted that I had, and he said brusquely, "You need to go wash your hands."

"It wasn't a lock made out of shit," I told him.

"You need to go wash your hands."

"I'm not going anywhere," I said.

Only after he threatened to sleep in the guest room did I get out of bed and race, freezing, to the bathroom. There I ran some water in the sink and looked at it being wasted, thinking, *What in the world is his problem?*

December 13, 2013
Paris
On a recent flight from the U.S., Patsy sat next to a female pharmacist who was born in Cameroon and now practices in Boston. The two got to talking, and the woman brought up

a teenager who had come in a few weeks earlier. "She was picking up a new prescription for birth control pills," the pharmacist said. "It only took a minute or so, and when I handed them over, she asked me, very quietly, 'How you get them to stay in?'"

December 14, 2013
Prague, Czech Republic

I'm so glad my Czech publisher contacted me. We met for dinner last night at a restaurant called Essence. It was a good distance from the city center, in the sort of neighborhood where the sewing-machine repair shops are. A hotel car took us at 7:15 for the equivalent of $20 and we arrived to find three people seated at a table. That was it—three people in the entire restaurant. The fourth member of their group, Milos, arrived shortly afterward, as did a party of two, who sat near the Christmas tree, but otherwise the place was empty.

My editor, Petr, was younger than I'd expected, thirty-eight, and newly married. Across from him sat a woman around my age named Hannah who translated *Naked*, and beside me was Jiri, which is pronounced "Yeasy." He translated *When You Are Engulfed in Flames*, which comes out in a few weeks, and had a gray walrus-style mustache. Jiri is in his early sixties, and before my book he translated the last Philip Roth novel. He's from what used to be Bohemia and still has a house there, one he inherited from his parents.

"Do a lot of people here go to church?" Patsy asked.

Hannah said that in Poland, 91 percent of the population identifies as religious, while in the Czech Republic it's just 20 percent.

"Well, Poland," Jiri said. "Outside of ten or so cities, it's just mud, isn't it?"

I asked if abortion was readily available here and Hannah

said, "Oh, yes. We're very liberal." She added that the Czech Republic gets a lot of abortion tourism, a term I'd never heard before.

Later we learned that this is a fairly industrial country. Its biggest export is automobiles, particularly the Škoda. "Does that word mean something?" Patsy asked.

Petr said it was the founder's last name and that unfortunately it means "pity, harm, and damage." He and Milos are leaving this morning for a week in the Italian Alps. The whole company goes every year, including the wives and kids, for a ski trip.

We asked what happens at Christmas and were told that in the Czech Republic, it's all about the twenty-fourth. "That's when we have the big dinner and open presents," Petr said.

I asked who brought the presents and learned that it's Baby Jesus.

"But He's just a newborn," I said. "How can He lift anything heavier than a candy cane?"

"That's the mystery of Christmas," Hannah explained. She said that, unlike Santa, there are no pictures of Jesus creeping into the house. "We don't say the Baby Jesus comes down a chimney or through a door, just that He comes."

Jiri said that they also celebrate on December 6, when Saint Nicholas arrives accompanied by an angel and a devil. "Of course, they're not a *real* angel and devil," he assured me.

We left the restaurant at around ten thirty and went with Milos to the main post office, which is open twenty-four hours a day. I don't mean there are machines, I mean there's an actual counter with clerks behind it. Patsy and I bought stamps and then Jiri walked us the rest of the way to our hotel. He's on his third marriage and his wife is eight years younger than he is. With every child you have, you're allowed to retire one year earlier. She had two. He also has two from previous marriages.

I liked a story he told about driving into Germany after the wall came down. He was with his father. The two of them were super-excited and arrived on a Sunday morning. "The Germans were getting out of church, all dressed in their finery, and we looked like tramps," he said. "We looked like people from a Communist country."

December 18, 2013
London
At the Gare du Nord yesterday morning, Hugh went to the table reserved for filling out immigration forms and brutally yanked the pen from its chain. "What?" he said when I gave him my What-on-earth-has-gotten-into-you look. "It's too fucking short."

It may have been, but he was already angry when he approached the table on account of the security guard who'd directed him there. The guy saw him jerk the pen and looked at him with amusement, the way one does when a wild card enters the scene. I often imagine Hugh being led away in handcuffs after a blowup at an airport or train station. Why does he have such a short fuse? It's nothing new—he's been like this ever since I've known him—but where does it come from?

December 19, 2013
London
Hugh and I left the house at ten yesterday morning and caught a cab driven by a man who often lays pipelines for oil companies. He was maybe sixty and gets an annual two-hundred-pound heating allowance. "Not that I need it," he said. "There are those who do—don't get me wrong—but it's completely wasted on me and my wife."

When told we were going to the job office in Tooting for my national insurance number, the man scoffed. "No one working there but a bunch of miserable Asians who all hate white people. Their own kind, they'll give anything to, but not an Englishman."

By this he meant South Asians, people from Pakistan and India. The driver told us that his son had recently tried to claim unemployment benefits and was turned down on account of a flat he rents out. "He got rid of his wife," he said, adding, as if this explained everything, that she was a vegetarian. "I ain't racist, though," he assured us. "I've shagged thousands of Asian women. How can you be racist and have sex with them—that's what I want to know!" He said that while Asians were miserable, the Scots were even worse. "The lowest of the fucking low. They can get under a snake's belly with a top hat on.

"The English are a bastard race," he explained. "Irish, Scottish, we come from all over." He told us he reads a lot of history and that for all we know, Queen Elizabeth had a pair of bollocks under her fucking skirt. This, somehow, got him on the subject of Poles, who are apparently as low as the Scots. "Their woman are like Persian carpets, pretty until you get up close and see all the flaws." There's a Polish woman who works at his local pub. "The most miserable cow who ever pulled a pint," he called her.

The man has spent a lot of time in the Middle East and will leave in January for Nigeria. "I don't care where they send me," he said. "Gets me away from my wife, doesn't it?"

December 22, 2013
Rackham

I called Lisa for her birthday. "So, what did Bob give you?" I asked.

"Bob? Oh, he's going to take me out to dinner."

"Is that all?"

"Well, it's not wrapped or anything, but we're also giving each other new grout for the bathroom."

This is a new low for the presents she and Bob exchange. A few years back it was an air-conditioning unit, something you can't even use in December. "My main present will be our trip to the beach," she said. "I told the dogs they could bring one toy apiece, so Polly chose her ball and Chilli picked out a fake bone." She'd bought one of the dogs a cape for Christmas, but Bob made her return it. "I guess if one or the other of them gets cold at the beach they can just wear Polly's ThunderShirt," she said, referring to a tight-fitting sweater that supposedly calms a dog down during storms.

She'd just finished a book called *Wild* in which the author, a young woman named Cheryl Strayed, walks the Pacific Crest Trail. It was a 1,100-mile journey and Lisa was thinking that after Dad dies, all of us might want to take that same hike. "Don't you think it would be a good idea? Maybe we could hire a cook to come with us, and a guide, maybe, someone who knows the area in case Gretchen breaks her leg."

"Um...sure," I said.

One of the things she'd wanted to give Dad for Christmas was a book called *A Good Death*.

"I don't know that that's such a good idea," I told her. "It might be jumping the gun a little."

She sighed. "That's what Bob said."

December 28, 2013
Rackham

Slate ran an article on inappropriate courtroom attire and included an arsonist who showed up for his sentencing in a T-shirt reading SNITCHES GET STITCHES. Then there was the woman who pleaded guilty to child abuse in a shirt that announced SEX IS A MISDEMEANOR. THE MORE I MISS, THE MEANER I GET.

In another example the message read DON'T PISS ME OFF. I DON'T NEED ANOTHER F#*KING FELONY CONVICTION.

This being *Slate,* most of the responses were humorless, many people pointing out that decent courtroom clothing costs money and the suspects are, by and large, indigent.

That doesn't quite fly, though. A button-down shirt at the Goodwill is only a few dollars more than one reading SLAVERY GETS SHIT DONE. The problem is stupidity—for instance, the guy who was accused of domestic violence and wore a T-shirt to court that had no words on it, just a picture of a handgun.

2014

January 5, 2014
London

At Marks and Spencer I emptied my basket onto the belt, saying, "I don't need a bag, thank you." Then I watched as my cashier, who wore a badge reading HEARING IMPAIRED, put my items into a bag and charged me ten p. for it. When we tell the disabled they can do anything they want in this world, don't we mean that they can invent a new kind of alarm system or write a book about loneliness—something, well, that can be accomplished at home?

January 10, 2014
Tokyo

Yesterday afternoon, at a store called Kapital, Amy and I found a curious sweatshirt. It pictured a bear on all fours idling beside a stream. That seemed normal enough but above its head, hanging in the sky like the sun, was a bright yellow swastika.

"What on earth?" we said.

The saleswoman noticed the tone of our voices and stepped over to see what the fuss was about. "Ah, yes," she said, addressing what, to her, seemed remarkable. "The bear, he have a salmon in his mouth."

January 22, 2014
Melbourne
Joining us for dinner after last night's show was an actor and comic named Josh. He's gay, and after a show last month, a young man approached him, saying, "Your act gave me the confidence to come out to my girlfriend."

"Isn't that awful?" Josh asked us.

I agreed that it was, adding that there ought to be a different word when the honesty involves someone you've been actively hurting for the past few years. You come out to your parents. You destroy your girlfriend.

January 23, 2014
Canberra, Australia
I groaned when I saw the word *Hyatt* on my schedule but it's actually a great place. My only complaint—and it extends to the whole of the country—is the coffee. It's all espresso-based, meaning that after I have one long black, my mouth is dried out. "Are you one of those who likes that watered-down American shit?" a woman asked during last night's signing.

"Indeed I am," I said.

She was a barista with huge breasts and seemed to perfectly sum up the Australian attitude toward coffee, that being that they know best. It's amazing how people go on about it here. Yesterday's flight attendant, for instance. The guy in front of me asked for an espresso and with great sorrow she explained that the machines couldn't work properly at that altitude. Then the two of them got onto the subject of coffee beans, both sounding very technical, like people do when they carry on about wine.

"I live quite close to a barista training center," Peta said on the way home from the theater last night. That's another thing that astounds me here—the reverence afforded to people who operate milk steamers.

I sat behind two middle-aged women in the hotel restaurant yesterday afternoon. Both were well dressed and Australian. "You could tell right off that he was of the Jewish persuasion," one of them said as I peeled a shrimp the size of an old-fashioned telephone receiver. "You know how those people are with money."

January 25, 2014
Perth

At last night's signing I met an Irishman. We talked about a diary entry I'd read toward the end of my show and he told me that his grandfather used to threaten his uncle by saying, "I'm going to take an iron poker and stick it in the fire until the point turns bright red. Then I'm going to shove the cold end up your ass just so you can burn your hands trying to yank it out."

"It's poetry, really, isn't it?" he said.

January 28, 2014
Dubai, United Arab Emirates

There's the Dubai everyone talks about when they talk about Dubai, and then there's the one that Dawn and I are staying in. We're not in the neighborhood of towering new buildings but of low shabby ones. It was 1:30 a.m. by the time we checked into our manger-like hotel, and because neither of us was sleepy, we left for a walk immediately after settling into our rooms.

Our first stop was a twenty-four-hour grocery store. "It's all Indian," Dawn observed, looking at the rows of spices and staples in their beautiful little bags. On the shop's second story were small appliances and some of the saddest clothing I've ever seen—a glittery sweatshirt, for instance, that had the word ACTIVITY written on it. We were the only customers, and I felt bad for the security guard, a young man with a single, thick eyebrow who marched back and forth between the toasters and the underpants.

It was perhaps in the mid-seventies last night, pleasant, especially for Dawn. It's been so cold in Minnesota, she's been unable to leave her house. Walking without a heavy coat on was a luxury for her, and so we continued up the road. I thought this part of town would be deserted but we passed quite a few people. No one was alone, and aside from two men in white robes, no one seemed to be from here. Rather, they were foreign workers, Indians and Filipinos in line at the kebab restaurant or KFC. We passed another grocery store, this one called Choconuts, and a shop with a sign reading IF WE DON'T HAVE IT YOU GET IT FOR FREE.

"How does that make sense?" Dawn asked. "I mean, if they don't have it, what's to get for free?"

Another sign, this one outside a place called Loyalukkas, read WIN 32 KILOS OF GOLD.

That's so curious to me. Not "a chest of gold" or "$10,000 worth of gold" but "32 kilos." It sounds like such a random amount.

Mainly we passed stray cats, dozens of them. I tossed one a treat made of caramel corn and peanuts and watched as she gave it a few licks. Nearby was a dying pigeon. I thought the cat would eat it, but instead, after a quick sniff, she walked on by. The stores we passed were not at all fancy. The clothes in their windows looked costumey and cheap. BED SPACE AVAILABLE FOR INDIAN MUSLIM BACHELOR read a sign pinned to a noticeboard. I'd read about places like the ones I saw advertised, and they sound horrible. All you basically get is a mattress, most often in a windowless room in a neighborhood where cats fight on the street all night.

Though sad, the area feels pretty safe. No one called out to us as we walked. I didn't see any trash or hear any music. Everyone seemed exhausted, though that could be me projecting. I hadn't slept in twenty-four hours but wasn't in the least bit tired when, after a shower, I climbed into bed. Not long afterward I awoke to a recording coming from the minaret. *A call to prayers!* I thought, wondering what it translates to. Is it scolding? What kind of voice was I hearing? Was it considered sonorous or did it just happen to be the voice of the imam? Regardless, it gave me quite a thrill. *I'm in the Middle East!* I thought. *If they don't have it, I get it for free!*

January 29, 2014
Dubai

After dinner last night we went for a walk on the promenade that runs along the waterfront. It was ten thirty or maybe even later, and families were out strolling with their children. Every so often we'd pass men holding hands or walking with their arms around one another. They're not gay, though at first sight you might assume otherwise. Then you take a second look and see that the touch has no hint of sex in it. It's the way kids touch each other, only they're grown up, and with beards. It's how I touch Ronnie sometimes, how I used to touch my mom, a way of saying "I love you" without having to say anything. All day long I saw men touching each other, and it was beautiful.

On top of affectionate males, the promenade boasted a camel. He was tethered to the ground within a small pen and I decided his name was Chris. "How many teeth have you got?" Dawn asked, and, as if he understood English, Chris lowered his head and opened his mouth. It was nice to be out late in a place where everyone was sober. Never did anyone raise his

321

voice, there were no beer cans on the ground, and, best of all, there wasn't that aggressive energy you get in places in the UK, where at that time of night anything can happen.

January 31, 2014
Abu Dhabi, United Arab Emirates

We began our day at Starbucks, where Hugh had a coffee, and Dawn and I watched him drink it. On the table was a copy of the daily paper. It was all in Arabic, and pictured on the front page was a woman shrouded in black with a graduation cap on her head. It was like promoting a chess piece from rook to queen. Later, at dinner, we saw a woman veiled in black but with glasses on. There were no holes for her eyes or mouth. You couldn't see anything except her hands. *They're the perfect shape for you*, I imagined her optometrist saying.

Then I pictured her friends at a party. *You seem different somehow, Samira, but I can't quite put my finger on it.*

One of our drivers yesterday was female. Her cab was intended for women and families, and because Dawn was with us, she stopped and picked us up. Like everyone else we'd dealt with since arriving, the driver was not a native but had moved here, in this case from Eritrea. "I have this purple scarf on my head, but it is just a part of my uniform," she told us. "After work I can take it off and nobody says a thing to me about it. That's why I like it in the Arab Emirates. I can be free here."

I asked if she ever went to Saudi Arabia and she groaned. "Who would want to? I hate those people." The driver told us that our fellow guests at the Shangri-La were mainly from Qatar and Kuwait, two countries she doesn't mind so much, not that she'd want to pack up and move there. "I have a good life," she said.

"Do you live in an apartment?"

"A room," she said. "About as big as this car."

"Does it have a window?" I asked.

She was silent for a moment. "No. But there's a fan in the bathroom."

All the heavy lifting here is done by foreigners, who, like the cabdriver, live in miserable boxes. At a newsstand yesterday I watched as two Frenchwomen laid their items on the counter. "That will be twenty-five dirhams," the clerk informed them.

"I'll give you fifteen," the taller of the Frenchwomen said.

"Twenty-five," the man repeated; his right, I think, as the goods in his store had price tags on them.

"You're supposed to bargain," Hugh said, but I can't bring myself to nickel-and-dime someone who doesn't have any windows. So what if I pay an extra ten cents for something?

We took a cab yesterday morning to the Sheikh Zayed mosque, which is reportedly the biggest in the world and one of the few that allow non-Muslims to visit. Men can't wear shorts or tank tops, but apparently they can wear T-shirts reading DON'T MESS WITH TEXAS. Women, on the other hand, have to dress like the Grim Reaper. Hugh and I waited as Dawn was outfitted in a black hooded robe. Then we stuck close by her side, as once we entered the building, she looked just like every other female. The mosque was built in the 1990s, I think, and looked like a terminal for Aladdin Airlines. It surprised me that they allowed photographs. A few people took them of the walls and ceiling, but most wanted pictures of themselves. "Do you mind?" they'd ask, handing you their cell phone. Then they'd smile or put their hands on their hips.

"What did people do before they took pictures of everything?" I whispered to Dawn as we accidentally invaded one photo after another. It was just as bad later on at what amounted to the Village of Yesteryear, a re-creation of a Bedouin encampment. There were a lot of Russians there,

323

all raising their cell phones. The camera has replaced actual looking and turned life into evidence. It drives me crazy.

Sohar, Oman

If I didn't sleep well last night it's because I kept worrying about the time. Rather than leaving the hotel at noon, we're taking off at nine a.m., this at the suggestion of Jacob, our driver, who is thirty-two and got married too early. "I have four children," he wailed. "Four!" Over dinner at a Pakistani restaurant called Al Nakhalah, he told us that his wife would like to get a job in an office. "But I forbided it," he said. "I say to her there are things more important than money—having good childrens, for example. I say if my money isn't enough for her, then too bad!"

Jacob lives, we learned, in the house of his dead father, which he shares with his three brothers and all their wives and children. "We have two rooms, so it's good," he said.

We'd taken a table outside. It was low and the chairs we sat in were high-backed, like thrones. Next door was a Shell station, and down the busy, chaotic road were places where people could buy tires or used furniture or have their teeth cleaned. After we ordered, a calico cat came around. "Oh, look at you!" Dawn whispered. The air smelled of gasoline.

I like Jacob's English. At one point in a rather long story, he used the line "He was just sitting there, watching the newspaper." He meant to say *reading* and the easy mistake prodded his sentence from banal to fascinating. He's a big guy, over six feet tall, and bulky. "What do you wear under your dishdasha?" we asked, and he roared with laughter. "That is always the first question with you people."

The answer—shorts and a T-shirt—was sort of disappointing.

"How many do you own?" Dawn asked.

"Eleven."

"And how do you keep them so white?" I asked.

"Good wife," he answered.

Hugh thinks Jacob is okay. Dawn hates him but I can't make my mind up one way or the other. He met us at our drop-off point in Al Ain and was close to an hour late. This was unacceptable to our first driver, a prim Filipino in a coat and tie who also has children, though his are all back home in Manila. He met us promptly at noon in a black SUV and was good at answering our questions. "What's that?" I asked, pointing to a grim compound half an hour outside of Abu Dhabi.

"Workers' accommodations, sir," he chirped. The man's front teeth were capped and sightly oversize, and he said everything breezily, the way I might say, "Merry Christmas!" "The UAE is a great place, sir. You can do anything you want here!"

"*Anything?*" I said, wondering what it's like for gay people.

"You may want to look at a bideo called *Slaves of Dubai,*" our driver sang from the front seat. "It is very interesting and educational!"

I liked that he said *bideo*.

Our first stop yesterday was the city of Al Ain. Most of it looks like the campus of a low-level community college, but we bypassed all that and went straight to the camel market. If it wasn't their equivalent of a Sunday, it would have been pretty lively. As it was there were a lot of Berbers and Afghanis sitting on the ground in small groups. "Want to see baby camels?" a man said to Hugh—as if anyone couldn't see them for free, standing in their pens the way the adult camels were. The next time I looked over, one of the men had forced Hugh to try on his headdress. Then he took Hugh's camera and snapped a photo. "Fifty dirham," he demanded after handing it back.

"But I don't have fifty," Hugh said.

"Thirty, then," the man and his friends countered.

"It was *your* idea to take my picture," Hugh told them. "I was just minding my own—"

"Thirty dirham."

Dawn and I came along just then and the three of us headed to a row of shops that sold camel accoutrements: leashes and harnesses and the like. There were also camel veterinarians. A few of the shops had their doors open. We'd poke our heads in and see the owners asleep on the floor or lying on blankets scrolling through their smartphones. As we walked, our driver followed slowly behind. At one of the few open shops, he stopped to buy a camel leash, saying it would be good for his German shepherd.

"What's its name?" I asked.

The man beamed, revealing the edges of his capped teeth. "Douglas, sir."

February 8, 2014
Paris

A Greek entomologist in Tennessee has named a beetle after me. The *Darwinilus sedarisi* is a predator that eats maggots. That'll be two things I'll have named after me this year: a bug and a garbage truck.

February 18, 2014
London

At my friend Valerie's antiques store yesterday afternoon I noticed a collection of four handguns. They were carved out of wood and life-size, maybe toys or perhaps props for a play. One's a Luger, one's some kind of long-barreled Colt, and the others are what I think of as simple revolvers. All are painted gray and have unmovable triggers made of metal.

Valerie reckoned they were from the 1940s or '50s, and,

rather than choosing one over the others, I bought all four, figuring I'll give them as presents to people over the course of the coming year. On returning home I put two in my gift cupboard and laid the others on my desk.

Hugh was out with friends for dinner, and at around ten, when I heard him come in, I took a gun in each hand and crept down the stairs. He was at the kitchen sink, pouring himself a glass of water, when I came up behind him. "That's right," I said. "Pour yourself some water. Fill that glass. Come on, *fill it*. Now turn the tap off. *Turn it off*, I said."

I know you're not supposed to laugh at your own stuff, but I think it's so funny to point two guns at someone and order him to do what he was going to do anyway. "Drink it!" I commanded. "That's right, empty the glass into your mouth. Now put it on the counter. You heard me. Nice and easy. And keep those hands where I can see 'em."

February 21, 2014
Athens, Greece

"You looked like your father onstage last night," Hugh said yesterday morning in the breakfast room of our hotel.

"I take that as a compliment," I told him, feeling suddenly better about myself.

Hugh refilled his teacup. "Your father is ninety-one."

March 2, 2014
Spreckelsville, Hawaii

After arriving yesterday evening, Hugh and I drove to the Safeway for groceries. We loaded our cart and had just gotten in line when I noticed that the fellow behind me had only four items, one of them a box of ice cream.

"After you," I said. "Please, I insist."

The cashier was my age and wore a scarf tied pirate-style

around her bald head. There was a smudged tattoo on her left forearm, and she had on brown, plastic-framed glasses. One of the items she scanned when my turn came was a jar of pickles. "Wait," I said. "I don't think those are mine."

She snatched them from the bagger. "Want me to take them off?"

"On second thought," I said, "maybe they are mine." I looked toward the door, where Hugh was reading the paper. "Maybe my friend picked them up."

"Ah, yes," the cashier said, scanning the quart of milk I'd selected. "Your imaginary friend."

When she finished, she announced the total and asked if I had a Safeway Savings Card.

I shook my head no.

"Well, let me sign you up for one."

"That's all right," I told her. "I don't live in your country."

"Are you a billionaire?" she asked. "Unless you are, I'm signing you up." She handed me a form and a pen. "All I need is your name, your phone number, and a signature."

A considerable line had formed behind me, so I moved quickly, knowing that everyone must hate me by now. When I'd finished, the cashier took a plastic card and scanned it. "There," she announced. "I just saved you fifteen dollars." Then she handed me the card along with the receipt and said, coldly, "Now be gone."

March 15, 2014
Indianapolis, Indiana
While waiting for my lost suitcase to arrive I walked to the Au Bon Pain outlet a few blocks from my hotel and ordered a chicken wrap. "It's my favorite," said the tattooed young woman behind the counter. "Actually, though, I like to add strawberries to it. Call me crazy, but I do."

"Freak," I said.

"What?"

"You're not crazy," I said. "You're a freak."

If I had a business, I'd have hired her away, not just because she was fast and efficient but because she had a winning personality. Making my wrap was her last chore of the day. After giving it to me she changed back into her street clothes. On her way to the door, she passed me and said, very warmly, "Stay unique, my kind sir."

April 2, 2014
Dublin

It was around 2:00 when we arrived in Dublin. A chubby fellow with very white skin and red hair picked us up at the airport and talked all the way to the hotel. "I don't let anything get me down," he said. "What's the point, right? My girlfriend, though, I call her Jekyll and Hyde."

I learned that he had a seven-week-old baby at home, a girl. "She's a fookin' monster," he said. "A fookin' nightmare. Got a real bite on her too. Clare had to give up breastfeeding. The pain was too much!"

The cabdriver lives on the other side of the airport, in a village on the coast. He's not right on the beach, but he can see the water from his house.

"Is it old?" I asked.

"Built in the sixties," he told me. "That means I can hang a flat-screen TV without making a big fookin' production of it."

I love how chatty Irish people are. It can take a real toll on a book signing, though. Last night's show was sold out and I didn't leave the theater until one a.m. One of the people I met, an American in her early thirties, had worked as an aerialist for the circus until she got hit by a car.

"You flew through the air holding on to someone's ankles and then *got hit by a car*?" I said.

She nodded. "In New York. Isn't it crazy!"

I later met a woman named Fanny Dyke. "Don't get me started," she said.

Then I met a retired German fellow who lives in Cork and who taught me the word *Flusensieb* (pronounced "fluzen zeep"), which means "dryer fluff."

Finally, I met a guy whose teacher would criticize him, saying, "You're so lazy you'd shit the bed and push it out with your foot."

The theater was beautiful, as was the lobby. On the stage manager's recommendation, I had a steak for dinner and ate it while signing. "Want to bring the bone home to your dog?" I'd ask.

"Oh, I hate dogs," everyone said. "I'm more of a cat person."

I loved meeting so many anti-dog people.

April 4, 2014
Rackham

A few days back I met a woman who'd just gone on a date with a man she'd met online. "He mentioned over dinner that he had a fear of the C-word," she told me, "and before I had time to think, I leaned across the table and said, '*Cunt?*'"

The word he'd meant was *commitment*.

April 6, 2014
Birmingham, England

At last night's signing I met a young woman named Melanie. "You're a Pisces," I told her.

"How did you know?"

"You have a sister and you spent some time in a hospital this past month."

She was too stunned to say anything for a moment or two. "How did you...how can you know all that?"

"I know everything," I told her. "Sometimes I wish I didn't, but I do."

April 29, 2014
London

I told Hugh yesterday that when I die, I want my body taken to an ice crematorium. There I would like a traditional sundae service.

May 9, 2014
Rackham

While picking up litter yesterday afternoon I came upon a pair of men's briefs with a soaking wet turd in them. Atop this turd, feasting, was a thumb-size slug. *Really,* I thought. *You eat that?* It might have been the most disgusting thing I've ever come across. Surrounding the briefs, which were perhaps a size 40, were six shit-smeared napkins. I picked everything up with my grabber and stuffed it into the trash can that was three feet away, wondering if these underpants were related to the ones I found a few weeks ago. Later on I discovered a microwave someone had thrown into the ferns.

Hugh returned yesterday afternoon and at 9:15 he went to shut in Tim and Helen's chickens. On his way back to the house he passed a toad. "What was its name?" I asked.

He thought for a moment. "Lane."

That is such a perfect name for a toad.

May 16, 2014
Rackham

I had just collected two dozen cans and bottles from the front yard of a cottage yesterday afternoon when a white-haired woman wandered out from behind the hedge with her hands on her hips. "I heard a noise!"

I told her I was picking up trash, that it was my hobby, and she said it was about time somebody did something. "All this rubbish, it's disgusting."

She saw my black plastic bag—full now—and said, "You're not going to leave that *here*, are you?"

"I'll have the council pick it up in the morning," I told her.

"No," she said.

"So, you *want* me to pick up all the rubbish from your front yard, but you *don't want* me leaving the bag it's in here overnight?"

"That's right," she said. "Put it over there." She pointed to her neighbor's yard.

I picked the bag up. "How about I just carry it a mile down the road," I said. "Would that work for you?" As I continued walking, I added, "Jesus fucking Christ."

"You shouldn't have used that language," Hugh said when I told him about it. "It was rude."

"Whose side are you on?" I asked. It was a dumb question, as clearly he was Team Hag.

I fumed for two hours after my talk with the horrible woman. What a hypocrite. These people moan about the litter but aren't prepared to make even the smallest of sacrifices.

May 19, 2014
Rackham

It was Sunday, and Storrington was quiet. Passing the square not far from the Waitrose, I came upon a fat boy of twelve or so sitting on a bench. "Are you picking up rubbish?" he asked.

"I am," I said.

He gestured toward my grabber. "And you bought that thing to make it easier?"

I admitted that I had, and then I asked if he occasionally littered.

"No," he told me. "Never."

"Picking it up is a nice hobby," I told him. "You should try it sometime."

"Nah," he said, not impolitely but decidedly. "It's boring." Then he returned to what he'd been doing before I came along: sitting on the bench and looking out onto the road.

Hugh announced the other day that slugs can travel a mile over the course of a single night. "There's no way on earth that that's true," I told him.

"Okay," he said, "a half a mile." He then claimed that in order to get rid of a snail, you have to put it in your car and drive it some great distance from your house, otherwise it will remember where it was and return.

That can't be true either. Surely he's confusing slugs with dogs.

June 11, 2014
Toronto

They bumped me to first class on the flight from Boston to Washington. I was on the aisle and across from me sat a fellow who was wearing dress shorts and chewing tobacco. In his hand was an empty juice bottle, and every few minutes he'd raise it to his lips. I'd watch the brown spittle ooze down the sides and wonder, *How much would someone have to pay me to drink that?* Thirty years ago I'd have done it for $50. Ten years later you'd have had to raise it to at least $5,000, and now you'd have to pay me twenty times that amount. *Look at how spoiled I've become,* I thought, still in first class but depressed now.

David Sedaris

July 5, 2014
London

I couldn't get over how unfriendly yesterday's flight attendants were. It was as if they'd taken a pledge of unity: *If anyone is caught being nice to a passenger, that's it—you're out.* Dinner was thrown at us, appetizer and main course at the same time, and I have no evidence they served anyone breakfast. I awoke forty-five minutes before landing to discover that they'd taken my headphones—reached around me and disconnected them while I was asleep. No one offered me coffee or juice. My coat was returned with the word "Here."

Conversely, I had a great driver from Heathrow. I think he was originally from Pakistan but moved here as a child. The man was tall with a black mustache and thick hair he'd treated with oil. Among his favorite clients were Bill Clinton and George Bush Senior, both of whom were talkative and friendly. "Politically they are day and night but in terms of their kindly spirit, they are twins!" he reported.

July 24, 2014
Rackham

At two o'clock Andrew Baldwin collected me in his car and drove us to the Old School House, where a garbage truck had been named after me. A crowd of twenty or so people were waiting, among them Tom, Thelma, Ben, Nicola, and Olivia. "All of my friends," I later said to Hugh, realizing how small that sounded. Also there were four garbagemen, several members of the Horsham council, and Susan Pyper, the lord-lieutenant of West Sussex. It was she who pulled the tarp off the truck and unveiled my sign. It was much larger than I'd expected—ten feet by six—and read THANKS DAVID FOR HELPING TO KEEP THE AREA CLEAN. There was a cartoon pig next to the message, and he had my hair.

After some photos, champagne was served, and I noticed that even Tom had a glass. I shook hands with all the garbagemen, returned to the truck for a few more pictures, then started on the A283 to Steyning. That road has never been cleaned by me, and it's a mess. While I was picking up cans, a big truck passed, and I was surprised and disappointed not to see my name splashed on the side of it.

Can't I be on everything? I wondered.

July 30, 2014
Rackham

Nicola and Ben came for dinner. We ate at around nine, and before that we sat outdoors. I ran in to make a cup of tea and when I stepped back outside, Hugh was repeating his ridiculous claim that slugs can travel an entire mile over the course of a single night.

"That is simply not true," I told him.

"It is, well, rather a lot," Nicola politely added.

Later I stepped indoors to pee and when I returned, Ben was looking through the before-and-after photo album Hugh made on the Swan Cottage renovations. "So you had that timber brought from Normandy?"

As other beams were mentioned, I decided that Hugh should have a TV show called *Timber Talk*. My show, meanwhile, will be *Trash Talk*.

Over dinner Nicola said that the juice of a boiled slug used to be prescribed for respiratory complaints. Can this be true? She then mentioned someone named Diggery Eden. That's such a great first name, Diggery.

Ben told a story about walking home from Pulborough and being called a cunt-head by someone in a passing car. They're such a good pair, him and his mother. Hugh roasted a chicken and served a pie made from fresh cherries for dessert.

August 2, 2014
Provincetown, Massachusetts

Before last night's show, Hugh and I rode bikes. The trail we took was hilly and cut through a beautiful forest of stunted pines. At the end was a beach, and as Hugh swam, the couple beside me monitored his progress. "That guy's an idiot. Look how far out he is!"

"And he's going out even farther! Doesn't he know anything? There are seals there. Seals spell sharks!"

"It's Shark 101," the man said. As the two spoke, they exercised. Both were tanned and in good shape. "We'll go swimming after he's finished," the guy continued. "After the feeding frenzy."

August 21, 2014
Colorado Springs, Colorado

Again this morning at seven o'clock, men with leaf blowers took to the grounds of the hotel. I looked out the window and burned as I watched a landscaper loudly chase what looked like a single pine needle down the sidewalk.

Awakened by the noise and unable to fall back to sleep, I went downstairs for a coffee. "Good morning, sir," said the fellow behind the counter. He was African, perhaps in his mid-twenties, and had several thick, deliberate scars on his face. "How are you?"

That's the thing about this hotel. I must have had fifteen people ask me how I was yesterday: the hostess at the restaurant, the waitress, the desk clerk, the shop employees. "How are you?" "How are you?" "How are you?"

"As long as you're asking," I said to the African fellow, "I'm kind of on the angry side."

"Oh, no!"

I told him about the men with the leaf blowers and he folded his hands. "They're probably just trying to keep things nice and clean."

"I appreciate that," I said. "But do you really need a machine that loud in order to get a single leaf? Just bend down and pick it up. Or use a broom!"

He nodded and smiled, the way you do at old, spoiled people who complain too much and want to take away the tools that make the lives of manual laborers a little less wretched. "Or just leave the damn thing where it is," I said. "I don't care if there's a leaf in my path."

Again he smiled, and my eyes fell to his name tag. D-U-M-I, it read.

"I'll just have a large coffee," I said.

Back in the room a few minutes later, I found Hugh standing on his head in his underwear. Quietly I passed him and opened my computer, hoping to learn if D-u-m-i was pronounced "Dummy" or "Doomy." I got no answer, so I looked up *leaf-blower haters* and spent a pleasant few minutes realizing that I am not alone. And isn't that really what the internet is for?

August 22, 2014
Aspen, Colorado

I like the oatmeal at our hotel but don't much care for the rest of it. "Where are we coming in from today?" the check-in clerks asked when we arrived. "How was your trip in?" There was a mix-up with the billing and after it was settled, they made keys and signaled for our personal butler, a small Filipino man in his mid-thirties named Rusty. "Can I help you with your luggage?" he asked. "I go to the gym and am strong!"

I gave him my tote bag and we followed him to the elevator. "Your suite has the best view in the entire hotel," he said, clearly untrue, as we are only on the second floor, practically eye level with the cars parked out on the street. "This desk, let me tell you, this desk was designed by Ralph Lauren," Rusty said after he'd ushered us in. He ran his hand admiringly over the surface. "I wear his cologne. Exclusively."

Hugh and I nodded, and as he moved on to the bedroom, I wondered if I was to tip piecemeal or hand over a lump sum upon leaving.

Breakfast was good, though. After eating we took a walk across town. Aspenites wander the streets like cows in India, never looking out for traffic, rarely even glancing up from their phones. It's fine when you're the pedestrian but maddening when you're a driver. We ate lunch in the town of Leadville and stopped for coffee sometime later at a Starbucks-type place on the highway. There were two men in line and one young woman behind the counter. "Actually, make that *two* hot chocolates," one of the men said to her as we walked in. He then turned to a woman I took to be his wife. "Does Deb want one too?"

"I think so," the woman said.

"Let's make it three hot chocolates," the man said.

A young man walked in from the convenience store attached to the coffee place. "And a caramel frappuccino!" he shouted.

"So that's the frappuccino and three hot chocolates," the man said to the woman behind the counter. "And me, I'll have a latte, I guess." He called out to his wife, "You want a latte too?"

She said no and then a teenage girl walked in from the parking lot and said that instead of a hot chocolate, she wanted an iced mocha.

"So that'll be two hot chocolates, a latte, the frappuccino, and an iced mocha," the man said. He looked like Raymond

Carver and wore shorts, Bass Weejuns, and no socks. "What about you, Mike?" he said to the man beside him.

"I'm going to get a cappuccino and probably a mocha for Pam," the man said.

"Well, let me get them."

"No, you've done enough."

"I insist!"

The second man relented and as the first one added the cappuccino and mocha to his existing order I groaned, and Hugh left the line, saying, "Just forget it."

That was when a second teenage girl came in from the parking lot, and the man who was ordering said, "You want a hot drink, Kimberly?"

We left then, and for the rest of the afternoon I thought back on the jerk who was ordering and treating the place like he owned it. The girl behind the counter was over the group as well. She had the blender going, the milk steamer, everything in the house, while the guy asked for one asshole concoction after another.

"You don't continually *add* to your order," I said to Hugh. "If the girl wanders in from the parking lot and decides all of a sudden that she wants a liquid Snickers bar, you tell her to get to the back of the line and ask for it herself."

"Let it go," he groaned.

But I couldn't.

August 24, 2014
Rackham
I'm thinking that the Washington Redskins should keep their name but change their logo from an American Indian to either a red-skin peanut or a red-skin potato. It really is the perfect solution.

September 10, 2014
Rackham

The weather was beautiful yesterday afternoon, bright and clear with a slight chill. I picked up a few things at the supermarket in Storrington, and then headed down the lane past the fitness center, which is narrow and winding, canopied by tall trees. I'd just started listening to Marc Maron, who was introducing his 2010 interview with Robin Williams, when a dog rounded a bend in the road and approached me, snarling. I don't know what breed it was. I was too busy being scared. Size-wise, it was big, like a German shepherd but not a German shepherd.

Twenty or so feet behind the dog was a woman on horseback. She saw what was happening but didn't pick up her pace or seem particularly concerned. Meanwhile, I slowly backed up. "Bramble," the woman called, and I realized that she and I had run into each other twice before. The first time was near the pub. It was raining buckets and I'd heard her tell a woman who was racing toward her parked car that she needed to put her umbrella down. "My horse is afraid of umbrellas," she'd called.

The second time was a few months after that. I was walking up this same lane, in almost the same spot as I was in yesterday afternoon. I'd been picking up litter and she approached, saying, "You there, you need to put your plastic bag away. It's scaring my horse."

"Your horse is afraid of a plastic bag?"

"Yes," she said. "So put it away." What struck me was how imperious she was—on her high horse in every sense of the phrase. She didn't even say thank you when I did as she asked; she just rode on by in her velveteen helmet. She's in her mid-sixties, this woman, thin and booted.

"Bramble," she called again, not in a scolding tone but one

she might use when summoning him for dinner. The dog ran toward her, and as I stood there glaring, she said, "Don't you look at me like that."

I was like, "Excuse me?"

"He was barking because he was *frightened,*" she said.

How many times have I been walking down a road in the U.S. or France or England and had someone's dog race toward me, growling? Then the owner will call, "Don't worry, he doesn't bite!"

You, I always want to add. *He doesn't bite* you.

Dogs had had no problem ripping out part of Maja's arm or nipping my sister Gretchen in the face. One attacked Hugh in Paris a few years back while the owner stood there passively as if to say, *What he does while he's off the leash is none of my business.*

I resent the implication that everyone's supposed to know your dog and have an understanding of what makes him tick. The woman on the horse acted as though I had this coming. "You were standing by the edge of the road and that *scared* him," she said, as if my position were somehow perverse and I was supposed to be *under* the pavement rather than on top of it. Then, too, this wasn't her private lane. And wasn't Bramble supposed to be tethered?

"Lady," I said, "I don't know you *or* your fucking dog."

She said something in return, and I stuffed my earbuds back in, surprised to hear Robin Williams not doing a dozen different characters but just being himself and talking about things that mattered to him. Four years after the interview was taped, he killed himself, and knowing that made my listening to the conversation all the richer. I fully support a person's right to commit suicide—who are we to judge what depressed people go through on a day-to-day basis?—but I wish that before they hung themselves or put the handguns to their temples, they would knock off a few of the characters on my hit list. This woman on horseback, for instance. My hands shook all the way home.

"Well, you shouldn't have cursed at her," Hugh said when I told him about it.

"But she didn't even apologize."

"It doesn't matter," he said. "You shouldn't have used that language. It wasn't right."

Then I hated both him *and* her *and* horses *and* dogs when all I'd ever wanted was to take a walk on a beautiful late-summer afternoon.

September 15, 2014
Ho Chi Minh City, Vietnam

It was midnight by the time we checked into our hotel, and after setting down our bags, Hugh and I headed out for a short walk. "You want ladies?" a man asked fifty or so feet beyond the front door. "Girls? Young girls?"

I'm always shocked when someone offers me a woman. *Really?* I want to say. *Do I look like that guy?*

Apparently I do. So did Hugh on this occasion. "You want lady?" another man asked thirty seconds after we said no to the first one. We were out for ten minutes and were probably asked a dozen times if we wanted a woman. One guy offered women and drugs—"Anything you want"—so that was a nice change.

At around two we went to bed. I should have been beat, but I wasn't for some reason. At eight we went to the breakfast restaurant and were seated in the atrium overlooking the street. The Westerners were kind to the waitstaff, but the Asians were terrible. Two young women moved to another table after being seated and refused to look at their waitress while ordering, as did the Chinese guy who sat next to us. He had a shaved head and wore a towel around his neck. After demanding four hard-boiled eggs and some sausage, he put his earbuds in. The waitress asked if he wanted coffee or tea and he waved his hand at her as if to say, *You and I are finished.*

When the food arrived, he did not acknowledge the prompt service. Again he waved away the person who brought it. Then he poured some of his bottled water over the hard-boiled eggs, speared a sausage with his fork, and ate it held before his mouth like something on a stick.

September 16, 2014
Ho Chi Minh City

Yesterday was spent alternately napping and walking around. Crossing the street here is a real headache. There are red lights, but they don't mean anything, and people seem to honk just for the joy of it. The guidebook encourages one to wade into traffic—"Cars will go around you," it promises, "just don't make any sudden moves." Two-lane streets are bad enough but on the boulevards you're really putting your life on the line. After a midmorning coffee, we walked to the river. There's a promenade of cracked, uneven concrete along the banks and on it were many people who wanted to sell us barrettes or a watchband. Others offered to shine my new shoes, and when I said no, they pointed to the slightest of scuff marks and said they had no money.

The river was mud-colored and on the opposite bank stood six billboards. Half concerned themselves with the Communist Party and the other three advertised Heineken. Back in the thick of it, we passed countless men sprawled barefoot on motorcycles and scooters. They treated them like beds, many napping or talking on their phones. Every business seemed devoted to some small aspect of scooter or shoe repair. One shop fixed starters while another replaced wheels. At the market recommended by the guidebook, they sold shampoo and plastic pails and novelty T-shirts. As people called out to us and grabbed at our shoulders, I wondered where they lived.

At around one I started getting hungry. People were gathered at preschool-size tables on the street but I didn't understand what they were eating or how they had ordered it. Then we visited a market where something smelled so terrible I forgot I was hungry. When my appetite returned, we had lunch at a restaurant staffed by orphans. It was on the second floor of a colonial-style building in a high-ceilinged room with shutters on the windows. Behind us sat two Japanese girls, one of whom had a hunched back. Then an American family came in and took a table near the kitchen. There was music softly playing, and one of the songs was "Misty Blue," which I hadn't heard in years. Our waiter was named the Vietnamese word for "ten," as he was the tenth child born in his family.

"I have sisters name Four and Six," he said. Like a lot of the people we've dealt with here, Ten spoke English well. His accent, though, was so heavy I found it nearly impossible to understand him.

It was the same at dinner, which we ate on the second floor of the hotel. Again, we had the set menu, and for the second time that day I worried I was using the wrong sauce or making a fool of myself in some other way. I'm pretty sure, for example, that I ate one of the skewers my shrimp came on. The only thing I really felt confident about was the coconut ice cream, which arrived at the end of the meal. I complimented the waiter on it, and he kindly brought us a serving of sugarcane ice cream, on the house. It was presented in a single bowl with two spoons, so he must have known we were gay. The four straight men at the next table—three Americans and an Israeli—would have just stared at it, the way they might if it were served in a jockstrap.

September 29, 2014
Rackham
Yesterday was Viv Anderson's memorial luncheon, so at 11:00 I got out my bike and headed to Sutton. It was a good distance, lots of hills, and I arrived at the village hall to find a crowd of seventy or so people standing out front. A four-piece jazz band was playing in the parking lot and led the group up the road to the churchyard. I caught up with Gretchen along the way. She was talking to an old friend whose husband had had both his legs amputated due to poor circulation. Afterward the couple moved to London, and in time he died. "One keeps saying, 'I can't believe it,' though of course one does," Gretchen said, looking wonderful as always in her Egg dress with a light coat thrown over it.

The memorial marker is a plaque set into a stone wall. Oliver said a few words, then someone read a letter from Gretchen's sister, and we headed to the village hall for a luncheon. I sat at a table between two delightful women I didn't know. One had a husband on the other side of the room, and he moved over and joined us when the coffee was served. "I think they should remove seat belts from cars," he told me. "They should take away the airbags as well and replace them with sharp spikes. That'll teach people to be careful. As it is, they feel invincible, especially in these damned SUVs."

It's such a good idea.

October 14, 2014
Purchase, New York
The news I've been waiting on for over a decade arrived yesterday morning when Madame Sheppers called Steven and reported, sobbing, that her dog had died. Robinson was a miniature collie, and I could not bear his nonstop barking.

345

I'm praying she doesn't run out and replace him, but we'll see. Madame Sheppers is in her eighties now, and the daily walks might be a bit too much for her, given the five flights of stairs she has to climb. I feel bad that she's lost her beloved pet, but...yippee!

October 23, 2014
Blacksburg, Virginia

I flew into Roanoke yesterday afternoon and was met at the baggage claim by a tall, silver-haired man in his seventies. He wasn't dressed in a suit, the way most drivers are, and his car was tan, not black. I liked that he didn't ask how my flight was, and when I thanked him for it, he scrunched up his face, saying, "They's all the same, really, isn't they?"

At first we talked about the trees. I told him that in England we don't get the red leaves that they have in America, and he pointed to a stand of maples, saying, "There's you some red." We were in the mountains, and climbing. I asked what sorts of animals there were up here, and he said that just yesterday he'd passed a bear cub, dead, on the side of the road. "It musta somehow got away from its mama and been hit by a car. First time I ever seed a thing like that, but, oh, we got all kinds of things: deer, of course, bobcats, mountain lions sometimes, but no elk."

I asked why not, and he thought for a moment. "They flourish in the higher altitudes."

I was so surprised by his wording.

We talked about moose for a few minutes, and then he announced that Barack Obama hated America and had done everything in his power to destroy it.

"Is that so?" I asked.

"Yes, sir," he said. "That man hates this country. The fact is that he wasn't even born here."

"No?"

"No, sir. He was born in Kenya and went to college under his real name, which is Barry Saretto. He ain't even a Christian."

"So what?" I said. "Why does everyone in this country have to run for office on the back of a Bible?"

"He's the worst president America has ever had," the driver continued. "He's destroyed our economy and our whole way of life. We used to be a moral country. People used to look out for their neighbors and now they can't even pray. He's taken away all our freedom and left nothing but abortion."

"Really?" And I said the dumbest thing. "I love abortion."

November 13, 2014
Tulsa

At last night's book signing a young woman approached me, asking, "If you were a pedophile, and you knew you could be cured after having sex with a single baby, would you do it or would you continue on with a life of celibacy?"

It was a good question but, for me, an easy one. "Sex with the baby."

"But it would scar him for life."

"Not if he just blew me," I said. "I mean, you never said intercourse."

"That's true," she whispered.

"But he'd have to be white," I told her. "For me, it's a white baby or nothing."

Why did you have to take it there? her look seemed to say. Like it's fine to joke about sex with a baby, but the moment you bring race into it you have crossed the line, mister.

November 16, 2014
San Francisco

After breakfast yesterday morning, Hugh and I walked down Market Street in the direction of Sanchez, passing scores of mentally ill people who drooled and cackled and shook their fists at the sky. The city is an open-air psychiatric hospital. As we waited for a light to change, one man threw his empty beer can to the ground while another scowled at the oncoming traffic and cursed. Farther along we came upon two young women pushing carts. One shouted at the other, and as she stopped to repeat what she'd just said, I thought, *This is going to lead to a fistfight.* And indeed it did. What always surprises me is how quickly these things start and then pause, most often when each party is yanking on the other one's hair. It makes me think of the way stags joust. The two women would go at it, take a short breather, and then recommit themselves to their hatred.

November 25, 2014
Tallahassee, Florida

It was announced that charges would not be brought against the police officer who shot Michael Brown in Ferguson, Missouri. I don't understand how shooting an unarmed teenager multiple times can be justified and neither do a lot of other people, many of whom set fires. The news was broadcast on the lobby TV and it felt weird to return after dinner and hear the woman at the front desk, who was black and is forced to do such things, welcome me back.

November 30, 2014
Emerald Isle

The only discomfort on this most recent beach trip came on Friday evening. Someone mentioned Ferguson, Missouri, and Dad, probably repeating Rush Limbaugh, insisted that

Obama was using Charlie Rangel and Al Sharpton as his mouthpieces.

"How do you know?" I asked.

He shook his head. "Man, oh, man, everyone knows that." He took a bite of a biscuit Bob had made. "And who's that other black guy?"

"Bill Cosby?" Amy said.

"Gil Scott-Heron?" I asked.

"Stevie Wonder?" Gretchen called from the living room.

Lisa said, "Denzel Washington?"

"You know who I mean," Dad said. "He's got that son."

"Jesse Jackson?"

"He's the one. Always stirring up trouble."

December 1, 2014
Emerald Isle

Late yesterday morning Hugh laid out the little seascapes he's done since arriving on Emerald Isle. While he wasn't looking, I took a pen and wrote prices on the backs of them: $1.75, $2.15, etc. I think the most expensive went for $3.25.

He's gotten some sun, and it brings out the color of his eyes and the beautiful silver his hair has become. "What's it like to be so good-looking?" I asked him.

"I was just thinking the same thing," Gretchen said. She turned to me and asked, "How did you get so lucky?"

There must be a better way to phrase that, but she's right. I've always had boyfriends who are way more attractive than me. How did I do it?

December 10, 2014
London

I'd just walked through the door yesterday afternoon when

an Indian woman called and asked if I could answer some questions. "It will only take one minute, ma'am."

I told her I was a man and she forged ahead. "Is your house owned or rented?"

"Owned."

"What?"

"I own it."

"Let me say, ma'am, that you have a lovely voice."

"I'm a man."

"And how would you describe your work situation? Are you retired, employed, self-employed..."

"Self-employed."

"Oh, madame, how lucky you are. That has always been a dream of mine."

"I'm a man."

And on it went for well over a minute. Close to five, actually.

December 13, 2014
Bucharest, Romania

Our flight from Paris to Bucharest was full, and even at the airport, you could tell who was French and who was Romanian. There's a look that women have here, and I find it fascinating. First there's the makeup—so much you'd think they were backstage, ready to take part in a play. Their role is the villainess, hence the arched eyebrows and severe hairstyles. The overall effect is stunning, especially on someone over sixty. The Romanian men on our plane tended to be sloppy, and when they reached into the overhead bins—they all had carry-on suitcases—their sweaters rose, revealing big bellies. I had an aisle seat, Patsy was beside me, and at the window was an unkempt guy in his late thirties who picked his nose a lot and dropped the rolled-up boogers into the canyon between his armrest and the wall.

The flight lasted an hour and a half. During it, Patsy read the guidebook I'd downloaded while I studied my Pimsleur. The first words of Romanian I spoke were to the fellow at the passport counter. "Hello, sir. Good day! How are you?" It went over well and I tried it again ten minutes later, after we'd gotten our luggage and passed through customs. There, we were met by our guide and driver, Ion. *"Bună ziua domnule. Ce mai faceti!"*

Ion looked at Patsy and then back at me. "Oh," he said. "Okay. We go to the car, then." He was a nice-looking guy, around five nine, with a short stubble of hair. He wore jeans with a local version of Red Wing boots and was, I guessed (correctly), thirty-three years old. "Do people tell you you resemble James Franco?" I asked.

"Who is he?"

"An actor. Did you see *Planet of the Apes* or the one, I forget the title, where he cut his own arm off?"

"I don't know it."

Ion's English is pretty good. Most of the mistakes he makes have to do with verb conjugation; plants were "putted" all over the place, for instance. The building "rised" in 1920. Referring to a missing mirror on his passenger-side door he said, "It fell down," rather than "It fell off." No big deal. It's charming. I just don't see why my baby Romanian can't be equally charming. "Girls are going to laugh at you when you talk," he predicted.

"Why?" I asked. "Is my pronunciation that bad?"

I later learned that because Romania has so few immigrants and because few visitors bother to learn so much as the word for "thank you," they never get the pleasure of hearing their language mangled. It turned out that Ion was right: people did laugh at my Romanian, but never in a way that hurt my feelings. They were, by and large, the reactions I was hoping for, amused delight, for the most part. I'm like a dog walking on his hind legs—"Look at that!"

On the way into town we passed an Ikea and a massive hardware place called Brico Store. I noticed no litter whatsoever, not a can or bottle. Not so much as a tissue. Closer to town we saw a billboard for a Dove brand deluxe prawn ring, a wreath of shrimp with two different sauces in the middle. "Do you eat a lot of prawn rings?" I asked.

Later I looked at a sign on a massive concrete building and tried to make it out. "I'm afraid you are reading the pigeons," Ion said, at which point I realized the accent marks atop each letter were, in fact, alive.

I'd thought no one would show up for my bookstore event but the place was full. A few years back Marlena taught me to say "I shit in your mother's mouth" in Romanian, so I trotted that out and asked if, when getting their books signed, people could give me some equally good curses. "Things you might hear on an average day in your country." At the end of the night my list included the following:

I fuck your mother's cross.

I fuck your mother's dead.

I fuck your mother's Christ.

I fuck your mother's icon.

I fuck your mother's Easter.

I will make skis out of your mother's cross.

You should go back into your mother's cunt.

I fuck your mother's onion.

And the best:

I drag my balls across your mother's memorial cake, from cherry to cherry, and to each of the candles.

"Wow," said everyone I repeated that last one to. "There's nothing you can say after that!"

Of course, the curses showed up in my inscriptions.

"This book is for my mother, who loves owls," one young woman told me.

I fuck your mother's owls, I wrote.

"Perfect!" she said.

I loved the book signing. Everyone I met spoke beautiful English and eagerly answered all my questions. Afterward, eight of us headed to a restaurant housed in an old seed company. I walked beside a young woman who comes from a small town that's just large enough to have an airport and whose name translates to something like "Fucky." Her mother worked at the slaughterhouse there and now, at a very advanced age, has moved to Bucharest to be closer to her daughter. "How old is she?" I asked.

"Sixty-four!" the young woman said.

A dense fog had settled in during the bookstore event and I peered through it to the building we were walking toward. *Fuck you* was scrawled on the side of it. "Usually they write 'Suck my dick,'" said the young woman with the sixty-four-year-old mother.

In the restaurant we were given a private room; half was for smoking, and it was within spitting distance of the non-smoking half. By the time we left, three hours later, my eyes were burning and my clothing stank. It was worth it, though. They were a terrific group of people, very interesting. I learned while eating my salted mutton that the dog problem I'd anticipated had pretty much been solved. A great number of strays were killed last year; shot, if I'm not mistaken. I also learned of a pastry made of phyllo dough, nuts, and rose water called Jesus diapers.

December 19, 2014
Rackham

For the first time in what feels like ages, the sun is out. Yesterday it was wet and gray. I left the house at 1:30 thinking I could make it to Storrington by way of West Chiltington before 4:00, but I was wrong. It was just getting dark when a beautiful young woman with two equally beautiful daughters, one of whom wore braces on her teeth, stopped to say she'd twice seen me read in London. We talked for a minute, then half a mile up the road, with the aid of a flashlight, I found a strap-on penis. It was perhaps three inches long, and very realistic-looking. I thought of bringing it home but was convinced that if I put it in my knapsack, I'd get hit by a car. Therefore, it's in a trash can next to the bus stop.

I also found a bucket that someone had shit into.

2015

Late yesterday morning a monk seal flopped onto the beach behind the house we're renting. I saw it at eleven and then again at four when I joined Hugh and Gretchen for a swim. "A baby," people called it, though it seemed at least as long as I am. It was funny to watch it shift position, sometimes lying on its back with that strange hand-like flipper on its stomach. By that time of day there were only a half a dozen people about. One was a pretty young woman with a black Lab she was walking without a leash. She'd just passed the towel we were on when a newcomer arrived. She was a woman as well but much paler and older, in her early seventies maybe, with hair that was red in some places and white in others. "Hey," she called to the younger woman. "We got a seal on the beach so that dog of yours needs to be tethered."

"That's okay," the young woman said. "She doesn't bother the seals." She offered a quick, tight smile and headed toward the path that leads to the road. "Besides, I live here."

"Well, I live here too," snapped the older woman. "Asshole!"

A man who also looked to be in his early seventies came round the bend, and the woman with the red and white hair told him what had just happened. "She said, 'I live here,' and I said, 'Well, guess what? So do I!' Twenty-five years I've been on this island and this is the first time I've seen her."

The man and the woman got to talking about the seal. "Did you call it in?" she asked.

"Hours ago," he told her.

"Call it in?" I asked.

"To the seal patrol," the woman said. "This is a protected species. There are only nine hundred left, so when they beach, we need to make sure they're left alone. Without their sleep, these beauties are shark bait, so we need to keep the tourists from coming up and bothering them."

She reminded me of one of those self-proclaimed turtle protectors you see on Emerald Isle, the kind who force kids to destroy their sandcastles lest some hatchling get trapped in a moat. I'm not saying it's an unworthy pursuit, only that it calls for a certain degree of self-importance. Just as I thought this, the woman with the red and white hair cupped her hands around her mouth and yelled at a figure whose sun-ravaged skin looked like beef jerky, "Hey, you, back off from the seal!"

"It's all right," the man said. "That's my wife. She's been helping me stand guard."

"Well, okay, then," the woman said. "That's good. Excellent work."

February 20, 2015
Hilo, Hawaii

After checking into our hotel yesterday afternoon, Hugh and I took a walk to the center of town, which had an odd, frontier-like feel to it. There were fewer knickknack shops than I'd expected, fewer places selling ukuleles and puka-shell necklaces. We bought a shaved ice at a little stall and ate it on the lawn where a panhandler in a Hooters T-shirt played a plastic recorder.

A few doors down a thin man in his fifties sprawled in the

grass with a guitar and argued with a seven-year-old who was holding a newspaper and standing with his brother in front of a food store. "The news is just bullshit, man," the adult said. "Why are you reading that crap?"

The boys were pale and dressed in new-looking vacation clothes. "It's not...what you just called it," the seven-year-old said. "ISIS just killed three people!"

"Three, ha! China killed a billion people. How come you don't care about them? I'll tell you why—it's because they weren't Americans. It's because you think you're better than everyone else."

"Do not," the seven-year-old shot back.

"Do too," the full-grown man sitting on the ground said.

February 27, 2015
Nashville, Tennessee

Last night's signing lasted for five hours, and during it I met a man who asked me to inscribe a paperback for a friend of his. "He just for the second time peed in his wife's ass, if that'll help any," he said as he handed me the book.

I reached for my pen. "I'm sorry, but did you say *on* her ass?"

"Nope," he said. "In it. He peed *in his wife's asshole*."

I winced. "And for the second time?"

He nodded, and I thought that if I were this woman, there wouldn't have been a second time. That's the rule: Pee in my ass once and that's it.

Odder still was that the fellow handing me the book thought there was an inscription that went with this, something standard like *I'm sorry you're in the hospital* or *On the occasion of your forty-seventh birthday*. What do you write to someone who twice peed in his wife's ass?

That's why the signing lasted for five hours.

March 17, 2015
Rackham

While cleaning the road to Storrington I picked up a McDonald's bag. Its weight was unsettling, and inside I found, in addition to napkins and a Big Mac container, a rubber surgical glove filled with urine. *What on earth?* I thought, wondering how a person could pee into a glove and then tie it off while driving. I found a great deal of McDonald's trash yesterday, especially as it relates to the McNugget.

April 10, 2015
Harrisburg

"Are you going to church on Sunday?" I asked a woman at last night's book signing.

She looked at her husband and then back at me and said, "We, um...home-church."

April 12, 2015
York, Pennsylvania

At 9:45 yesterday morning, Marlena picked me up at my hotel and drove me to the Cracker Barrel, where we met up with her dad, her husband, one of her sisters, her brother-in-law, her nephew Alex, and her two nieces. It was a Saturday and the place was packed with large groups. At the long table next to ours sat four chubby kids and two women, one of whom was cradling a monkey dressed in baby clothes.

"It's a service animal," our waiter explained when we asked about it, adding that the customer comes in all the time and has trouble with anxiety. The woman's back was to me, so I saw her monkey only twice, and very briefly. It looked like one of those kids with premature aging disease, though smaller, of course, around the size of an adolescent house cat.

"I want to see it," six-year-old Alex said, fidgeting in his seat. "Make her turn around or something."

The woman, who had blond hair that fell loosely to her shoulders, moved like a celebrity—like someone who knew she was being watched—and it bothered me that when it came time for her to leave, she took great pains to conceal her monkey. "Where did it go?" Alex whispered. "Did she put it in her purse?"

She struck me as someone who wanted attention and then got all snippy when it came her way. I mean, really, if you don't want to be looked at, don't bring a monkey dressed in baby clothes into a family restaurant loaded with children on a Saturday morning.

April 15, 2015
Red Bank, New Jersey

Waiting for my suitcase at Newark yesterday, I thought of how great and startling it would be if a child's coffin appeared on the baggage carousel. A white one, with maybe a little blood on it. It would be interesting if a grieving couple dressed in mourning clothes stepped forward to collect it, but better still if the couple was laughing.

I was driven from Newark yesterday afternoon by a towering black fellow who until recently weighed five hundred pounds. "How tall are you?" he asked as we got under way.

"Five foot five," I told him.

"Child, I think I was *born* five feet five," he said, laughing. A few of his teeth were missing, and he had a slight lisp that was charming. I don't know how it came about, but on our walk to the car I learned that he has an ex-girlfriend named Tammy Santana.

God, that's a good name. I've had such good luck with drivers lately.

April 17, 2015
Atlanta

I was heading from the lobby to my room at the Four Seasons yesterday when a tall black fellow, maybe thirty-five years old, exited the elevator. On seeing me, he held the door open, and after I thanked him, he stepped back inside. I'd later realize that he hadn't pressed a floor button, but at the time I was oblivious.

"So how's your stay?" he asked.

"Great," I told him. "They put me in the Presidential Suite!"

"Wow!"

"I didn't do anything to deserve it," I said. "They just gave it to me!"

The guy cocked his head and smiled. "Well, you seem like a nice person. You have a nice face, a friendly face."

I said something like "Oh" or "Gosh."

"You have a good spirit," he continued. "I bet you never meet a stranger."

"Oh, I meet them all the time."

He smiled wider. "What I mean is that they probably don't stay strangers."

Again, I said, "Oh," or "Hmmm."

"Are you gay?" he asked, lowering his voice on the last word, though it was just the two of us in the elevator.

I told him I was, and he said, again very quietly, "Want to hang out?"

"That's all right," I told him. "I'm fine."

We had reached my floor, the nineteenth. My suite was right there, across from the elevator, and just as I realized he hadn't pushed a button, we were standing at my door. "I'll be honest with you," he said. "My parents are staying at this hotel. My car just broke down and I need eighty dollars to fix it. Can you give me eighty dollars?"

"Oh, no, thank you," I said, thinking, *Your parents aren't staying here.*

"I'm not offering to give *you* money," the guy said. "I want *you* to give it to *me.*"

"Oh, no, thanks."

"So you're not going to do that for me?"

"Nope." I opened my door then. "Bye!" Through the peephole I watched him summon the elevator. It arrived and after I was sure that it had left, I raced downstairs to tell on him, realizing as I related the story how complicit, or at least astoundingly naive, I sounded. "I told him I was in the Presidential Suite and when he asked if I was gay I said, 'Well, sure...'"

April 27, 2015
Champaign, Illinois

I'm wondering if there has been a contest offered on my Facebook page: See who can be the most outrageous at a book signing. On every tour there's someone, but lately it's so consistent I'm starting to get suspicious. The other night it was a woman who asked for a strand of my hair. She looked normal enough and so I said, "Okay, sure." She then proceeded to yank out an entire fistful. Aside from it hurting, I couldn't believe my scalp had surrendered it so easily—and so much!

In the next city it was the woman with tattooed wrists who reached over and would have taken half my dinner if I hadn't snatched my plate away, but last night's kook is the hands-down winner. Again it was a woman—the last person in line. She was a few years younger than me, dressed in a business suit, and she started by saying, "Well, finally!" Her books were in a tall stack and I'd just started signing them when she handed me five fresh hundred-dollar bills loosely held together by a rubber band.

"What's this?" I asked.

"It's money," she said. "It's for you."

"I can't accept this!" I told her.

"Sure you can. Besides, it's nothing to me. My husband's a surgeon and won't even come to our kid's parent-teacher conferences. 'Are you kidding?' he says. 'An hour of my time? That's ten thousand dollars!'" She bent forward and nudged the money closer to me. "I've been very fortunate."

"Well, so have I," I said.

"Just take the money." She sighed. "Everyone else does. My kid's doctor, for instance. My son is autistic and will throw up if he sees you eating potato chips. Can you believe it—if he sees *another person* eating one! Then there's my brother, who's schizophrenic, but that's another story. But anyway, take the money."

"I don't want it," I said, thinking that while my former twenty- or even thirty-year-old self might possibly have believed I'd one day tour the country reading in theaters, there's no way he'd imagine me turning down five hundred dollars, especially when the other person kept insisting. What my former self didn't know is that it's never really free. There's always something attached to it.

"I just thought we could maybe hang out," the woman continued. "Even if I just walk you from the desk of your hotel to your car tomorrow morning. But you don't even have to do that. We could write or talk on the phone or whatever. So, please, take the money."

Adam, who produced last night's show, stepped in just then, saying, "We really need to get going."

"Oh, shut up," the woman said.

"Now you've crossed the line," he told her.

"I'm sorry," she said. "Please don't—"

"That's it. I'm going to have to ask you to leave."

She started to argue and I slipped the money into one of her signed books and placed it back in her pile, which she took with her when she left. "I messed up, and here it meant so much to me," she said as she walked out the door. "Now I'm going to cry."

April 28, 2015
Chicago

While checking into the Ritz-Carlton yesterday morning I told the desk clerk about the run-down Marriott I'd stayed in a few days ago in Cedar Rapids. "I walked into the room and there was a toenail, the entire thing, sitting on my desk." Then I added, just to creep him out, "At least, it tasted like a toenail."

Honestly, I hadn't immediately known what it was. A toenail on a toe you recognize right away, but when you see it out of context, lying on a flat surface between the phone and the desk lamp, it takes a few minutes.

April 30, 2015
Oklahoma City, Oklahoma

"How are we this afternoon?" a woman named Renée asked as I settled into her barber chair yesterday afternoon.

"Do you have a godchild?" I asked.

"Me?" she said, as if it should be evident. "Goodness, no. I got my hands full with my own kids." There had been, I learned, four of them, but now there were only three. "Becky was the biggest blessing I ever had, even in her wheelchair, even with all her troubles. Doctors said she wouldn't live past two months but she made it seventeen years!"

Becky, she explained, had no brain stem, or had a battered one. Or maybe her head hadn't developed properly. Regardless, she couldn't walk or talk or swallow. "She sure could smell french fries though," Renée said. "Sometimes for a treat I'd let her suck on one." She showed me a picture on her phone: a child of two, laughing. "So don't tell me miracles can't happen."

Renée was around my age, dark-haired and thin. "You know what I love?" she asked as she trimmed my eyebrows. "Giving perms. I wish they'd come back."

"Well, they have to eventually," I said. "I mean, don't they?"

"Are you okay to walk through the scanner?" a TSA agent asked me this morning. She shouted the question, the way you would to a very old person, and I wondered what might have possibly happened between yesterday, when I looked my age, and this morning, when I apparently didn't.

May 9, 2015
Eureka, California

There was a Starbucks-type place next to my San Francisco hotel and I was in it on Thursday afternoon when a street person entered. He'd panhandled enough money for a small coffee, and the young woman behind the counter upped his order saying, loudly, the way you might when you want to be overheard and subsequently admired, "I'm giving you a large instead!"

The street person did not say thank you. Rather, he took his coffee to the milk station, where he poured a good deal of half-and-half onto the countertop. Then he tore open a dozen sugar packs. Some he emptied into his palm and lowered his face to, the way a horse might, and others he dumped into his cup, the end result being that it got everywhere. Mixing it involved at least a dozen stirrers, which he left on the counter in the puddle of half-and-half and sugar that was dripping onto the floor as he stepped back outside.

May 21, 2015
Emerald Isle

We had the fellow across the street over to dinner last night. Lee lives in Maryland and tries to spend at least ten days a month at his beach house. The rest of the time it's rented out.

"And what's that like?" I asked.

"One damn thing after another," he said. "Someone will complain, 'The dishwasher's broken,' and I'll be like, 'Yes, because you broke it!' Then there are the comments, right? One guy wrote in our guest book, 'I was shocked by your outdoor shower.' I was thinking, *How surprising can it be? I mean, you're at the beach, for God's sake.* Then I went out to wash up and when I touched the handle for the hot water, I got thrown clear across the room."

June 12, 2015
Bradford, England

"Have you ever been stabbed?" I asked people as they came through the signing line on Monday night in Nottingham.

"I was," said a fellow with noticeably big hands. "They got me in the back with the sharpened tip of an umbrella ten years ago when I was working as a bouncer at a nightclub."

"I almost was," said a retired social worker who'd once been threatened with a kitchen knife.

"Well, yes and no," a teacher told me. "It was with a compass point, but the student apologized afterward."

On Tuesday in Leicester, I picked up where I'd left off.

"Does a dart in the head count?" one woman asked.

"I'd say it does," said a man I repeated this to last night in Bradford. He'd never been stabbed but was once glassed on a Greek island. That, he explained, is when someone hits you with a broken bottle or, in his case, a broken mug. It took over thirty stitches to close the wound.

"Have you been stabbed?" I asked a young woman a few places behind him.

"No," she said. "But I did once stick my finger into a Mexican dolphin's blowhole."

I'm not sure how this answered my question, but it did, and then some.

June 19, 2015
Rackham

On Wednesday night a baby-faced twenty-one-year-old white man entered the Emanuel AME Church in Charleston, South Carolina, and killed nine people, saying, "I have to do it. You rape our women and are taking over our country. You have to go." He then got into his car, which had a Confederate-flag plate on the front of it, and drove away. He was caught the next day in Shelby, North Carolina, and identified as Dylann Storm Roof. An article I read yesterday quoted one of his high-school classmates as saying, "He used drugs heavily a lot."

I'm not sure how that's wrong, but it is somehow.

After reading about the arrest in this morning's *Times,* I turned to an article about the summer solstice Lychee and Dog Meat Festival set to take place in Yulin, China. When it comes to eliciting outraged reactions, nothing else comes close, not even the church shooting. "Dogs are people too," someone named Paw wrote in response to the article. "Not human people, but people nevertheless."

Is there such a thing as a nonhuman person?

August 26, 2015
Copenhagen, Denmark

Over dinner last night at a place called U Formel ("Oof Ormell") I learned about a Danish man who had recently killed a rabbit live on the radio. "Listeners complained afterward that they were traumatized," said Charlotte, a woman my age who works with my publisher. "His point was that they're murdered every day in the slaughterhouse, so how was this any different?"

I guess it's a question of doing something in the place where it's not usually done. You don't shit on the floor at the airport or practice archery in a library, so his point seems pretty weak to me. The restaurant was fancy, and while eating I learned that having sex with animals was only very recently outlawed in Denmark.

"So it was okay before now?" I asked.

My companions looked at each other and shrugged. "I think it was always...frowned upon," Susanne, my publisher, said. "Law-wise, I guess the government had other things to get to first."

The second of yesterday's three interviews was canceled, so in the hour and a half that we now had free, Susanne and I went shopping. One of the places on my list was the luggage store I'd passed on my walk last night. In its window was a rolling suitcase with leather trim, expensive, but the sticker read MADE IN EUROPE, which means it was probably cheaper here than it would be in the U.S. The person who waited on me was perhaps in her early sixties and had a big gap between her front teeth, just like I do. The suitcase I wanted was in the window, and though she had to move things in order to get it, the woman remained talkative and cheerful, asking what had brought me to Copenhagen and wondering how long I'd be staying.

The more energy a salesclerk expends to show me something, the more obligated I feel to buy it. Once the woman had freed the suitcase, though, and I'd walked back and forth, testing the wheels and feeling the weight of it, I still wasn't sure. Did I really need this thing? What would I do with my old suitcase?

Sensing my indecision but not pressuring me in any way, the woman led me to the other side of the room. "Here," she said, "why don't you look at yourself standing next to it in the mirror."

"Do people do that?" I asked.

"All the time," she told me. "Please, feel free!"

It was such a silly invitation I couldn't possibly turn it down. And so I stood before the mirror and struck a number of poses, my favorite being the one where you touch the suitcase with one hand and raise the other in order to hail a cab. "Taxi!" I said.

I imagined the driver saying, *What nice luggage you have! Was it made in Europe?*

And then quick, before I could change my mind, I said, "I'll take it!"

One of the odd things I learned yesterday is that the Danes have no word for "please." Susanne told me this in a cab from the television station. Later, at a department store, I learned that Danish ghosts say *bøh* ("buh") rather than boo. It's so lackluster. *Bøh*. Who's that going to scare?

September 10, 2015
Imerovigli, Greece

The heat here is startling. Shocking. It's an affront. Hugh and I are staying in a cave overlooking a volcanic crater filled with seawater. I'm at a table on our private terrace, next to our private plunge pool, the same spot I was in late yesterday afternoon when I learned that Madame Sheppers died. It happened three days ago. A heart attack, apparently. Up to the end, she colored her hair dark brown. It was done on the cheap and looked like paint. She also continued to leave notes everywhere—*Please make sure you close this door behind you,* etc.

My only beef with her, really, was that dog of hers, Robinson. I had been delighted to hear that he'd died and happier still to learn she would not replace him. Now the apartment will be sold. It's worth a fortune, though, according to Hugh, it's a wreck, a warren of small cramped rooms. Because her place is so high up and we have no elevator, the person who eventually buys it will probably be young and, perhaps, loud. There's a chance—and a good one—I'll long for the days when Madame Sheppers and her yapping dog were still upstairs from me.

September 11, 2015
Oia ("Ee-yah"), Greece
One of the things Hugh brought with him to Greece is the ridiculously oversize newsboy cap we bought in Japan last year. It's dough-colored, as big as a manhole cover, and embroidered with names like *Litter Bug, Violet, Mary Jo,* and *Stinny.* I'm thinking that should be *Stinky* and that *Litter Bug* should have read *Jitter Bug,* but they're inside out anyway and aren't the part that grabs attention.

"It looks like something a Dutch painter might have worn," someone observed yesterday. Others just stare in stunned silence.

"Welcome back," said our waiter at Katina's last night.

"How do you think he remembered us?" Hugh asked from beneath what looked like an uncooked pizza. I have to hand it to him—he wears it with confidence and marches ahead, oblivious to the stares and comments.

"Did you see that man's hat?" a child asked yesterday morning.

"Shhhh," his parents hissed. They in their baseball caps, so bland, so un–with it.

September 13, 2015
Oia

I got a lot of political questions during last night's Q and A, which is typical when touring in another country, especially when there's an election coming up. "What do you think of Donald Trump?" a Greek person asked, and I wasn't sure where to begin. I first became aware of him in the late '80s when Alma, the Lithuanian woman I was working for at the time, bought his book *The Art of the Deal* and decided that he was wonderful. A short while later I saw him on *Oprah,* and ever since then he's always been in the background, this ridiculous blowhard, part showman and part cartoon character. I see his presidential bid as just another commercial for himself. It wouldn't surprise me if he were to name the Hamburglar as his running mate. So I said that onstage and then had to explain who the Hamburglar was.

September 20, 2015
Rackham

One of the closing questions during this week's Republican debate was "What woman would you put on the ten-dollar bill?" John Kasich chose Mother Teresa, who turned her back on money and devoted her life to the poor, while Marco Rubio, Ted Cruz, and Donald Trump all chose Rosa Parks, apparently not knowing that she used to attend meetings of the Communist Party and was on the board of Planned

Parenthood, an organization that Cruz in particular is determined to defund.

October 3, 2015
Rackham

I learned while finishing Mike Paterniti's new book that the great Greek poet and playwright Aeschylus (525–456 BC) died when an eagle mistook his bald head for a rock and dropped a tortoise on it, hoping it would crack the shell and allow him easy access to the meat. I read that and thought, *Eagles make mistakes?* How had I come to think they were infallible?

October 22, 2015
Portland, Maine

Twenty-five years ago today, Lilia Montero took me to Canal Street, where I met Hugh. I knew on seeing him that I would make him my boyfriend. I don't think I knew it would last so long, especially during those first few years on Thompson Street when we were fighting so much. The only thing standing between us and a fiftieth anniversary is age. In another twenty-five years I'll be eighty-three and probably dead, hit by a car, most likely. But let's not think of that today.

October 23, 2015
Washington, DC

The car that picked me up yesterday took me directly to the White House. There I hooked up with David Evans and David Litt, the twenty-nine-year-old speechwriter who'd invited me to lunch. He's a bright, slightly built guy, baby-faced and serious.

After going through a scanner and presenting our IDs, twice, we were led to the Navy Mess, a small, wood-paneled restaurant located in the West Wing next to the Situation Room.

There we were told that if we wanted Chocolate Freedom—a dessert—we'd have to put in an early order. There were specials and a regular menu. I chose a salad with shrimp on it, served with a green goddess dressing. It was like something you'd get at the Sheraton and was served with tortilla chips rather than bread.

Still, though, the West Wing! David Litt was working on a speech Obama would deliver to the National Association of Police Chiefs. It involved a good deal of research, of contacting people and finding out what their concerns were. Some of his talking points were being critiqued, so he kept his BlackBerry on the table and would look at it every few minutes as I rambled on, doing my little David Show.

After lunch, we were led to another building, where I was introduced to a number of other speechwriters, all of whom were young and several of whom had pierced noses. They wrote for senior staff or Obama or Michelle, who was roundly adored. The questions they asked me were really thoughtful, and they all seemed to be actually listening.

When it seemed time to wrap up, we wrapped up. David led me outside and just as we hit the sidewalk, a Secret Service man told us to stand back. "POTUS is coming," David Litt said. I looked at him with my head cocked. "The president," he explained.

And there he was, all of a sudden, maybe twenty feet away, tall and smiling. I tell people that he looked at me and waved, but David Evans swears the wave was most definitely directed at him.

"The president!" we said. I thought I might cry. After he went by, we were led past the Oval Office. "Lower your voice," David Litt whispered. Not that we were loud; it's just what he has to say. Then we were outside the compound where a number of tourists were standing around. I went to a plump woman with jeans on and said, "We just saw the president. We had lunch in the West Wing, and we saw him! We did!"

The driver who picked me up at the airport yesterday was black and in his sixties, wearing a flat-topped cap and listening to a live broadcast of the latest Benghazi inquisition. This is the third time Hillary Clinton has been forced to testify, which means being interrupted while congresspeople compete for sound bites. "Four Americans lost their lives, and you think this is *funny*? You think it's *nothing*?"

I had the same driver this morning. "What a bunch of assholes," he said, referring to the Republicans. "She showed them, though, she kept it together. Eleven hours of that bullshit and she didn't flinch."

We speculated on what Obama might do after leaving office and he said that whatever it was, it'd be a damn sight better than what Bush had done. "His presidential library ain't nothing but a coloring book and a box of crayons."

November 1, 2015
Chicago

Over dinner last night, Lisa turned to Adam. "Are you familiar with a newspaper called the *Onion*?" she asked.

"Of course," he said.

"Well, I didn't know what it was, and I read an article claiming that in order to save money, schools in America were going to eliminate the past tense."

"Oh God," Adam said, and he covered his mouth the way he almost always does when he laughs.

"After I finished it, I phoned my husband and said, 'This is the last straw.' Because I used to teach, and the way budgets are being cut nowadays, this seemed entirely possible to me."

"How do you save money by eliminating the past tense?" Adam asked.

"I don't know," Lisa said. "I guess I didn't think that far."

Breakfast was taken at the same place we went to yesterday, only this morning we were waited on by a young man instead of a woman. He might have been in his late twenties and was tall and powerfully built with black curly hair and a wavy beard that was four inches long. His lips were well defined, and his mouth was oddly small, almost like a child's. The fellow spoke with an accent I couldn't quite place, so as he handed us our menus, I asked where he was from.

"Iraq," he said. "I have been in the United States for one year and a half."

"Are you an actor?" I asked. "Have you been in the newspaper? I feel like I know you from somewhere."

He stood there for a moment, helpless, and then went to fetch our coffees.

All through our meal it drove me crazy. "Where have I seen that guy?" Our food was delivered, and just as I was finishing, it came to me. "You know who he looks like? Neptune, the Roman god of the sea."

"Oh my goodness," Lisa said. "You're right!"

"It's his build coupled with his beard and his tiny mouth," I told her.

She nodded. "The spitting image."

"You know how yesterday's waitress drew a smiley face on our check?" I said. "I bet he draws a trident."

Lisa laughed. Then she looked out the window and told me that her ears itched.

"Then scratch them," I said.

"I mean on the inside," she explained. "Where I can't get at them."

We had a lot to do this morning, so I caught our waiter's attention and made the international symbol for "Check, please." It's supposed to resemble a hand writing something, but perhaps to him, it looked like a person drawing the waves.

"Oh, Poseidon," Lisa said as we left.

I pointed out that Poseidon was the Greek god of the sea while our waiter had been the Roman one. "Isn't it great that we know that?" I asked as we walked back to our hotel. "Or, I mean, great that *I* do? Who says an elementary-school education is worthless."

Lisa zipped up her jacket. "Not me. I used to teach."

November 13, 2015
Spokane

I was in a murderous temper yesterday. Part of it was lack of sleep, part was general tour fatigue, and part was left over from the night before, when the producers in Olympia stuck me in a sweltering black box for my book signing. Adam was supposed to collect me in Spokane at around noon but his flight from O'Hare to Denver was canceled, so instead he sent a car service to pick me up. The driver, a stout woman in her early thirties, met me at the baggage claim, and when she asked how my flight was, I knew it was going to be a long ride. It's not her fault, but I've had it with small talk. The same lines day after day. I just can't do it anymore.

I never caught her name, this woman. She wore a flat-topped cap and a hideous tan dress that looked like she'd made it herself in the dark. On her left shin was a tattoo that was perhaps four inches high and seemed fairly fresh. "What is it exactly?" I asked.

"Well, an anchor, obviously, surrounded by some scripture."

"Hmmm," I said.

She smiled. "I see you didn't bring the sunshine with you!"

I gritted my teeth and was quiet until we got into her car, a big SUV that smelled like a Yankee Candle shop. "Do you sew?" I asked as we headed into town.

"Me? Gosh, no," she said. "But that's a funny question."

I stayed at the Davenport. "How's your day going?" the check-in clerk asked.

"I've been here before" was how I answered.

"Well, welcome back. I wish you'd brought us some sunshine!"

I moaned.

This morning at breakfast I was escorted to a table by a beautiful young hostess. "How are you?" she asked.

I said nothing.

"How are you?"

The third time she asked, I told her that I was no longer answering that question. "It's just not important," I said.

She gave me the look people do when they work in the service industry and need to tell someone, as subtly as possible, that he or she is being an asshole.

I returned her look with one of my own that said, *Actually, you're the asshole.*

She walked away and as I lowered my napkin to my lap, I noticed that my fly was down. *Of course,* I thought.

Adam was originally going to drive me to the airport at 8:20 this morning, but instead he changed his flight, so I took a car driven by the same woman I had yesterday. "How was your stay?" she asked.

"Okay."

"How was the show?"

"Fine."

We were silent for a few minutes, and then I apologized for being in a bad mood. "I think I've been on tour too long," I told her. "I just can't take the small talk anymore. Here it is, not even eight-thirty and I've already been asked how I am six times."

She nodded.

"It's just a lazy question," I said. "Why not ask, I don't know, 'Have you ever donated bone marrow?' If the person you're talking to is in a bad mood, it'll still come back to bite you, I suppose. I guess there's just no way to win."

"I see your point," the woman said. "I'm not an intellectual like you, so maybe I wouldn't put it that way, but I understand what you mean."

"I'm not an intellectual," I assured her. "Far from it."

We were quiet again, and then I asked what she planned to do for Thanksgiving.

"I'm thinking I'll get one of those kits," she said. "The kind that has everything in them—the turkey and stuffing and so forth—and then in the day I'll maybe play football."

"You play football?" I asked.

"Just tag," she said. "Our family does it every year. I got boys."

She seemed so young then. "How many?"

"Two," she said. "One seven and the other eight."

I asked their names and after she told me, and after I had winced, she turned onto the road that led to the Alaska Airlines terminal. "My husband died nine months ago, so the holidays, they're hard. I'm not sure if I should do the same things we did last year or try something different, you know."

If she were savvy, she'd say this every time she dropped someone off at the airport. It's what I'd do—claim my husband just died and rake in the tips. But she wasn't like me. She wasn't a snob or a grump, just a young widow in an ugly dress who had two children and was trying to put one foot in front of the other. God, do I feel like an asshole.

November 21, 2015
Reno, Nevada

I got to LAX earlier than I expected yesterday and decided to have lunch there instead of in Reno, where I'd be trapped in a sad casino hotel. There was a place not far from my departure gate, so I took a seat at the counter and ordered a salad. On one side of me a young woman fiddled with her phone, and on the other, a young man did the same. He was well dressed without being dressed up, and eating a small pepperoni pizza. When he walked away leaving half of it, I looked over and thought, *Why not?* If I didn't finish it, it would just be thrown away, and why waste food?

The real question was whether I wanted pizza or, rather, all the calories that came with it. I'd had a soft ice cream cone the day before in San Francisco, and wasn't that enough? Just as I decided one slice wasn't going to kill me, the fellow returned from what I guessed was the bathroom and picked up where he'd left off.

What would he have thought if he'd come back and found me finishing his meal? I wondered. Even if it wasn't all of it, even if I'd taken just one slice, he'd have looked over and known it was me. That's where being old comes in handy. *I thought it was mine,* I could have said. *Aren't you me when I was your age?*

November 30, 2015
Emerald Isle

I heard yesterday that the day after Thanksgiving is the busiest time of the year for plumbers, who refer to it as "Brown Friday."

December 12, 2015
Lisbon, Portugal

After checking into our hotel, Patsy and I reunited with Carlos, who is unfortunately more of a tour guide than a driver. I had a list of stores we wanted to go to, but every three minutes he'd stop the car and say, "David, turn to your right. Do you know what you're looking at?"

"A statue."

"Yes, but of who?"

I whimpered, thinking, *Do I really have to care?*

At one point he showed us the bullfighting arena that's been turned into a mall. "As bad as people think it was, we never killed the animal in public view the way they do in Spain. Instead, here, we would do it backstage."

Americans think that bullfighting is savage and backward, but if you could do it with guns I'm sure we'd be all for it. "Can you imagine?" I said to Patsy. "The bull would be released and someone with a sawed-off deer rifle would blow its front legs off."

She can't bear to *hear* about things like that and covered her ears.

Meanwhile, Carlos had moved on. "David, look to your left..."

Dinner was taken at the hotel restaurant. "The chef won Best in the City in 2013," we were informed as we took our seats. Our food was good but at the same time ridiculous. "What was that?" I asked after eating what looked and tasted like a miniature storm cloud.

"That was a sponge made from bread and squid ink," I was told. Ten courses and nothing was larger than a domino. Still, the room was pretty with its brick vaulted ceiling. It was lively. While eating, Patsy told me about her trip to China. "We had a driver and his car was really dirty. Everything everywhere was." She paused, then asked, "Do you know your eyes are twitching? When did that start?"

"Third grade," I told her.

December 20, 2015
Rackham

One of the documentaries Mike Sacks recommended to me last week is about the punk-band leader GG Allin, who was born, like me, in 1956 but died in 1993. His music seemed sort of beside the point. It was just a noise to be made while inviting people's hatred. In one part of the movie, when he's playing at the Loeb Center at NYU, he punches a girl in the stomach and throws her to the ground. He's naked at the time, and his dick is as thin as a pencil. Later, at another show, he's naked again. This time he squats with his back to the audience and defecates onto the stage. What kind of mind would then think, *No, this is not enough. I must now rub my stinking feces onto my face and torso. Then I need to throw them at the audience that has paid to come see me?*

What would Tony Bennett make of this? I wondered, watching as people fled. I mean, you'd have to be crazy to do that. Then he died of a heroin overdose and had an open-casket funeral with no makeup on. His face was brown and bloated. He wore no trousers, and his hands were arranged so that they both touched his dick.

I went to bed feeling filthy and had a dream that I ran into Julia Roberts at a bar and told her about the documentary I'd just watched. "Hmmm," she said, and she wrote *GG Allin* on the script she'd been sitting there reading.

December 25, 2015
Rackham

It's so warm in New York that confused flowers are starting to bloom. Trees are budding. "Do you think toads are waking up?" I asked Hugh in the kitchen this morning.

Leslie was at the table a few feet away, looking at Facebook. "I would imagine so," she said.

It seems so...doomy, the heat. A tornado ripped through the Bible Belt yesterday and killed a number of people. Here in England, though, where no one seems to care about God, the weather is fine. Yesterday morning it rained. A while later it tantrummed, but for the most part it was beautiful and at least cold enough to see your breath. In the morning I scrambled to get the house ready for Frank and Scott.

Their train arrived at around two, and while Hugh headed to the station to pick them up, Leslie and I walked to Amberley for the annual Follow the Star Nativity procession. It was a lovely walk and we arrived to find seventy or so people gathered in front of the bus shelter. Stragglers trotted toward us from freshly parked cars and I thought of Shirley Jackson's "The Lottery."

The event featured the Amberley Singers and involved the audience on four numbers, starting with "The First Noel." We got the lyrics after dropping change into a bucket the vicar was carrying that had *Freedom from Torture* written on the side of it. Then we moved with the crowd from one house to another. At each stop, a brief skit was performed. Shepherds appeared early on, and while the upper two-thirds of them was convincing enough, they lost me every time on the footwear. "Sneakers?" I whispered to Leslie.

That was nothing. Both Mary and Joseph had glasses on. We came upon them after we'd sung "We Three Kings," which here includes the lyric "Myrrh is mine; its bitter perfume / Breathes a life of gathering gloom / Sorrowing, sighing, bleeding, dying / Sealed in a stone-cold tomb."

They've got to be making this up, I thought. What Christmas song has the phrase *stone-cold tomb* in it? And is *sorrowing* even a word?

The procession ended in the Lyons' barn, where mulled wine and star-shaped cookies were served. While standing there, I met Mrs. Lyon, an American, very beautiful and charming. Her husband, David, had played one of the Three Kings and still had his crown on. He wanted a picture of everyone assembled, and as he climbed a ladder with his camera, his wife rushed to steady it, crying, "My king!"

Children raced across the gravel drive, the carolers congratulated one another, and as the sun began to set, we walked to the pub and got a corner table beside the bar. They were playing the sorts of Christmas songs I'm not too crazy about— pop, mainly by boy bands—but I'd had enough of the others for one day. In my office before lunch, I'd wept to the Roches' "Star of Wonder." Then I walked into the kitchen to find Leslie bawling to "Have Yourself a Merry Little Christmas," the saddest holiday song there is. Her mother died a few months ago, so it hit her extra-hard. I'd cried to it the night before while walking in the moonlight across the grounds of the Parham estate. It makes me ache for the Christmases we had in the seventies and eighties, all of us young and together— high, most often—our whole lives stretched before us. Mom was still alive, and Tiffany. I wonder how we manage to live with such, well, sorrowing, then remember that twenty years from now, this might be the Christmas I pine for. Hugh and I together, both of us fit and untroubled, surrounded by dear friends.

December 27, 2015
Rackham

Because of the holiday there were no trains yesterday. Hugh arranged a cab to pick up Sam and Jeff at Heathrow. The driver was to meet them at the exit you pass through after clearing customs, and on being told to look for two men, he asked, "Are they flamboyant?"

"I'm pretty sure that qualifies as a microaggression," I said to Frank. "I mean, really!"

December 28, 2015
Rackham

My father went to Paul's for Christmas and everyone winced when a friend of Sandra's dropped by. The woman had just lost 165 pounds, and on hearing it, Dad said, not "Congratulations" or "That must have been tough," but rather "I'll bet you're a real sight to see in the shower."

And people accuse me of having no filter.

2016

January 3, 2016
Tokyo

While searching for somewhere to eat last night we passed a salon called the Joker of Hair. Later we came upon a restaurant that offered fried chicken knees.

"Do you think they mean 'legs'?" Amy asked.

The place we eventually settled on was on the third floor of an eight-story building. "Isn't it scary when you can't tell if you're looking at the menu upside down or right-side up?" Gretchen said. We were given a private room, and she was delighted to realize that the ashtray-looking bowl on the table was, in fact, an ashtray.

I got up at one point to use the men's room, and when I returned, Amy was saying to Hugh, "Well, just tell him that you want to break up, then." She does this a lot, pretends to be engaged in a conversation I wasn't meant to hear. "AIDS isn't the death sentence it used to be, I'm sure he'll be fine with it," etc.

January 23, 2016
Melbourne

Pat picked me up at 8:30 yesterday morning and took me to a number of places that have special meaning to her. With us was her friend Laurie, who's on a hundred-day shopping fast. "It's to teach me to appreciate the things I already have," she said. "I can buy groceries and food, but nothing else—no clothes or music. Not even newspapers."

On our route we passed the campground where Pat and her family used to spend their summers. "Before Dad went to prison," she said. It was a dismal-looking place, though that probably had a lot to do with the weather. Still, you could see how a kid would like it. Over our coffees Pat showed us pictures. "I was a plain girl," she said, handing me a blurry black-and-white photo. "Plain and fat." She showed me a snapshot of her dad in his thirties, a handsome man with thick, oiled hair. "A charmer," she called him. It came out "chama," rhyming with *llama*.

Pat grew up poor. Her father was a butcher and they'd have been all right were he not also an alcoholic. We talked about her new boyfriend, Mark, and when we moved on to relationships in general, Laurie said from the back seat that she gives her wife, Louise, two minutes of uninterrupted listening time a day.

"Is that all, darl?" Pat asked.

"No," Laurie said. "That's just the *uninterrupted* listening time."

Lunch was taken in a small hotel in the port city of Queenscliff, which was where we got off the ferry. It had been a short, pretty ride. "Pretend the sun is shining," Pat said. "Pretend the water is sparkling and you're looking out at seals and dolphins."

We'd booked lunch for 1:30 but the place was almost empty, so they took us early with no problem. Both women ordered fish and chips that came with an aioli sauce Pat liked but Laurie didn't. She left the table to throw up and when she returned, Pat said, "Feel better, darl?"

Laurie said yes.

"We usually do after a nice chunder."

We then got onto the subject of a conference Pat had attended. She said that after the first day, the grievance committee requested that people refrain from applauding, as it stirred anxiety in certain attendees. "We were told to use twinkle hands," Pat said, meaning what the English call jazz hands. Then someone complained about that too and people were asked to respond with a thumbs-up instead.

On the final day of the conference there was a scheduled seminar on menopause. Then the trans women complained that it left them feeling excluded, and it was canceled. "Can you believe it?" Pat asked.

Laurie allowed that they sort of had a point, and I looked at her thinking, *What do you know? You who haven't shopped in twenty-two days.*

After throwing up she wanted some candy so we went to a few places in search of it. Nothing appealed to her, so we stopped at a bakery and bought two kinds of slices. A slice is an Australian dessert made of puff pastry topped with custard and then either passion-fruit icing or Jell-O. "What flavor Jell-O is this?" I asked.

"Red," Pat answered.

March 9, 2016
London
While eating lunch yesterday afternoon Jeff told me about a friend of his who believes there's a secret planet hidden behind the sun that the U.S government knows about but is keeping to itself.

On the bus home I googled *hidden planet* and came upon the following, which was posted by someone named XZiled, who calls himself a journalist: "Proof of an Object Behind the Sun that NASA Has Removed from Their Images," it's headlined. "Almost 6,000 years ago, the ancient Sumerians told of planet

Nibiru existing in our solar system. The ancient Hebrew text, called the Kolbrin, also described this mysterious planetoid and called it 'The Great Destroyer.'"

A number of people responded to the post, including this guy:

OK, I am a little confused. A planet "behind" the sun? One that people who lived 6,000 years ago knew about even though they hadn't yet figured out that the earth was round? I think it's time to get some Science up in this bitch!

He then listed a number of reasons the hidden planet was bullshit.

Later Jeff told me about an American musician named Bill Callahan who recently released an album called *Sometimes I Wish We Were an Eagle*. God, I wish I'd thought of that.

March 20, 2016
Rackham
On this week's *Real Time*, Bill Maher predicts that, if elected, Donald Trump will do away with the eagle as the symbol of America and replace it with a turtle fucking a shoe.

April 6, 2016
New York
There are only two guest elevators at the Excelsior Hotel. You can wait quite a long time for one, so if I'm in the lobby going up, I always check to see if anyone else is coming before I press the button. Late yesterday morning it was a group of four middle-aged women, all plump and American. "Thank you, thank you," they panted as they piled in behind me.

"No problem," I said, changing my mind as each of them pressed a button for a different floor.

"We're all over the place!" one of the women cried, and the

others shrieked. Their laughter was sudden and shrill, and the sound of it caused me to wince.

"Marcie here's the crazy one," a woman in a brown turtleneck said, and again they all cracked up.

"Me!" the one named Marcie countered. "What about *you* on that double-decker bus!"

My floor was 11, but our first stop was 2, where I glared at the woman getting off and thought, *Couldn't you have walked? There are stairs off the lobby. I've taken them a thousand times.* Making it worse, instead of just stepping out of the elevator, the woman turned to hug her friends and say how much she was going to miss them. "You tell Gary hello from me."

"You say the same to Mark." The door started closing so one of them held it open and that set them all to laughing as well. *How funny! We're holding things up!*

Next it was 5, where again hugs were exchanged. "Thank you so much, Mary Beth, for organizing the trip."

"No, thank *you* for coming."

"Are you kidding? I'll take any excuse to get away from Brian and the kids."

On 9, the third woman got off. Hugs were exchanged and after the door had closed behind her, the one remaining woman turned to me, her eyes moist from laughter. "I bet you'd have never held the elevator if you'd known we were all so crazy!"

"Actually, no," I said, my voice flat and cold. "I wouldn't have."

Then it was just weird and uncomfortable up to 10, where she finally got off.

April 29, 2016
Dallas, Texas
"I've seen you four or five times in the past and have to tell you with all respect that you were out of control tonight,"

a woman said to me after my show yesterday evening. And it was true. The reading was fine but often during the Q and A I'd hear something completely fucked up and realize it was coming out of my mouth. Which happens. At one point a young man raised his hand. "Yes," he said, "you made a reference in one of your stories to growing up gay in North Carolina in the 1970s. You spoke of how alienated and unwelcome you felt, and speaking to you as a Muslim man living in Texas, I'm wondering what advice you might have?"

I thought for a moment. "Accept Jesus Christ as your personal Lord and Savior."

And that wasn't even the bad part.

May 17, 2016
Emerald Isle

I thought it would be hot in Raleigh but it was only in the high sixties. Hugh and Candy got into the front seat, Amy and I took the back, and by 3:30 we were on our way to the Sea Section.

"Whatever you do, don't tell the people in the pink house next door that we're its new owners," Hugh said.

"Why?" I asked. "Who's there?"

"It doesn't matter. Phyllis told me that if they know, they'll never stop asking for stuff." He then announced that he'd come up with a name for it. "Dune Buddy," he said.

Amy and I both groaned, not the way you do when you hear a pun, but the way you do when someone suggests basting grilled fish with NyQuil.

"That's awful," I said.

"The word *buddy*, that's as bad as *awesome*," Amy said.

"Well, then, what are *your* suggestions?" Hugh asked.

"I still like the idea I came up with yesterday," I said.

Hugh drifted into another lane. "Remind me what that was again?"

"Country Pride Strong Family Peppermill," I told him. "It's not a pun, but it has a nice ring to it."

"It's way too long," Hugh said. "Remember this has to go on the Emerald Isle Realty site, so it can't be anything dirty— nothing with *Semen* on it, no *Conch Sucker*."

Throughout the rest of the ride we tried coming up with a name, but nothing was perfect. It's the same way with an essay title: you know when you've got it and when you're just settling for something.

While each of us thought, separately, Amy brought up Fran Lebowitz. "Someone asked her what her favorite animal is and she answered, 'Steak.' Isn't that perfect?"

In Beulaville we stopped at Miss Madison's strawberry stand. We first went three years ago, when Hugh, Amy, and I drove from Raleigh to the beach house we rented a few weeks after Tiffany died. That was such a dark time.

Next we went to the ABC store. "Wow," I said to the cashier. "You people are giving liquor away."

She was around my age with beige hair piled upon her head. "Why?" she asked. "Where are y'all from?"

"England," I told her. "Liquor's really expensive there."

Beside the register was a large sign announcing that cell phones were forbidden.

"Doesn't everyone just ignore that?" I asked.

"Yes," said the woman whose name tag identified her as April. "And when they do I just ignore *them*."

Amy pulled her wallet out of her purse and held it up to her mouth. "Listen, they won't let me use my phone in the liquor store, so I'm calling you on my wallet, okay?" She paused. "The lady who works here, April, her name is, she won't let me use my phone. Can you believe it?"

April laughed.

"All right, well, I guess I'll see you when I see you," Amy said. "I love you too."

"Lord, that's funny," April said as we headed to the door. "Y'all have a good rest of the day."

"Is there anything in Clamydia?" I asked as we got back in the car. "It *is* next to the Sea Section."

"No way," said Hugh. "I still like Dune Buddy."

May 21, 2016
Emerald Isle

I returned from my walk last night to find Dad in the living room. "Hey there, paunchy," he said.

"I don't have a paunch," I insisted. "It's my shirt billowing."

"You're just sucking your stomach in," he said.

At breakfast this morning, I asked Dad what he thinks about Trump.

"Well, he's a businessman. I think he's got a lot of courage."

"Courage like when he said that Ted Cruz's father was responsible for the Kennedy assassination?"

"I think the bigger problem is the news media," he said. "Places like the *New York Times,* they have a definite... agenda."

"I bet the only place that's not biased is Fox News," I said.

"Well, as a matter of fact, that's right," Dad told me.

"It's because they say so on air," I continued. "'Fair and balanced.'"

"They do say it, but only because it's true," Dad said.

He was an old-school fiscal Republican until the advent of cable news. Now he believes whatever Bill O'Reilly tells him to, though he gets a bit confused as to why.

While walking along Ocean Drive yesterday, the stretch that's located off the Coast Guard Road, I passed a house with a sign out front reading TEAM TRUMP: REBUILD AMERICA.

*   *   *

Over dinner last night, Amy recalled the time her sixth-grade health teacher separated the girls in class and asked, "If you were naked and had only a washcloth, which would you cover, your top or your bottom?"

Amy's answer—"I'd cover my face"—is, I think, the best possible response. But still, what a question.

May 22, 2016
Emerald Isle

After dinner last night we took a walk. Amy and Hugh plowed ahead while I lagged behind with Dad. "How's Cindy?" I asked. "What's Keith up to?"

"She's fine but he has cancer of the esophagus, so I haven't heard from him in a while."

It was murder trying to make conversation. I told him I'd gone to Binghamton and had been driven by Cortland on my way to Syracuse last month. "Is Fanny still there?" I asked.

"The last I heard," Dad said. He was wearing the drawstring jeans we bought in Tokyo last winter, and they looked great on him. On his feet were black Rockport Dockers. "These are so comfortable. Say, what's your size? I'm going to get you a pair."

"That's okay."

It was a clear night. The moon was full and no cars passed us. After we all returned to the house, Amy and I went out on our own. At one point, an animal ran across the road ahead of us. "What was that?" she asked, clutching my arm.

I hadn't gotten a clear view but knew that it wasn't a dog. It moved differently. "I think . . ." I said. "You know, this is crazy, but I honestly think it's a panther."

I'd normally never venture such a crazy guess, but it's the

name of the state's NFL team, so they must exist, right? I told myself this but thought later, *Right. Like there are eagles in Philadelphia and bears in Chicago. Like New York has actual giants in it.* As we approached the yard the creature had run into, both of us trembling, we saw that it was a fawn.

"Baby deer, panther, they're the same thing, essentially," I said.

Afterward we watched an episode of *My Six-Hundred-Pound Life.*

May 30, 2016
London

I worked until three thirty yesterday and then cut through the park. It was warm and sunny, and among the couples lying on blankets in the grass I saw two young men with their arms around each other. I could never have done that when I was their age, not unless it was Pride Day and every single person in the park was a homosexual. How different young gay people's lives are today. How wonderful.

While walking I listened to a long Ian Frazier profile of the woman who now writes the Hints from Heloise column and is the daughter of the original Heloise. She lives in Texas and has a cockatoo named Fussy. She also has an albino ferret.

June 6, 2016
Rackham

I was working yesterday and looked out the window to see Hugh on what was surely the world's first riding mower. It looked like a buggy almost, and he was bobbing up and down in the seat. I laughed so hard. "It's like a Model T," I said, "but it's also like you should have a whip in your hand."

"It's Tom and Thelma's," he explained, which would make it a Model T&T. Later in the day he tried transplanting some sweet peas he'd grown from seeds. "Neela tells me they're like caviar to slugs," he said, sighing. His painting studio is closed for the summer. Now it's just piano and gardening. I came home from picking up trash last night and found him on the bench beneath the tree drinking a manhattan and surveying his freshly cut lawn. This is my favorite encounter: him at the end of the day, drink in hand, sun-kissed and in a good mood. The house feels like a wonderful decision then—no matter how much trash I've picked up, it's all worth it. We always seem old in these moments, but not in a dreary way. It's rather like we're celebrating something that was hard-earned. We were young once, and now we have all this.

June 9, 2016
Rackham

On the *Daily Beast* yesterday morning I read a list of demands presented by the students of various colleges and universities this past year. Included was "No 'ethnic' food in the cafeteria." Taco Tuesdays amounts to cultural appropriation, as does stir-fried chicken. On one campus they're insisting that white people should not be allowed to have dreadlocks, which is something I've been saying for years.

June 12, 2016
Rackham

Kerry and her seventeen-year-old daughter, Grace Anne, arrived shortly before noon yesterday. It's such a pleasure to spend time with a vibrant, talkative teenager. Even when they break into French for no reason or just start singing, you forgive it because they're young and anything's better than just grunting and poking at a cell phone. She's lovely, Grace Anne, and will be lovelier still when her braces are removed. We probably should have headed straight out to Sussex but instead I took them to Portobello, where at my favorite stall I saw another hand-carved eighteenth-century snuffbox in the shape of a figure shitting. This time instead of a French hunchback, it's a schoolboy with a grotesque face. I think I'll ask Hugh to get it for me for Christmas.

"So what are you going to do in Paris next week?" I asked Grace Anne as we walked back to the house.

"Listen," she said.

It's the best answer I've ever gotten. She's been studying French for four years, and while she has a great accent, she's hoping to make it better.

Our train got canceled at Horsham so we waited twenty minutes and caught the next one. It was overcast when we arrived, and after a cup of tea, Hugh drove us into Amberley so we could look around and walk back. There was no talk of jet lag, no "I need a nap." On our way home, Grace Anne noticed a dead goose in a tree. I couldn't figure that out for the life of me. Had someone shot it, and this was where it had fallen? Did it die of a heart attack? A stroke? Not long afterward, she noticed a live mole by the side of the road. It was good-size and just as I was looking for something to put it in, Grace Anne offered up her sneaker. The mole, we decided, was named Margaret. At one point she stuck her head out from between the shoelaces, and we all agreed it was the cutest thing we'd ever seen.

We showed Margaret to Hugh, and just as we started searching for a place to let her go, one of the neighbors pulled over. She thought we were visitors who needed help, and when we told her we had a mole in a sneaker, she said, "Just don't let her loose in *my* garden."

I've wanted for years to catch a live mole.

Hugh made fish pie for dinner, and again Grace Anne was a model teen—no picking things out or deciding she doesn't eat haddock. Every now and then she'd ask her mom for a sip of wine and get it. Hugh can be tricky with company, but he liked both Kerry and her daughter. "I read somewhere that up to one-quarter of all birds are gay and that a majority of giraffes are bisexual," Grace Anne commented, apropos of nothing, when her water glass was refilled.

Later in the meal, Kerry told a story about living in Chicago in married-student housing while her husband, Win, was finishing school. "We had a car and came out one morning to find a note on the windshield that read *Never you park here again. Next time you must be tode.*"

June 13, 2016
Rackham

A gunman opened fire in an Orlando gay bar on Saturday night, killing fifty people and wounding another fifty-three. An article in this morning's *Times* described the weapon he used—an assault rifle that was easy to buy. After the bodies were carted away, the president made a speech, people piled flowers and teddy bears on a curb, and an NRA spokesman undoubtedly released a statement saying that one lone crazy person shouldn't be allowed to ruin things for everyone else.

But one lone crazy person is *always* ruining things for everyone else. Some nut puts a bomb in his shoe and suddenly everyone has to walk through the security arch in stocking feet. One person sneaks a liquid bomb onto the plane, and the next day you can no longer fly with more than three ounces of shampoo. A handful of people who jumped from the high floors of hotels made it so that all the windows are sealed.

So why can't one lone gunman ruin automatic rifles for everyone else?

"Shame about the killings," the FedEx driver said this morning when he came to deliver a package. We got to talking about guns, and he said that a few years ago he took his kids to New York. "They wanted to have lunch at McDonald's but I made us go to the Wendy's across the street, because you never hear of shootings there. McDonald's, on the other hand..."

Also curious is that the Orlando shooter dialed 911 shortly before his rampage and pledged his allegiance to ISIS. To 911? Trump tweeted what amounts to *I told you so,* but I don't think this qualified as an ISIS attack. Rather, it sounds like a lone crazy person who decided, *What the hell, might as well join the club,* before killing a lot of gay people. It's like a deathbed conversion.

Trump gave a speech and said that the killer was born in Afghan.

"Like the blanket?" Hugh said.

The guy was actually born in New Jersey.

June 14, 2016
Rackham

Walking home from Storrington I passed a pro-Brexit sign reading VOTE LEAVE. It's the first one I've seen, but it's not surprising, given the area. City people and the young are more in favor of remaining in the EU, but will they vote in sufficient numbers? What would it mean for everyone who works at Starbucks and Costa and Whole Foods and Ryman's and everywhere else that relies on foreign workers?

June 16, 2016
Rackham

On my walk I listened to a bit of a sermon delivered on Sunday by Roger Jimenez of Verity Baptist Church. "What if you asked me, 'Hey, are you sad that fifty pedophiles were killed today?' Um, no, I think that's great. I think that helps society. I think Orlando, Florida, is a little safer tonight. The tragedy is that more of them didn't die. I'm kind of upset that he didn't finish the job. I wish the government would round them all up, put them up against the firing wall, put a firing squad in front of them and blow their brains out," he said. "I'm not saying we should do it. I'm not saying we should go, you know, blow up Planned Parenthood. All I'm saying is this, if God had His way, that's what He would do."

Then I listened to a similar sermon from a church in Sacramento. This guy too used the words *homosexual* and *pedophile* interchangeably and said that the tragedy was that more gay men weren't killed.

Hearing the snippets, I wondered if I haven't missed feeling hated and discriminated against. Just a little, maybe. Here in Sussex, everyone's so welcoming. "And where's your partner? Are you married?" There's no outside anymore.

Hugh and I were talking about the Orlando shooting, and when I got into how easy it is to buy an automatic weapon in America, he said it didn't matter. "If it was more difficult, the guy would have just made a bomb."

"Certain people might, but most won't even make their own pie crust," I argued, "and I think that if you made the guns more difficult to get, they'd do like everyone else and just yell and scream when they got angry."

"What kind of person wouldn't make his own pie crust?" asked Hugh, whose question makes him gayer than all of the shooting victims combined.

I pointed out the window at the greater world. "There are people out there," I told him, "who don't even make their own eggnog."

"But that's so ... easy," he said, finally as sad and confused as the rest of us.

June 20, 2016
Bucharest

It's always tricky when you visit another country and your hosts, invariably kind and well-meaning, ask what you'd like to do. If you're in Copenhagen or Stockholm or Milan, the answer is simple: "Go shopping." In Romania, where there's nothing to buy, it can get more complicated. "What would you like to see in Bucharest?" Ioana asked when we met her yesterday morning. It was a holiday, so the streets were deserted except for the lot across the street from the hotel where a loud, filthy machine spat mud onto passersby.

"I'd like to see angry orphans and drunk people fighting, if that's possible," I said.

She nodded. "Okay, then."

Having watched the documentary *Children Underground* something like eight times, I thought angry orphans would be everywhere, running wild with spray paint on their faces, but I haven't seen a one. Ditto drunk people fighting. We saw alcoholics, but only a few, and the only one with scabs on his face was politely begging from diners seated on the terrace of a café. He wore a woman's coat with a zebra-striped pattern despite the punishing heat.

Most stores and businesses were closed because of the holiday, but there was a bookshop Ioana thought was okay, so we followed her there. Like the big chains in the U.S. and England—Waterstones, B and N—this place sold a lot of toys and games, all of which were made in America or Western Europe. I wanted something Romanian. "What's your biggest export?" Hugh asked Cristian on the day we arrived.

Immigrants, I thought.

After the bookstore, Ioana led us to a park. Along the way we passed some of the largest bottles I have ever seen in my life—for water, for beer, for detergent; they're huge here.

Some were half filled and stood in the street to save someone's parking space, and others were partially stuffed into garbage cans too small to accommodate them. They were as big as fire hydrants, some of them. I noticed a lot of people crossing themselves when they passed a church, and one woman crossed herself while passing a church-supply shop.

The last time I was here it was December, and the city was a lot bleaker-looking. Now, with the trees in bloom, it's more inviting, softer. The park we visited had a pond, and we stood on a bridge for a while watching as people paddled below us on little boats. "Have you gotten a lot of Syrian refugees?" Hugh asked.

"One," Ioana said. "He got lost, and when he found out that he was in Romania instead of Austria, he started crying."

Poor Romania—not even Syrians want to live here.

A short distance from the pond was a large cage with peacocks in it. One of them had a tumor on the side of his face so large it covered his eye. I noticed while walking that everyone was white. "Well, yes," Ioana said. "We have no black people in Romania."

An hour or so after lunch we went to a café and waited an insane amount of time for our drinks. While sitting there, I watched a pair of street cleaners sweep up stray leaves. The man was diligent, but the woman had little interest in working. Rather, she leaned against her broom and stared dumbly into her phone. "Where do you think she lives?" I asked.

Ioana named a neighborhood she tries to avoid, saying that it was dangerous. "That's where you go to see fights and angry orphans."

Then what are we doing sitting here? I wondered.

On the way back to the hotel, I asked who Romania's biggest pop stars were. "Well, there's Ina," Ioana said. "And Antonia. Delia's big now, and Andra." All of them went by one name.

In the late afternoon I sat for two interviews. At 6:15 we

headed to the theater, which was small and pleasant and sat 180. The air-conditioning worked, the lobby was spacious, and I really liked the audience. The show was sold out and it was the most glamorous-looking crowd I've ever had. Almost all the women wore dresses, many of them new. I signed for two and a half hours while drinking water from a bottle with a ridiculously large mouth.

June 22, 2016
Bucharest

On Monday our babysitter from the publishing house was Ioana but yesterday it was Gabi, who is thin and twenty-seven and relentlessly negative. She's not a complainer, necessarily, just a storm cloud, though not without reason. Her parents had her late in life and suffered relatively early from poor health. Her father died of cancer a few years ago, and her mother has Parkinson's. "What with my genes I'm really looking forward to aging," she said.

Gabi had nothing good to say about Romania: all the politicians are crooked, there's no hope of improvement, etc. If I tended to believe her, it was likely due to the heat. She met us at the hotel at eleven and by the time we reached the Village Museum it was easily 97 degrees outside. It's a beautiful place, on a lake, and the old houses were stunning. Most were wooden and simple, with roofs that were peaked, sometimes thatched and sometimes covered in small shingles.

"Now all the houses in villages are so ugly you would not believe it," Gabi moaned. "Most are painted the most horrible pink you ever saw in your life, or orange." She frowned at a nearby tree. "I hate orange."

There were a lot of stray cats living at the museum. Food was left out for them, and they dozed in the staggering heat, some with their tongues hanging out of their mouths.

"It can be like this until October sometimes," Gabi said, sighing. "A lot of people go to the seaside or mountains but all of my friends are too lazy to take me. And so I stay and am baked alive."

For lunch we walked to the Museum of the Romanian Peasant. There's a beautiful restaurant there so we sat and were waited on by a woman who looked so much like my sister Tiffany when she was young that it stopped my heart. She was blond, but her nose was the same, as were her eyes and her build. *It's her,* I thought. It was insane to believe that instead of dying, Tiffany had moved to Romania, drunk from the fountain of youth, and found a waitressing job, but for a moment, I was convinced that it was actually her. It was so eerie, seeing this young woman. I couldn't stop staring at her.

June 24, 2016
London
England voted by a slim margin to leave the EU and already the pound has dropped to its lowest level in over thirty years. It's now at 1.35 against the dollar. When we bought this house it was 2.06. These are just the first rumblings. If I believe what I read in the *New York Times,* wages will fall, and median incomes will shrink, yet still on the radio I hear people cheering: "We won! No more Brussels telling us what to do! We have our identity back!" You hear that word a lot, *identity.* It's like me saying, "I don't know if I'm a North Carolinian, an American, or a North American!"

Do people really lie awake at night worrying about such things?

In London it's like someone died. "The important thing is not to make any snap decisions," Hugh says. Frank and Scott said they'd move back to the U.S. if England voted to leave.

Can it be as bad as all that? I'd wanted to get my British

passport, as it meant I could live anywhere in Europe. Now it means I can just live here.

As we were sitting in traffic on our car ride from Ruse, Bulgaria, to the Bucharest airport yesterday, our driver, Arthur, asked if we'd like to hear some traditional Romanian music. We said yes, and as the first song played, he translated it. " 'I sold my soul for a...few bucks. I am having some bad habits and when I sleep in the morning...I said some bad words about myself.' "

The next song amounted to "I am old. No one has any use for me." The song after that was also about being ugly and unhappy. Then came one that was just about regret. " 'At a restaurant I used to like there was a girl with...black hair and dark eyes and...a red face who had a very nice body. Then I find out that...she loves somebody else.' "

After our passport control on the border we stopped for gas, then drove on unimpeded, passing farmers in horse-driven carts and grand houses—or, rather, the shells of grand houses—built by gypsies. "Many times they live in tents in the backyard and the horses live inside," Arthur explained. It was 100 degrees outside, and I felt sorry for everyone we saw.

At the airport we got our tickets and moved easily through security. The sad lounge was upstairs and it had no air-conditioning. I sat there sweating until six, when we boarded and I learned that I had a middle seat. Our plane was delayed due to striking air traffic controllers in France, so we sat on the runway for another hour, waiting to get clearance from London. After taking off, the woman in front of me shoved her seat all the way back and the woman next to her put on some horrible melon-scented hand cream. I couldn't have been any more miserable. When we got back to London it was so muggy, I had to pull the fan out. Today it's drier. The sun was shining when I was woken up at six by Hugh, who looked at his phone and said, "It's done. We're out."

It took me a moment to realize what he was talking about— Brexit.

June 29, 2016
Rackham

At dusk Hugh watched a fox walk across the backyard, not darting into the shadows but going at a leisurely pace. He's named her Carol.

July 12, 2016
Rackham

Pat and Mark arrived from Australia at five yesterday. I'd spent the afternoon cleaning, and Hugh had spent it cursing the slugs that had decimated his garden. It's in ruins now, all his vegetables gone.

I'd met Mark briefly in Melbourne last January but got no sense then of how dry and funny he is. I've been laughing since they got here, quite often over words. Recounting a recent flight, Pat, referring to the flight attendants, said she'd much rather have an old boiler than one of these young ones.

"An old boiler?"

"You know," she said, "an older woman with experience. She might be a bit mean, a bit hardened."

"It's the opposite of a spring chicken," Mark explained. "An old bird is tough, so it needs to be boiled if you want the meat to be tender."

God, that makes me laugh. My sister Gretchen might be an old boiler.

I'm also getting a kick out of "having a blue," which means having a fight. You could say, "It was a serious blue," or "We had a blue," or "If I talk to this woman there's going to be a blue." You could also say, "I'm ready to put the blue on."

We went to the pub for dinner, and while eating, Pat talked about her former maid, Hazel, whom she looked after until her death. "When she was sixteen, her father took her to the dentist and had all her teeth pulled," she said. "This was done quite often back in the twenties and thirties to save the girl's eventual husband money."

"How did that save money?" I asked.

"No dental bills," Pat said.

I was as shocked as I'd been when I first heard of a clitoridectomy. Pulling every tooth out of a sixteen-year-old's head to make her financially attractive to a potential suitor! And of course nowadays there are other considerations: What if she was a lesbian and finding a husband wasn't a priority? Plus, back then, especially in the country, if you had a tooth problem, they'd just pull it, and how much could that have cost? How much was it actually saving to have it done all at once?

Pat's maid literally could not bite the hand that fed her. She could just gum it.

July 17, 2016
Rackham

I was in my office working yesterday afternoon when Hugh yelled, "David, come here." His tone suggested wildlife on the run—it's the voice he uses when Carol the fox sprints across the backyard or when the barn owl whose name I've now forgotten would alight on a fence post. "Quick!" he said. I stepped outside and as he pointed to a cleared space at the base of the house, I saw a snake pass into a clump of yellow flowers.

"Kill it!" I yelled.

"No," he said. "It's not hurting anyone."

"*Yet*," I said. "Hurry, get a shovel and kill it."

"Snakes are protected. I can't do that."

"You're just making the protected bit up," I said. "Besides, who's to know? I won't tell anyone. Kill it."

The snake had by this time rounded the corner and curled itself up beneath the drainpipe.

"Throw gas on it," I whispered. "Light it on fire."

"I will not," Hugh said, and he went inside for his binoculars.

There is only one kind of poisonous snake in England, the adder, and according to our wildlife book, this was not one of those. Rather, it was a grass snake. "Completely harmless," Hugh said.

"Not to toads," I told him. "What about Foster, the one we found last week? This is where he hangs out. It's not fair to him to let this snake live."

As if it could understand me, the snake uncoiled and took off across the yard, me following at a safe distance and yelling, "Kill it! Kill it!"

My father would have. He's the only person in the world more afraid of snakes than I am. I don't know where our phobia comes from, but the Hamricks sure don't share it. Hugh grew up in Africa, where I don't think there's a snake that *can't* kill you, yet he and his brothers have no fear of them. You'd think they were butterflies they were chasing, all "Look how beautiful," and "Hey, there, sweetie, you lost?"

Hugh's father retired to a farm in Virginia and would catch three-foot-long rat snakes with his bare hands, grab them behind their heads, not to squeeze the life out of them but just to say hello. "Are you people crazy?" I asked when Hugh showed me a picture of his father holding what looked like a belt for a really fat person—what *should have been* a belt.

I must have been in the first grade when I walked out our door in Endicott, New York, and there, beside a rock wall, I saw a snake eating a toad. He'd come up from behind it and had the back half of it in his mouth, which was open impossibly wide. The toad was still alive, and what struck me was its expression, which was no different than it would have been had it not been half inside a snake's mouth. Every so often the toad would blink, but that was it—no cry for help, no expression along the lines of *Tell me this is not happening*. That's the way it goes for amphibians.

Reptiles don't change expression either, of course, so in that sense the two of them were made for each other.

After the grass snake had disappeared into the hedges, Hugh told me that it didn't even have fangs, and that its only defense was a garlic-smelling fluid emitted through its anal glands. As if that mattered. With snakes, it's not the bite that will kill me, it's the heart attack. What if one got into the house?

"That's it with me and the yard," I said to him over lunch. "I just want you to know I'm never setting foot out there again. You want clothes on the line, *you* hang them."

"Me?"

"You wouldn't kill that snake, so from now on, fine, the whole outside is yours. I'm having nothing to do with it."

It's no big sacrifice, really. Before we bought the house, on the day we came to look at it, I thought I'd spend a lot of time in the side yard, beneath the copper beech. The grass is soft there, almost like it is on a golf course. That was six years ago and I sat on it once for all of two minutes before I remembered why I don't sit on the grass: it's grass. Hugh's the one who mows and gardens. He lives outside.

The only thing I'll miss is an occasional stroll beyond the fence, where the backyard becomes a meadow. That's where we toss our chicken carcasses and the fat cut off the lamb. Pork chop bones, gristle, it all goes to Carol the fox. I like dumping it onto the tall grass at dusk and returning in the morning to look at the spot where it was. I like imagining her coming upon it and turning to the light that's likely still on at my office. At one a.m., sometimes as late as three o'clock, the two of us wide awake and her thinking, *Thank you, David*.

July 18, 2016
Rackham

Every night at dusk Carol the fox arrives. "Bold as brass," we say. On Saturday she trotted by the open kitchen door. We put the bone from that night's côte de boeuf in the pasture and peeked out of the house at 8:30 to see her in the spot where we'd left it. She walked away as if she'd been caught at something, as if to say, *I was just standing here, but now I think I'll stand over there instead*. She ambled over to the orchard, but a few minutes later she was back and had the bone in her mouth.

We're just crazy about Carol. I think of her as half dog and half cat. I'd considered leaving her some canned food but read this morning that foxes are naturally pretty lazy, and if you feed them they're likely to stop defending their wider territory. Then you go away on vacation and they're like, *Fuck*.

August 8, 2016
Emerald Isle

As Hugh and I went for a swim yesterday I tried to think of a name for the pink house. "What about Come Shell or High Water?"

He loved it, which is nice but puts it squarely in the "no" category. A "yes" is when he moans or says, "That's disgusting. That's awful."

He's happy here but I just don't get it. Walking anywhere, in any direction, is a pain, even if it's not 100 degrees outside. I've passed a house called the Fighting Cocks in West Sussex a thousand times, always happily, but if I have to walk by the Emerald Isle CVS once more, I'll scream.

"But look at it," he says. "Look at the ocean!" He sits on the landing and stares at the water in the morning with a cup of tea in his hand, in the afternoon with coffee, at dusk with a gin and tonic or a manhattan. "It's like Somalia," he says. "I have my youth back."

I say, "You're crazy."

He says, "You don't understand."

After our swim I went out again and walked to the Food Lion, where I bought three boxes of Jell-O for myself and a pack of hot dogs to throw into the canal. The store was jammed with newly arrived vacationers, their carts heaping. "I ain't never seen it this bad," said the woman in front of me. She was buying frozen chicken fingers and a jug of water, and when she turned around I saw that a big chunk of her nose was missing. Skin cancer, most likely. She was as small as a child— four foot ten maybe—and wore a sun hat, a sleeveless top, and long pants. When we finally got close, the woman placed her items on the belt. I did as well and watched as she studied what I was getting. "Looks like you eat about how I do."

I wanted to tell her that the Jell-O was ironic and the hot dogs—the cheapest there were, red hots, actually, the color of dynamite—were for snapping turtles, but it seemed pretentious.

"I don't cook either," she said. "No time—not that I'd do it if I was retired. I'm eighty-one and still work. My husband died five years ago."

"Where do you work?" I asked.

"Yonder at the campground," she said. "I manage it."

I bet you do, I thought admiringly.

August 14, 2016
Emerald Isle

Dad is incensed over a woman my age he recently saw at a funeral. "I don't understand these people with no discipline.

I mean, she's enormous—legs that go straight down into her shoes. Just...Jesus. And makeup an inch thick. There's nothing...feminine there. Nothing of beauty." He made a series of disgusted faces, and Amy and I laughed. "It's not funny," he said. "You should have seen her!"

He arrived yesterday afternoon wearing white shorts with a matching T-shirt. We hugged and he was just bones with a slightly humped back.

"So how's the Muslim situation over there in England? Do you feel targeted because you're homosexual?"

Dad either hopes or worries that ISIS will blow up a theater during one of my events.

I said, "Where do you get these ideas from?" Though I know exactly where he gets them from: Fox News.

Later, when talk turned to guns and how easy it is to get one in the U.S., he said, "Well, that's just the media."

There were reports of a shooting in the food court of Crabtree Valley Mall yesterday. "I'm sorry to have to tell you, Maddy, but all your friends are dead," I said. "All of them."

Was it ISIS? everyone wondered. Was it a disgruntled employee?

As far as I know, it was a false report. Police closed the place but found no victim and no shooter. Still, we thought of it on the beach yesterday, under the umbrella, tan-talking. This is different from regular talking. It's lazier and more meandering.

"Is Jack Frost married?" I asked.

"That's a good question," Amy said.

Nearby a fat man waded into the ocean. "Is he wearing suspenders under his T-shirt?" Gretchen asked.

He was.

We talked about Simone Biles, the Olympic gymnast who's captured the nation's heart. Not only is she lovely and enthusiastic, but she's got a great story, one that sounds almost invented for TV.

August 20, 2016
Rackham

I had the kitchen door open and looked over at around midnight to see Carol not exactly peeking in but standing not far away, waiting to be noticed. "Well, hello!" I said. "I've been looking all over for you."

And it's true. I've been calling for her since we got back from our trip. On Thursday and Friday night I put out dog food, over Hugh's strenuous objection.

Last night I returned from my walk and found him at the table outside my office, drinking a manhattan. He's been cranky and depressed, threatening to get on the next plane back to North Carolina. When he saw the dog food I'd bought, he said that if I put it out, he wasn't going to make me dinner.

"Oh, you are so."

He insists that my feeding Carol will ultimately make things harder for her—"What happens when you take off for three months?"—and I argue that she could get hit by a car tomorrow. "How nice for her to come upon a windfall. You don't know what it's like out there night after night, lucky if you come away with two grubs and a millipede."

When Carol arrived, I took off my iPod and sat on the top step outside my office with a bag of frankfurters. They were all I could find at the Waitrose, no big hot dog selection like you'd get in the U.S. Carol came pretty close and might have taken it from my hand had I been more patient. As it was, I felt like I was causing her undue stress. She doesn't like making eye contact and isn't crazy about eating in front of people. The three thin frankfurters I gave her were carried away and looked funny hanging from her mouth. "Carol, you nut!" I said.

The chicken back she ate in front of me, ditto the dog treat. Between feedings I tried to wake Hugh. "Come downstairs, our friend is here. We're fellowshipping."

"What does that mean?"

"You know what it means. We're hanging out. It's beautiful."

He says I'm manipulating her. "It's what you do, the puppet master. It's the same thing with people—you try to buy them."

He's just jealous. Oh, Carol.

August 26, 2016
Rackham

In this morning's *Times* I read about Martin Blackwell, a Georgia man who threw boiling water on the gay son of his girlfriend. He got the son's boyfriend as well, and the both of them had to have skin grafts. "They were moaning and hollering, like two hot dogs stuck together," Blackwell said. "They'll be all right," he insisted when the police came. "It was just a little hot water on 'em."

Yesterday he was sentenced to forty years in prison. His picture was in the *Times* this morning, and looking at it, I noticed that his fingernails were long, like a woman's.

September 12, 2016
Rackham

At around ten fifteen Carol showed up, and I let out a little cry. "Where have you been?" Because I hadn't seen her since returning from London, I'd decided she was punishing me. Then an even worse idea presented itself: *She doesn't think of me one way or another. I am nobody to her.*

"Nothing a little pork shoulder can't fix," I said, adding a few raw chicken legs for variety. Those she ate right there on the grass, while the shoulder, which is in bite-size nuggets, she carried into the darkness, burying for later, maybe. She didn't know what to make of the hard-boiled egg until I broke it in half, and she went, *Oh, great!*

At one point, returning from the yard, she had the choice of either brushing my leg or jumping over a flowerpot, and she chose the latter. "Really?" I said. "And *how* long have we known each other?"

Lately I feel I'm embarrassing her and that a better person would just leave her food in the field and allow her to get it in her own time. Then I remind myself that if I did so, the beef or chicken or whatever it was would, within minutes, be covered by slugs.

September 29, 2016
Rackham

I was getting ready to take a bath and was in the bedroom undressing when I felt a sudden, severe pain on what would be the instep of my left foot if I had an instep. I was in my stocking feet and had just removed the sock, expecting to find a sliver of glass, when I saw a wasp writhing on the floor beside my bed. "Son of a bitch," I said. "You come into *my* house and sting me on the foot when I've never done anything to you?"

What was he doing *walking*? Had the joy of flying worn off? I picked him up with Kleenex, and after throwing him in the toilet, I continued to berate him. "Asshole. That's right. Who are you going to sting *now*?"

God, did it hurt. If I'd been a child, I'd have cried for at least twenty minutes. As it was, I winced for a while, took my bath, and was in bed by 1:45. A few hours later I awoke, my foot alternately throbbing and itching. I've never been one to make a fuss when wasps alight on an outdoor restaurant table, but maybe I'll change that. I'm also going to stop feeling sorry for whatever it is that's going on with bees now, whatever that problem they're having is, confusion or mass suicide. From this point on, bees can kiss my ass. I mean it.

October 25, 2016
New Orleans, Louisiana

At the Walgreens on Canal Street, not far from my hotel, the laundry detergent is locked into bins, the way razor blades are. *Really?* I thought. The line at the counter was short but seemed not to move. The holdup was a homeless guy, maybe fifty years old and not bad-looking, who was buying a pack of cigarettes. He wore filthy corduroy pants and an even filthier long-sleeved sweater, and when he stepped in my direction the stench was overwhelming, like what I'm told a bear smells like. It made my eyes water, and I winced as I looked at his hands, the nails long, dirt packed underneath them.

After he was gone, the cashier reached for a can of air freshener. "Every day," she said. "Can you believe it? Every day I go through this, and I'm sorry and all, but that shit *lingers.*"

At dusk the streets became all the more nightmarish. "Hey, sir, can I ask you a question? All I need is fifty cents. I just got out of the hospital—look, I got the wristband and everything."

There's an IHOP four doors away from my hotel and the young women hanging out in front of it had to be prostitutes. None of them looked older than sixteen. Beyond them, four women fussed over a man in a wheelchair who had a head wound and was yelling at them. As I approached, one of the four was holding a disposable diaper to what looked to be the source of the bleeding. "Motherfuckers," the man said. "Just a old bunch of old motherfuckers."

Near the restaurant, a man my age came over to me with

a folded-up document in his hand. "These are my discharge papers from the army. I'm trying to get me a place for the night. I'm a vet."

Near Harrah's Casino I found a driver's license and credit card on the sidewalk. They were a woman's and she lived in Louisiana, in a town I'd never heard of. I put them in my pocket, thinking I'd mail them off when I got back to my hotel, and a block later I came upon a couple and a child searching a patch of ivy outside what looked to be a hotel. The woman was heavier than the person pictured on the driver's license, but that didn't mean anything. "Excuse me," I said. "Are you looking for something?"

When they turned around I understood that they were drunk, or at least the adults were. "She done lost her damn driver's license and credit card," the man said.

I held them out. "Are these them?"

"Hallelujah," the woman said. "Sir, you got good karma."

It was a surprisingly brief encounter, and disappointing. Being that drunk, she sort of deserved to lose her credit card and license.

I walked back to the hotel through streets smelling of sour milk, passing people holding drinks in what looked to be goldfish bowls. After dinner I walked that route again, thinking that this is what hell must be like, a combination of prostitutes, homeless people, drunk white kids, and out-of-towners in T-shirts and spanking-new sneakers talking about how much fun they're having.

The daytime's just as bad. On my way for a coffee this morning, I passed a man with an umbrella on his head, the kind that's been turned into a hat. He held a microphone and was talking about Jesus. "The thing about the devil is, the devil will fool you," he told me.

November 8, 2016
Santa Fe
I was driven to the airport this morning by a tall, pale blond fellow who referred to his bosses as "gals"—two gals who were married to each other. Here it was, Election Day, he said, and he had no idea who he was going to vote for or if he was even *going* to vote.

"Of course you are," I said. "You're going to vote for Hillary Clinton." What I thought was *Gads, man, pull yourself together!*

"I'm just not sure," he continued. "I mean, I drove Ivanka once and she gave me a pretty big tip."

"That's no reason to vote for her father," I said. "Chelsea Clinton would have tipped just as big, she just never happened to get into your car."

"I just hate not to vote."

"Then do it," I said. "And do it for Hillary. That tape that leaked, Trump saying that because he was famous he could do whatever he likes with women—that's not what a decent person would say. Hillary Clinton has her drawbacks but she's qualified and you're going to vote for her—end of story."

I wonder if he will.

November 9, 2016
Portland, Oregon
"How are we doing this morning?" the hostess of the hotel restaurant chirped.

I said, "Really? You're honestly going to ask me that?"

Trump won, and I'm in shock. Here it is, not even eight, and already three American friends have written to ask if they can live in our backyard in Sussex.

I got into bed early, before Clinton lost, and every fifteen minutes I checked my iPad. He won North Carolina. He won Florida, and Ohio. Like everyone else I know, I started getting uncomfortable.

He flipped Wisconsin, Michigan, Iowa, Pennsylvania. He won.

Every pundit was wrong, as were all the polls. Trump won by uniting white working-class Midwesterners without a college education. They're people who voted against their best interests. Bye, health care; bye, fifteen-dollar minimum wage.

Like always, I blame those who didn't vote. I mean, he won *Pennsylvania*? I think back to when I was in York and ask myself: *Why didn't I do anything?* But, like, what? Kill people?

November 24, 2016
Emerald Isle

I waited around for Lisa, Bob, and Dad to arrive, but by 5:30 they still weren't here, so I set off on my walk, which took me past the Pacific Superstore. Like any number of other places along the main road, it sells rafts and T-shirts and bathing suits. In its enormous windows hung two extra-large beach towels with Confederate flags on them.

Really? I thought.

When I returned to the Sea Section, the others still hadn't arrived. Kathy planned to grill fish for dinner and just as she was carrying it downstairs, they pulled up. Lisa has continued to lose weight since I last saw her. You can see it clearly. "I told Dad I was down twenty pounds and he said, 'Lose any more and you and I are going to have a love affair.' Isn't that creepy?"

It made me think of what Trump had said about dating his daughter Ivanka. "Since when do men do that?" I asked Lisa.

At the table I told everyone about the Confederate-flag beach towels I had seen. "That's just terrible," Dad said, forking asparagus into his mouth.

Lisa mentioned the recent rise of hate crimes and Dad said

he'd heard there was a lot of bad stuff going on. "I wonder what precipitated it?"

"You wonder?" we all said in unison.

"It's Trump," Lisa said.

"Baloney. He has nothing to do with it."

This was the conversation we were all hoping to avoid, or at least postpone until Paul arrived, but now we were having it.

"He actively courted racists," I said. "They were front and center at his rallies, and since winning, he's done nothing to disavow them."

"He doesn't have time for crap like that," Dad said. "He can't disavow every group he doesn't like, he's too busy."

"Not too busy to tweet about *Hamilton* at three a.m.," I said. "Or to complain that *Saturday Night Live* is one-sided."

"Oh, baloney. You don't know what you're talking about."

"How could you vote for that asshole?" I asked.

"Donald Trump is *not* an asshole!" Dad shouted, which I thought was funny. I mean, he pretty much ran on it.

"Any kid in America can go online now and hear his or her new president say the word *pussy*," I said, my voice raised, my heart in my throat. "Is that the person you want your children to look up to? What kind of a man says that sort of thing?"

"It was locker-room talk."

"He wasn't *in* a locker room, he was *at work*," I shouted. "And don't tell me about locker-room talk. I'm in them five days a week and never hear anyone speaking like that. And if I *did*, the last thing I'd think is *Oh, I wish that guy were my president.*"

Amy jumped in. "It's the most important job in the world and you voted for someone with no experience?"

"He has plenty of experience, business experience."

"Steve Bannon in the White House?" I said. "Steve Bannon, who said he didn't want his kids going to a school in LA because there were too many Jews there?"

418

"He never...I don't know where you're getting this crap. Trump is a wonderful man, the best thing that's happened to this country in a long time."

"He's a con artist. He's a huckster."

"You're *wrong*," Dad said. "All of you are *wrong*."

"You want to go for a walk?" Lisa asked.

"I'd love to," I said.

We went five miles on steam. *Idiot...asshole...how dare he...*

"I was going to write Dad's obituary in the car on the way here but I was too upset," Lisa said. "I'd wanted to get all the facts straight but now I really don't give a damn."

By the time we returned, it was midnight. Dad had gone to bed and we stood in the kitchen outside his room rehashing the argument with Amy and Hugh until we were all repeating ourselves. "Well, I'm going to go to bed," Lisa said, sighing, at 1:00.

"With Bob or Dad?" Amy asked.

I've never seen Hugh laugh so hard.

December 4, 2016
Rackham

It's bright and bitterly cold this morning. The yard is white with frost, and lying on the ground outside my office—frozen now, but still glistening—are the four slices of lamb's liver I bought for Carol on the night I returned to Sussex.

"Thelma hasn't seen her since we left in early October," Hugh said over dinner last night. "Face it—she's dead."

But I don't want to face it. It's too early for that. I called for her after sunset, great clouds of steam coming from my mouth and dissipating. I read last summer on some wildlife site that 58 percent of foxes die before they're a year old—hit by cars, most of them. Others are poisoned or maybe they starve to death. Carol seemed pretty young to me. I expected that she would mate right about now and take a turkey leg from my hand on Christmas Day. I had it all planned out. In the spring she'd have her litter. I imagined her bringing the kits straight to me, and I thought of how I'd spoil them and their children in turn. This is different from having a dog or cat go missing. Carol was/is a wild animal. There's no collar around her neck. I can't put signs up. She wasn't "mine," but that didn't stop me from being hers. And so the lamb's liver remains where it is. I'm just surprised that crows haven't taken it.

December 5, 2016
Rackham

I can't seem to put this election behind me. There was hope last week—crazy hope—that Jill Stein's requested three-state recount would go in the Democrats' favor, but if it were likely, the *Times* would have mentioned it. Hugh promised last year that if Trump won, the CIA would "take him out," but I don't see that happening either. By this point, Clinton won the popular vote by three million, a claim that Trump, with no evidence, is attributing to "massive voter fraud" and that his surrogates, with no evidence, are supporting. I've never been this upset by an election and can't shake the feeling that it's somehow my fault, that I could have done more. That makes me sound very grandiose—what do I think I had the power to do? It all comes down to ten thousand people in Ohio, Pennsylvania, Michigan, and Wisconsin. Ten thousand in each state, and the stupid Electoral College that allows a vote in Wyoming to count more than a vote in California. In the paper I look at people who attended his victory rally and wonder, *Who are you?* Then I think of Paul announcing with great authority that Trump is a man of peace and of Dad saying he's the best thing that's happened to this country in ages.

My God, I think. *Those people share my last name.*

*   *   *

At 4:00 yesterday Hugh and I drove to Storrington for his piano recital. There weren't any cars parked in front of the teacher's house so we knocked and learned we were an hour early.

"Really?" Hugh said. He'd been a nervous wreck all day and probably would have played his brief piece (Schubert's "Serenade") then and there if he could have. Rather than leaving with me, he stayed and helped his teacher set the buffet table. I picked up a big sackful of trash and returned at five to find the small parlor packed with people. Kids sat on the floor while adults occupied the chairs and sofas. There was one seat left in the back of the room and I took it just as an eighteen-year-old named Hannah stepped forward to play a piece that she had memorized. She and a serious-looking ten-year-old named Tom were clearly the best, but they seemed to take no particular pleasure in their superiority. Neither of them smiled at the accomplishment, much less pumped a fist. Is it an English thing, this modesty?

I liked that everyone was brief. "Now here's William to play 'Tearful Mouse.'"

"Charlie is a bit sick today, unfortunately, but had hoped to entertain us with 'The Stegosaurus Stomp.'"

Hugh practices every day for hours, so I thought he'd do much better. It was painful watching him approach the bench. He was the only one who spoke to the teacher while playing, who acted like this was a lesson rather than a recital. I've never seen him so vulnerable. That said, he was a good sport about it. "I wanted to be perfect," he said over dinner. "I...*need* to be perfect."

It's such a burden to place on yourself. Say you *are* perfect—who's going to recognize it? Few things are like the Olympics, where judges hold up score cards. How does one paint perfectly? Or lawyer perfectly?

The key is to fill the space between your skill level and perfection with charm. That said, you can't do it consciously. Charm can't be constructed that way. Maybe the word I'm looking for is *self-forgiveness,* the contagious variety. *There, that happened, so can we all now agree to put it behind us?*

After Hugh, a twelve-year-old blasted "My Heart Will Go On" on the trumpet. It was such a jarring instrument for that song, I loved it. A man played the Irish pipes with great skill, and then another child played, and another after that. It was such a lovely way to spend an early evening.

December 8, 2016
Paris

"Ah!" cried Dr. Barras when I showed up for my semiannual periodontal appointment. "You wore green socks to match our walls!"

She was in a good mood yesterday. "I got a pain in my side after your election and worried I'd have to be hospitalized," she said. "It's Trump! How can so many people in your country be so stupid!"

Her assistant agreed. "Horrible. What a stupid, stupid man."

I didn't have as much plaque as I did the last time but it was a bloody undertaking nevertheless. Afterward I was given a training session with an electric toothbrush. Dr. Barras held up a mirror, and after thinking that my teeth look pretty good, I realized I was looking at my implants, which are only "mine" in the way that my socks are, meaning I bought them. My real teeth look slightly better and slightly worse than I thought they would. Basically, they're just old-person's teeth, tea-stained and chipped. I'd love not to have so many gaps between them but am not sure I want braces again at age sixty. I'll get them off just in time to be cremated.

2017

February 10, 2017
Honolulu, Hawaii

I walked up the street yesterday afternoon and bought a shirt to give to Hugh for Valentine's Day. Afterward I wandered around and was passing a shoe store when a Hawaiian guy in his twenties looked at the shorts I got last summer and said, "Hey, man, those are sick!"

Later, nearing the hotel, a young man approached me saying, "I like your style." He was working at an outdoor booth in the open-air shopping center, and stopping people was his job. He was, I learned, from Israel, maybe thirty years old, and slightly chunky. "Let me ask you a question," he said. "What do you do for yourself, for your skin?" He handed me a free sample of rejuvenating cream. "This will bring down those bags under your eyes."

"What bags?" I said, pretending to be offended. Then I told him I moisturized, and he said, as if I'd confessed to bathing in cough syrup, "Listen, my love. What you are doing is not helping at all unless you are first removing all your dead skin."

"Okay," I said.

He put his hands on my face and I noticed he was an inch shorter than me. "Know why the skin on your cheeks is better than the skin on your nose? Because you shave away the dead cells on your cheeks every morning. You need to exfoliate before you moisturize, so I want you to hold out your hand, my love. Come on."

I presented my palm and he dropped a bit of potion into it. "Who are you here with?" he asked as he rubbed it in.

"My boyfriend."

"You should buy this Dead Sea salt mixture, then, and rub it into each other's body—not the face, just the body."

"We're old," I said.

He put his hands on his hips. "Nonsense. Now I want you to rub the salt into your hands."

I did as I was instructed.

"Pretend it's my body you're rubbing it into," he said, so bold.

Meanwhile I watched his associate, a young woman, attempt to snag a customer. "I like your dress..." "Hey, where are you here from?"

The Israeli guy had instantly read me and appealed to my vanity: "I like your style."

Now he was inviting me to imagine him naked. What made it less than an insult was that he wasn't gorgeous. Not that he was ugly—far from it—but he was probably only beautiful to someone my age.

"Great haircut," his associate said to a woman, who, like all the others, scurried away.

"I have a boyfriend too," the Israeli said. "He and I do this to each other once a week. No more, no less. Now here, my love, let me rinse your hands."

He poured water from a pitcher into a basin and as I washed myself, the water turned oily and my hands became like those of a baby. "Now I will put some shea butter on them," the Israeli said. "Can you believe how soft you feel? Imagine that on your whole body. On your boyfriend's body!"

The question "How much is this?" received a complicated

answer that involved the phrase "For you?" If that doesn't signal a rip-off, nothing does, but I thought the salts would be good either to give to Ronnie or to bring to Emerald Isle for our annual spa night.

"Where are you here from?" the Israeli's colleague asked a middle-aged couple who veered sharply to the right in order to avoid her.

I tried to pry my wallet from my back pocket. Because of its size, it was hard to get out. "Need some help?" the Israeli asked. What would he have done if I'd said yes? As perceptive as he was, I'm guessing he predicted my answer before asking the question. The encounter ended with a polite handshake and as I walked away, I wondered if he honestly liked my style.

Reentering the hotel, I got an idea for a restaurant called Waikiquiche.

February 16, 2017
San Francisco

Ronnie picked me up outside the recording studio at four yesterday and we drove in heavy traffic to Tail of the Yak, the store I like in Berkeley. From there we walked to Whole Foods and bought steaks.

"How's your day going?" the cashier asked.

"I'm exhausted," I told him.

"Me too," he said.

I put our steaks into a paper bag. "Probably not as exhausted as I am."

He took Ronnie's money. "Want to bet? I'm working a double shift!"

"Really?" I said. "You think that's tiring? I just performed surgery on a child for sixteen straight hours."

He looked taken aback.

"It was eye surgery," I continued. "This little girl didn't

425

have any. She was born with nothing so I made her a pair. Out of buttons." I took the receipt from his hands. "*And they work.*"

Try to out-exhaust me, will you.

February 24, 2017
Rackham

I continued watching *Westworld* at the fitness center last night but had to cut my episode short in order to make it to the grocery store before it closed. At the Waitrose I bought a small steak and some broccoli. Then I took a seat on the bench that faces the entrance and pulled out my iPad. The final few minutes of the show involved the saloon madam, Maeve, being operated on. But she hadn't been properly put to sleep and wound up jumping off the table. She was wandering naked through the place where her fellow robots, also nude, were washed and repaired when I heard someone say, "Sir?" It was a boy, maybe eleven years old. I'd noticed him skateboarding with a friend near the Caffè Nero and now he was talking to me for some reason.

I took out my earbud. "Yes?"

"I've cut myself, sir," he said. "And was wondering if you had a sticking plaster?"

"A Band-Aid, you mean?"

He held out his hand to reveal a quarter-size wound on his right palm. It was like he'd just pried himself off the cross.

Who asks people if they happen to have a Band-Aid? I wondered. Then, in the same breath, I felt certain that I actually had a Band-Aid on me. I looked through the pouch on my knapsack, realizing as I did so that my iPad was frozen on a picture of a naked woman. Surely he must have noticed, this eleven-year-old. Was I like the guy at the bus station with his nose buried in a copy of *Hustler*?

The whole show's not like this, I wanted to explain. *She's a robot, see, and even if she were real, this wouldn't turn me on. If anything, I feel sorry for her.*

"Here," I said, and I handed the kid my coin purse. "Maybe they sell Band-Aids at the Waitrose."

"I don't need all that money," he told me.

"How much do you think Band-Aids cost?" I asked. "I mean the sticking plasters."

He shrugged. "Three pounds?"

"Take four," I told him. "And come out if you need more."

I returned to *Westworld* but kept an eye on the door, thinking I'd turn it off before he came to give me my change. He was too quick, though. "They don't sell plasters, but thank you anyway," he said, giving me back my four pounds. "Thank you, sir. That was very kind of you."

I'm always so surprised when children are polite and wished I could have told his parents what a good son they have. That would have involved asking for his name and address, though, and no, that wouldn't have done at all.

March 8, 2017
Rackham

Yesterday morning shortly after ten, Dawn arrived, and an hour and a half later we were on the train to Sussex. It was bright and cold, and while I answered emails, she told Hugh about the charley horse she'd had on the flight from Minnesota. The plane was only a quarter full, and she was stretched out on her own row, happily asleep, when it struck her. "I used to get them all the time. Then I met a woman who told me I needed to put a bar of soap in my bed. I don't know why it works, but it does!" she said. "I started sleeping with soap four years ago and was charley-horse-free until last night, when I *didn't* have soap. I mean, I did, but it was in my suitcase in the belly of the plane!"

After lunch we walked to the Waitrose in Storrington. Heading home afterward, we passed the bridal shop. Dawn looked briefly at the gowns in the window, and when I asked what she had worn to her wedding, she said—no surprise—that she'd made her own dress.

"What color was it?" I asked, picking up a flattened can.

"Brown," she told me.

She has to be the only woman in the world who got married in a brown dress.

"It's my favorite color!" she said. "You know that."

Hugh made flattened chicken for dinner and afterward we sat before the fire in the living room and played two rounds of Sorry. I won the first, and Hugh won the second. There's something so innocent about playing board games. I always wish that someone would peer through the windows then or drop by to find us drinking things with no alcohol in them and crying, "But you drew the *last* two!"

If someone had told me forty years ago that this was in my future, I would have spit on him.

March 26, 2017
Rackham

We sprang forward last night, meaning I went to bed at 3:45 rather than 2:45. What kept me up was a call to Dad, who'd phoned on Friday and left a message. The conversation began the way it usually does nowadays: "How the hell are you!" followed by "So how the hell are you!" We talked for over an hour before he came to the purpose of his original call. "How would you like a drone?"

"I beg your pardon?"

"I was wondering what you get the guy who has everything and suddenly it hit me—a drone!"

"For, like, dropping bombs on people?"

"No," he said. "Surveillance. Picture taking, that sort of thing."

"I don't think my neighbors would appreciate that," I said, wondering how I might feel were I to see a hovercraft with a camera attached to it loitering outside my bedroom window, photographing the freshly waxed floor, the polished furniture, the beautifully made bed. "I mean, I wouldn't mind it, but they probably would," I added.

"Well, think about it," Dad said.

We also talked about Paul and Kathy. That led to Mom and her drinking. I was the one who brought it up. It's been on my mind since I started this latest essay. "Do you think she did it because of me?" Dad asked.

"I don't know that you can always attribute it to a specific reason," I said.

"I think she was unhappy because her looks were gone," he said. "She was starting to get lines on her face and so on and it made her lose her will to live."

What? I thought. Mom was always well put together, but it's not like she was Lauren Bacall. *Where did he get this idea from?* I wondered. It seems like something only a straight man would think: *She's sad; must be because she looks old now.*

That said, it was a good phone call. "When can I see you?" he asked, ending with "Hey, we need to do this more often."

I heard yesterday that one-third of Americans believe in ghosts.

March 29, 2017
Rackham
According to an article in the *Washington Post,* if spiders felt like it, they could devour everyone on earth between now and next St. Patrick's Day. As it is, they stick to insects, 400 to 800 million tons of them a year. It's a lot, given that there

are only 25 million tons of spiders in the world. The *Titanic* weighed 52,000 tons, therefore the weight of the planet's spiders is 478 times the weight of the *Titanic*.

That's really something to think about. The author of the article says that wherever you are, chances are good that there's a spider watching you. *Pish-posh*, someone in a high-rise apartment might think. Here, though, there's no doubting that statement. I bet there are at least fifty in the room with me right now. Every morning the first thing I do is check the tub and the kitchen sink to see who fell in while I was asleep. Then I pluck him or her out, always wondering what they think. One moment they were scrambling for purchase on the porcelain, and the next, they're free. It's nice to believe that they see me as a benevolent god, but more likely they just think I'm clumsy, that I tried to eat them and they got away. If it's gratitude you're after, rescue a dog. That said, I'd take a spider any day.

April 9, 2017
New York

At last night's book signing I met an eleven-year-old boy who'd come with his gay father. "Hey," the kid said. "I got a joke for you. What's good on a pizza but not on pussy?"

Shocked by his language, I said, "I beg your pardon?"

"What's good on a pizza but not on pussy?" he repeated.

Well, lots of things, I thought. *Mushrooms. Piping-hot cheese. The list goes on and on.*

"Crust!" the boy cried, looking up at his dad, who laughed.

"Oh my God," I said, reaching for my canvas bag. In it I keep little giveaways to hand out to kids and teenagers and people whose birthday it is. Quite often I'll offer bars of hotel soap, so I looked for one, thinking I could use it to wash out the boy's mouth. "Eleven!" I said. "That's way too young to be using that word."

"He gets it from his brother," the dad announced, smiling. "He's seventeen."

I thought I was pretty hard to shock, but I guess I thought wrong. *Pussy*. From an eleven-year-old! Wasted on a joke that's not even funny.

April 21, 2017
Miami, Florida

A joke Andrew sent me:

A Jewish man was leaving a convenience store when he noticed an unusual funeral procession approaching the nearby cemetery. The black hearse was followed by a second hearse. Behind that was an Italian fellow walking a dog on a leash, and behind him were about two hundred or so men walking in single file. The Jewish man couldn't quite figure out what was going on and approached the Italian guy with the dog, saying, "I am sorry for your loss, and this may be a bad time to disturb you, but I've never seen a funeral like this. Whose is it?"

"My wife's," the Italian said. "She yelled at me a few days ago and my dog attacked and killed her."

"So who is in the second hearse?" the Jewish man asked.

"My mother-in-law," the Italian said. "She came to help my wife and the dog killed her as well."

The Jewish man thought for a moment. "Can I borrow your dog?"

The Italian gestured behind him. "Get in line."

April 22, 2017
Little Rock, Arkansas

The breakfast room at the Capital Hotel is one of my favorites. I was there earlier this morning, and was waited on by a fellow who complimented me on my glasses, adding, "Do you mind if I try them on?"

It was such an odd request. "Of course," I said. "Be my guest."

He told me where he'd bought his frames and explained that they were called Tokyo Tortoise. "That's going to be my nickname for you," I said.

I later returned and brought him my black pair so he could try those on as well.

"Thank you, Mr. Sedaris."

"My pleasure, Tokyo Tortoise."

May 2, 2017
Austin

At last night's signing I met a young bearded man who, at the end of our encounter, extended his hand. I took it and found it nearly impossible to let go.

"What's happening here?" I asked. Nothing felt better than holding this guy's hand. He was plump, and it was soft and pillow-like. "Don't let go," I said, noticing that his knuckles and forearms were hairless, like a baby's.

It was like holding dough. "Can I hold the other one as well?" I asked.

"Sure!"

I closed my eyes and wished I could stop time and spend the next hour holding hands with this young man. It was crazy.

I later met a young woman who works as a professional cuddler. I'd read about this in the *Times* and thought it was a good idea for lonely people. She'd come with one of her clients, who was a bit older than her and remarkably pale.

Finally, I met a guy whose mother heard him say the word *fucker* when he was ten and made him eat an entire bar of Lava soap with a knife and fork.

May 5, 2017
Las Vegas

Yesterday was a real nail-biter. My flight from Santa Barbara wound up taking off an hour and ten minutes late. I ran for my connection at LAX and was heartened to find a couple of people still boarding. "If you're here for Vegas, forget it," announced the gate attendant, a tall, powerfully built fellow with graying temples.

"But..." panted the woman who ran up behind me.

"We already gave your seats away," the gate attendant told her.

Steven had backed me up on a later flight and just as I was about to turn away, I got a sudden urge to assert myself. "I'm first class," I said.

The attendant sighed and gave two standby candidates boarding passes. Then he took mine and tapped some information into his computer. "If you're not here ten minutes before takeoff, we give your seat away."

"I wasn't dawdling," I said.

"Excuse me?"

"I wasn't shopping or having a coffee with friends," I told him. "My flight was delayed. I just landed two minutes ago."

"I'm just explaining that that's the policy," the guy said. "Ten minutes before takeoff, don't come here expecting your seat."

I gave him the look one learns to perfect in first class, the one that means *Just do your little job.*

The surprise was that I was still in first class, though it wasn't my original seat. Rather, I was beside the window, next to a guy who looked to be around thirty-five and vaguely resembled Wisconsin governor Scott Walker. He had black hair that was thinning on top, and thick lips. His eyebrows joined together as one—the way my own once did—and he was watching a knockoff iPad disfigured by a bulky plastic case. It was a short flight—only forty-five minutes—and during every moment of it, my seatmate feasted on himself. If he wasn't picking his nose and then sticking that finger into his mouth, he was eating his ear wax or nibbling at the crust in the corners of his eyes. Or chewing his nails or the skin that bordered them. It made me sick, but I couldn't stop watching him and wondering, *Do you know what you're doing, what you look like?*

When the flight attendant came with the snack basket, I fought the urge to brush it away. *That's okay,* I wanted to tell her. *He's already full.*

The cannibal took two bags of chips and I thought, *Good, maybe he'll eat those instead of himself.* No luck, though. Rather, he saved the snacks for later and returned to the gold mine of his nose.

That's the thing about first class, I thought, watching him go at it. *You think it's fancy, but it's snot.*

May 11, 2017
Seattle

"How's your morning going so far?" chirped the Alaska Airlines agent at the check-in desk in Victoria yesterday.

I winced.

"How's your morning going so far?" she said, a bit brighter this time.

"I'm sorry," I said. "But I just hate that question."

"Really?" She moaned. "But it's such a good one. You could answer, 'My morning's been crappy. I burned my toast and was late for work and I wish I could start all over again.'"

Yes, but who would care, I thought.

The woman handed me my boarding pass. "Have you got something better I could ask?"

I thought for a moment. "How about 'Do you think I'm pretty?'"

It's actually the perfect question, guaranteed to make people uncomfortable.

"Do you think I'm pretty?" the ticket agent asked.

"Um...sure," I said, dying a little as I lied to her.

May 14, 2017
Anchorage

I met a male nurse at last night's signing. "I thought of you not long ago," he told me. "I was putting a catheter in a patient, a woman in a coma, when she started to pee. That's common enough," he continued, "but then she farted. The air blew through the urine and a drop of it flew into the air and went right into my open mouth."

"Oh my God," I said.

"My hands were full, so there was nothing I could do," he told me. "Anyway, it made me think of you!"

May 17, 2017
London

I'm in the British Airways Lounge, where the Wi-Fi password is always a destination; Budapest is today's. How much more interesting to have it be an illness—pneumonia, for instance, or colon cancer.

June 6, 2017
Grand Rapids, Michigan

At last night's event I met a woman who wanted a book inscribed to her son's godmother. "When she was little we convinced her that as long as she was naked, she was invisible, so the family has all these great videos and pictures of her with no clothes on taking sodas from the fridge and climbing onto the kitchen counters for candy."

It's a great story, and one wonders how long she believed her nudity kept her hidden. I can see her as a teenager not sneaking out of the house but boldly walking naked down the stairs and out the front door. I see her marching into a store wearing nothing at all and heading for the register.

June 19, 2017
Denver

I phoned Dad last night to wish him a Happy Father's Day. I assumed I'd get his machine, that he'd be off at Paul's having dinner, but he was at home alone. Dad likes talking about my health, so I told him about the gastrointestinal virus I had last month and the fear I'd had that I might shit in my pants onstage. "I worried I'd need adult diapers!"

"Well, they're not all that expensive," he told me.

I laughed at his assumption that the price was what scared me.

"I've been wearing them for the past few months," Dad confided. "No one in the family knows it, but I'm incontinent."

You're telling me? I thought. *Mr. Big Mouth?*

"You won't be laughing when it's your turn, I can guarantee you that," he said.

"I'm not laughing now," I told him.

"Yes, you are."

He didn't sound delighted to hear from me but was hardly a crab. We talked for half an hour or so and I hung up feeling terribly sorry for him.

June 24, 2017
Portland, Oregon

During last night's eight-hour book signing at Powell's, I met a young woman named Raney with a large tattoo of Carl from *The Walking Dead* on her left thigh. "I got my mom to sign off on it when I was seventeen," she said, sighing. "I thought I was going to be into that show and that comic forever, right? Cut to now and I haven't watched it in years, couldn't give a damn about it." Raney was twenty-three with dyed-blond hair. "Then there's this one," she said, backing up so I could see the portrait of Bryan Cranston as Walter White on her right calf. "Who'd have thought that tattooing a famous meth addict on my leg would mean that wherever I go, creepy guys would try to sell me crystal?" Again she sighed. "I'm wondering if I can't turn him into someone else—Walt Whitman, maybe."

July 1, 2017
Raleigh

My favorite person at last night's signing was a fifty-year-old man who lives with his mother. "What do you do for a living?" I asked.

"Well," he said, "I'm mentally ill. And that keeps me pretty busy."

Earlier I met a woman from Gastonia. "There was an IHOP in our town that was located on Cox Road, and they'd answer their phone saying, 'IHOP on Cox!'" she told me.

July 14, 2017
London

Walking through Hyde Park I passed a woman pitching a cricket ball to her son, who looked to be seven and was staring past her at a group of boys who had hold of a tree branch and were jumping up and down on it. The mother followed her son's gaze and called, "Hey, be careful or you'll snap that off."

The oldest of the boys put his hands on his hips and yelled back, "We're *kids*," meaning either "We don't have the strength" or, likelier still, "You're not allowed to talk to us."

July 18, 2017
London

As of yesterday, the London Underground announcements will no longer begin with "Ladies and gentlemen." Gender-queer people said it made them feel excluded, so from now on the conductors will say, "Hello, everyone."

There's something sad about this to me. It's like a casual Friday for language, only it's not just on Friday. I rather liked being thought of as a gentleman. *Yes,* I'd think whenever I heard it, *I believe I'm up for this.*

As for the people who once felt excluded, what will this honestly do for them? Whatever news follows "Hello, everyone," like whatever followed "Ladies and gentlemen," is bound to be bad—a stalled train ahead of us, a signaling failure—so actually, they should just change it to "Sorry, everyone."

July 20, 2017
Rackham

We took a 12:06 train from Victoria and things were fine until we reached Gatwick. That was when a couple in their thirties boarded. Watching as they took my bag and rearranged it on the rack so as to make things easier for themselves, I wondered, *Are they French?* The two took seats across the aisle from me and Hugh—facing us—and a short time later they started making out.

Oh no, I thought.

After a while the guy lay down with his head in the young woman's lap. His legs blocked the aisle, and as she bent to kiss him, the two spoke, and I realized with some satisfaction that I was right—French. The couple ticked all the boxes: re-arranging luggage, making out, and blocking the aisle. Had they been in reserved seats and refused to move, it would have been a clean sweep.

July 22, 2017
Rackham

I was heading toward the front door of the fitness center yesterday when a woman stopped me. She was around my age with two small dogs, and she pointed to a bench on the other side of the cricket pitch. "Excuse me, but there were some teenagers over there eating and drinking and I'm afraid they've left a terrible mess."

"Oh, I don't work here," I told her.

"No? Well, I think it's brilliant what you do. You're my hero. I'd pick the cans and bottles up myself, but of course I have the dogs to care for."

I told her I'd get it all after I finished exercising. "Don't you think they should give me free membership?" I asked. "Given all I do to keep this place clean?"

"Absolutely!" she said.

An hour later I went to pick up the dozens of cans and bottles the young people had left. They completely filled my bag and as I went to empty it, I came upon another woman my age. She, too, thanked me. "It's kids, isn't it?" she said.

In this morning's *Times* I read about a group of teenagers in Cocoa, Florida, who videotaped a drowning man and called out insults as he died. None of them reported the incident, much less phoned 911. All the English teens did was litter, but still, at least for now, I'm painting them with the same brush.

While I was talking to the first woman, some boys passed on bikes, and one, a fat kid, called out in a mocking tone, "Hello, David."

How does he know my name? I wondered.

August 11, 2017
Emerald Isle

Hugh was in a great mood on our plane from London yesterday. He was in a good mood driving from the Raleigh airport to the beach as well. Amy was with us and talked a bit about her new TV show. "My goal on this trip is to die," she said from the back seat. "I hate, hate, hate our production schedule."

The clips I've seen are really funny, but she worries the pace is off. "Everything's too slow."

It took three hours to reach the coast. Along the way we passed a Taco Bell with a sign out front that advertised the new Beefy Potato-Rito. We passed an Arby's and Amy said that when she was in high school she stole a straw dispenser from there.

"How?" I asked.

She shrugged. "Just walked over and took it. Then I stole a portrait of the Colonel from Kentucky Fried Chicken. I stole wigs off of department-store mannequins too, on a dare. It was just high-school stuff."

I'd had no idea.

Just outside of Beulaville, Hugh stopped at a Food Lion. We got out of the car, all of us sore from our plane rides and sitting. "In twenty years, we'll be eighty," I said to Amy. "Can you imagine what we'll feel like then?"

"Eighty!" she said.

"We'll have wattles," I said. "And I'll be walking with a cane."

When the cashier bagged our groceries, I told her that never happened where I lived.

"And where is that?" she asked.

"In England, and it's worse in France, where you have to have exact change."

"They don't give you no change?"

"Not without a fight," I told her. "Plus they sit down the whole time."

"We ain't allowed to sit down 'less we're on break," the cashier said. She was pale and had lank hair the color of dead pine needles.

"Do your feet hurt at the end of the day?"

"Lord, yes."

"Do you soak them?"

"It's too much work to get out the bucket," she said, sighing.

August 17, 2017
Emerald Isle

We were in the ocean yesterday, crowded onto inflatable rafts, when I brought up the Beefy Potato-Rito.

"The what?" Maddy asked.

"It's something Taco Bell is offering," I told her. "We passed a sign for it on our way to the beach."

"Ugh," Gretchen moaned. "Taco Bell."

"I don't think I've ever been," Amy said, looking beyond us at an incoming pod of pelicans.

Maddy said she didn't like Taco Bell and then told us about a place she'd heard about that had an incorrectly spaced sign out front that read FRE SHAVOCADO.

"Huh?" Amy said.

"Fresh avocado," Maddy explained. "Only they separated the two words wrong."

Hugh crept up from behind me just then and grabbed my

foot, causing me to scream like a girl. "What are you so afraid of?" he asked, laughing.

"Sharks," I told him.

He rolled his eyes. "There are no sharks here."

"Go to the pier and look over the edge," Maddy said. "You'll see dozens of them."

Hugh rolled his eyes again. "The pier—that's a mile away."

Maddy is fourteen now and it's hard to believe she's the same girl she was last summer. She's much more relaxed and will talk without being asked a question. "Daddy" is how she refers to Paul, as in "Remember the time Daddy..."

Tonight is the Miss Emollient Pageant, so Gretchen, who is the color of a wet pine stump, is going at it full force. "I know there are people with nicer skin than mine," she said late yesterday afternoon. "But I think the judges need to think about commitment. It takes hours to get this dark, and I don't mean, like, one day for a few hours but four or five hours a day for weeks, for months!"

She was on her back at the time, her hands at her sides, palms up. "And I'm also *even*—the same color coming as I am going." She lit a cigarette. "I just think it's something the judges need to consider."

October 4, 2017
London

At the Decorative Antiques and Textiles Fair I bought a cushion made by a convict. I really wanted the one that read HAND-STITCHED IN PRISON, but that was just for show, unfortunately. The one I got cost 120 pounds, and after I paid, the saleswoman suggested I write a thank-you letter to the guy who'd made it. "It's a good gesture," she said, "and it does wonders for the prisoners' self-esteem. You'll find the man's name and address on the slip of paper that's attached to the cushion."

If he was giving *me the cushion, I'd write him a thank-you letter, and without your prompting, thank you very much,* I thought. *But seeing as I'm* buying *it, I don't really know that it's necessary.*

I then moved on to the next booth, which was run by two brothers I'd bought some paintings from a few years back. They're shorter than I am, and once the older of the two accidentally filled his steam iron with white wine. "I was pressing a shirt and suddenly the room smelled of fruitcake," he told me. "So what have you got there, a cushion?"

October 11, 2017
New York

Cristina and I met for breakfast at my hotel, the Langham, and listened as the Italian couple next to us ordered in not-so-great English. "You will bring me a smoothie," stated the woman, who was very pretty and had no makeup on.

When she learned that the kitchen was not equipped to make her one, that they didn't have a pulverizer or whatever it's called, she commenced to pout. "A five-star hotel and you will not do this for me? Five-star!" She looked the waiter up and down. "You are disgusting," she spat.

"I don't know that that's the right use of that word," I whispered to Cristina.

The waiter later told me that the couple left without paying. "They each had a pastry and, for him, a cappuccino. Then they just walked out!"

Cristina told me that her office keeps a file of complaints registered against me. A recent one involved my use of *flesh-colored*. "What's that supposed to mean?" the author of the email demanded. "In case he doesn't know, flesh comes in many colors!!"

I'd meant "Band-Aid-colored," but I suppose those come in a variety of shades as well.

October 13, 2017
Baltimore

The actor who played Puck on *Glee* was arrested a couple of years back for possession of child pornography. They found all sorts of pictures on his computer, apparently, and last week he pleaded guilty. The general consensus is "Kill the monster," but I feel sorry for him. A person can't help who he's attracted to, and it must be terrifying to realize it's kids that you want. Being a pedophile—or at least, being a "good" one—means a lifetime of celibacy, which can't be easy. Those who are trying—the *Glee* actor among them—at least deserve a little pornography to masturbate to, but making that pornography would scar a child for life and so is out of the question. My solution, then, is to use dead children.

I explained this to Lee, who thought for a moment and then asked, "How dead?"

October 22, 2017
Charlotte

Adam met me at the airport yesterday and together we drove to the Ritz. It was a Saturday afternoon in downtown Charlotte, and the Black Israelites had installed themselves across the street. I used to see them in New York. "Cracker Faggot," they'd bark into their microphones as I passed.

"Welcome to the Ritz-Carlton," the bellman said as he took my suitcase out of the trunk. "Are you here for business or pleasure?"

I pointed across the street. "Oh, I'm with them."

November 10, 2017
Breckenridge, Colorado
I met a guy last night who stays home all day while his wife works. "I'm living off the sweat of my Frau," he said.

November 13, 2017
San Francisco
A joke Ronnie told me:

It's night, and a cop stops a car a couple of priests are riding in. "I'm looking for two child molesters," he says.

The priests think for a moment. "We'll do it!" they say.

November 17, 2017
San Diego
After checking into my hotel, I walked to the harbor front, where I passed a store called America's Heroes. The men's T-shirts in the window read ARMY or USMC while the women's pictured a shapely female silhouette above the words BOOTY CAMP.

December 9, 2017
Odesa, Ukraine
Most of the men I've seen in Odesa look like thugs. Their hair and beards are the same length—too short to pull—and they all tend to swagger. "It really is amazing," Patsy whispered at the restaurant last night. We ate at the hotel in a room that looked like it was decorated by Donald Trump. The curtains were the shade and texture of pantyhose and hung in limp swags behind the heavier pea-green drapes that went over them. Chairs were high-backed and velvet, some gold and others the same color as the drapes. There were chandeliers overhead and, at our feet, a mosaic-tiled floor. Carols played,

but so did music from the white grand piano in the next room. And everyone around us was a thug.

"Incredible," Patsy said. She looked at the menu, noting that a vodka was only slightly more expensive than a Coke. The restaurant was far from full, perhaps because of the prices. We each had appetizers and an entrée. Patsy had a few glasses of wine and it came to around ninety dollars, which is a lot in this country.

As we ate, a man took glamour shots of his wife, who was maybe forty and attractive. She wore thigh-high boots and was not afraid to pose in front of people. "She's pouting now," Patsy would whisper, looking over my shoulder. "Oh, here we go, now she's got her hands on the back of her head."

My first bit of Ukrainian was wasted on the guy who checked my passport. "Hello," I said. "Good day. Are you a Ukrainian gentleman?"

"*Tak.*"

"I am an American gentleman," I told him.

He looked up and sighed.

I heard someone use the Ukrainian word for "hour" and someone else say in that language, "I don't know." It was exciting.

Our luggage arrived and we exited to meet our driver, Gunadi ("Gun-odd-ee"), who doesn't look like a thug but sort of acts like one. "We have to change money," Patsy explained, moving toward the currency-exchange booth.

"I do that in car," Gunadi said.

"Excuse me?"

"In car I have money."

"But..."

"In car."

"Ride?" a thug asked, approaching from our left. "I give you better deal."

The neighborhoods we drove through to reach the hotel were bleak and unlike anything I have seen anywhere else in the world. Buildings were two and three stories tall, crumbling, many fronted by wretched-looking shops. A great many people stood bundled by the side of the road near piles of onions or potatoes, the women with scarves tied under their chins. "Is this where you're from?" I asked Gunadi, who was maybe fifty and driving us in a very noticeable BMW.

"Yes, is my town."

Other cars were grime-covered and dented, many looking like toys, holdovers, I imagined, from when this was part of the Soviet Union. It was perhaps 50 degrees and slightly overcast. Trees were bare. Everything looked dirty.

I used my Ukrainian to fine effect at the check-in desk, which was staffed by two young women. Our rooms are on the top floor, and though a good size, they have no windows, only skylights, which is disconcerting. A young bellman with a mullet brought up our bags and led us to the spa, where a tall, beautiful woman showed us the hot slab where massages are given. There was a sauna and steam room along with a pool that stank of too much chlorine. Floor-to-ceiling windows offered the grim view we'd have in our rooms if we had windows.

"Beautiful!" Patsy said.

We went to a place across the street for some spinach pie. The restaurant was cozy and reminded me of every coffeehouse I'd visited in Warsaw, decorated with dark, too-heavy antiques. I complimented the waiter in Ukrainian on his English and he responded that he was trying the best that he could—he said it as if I had criticized him.

By five it was dark. Patsy's ankle was bothering her so she took a bath while I went out for some excercise. All the sidewalks were broken, like they are in Athens, even though this is the fancy part of town. I passed groups of drunk men and old women begging. I gave one the equivalent of forty cents and continued on, feeling very generous. It was getting colder. A bus passed and I saw that it had curtains over the windows, not attached on the top and bottom, but only on top, and they fluttered.

December 10, 2017
Odesa

In the bright light of morning Odesa didn't look so bad for a while. There are plenty of trees and when there are leaves on them, they must vastly improve the streets, or at least hide some of the sadder parts. Our day started in the hotel restaurant. Patsy and I agreed to meet at eight for breakfast and I came down an hour early to drink coffee. I tried to tune out the Christmas carols, most of them American, but failed.

The buffet included cold poached eggs served on bacon and round pieces of toast, head cheese, and vodka. There was a bottle beside a stack of glasses and I watched as an Asian fellow helped himself. *What must it be like to start your day like that?* I wondered.

The driver Gunadi met us at ten and drove us a mile away to a dismal flea market where people sold crap on the ground. It wasn't one of those places where you're reluctant to look someone in the eye, afraid he'll give you the hard sell. No one seemed to care whether or not they sold anything. Even if you picked something up, the seller would leave you alone until you asked a question.

Gunadi had given us both the Ukrainian and the Russian for "How much is it," saying that people spoke both languages, though more of the former than the latter. He seemed sulky in the car and spent a lot of time talking to a woman on the phone. Every so often, though, he'd point something out. "Very old synagogue. Two hundred years."

"Were Ukrainian Jews killed in the Holocaust?" Patsy asked.

"Now is a . . . archive," Gunadi said. He wasn't being evasive. His English just wasn't very good. *Archive* is apparently the same in English as it is in Ukrainian. That's the only reason we got it.

Patsy got a lot at the flea market: a Roman coin, dish towels, more dish towels. We both bought postcards (they're too flimsy to send) and Communist pins and buttons. Then we wandered through the animal section, where puppies and kittens mewed and barked from too-small cages and the trunks of cars. It was a bright, clear morning, cold but not annoyingly so. The people we dealt with were all kind and good-natured. I never felt like I was being ripped off or targeted.

At dusk I went out on my own and came upon a warren-like outdoor market where women sold spotted fruit from card tables. One sat before a few dozen sad-looking tangerines. I liked the sign that she'd made from a piece of cardboard. Most likely it stated the price, though I suppose it could have been saying anything—*Hi!* or *I'm Cold, How About You?* "Do you understand English?" I asked in Ukrainian as I pulled the equivalent of a five-dollar bill from my pocket.

She didn't.

"I will give you this for your sign," I said.

She started filling a bag with blighted tangerines.

"No, just the sign."

As she continued two young women stepped up. "Oh my God, are you speaking English?" one of them asked. "I haven't heard English in, like, days. Where are you from?"

The woman's friend was Russian and spoke English with no

accent. "Can you explain to this woman that I just want to buy her sign?" I asked.

The young woman translated my request into Russian and all the other vendors began to laugh, saying, I imagine, *Now I've heard everything! The sign! Ha!*

I handed the vendor the money I was holding and she handed it back.

"She says it's a gift," the Russian girl said.

"No, I insist! Please." I jabbed it back.

"You would be insulting her," the young woman explained. "Please, just take the sign."

And so I did, realizing later that I should have at least bought five dollars' worth of tangerines. How dumb was I.

From the market I walked to the avenue the Bristol was on and then went on a mile-long detour. The streetlights were weak and widely spaced, and all the sidewalks were broken. *This,* I thought, *is what happens when people don't constantly sue one another*. The streets feel safe enough crime-wise but treacherous for old people, especially when snow- and ice-covered.

December 11, 2017
Chişinău, Moldova

Moldova is supposedly poorer than Ukraine, though you sure wouldn't know by driving on its roads or walking down the street. It has more hideous tower blocks than I saw in Odesa—they seem to go on for miles here—but there's very little graffiti, and the sidewalks aren't broken up, or at least the ones that I've seen so far aren't. Our hotel is beautiful and modern. My windows open, there's a sitting area, and the floors are bare wood but for some area rugs. My view is of a doleful housing complex, but it looks less depressing in the snow.

Driving here from Ukraine meant traveling through the

breakaway state of Transdniestria. It's under Russian control and was far more modern than anything I saw in Odesa. We passed a monument to Lenin and a big tank on a pedestal, both looking like something you'd see in a 1970 *Encyclopædia Britannica* entry on the Soviet Union. At one point we stopped at what seemed their equivalent of a Walmart to use the toilet. The store's aisles were like boulevards, brightly lit and empty on a Sunday morning in December.

I'd thought the countryside outside of Odesa would be grim, but it wasn't. True, the land was flat, but the roadsides were clean and there were plenty of trees. The villages we drove through were not picturesque and the people we saw all seemed to be carrying plastic bags, though I had no idea where they were coming from, as I saw no stores. As in Romania, a number of them seemed to be staring into oncoming traffic, hoping someone might stop.

It started snowing as we neared the border. This meant stopping alongside what seemed like several hundred people who were on foot and had come from ... where exactly?

"It good for shopping," Gunadi said. "Many things cheaper."

The villages we passed after crossing into Moldova resembled those in Romania. Backyards were fenced in and had wells and outhouses in them. The land was hillier than it was in Ukraine and the trees were laden with snow. I slept for a while and awoke as we entered Chișinău. It's a hard-looking city, mainly because of the tower blocks. Everyone was dressed in a heavy dark coat and hat. Everyone carried a plastic bag.

After lunch at the hotel I followed the bellman's directions to the center of town. In time I came to the world's saddest department store, five brightly lit floors of crap. There was a "Parada" boutique and acres of heartbreaking shoes for men and women ("VIP Collection"). I bought a pair of socks with roses on them at the counter that sold native costumes.

Once I left the department store, the sidewalks were easier to navigate. I was able to move quickly and tick off all the exercise minutes on my watch. It was lovely, the central area. I came to a park with snow-laden firs in it and a monument. I walked for two and a half hours. On my way back to the hotel I came upon a beggar with two false legs and no hands.

December 12, 2017
Paris

After breakfast at our Moldovan hotel yesterday, I accompanied Patsy to the clean, bright supermarket a quarter of a mile up the road. It was 10:30 on a Monday morning and maybe a dozen people were shopping. I saw some interesting matches, Patsy filled a basket with little things for her friends back home, and then we parted, her limping back to the hotel and me walking to the mall I'd seen the night before. It was massive from the outside but strangely small once I'd entered. *What is it, padded?* I wondered, taking the escalator to the second floor and peering into sad, empty clothing shops. At one point I heard a bird screeching and followed the noise until I came to what was essentially the pet department of a pizza restaurant.

The mice and snakes I saw seemed normal enough. Then there was a goat and a pig who was lying alone in the sawdust beside two potato-size turds. These were overseen by an angry monkey with needle-like teeth who was no larger than a chipmunk. *Who will buy these things?* I wondered.

On that same floor I found a sex-toy shop.

From the mall, I walked up a hill and came to the same boulevard I'd walked down the night before. It was cold and sunny, and I passed a guy in a folding chair who was seated across from the National Theater. At his feet was a bathroom scale and a sign that translated to "Your weight, 1 lei."

It was strange to see a bathroom scale on the sidewalk, but I saw another on the next block and a third on the block after that. Near the Ministry of Internal Affairs I saw a card table displaying a dozen or so tubes of something called Glister, which is apparently a toothpaste distributed by Amway.

While walking I noticed that occasionally an approaching man would scan me up and down with his eyes while frowning. It's the look you employ when judging someone, and I thought, *What did I do?* They were all dressed alike, in dark trousers and coats, most with dark hats. You'd think I had a dress on, though my only deviation was the color of my coat—tan—and a red scarf rather than a black one.

Well, excuse me, I thought.

December 17, 2017
Rackham

Included in the mail Little, Brown forwarded was a letter from a woman in Wappingers Falls, New York, who listened to part of *Theft by Finding* while in the car with her eighty-six-year-old mother, who, surprisingly, seemed to enjoy it. "Does the whole book continue this way?" she asked when they reached their destination. "Is it all that woman reading her diary?"

December 23, 2017
Rackham

Since we returned to Sussex from London, every day has been the same, with leaden skies and temperatures in the fifties. It's so gloomy I have my desk light on at nine a.m. I haven't looked at the forecast for the twenty-fifth. All I ask is that it be cold, please.

While the outside remains uncooperative, indoors, we're ready for Christmas. Last night after dinner we trimmed the tree while drinking eggnog and listening to carols. "Every ornament carries a very special memory we'd like to share with all of you," I announced to Hugh's cousin Robert and his wife, Cindy. It was just a joke—what could be worse than having to listen to such talk? Though it *is* true about the memories.

Apart from going in to open gifts, I will now avoid the living room, which I hardly ever spend time in anyway. The tree depresses me. I wish we could put it up on Christmas Eve and take it down two days later, but it brings Hugh great pleasure to sit before it, especially at night with the colored lights on.

December 27, 2017
Rackham

We awoke to snow. It doesn't happen terribly often here, so it was a real occasion. "Look!" Hugh said.

"I'm looking."

"Yes, but *look*!"

It's stopped now, and though there was no real accumulation it was nice to see random patches of it on the lawn and heaped on my outdoor table. I built a fire in my office yesterday and stayed in until two thirty, when I headed to Pulborough. At three it began to rain and it continued until seven thirty when I got home. There's a spot in the road that tends to flood, and the cars speeding past doused me with cold bucketfuls of water. "Fuck you!" I shouted, for surely they saw me and could have slowed down. My coat got wet, my hat, everything. And I still had eight miles ahead of me. *And it's my birthday!* I thought. Later I'd wonder at all the people who drove by, none of them stopping to ask if I needed a ride. I can understand not wanting a wet person and his bag of garbage in your car, but would you really let that stop you?

It's not that I would have accepted a ride, but shouldn't someone have offered? On my birthday?

2018

For what might be the first time ever, I have no idea where I was when the clock struck midnight. At my desk writing letters? In the tub? I was nowhere exciting, that's for sure. I said to Hugh over dinner, "Were we even invited anywhere?"

He said yes, that Ewan had asked us to dinner in London. In Hugh's condition, though, there was no way. He's had this flu for five days. Just when he thinks he's getting better, he relapses and feels worse. "It's overtaken the country," he moaned, huddled in the kitchen this morning. "There aren't enough doctors to treat all the people who are coming down with it."

Meanwhile the NHS is reminding everyone that it is not the National Hangover Service.

Had Hugh not gone to bed at eleven, I'd have known when the New Year hit. Instead, I was on my own. Weather-wise, yesterday was awful. All it did was rain. I got ready to go out after lunch, but just as I put my shoes on, it went from a drizzle to a downpour, so I stayed in for another few hours and answered letters. Little, Brown sent dozens of them a few weeks ago, and before the day ended I'd reached the bottom of the stack. The sweetest of the batch was from Marion Wheeler, the woman I met in Bristol last year when I was on my book tour. "I root for you," she wrote. "You deserve all the success that comes your way."

What a nice thing to hear from someone.

The worst letter in the batch was from a woman in a suburb of Chicago who'd seen my show in November and was not having it. First off, she said, it started fifteen minutes late. Then I brought out some guy who talked about me for another fifteen minutes! *Then* the potty humor—if you can call that humor—and on top of it all, I had a cold and blew my nose *into the microphone*! She ended by tallying the price of her tickets, dinner for her and her husband, and what it cost them to park their car. I'm guessing she wanted a check for the total.

It goes without saying that the woman had three names. I looked at her picture on Facebook and thought, *Of course.*

January 11, 2018
Seattle

It's rained every day since I arrived, but today it's supposed to really, really rain—at least an inch. "Oh, well," says Dawn. "We'll just go to the fitness center twice."

She and I had an early night. By eleven we were in bed, but by four a.m. we were both wide awake. I fell back asleep at some point, but it wasn't the kind of sleep that felt restful. I thought I was reading the paper that entire time. Then I realized there was no *Times* article about puppets filling my suitcase with grapes.

January 12, 2018
Seattle

Lisa wrote that Dad fell a few days ago. He fractured a number of ribs and now has stitches in his forehead. "I'm patiently waiting for him to break his hip," she said a few hours later over the phone.

January 16, 2018
Perth

"When was the last time you cried?" I asked a woman at last night's book signing.

"Just yesterday," she said.

"Why?"

"My father has dementia," she told me. "So we took him to the park and saw this girl, maybe five years old, on the slide. Other kids wanted to use it, but she just sat there at the top and wouldn't let them by. When she eventually went down, my dad said, really loudly, 'It's about time that little bitch got out of the way.'"

"And that made you cry?"

She shook her head. "I mean, she was five!"

January 19, 2018
Sydney

At last night's signing I met a guy whose dad used to threaten him, saying, "I am going to rip your arm off and beat you with the wet end."

January 27, 2018
Tokyo

On our way to the pottery shop we like, we passed an antiques store we'd visited on our second trip to Tokyo in 2007. "I bought a globe here," Hugh said to Amy, pausing to look in the window. "It was smaller than usual and on a beautiful stand. We shipped it back to England before leaving but for some reason or other it never arrived."

He frowned, and I put my hand on his shoulder. Poor Hugh. That globe meant the world to him.

January 28, 2018
Tokyo

Amy, Hugh, and I met Akira and Chiyoka for lunch in Yoko-hama yesterday. We went to the restaurant we ate at on our last visit and sat beside a family of three: parents in their mid-forties and a girl of around ten. Never once did they talk to one another. The man charged his phone from an outlet beside the table, and when they finished eating, the wife silently paid. Unlike in the U.S., people don't seem to speak to their servers or cashiers here. "Why not?" I asked Chiyoka. "Aren't they curious about the person who's waiting on them?"

"Not at all," she said.

Our waitress was around my age and was very formal. "That family not talk," I said in Japanese after the party of three had left.

The waitress seemed puzzled, so Chiyoka bailed me out. "He noticed that the people at the next table never spoke to one another."

"Ah, that's normal now," the waitress said. "Everyone is on their phone, aren't they?"

"Not us," I said. "We talk."

A short while later Amy asked for help locating a knife she was hoping to buy. That led to the verb for "to stab" (*sassumas*) and the news that a lot of kids are stabbing their parents to death in Japan now, though I'm not sure what Akira meant by "a lot." Surely not, say, 30 percent of children. It's not a gun culture, though, so stabbing is the way most people dispose of one another.

When our food came we asked Akira what this or that was — the marble-size ball at the bottom of a box, some damp shredded thing. He answered with a shrug, saying, "It's not just Western-ers. Japanese people don't know what we're eating either."

January 29, 2018
Tokyo
At one point late yesterday afternoon in the Christopher Nemeth store in Omotesandō, Hugh pooh-poohed a pair of trousers I was considering. Technically I guess they're sweatpants, as they stretch and have no fly—no closure, even. They're black and the pockets—which, surprisingly, function—look like organic holes. I feel like an old tree in them. The stitching is yellow although the rest of the pants are black, and they're designed to turn in at the ankle, making me look bowlegged.

"You *have* to get those," Amy said.

Hugh said they were clown pants, and Amy corrected him, saying, "Clown *sport*."

"They just...do nothing for you," Hugh complained, adjusting his stovepipe hat.

This, of course, changed things, especially given that the hat had smears of paint on it. I'd bought it for him hours earlier at the Yohji Yamamoto counter of a department store in Shibuya. We'd wandered in almost by accident, looking for lunch, and left hours later with several bags, most of them Amy's. The stovepipe hat is softer than we'd expected it to be. You can flatten it without causing damage, and, like most hats, it looks terrific on Hugh. It also makes him easier to spot in a crowd, which Amy and I appreciate. If it had a big red flower sticking up from it we'd like it even more.

February 3, 2018
Osaka, Japan
Before leaving the hotel yesterday, I considered the white shirt I'd just bought. "I don't know," I said to Hugh, looking at myself in the mirror. "Maybe if I dye it."

"You could just do what Todd and Cheryl are doing," he

said, looking up from his phone. "Cut out second helpings and sugar for a few months."

It took a moment for me to catch on. "I'm not saying it's too *small* for me, I'm saying it's too *white*."

March 21, 2018
Rackham

Over dinner Ingrid talked about an office she worked in for a year or so back in the eighties. "It was me and seven men," she said. "And this group, my God! They were constantly pulling their pants down to jump up on the Xerox machine, taking pictures of their bare bums and balls, which they'd leave on my desk. There was this one fellow, Devon, who'd approach with a ruler and pretend to measure the distance from my lips to the back of my head, calculating how far he could fit his cock in. Oh, we'd have such a laugh! It hardly felt like work, the days were so fun!"

It's shocking to hear that now. I mean, a Xerox machine!

April 6, 2018
New York

At 5:30 p.m. yesterday a very pale man in his seventies arrived to drive me to Morristown. He had white hair and baby-blue eyes and after wrongly guessing that he was Swedish or Russian, I learned that he was Polish. "But I did live in Stockholm two years."

At first the conversation was pleasant. Then he got on the subject of Muslims and how you simply can't have them living in Western countries. "My wife went to Paris not long ago and said she could not believe it. 'White people, we were like raisins in a cake,' she told me."

This led to black people and how lazy they are. "They don't want to work! And why should they when Uncle Sam gives them the welfare?" The driver said he'd gone to Charlotte recently and would gladly live there if only he were twenty years younger. He regretted working for a limo company after moving to the U.S. thirty years ago. "I should have worn the white collar and not the blue one because this"—he gestured to the wheel he was holding—"this has gotten me nothing. No house to own, only a shit apartment I rent."

Then it was back to black people leeching off the taxpayers. "I don't know how successful he'll be, but this is something President Trump is trying to change."

"Do you like birds?" I asked, desperate to get him onto another subject.

"Birds?" he said.

"With wings," I said. "You know. Birds."

He told me he'd had two parakeets he loved, but he asked a neighbor to watch them when he went to Poland and she'd let them escape. This led to his love of animals in general, not just pets but the things he sees out the window of his shit apartment: the squirrels that chase each other up trees, the occasional rabbit or stray cat.

I thought he'd be driving me back to Manhattan after the show but instead I got his exact opposite: black, liberal, born in America, and holding his nose until the Trump era is over.

April 8, 2018
Princeton

Lisa and Bob went to Dad's house yesterday morning to install the new TV and found him on the floor, soiled and disoriented. At his request, they put him in the bathroom, and on his way out he fell again. I got my information from Amy, who arrived shortly afterward and sent me the following report:

"Dad is spending the night in the hospital. He has a urinary tract infection. He slurs his words so it's hard to understand him. At one point he woke up and said very clearly and loudly, 'Outstanding. Fantastic. Wonderful. Marvelous.' He told the doctor Lisa was his wife and that he was in Syracuse, New York. It was very difficult to see him so vulnerable and sickly."

It's hard to admit, but my initial reaction was envy: *They're all there and I'm not! They're observing, they're having conversations in hospital rooms, they're seeing Dad as they've never seen him before. And I'm not!*

Isn't that awful?

April 23, 2018
Saint Louis

Adam met me at the baggage claim yesterday afternoon and together we headed to the airport's multilevel parking deck. This involved taking an elevator, and we'd just stepped inside one and pressed the button for our floor when a voice called, "Wait!" It was a woman with two daughters, aged maybe eight and ten. Adam held the closing doors and the girls ran in beside us, panting. Their mother, meanwhile, who was pushing a luggage cart, looked back in the direction she had come from, at her husband, I supposed, who was still a good distance away. The doors started to close again and she yelled to her daughters in a panicky voice, "Three! Go to level three and wait for us there!"

As the doors closed farther, I said to the woman what have to be the scariest words any parent can hear: "They're our girls now."

May 15, 2018
Vancouver

A woman in her late sixties came through the signing line last night and handed me a copy of *Theft by Finding.* "I'd like you to write something special, if that's all right," she said. "My daughter is being horrible to me, *has been* horrible for a long time now. One day I'll die, and I'm hoping she'll come across this book and feel terrible about the way she behaved. So how about something like, 'To Barbara, I'm sorry Cassidy didn't treat you better.'"

"Is Cassidy your only child?" I asked.

The woman nodded yes, and I picked up my pen. *To Barbara: I was fascinated by your story of the infant son you put up for adoption all those years ago.*

"Now, *that's* how you fuck someone up after you're dead," I said.

May 20, 2018
Rackham

It was beautiful when I arrived in London from New York yesterday. A chatty Lebanese man picked me up at the airport, and because it was a Saturday morning and the royal wedding was about to take place, there was no traffic whatsoever. We made it to the house in record time, and by noon I was on the bus headed to Victoria Station. It had just reached the High Street when a fellow in his late twenties boarded. He was wearing sweats, and when he fumbled in his pockets looking for his Oyster card, the man behind him, who was white-haired, moved ahead of him. "What the fuck," the young man said. "You can't just jump the queue, mate."

The older man apologized and touched the younger fellow on the arm. "So sorry, but—"

"Don't you fucking touch me," the young guy said. "Keep your fucking hands to yourself or I will *lay you out*. You got that?"

His reaction was vastly out of proportion to what had happened, which was, basically, nothing. He threatened twice more to knock the older man out, ending with "We queue in England, that's what we fucking do, you fucking bastard."

When the young man got off the bus ten or so minutes later, he stood on the sidewalk, glaring into the windows on the top floor, searching for the person who had done him wrong.

I sat there all the while wondering what I could have said or done to defuse the situation. Sweatpants in England translate to "quick-tempered."

On the train to Sussex I was struck by how green everything was. At one point I noticed a fellow passenger, a young man in a black coat that fell to the ground. It had a band around the waist that was a slightly different texture, and when the guy stood to disembark, I asked him about it. "That coat is really something," I said. "Is it part of a uniform?"

"I'm, um, a priest," he told me.

"Right," I said.

June 20, 2018
Albuquerque, New Mexico

What is it about Albuquerque? I'd been signing books for twenty or so minutes last night when a woman told me about a friend of hers who owns a pug. "He recently had an operation on one of his eyes so was having to wear a surgical cone around his neck, which he did not like one bit," she began. "All he did was whine and try to wrench it off, which was super-irritating. My friend removed it, just for some peace and quiet, and the pug scratched at his bandage with his back leg so hard that his eyeball literally popped out of his head. *And he ate it.*"

I made all the appropriate noises and facial expressions—horror, delight, horror again—and the woman said, "I knew you'd love that story."

She got that right. All night long I repeated it. "That is so interesting," said a woman I met a few hours later. She was a psychiatrist assigned to the county jail where a prisoner who was addicted to meth but had been clean for a month due to his incarceration dug both his eyes out with a teaspoon. He ate one but not the other, possibly because he couldn't find it.

I repeated the dog *and* the human story to someone an hour or so later, and she told me about another man—not a prisoner—who also dug his eye out with a spoon. "He was convinced there was a camera behind it," she said.

"So, was there?" I asked. Because after all that effort, you kind of want the guy to have been right.

Later still I met a woman with a friend who's in a gay gardening club called Fruits of the Earth.

Albuquerque!

June 27, 2018
San Francisco
Yesterday morning at 9:15 I had a radio interview. "Know who you look like?" the host of the show asked before we got under way.

"I'd rather not," I told him.

He shrugged. "Okay, fine." Then he held out his phone to a producer, who regarded it thoughtfully and said, "Sure, I can see that."

"Okay," I said. "Who is it?"

"Harry Truman," the host said. And I saw that he was right. He's not a terrible person to look like, though it's sort of grotesque when you picture him in Comme des Garçons culottes.

After the interview, walking to Wise and Sons for lunch, we passed an old tramp dressed in rags. He was lapping at a soft ice cream cone the way a cat might, and it was splotched all over his long white beard. "He should be in a commercial," Hugh said.

465

Later we passed an insane man with a pageboy haircut wearing a T-shirt that read IF SHE'S GOT A PULSE, SHE'S NOT MY TYPE.

July 12, 2018
Cambridge, England

I read my essay about cursing in other languages at last night's show. Later, at the signing, I met a woman from Istanbul. "When it comes to insults, the Romanians have nothing on us Turks," she said.

I set down my pen. "Hit me."

The woman put her hands on her hips. "I will plant a fir tree in your mother's cunt, then fuck your sister in its shade."

I said to Dave later, "Be careful what you wish for. It's going to take that tree a good long while to bear shade, and by that time my sister could be pretty rough-looking."

July 13, 2018
Glasgow

There are some good street musicians in Glasgow. I liked the jazz guitarist outside the Apple Store and a kid with a loud, clear Stacy Lattisaw–type voice on the pedestrian mall. I passed a lot of lads with fist-like faces. I passed drunks begging for money and bone-thin junkies buying drugs in an alley that might as well have been marked with a sign reading BUY DRUGS HERE at its entrance. I passed puddles of fresh vomit and then returned, with great relief, to my hotel.

July 18, 2018
Newcastle, England

I was on my way back from lunch yesterday, crossing through a crowded little park, when I saw a seagull pounce on a pigeon and stab her to death with his beak. "Oy!" people shouted, pulling out their phones. "Ha! Look at that!"

The gull stabbed the pigeon again and again, then flew a short distance with her body in his beak. Back on the ground, he returned to the serious business of decapitation, coming away at the end of each peck with a mouthful of feathers. It was traumatizing to watch, but not wholly unpleasant. It's not like there's a shortage of pigeons. That said, if I had to choose sides, I'd have gone with her, in part because she was smaller than the seagull and defenseless. When you're just passing through town, it's easy to like seagulls, but when you live in a city that's overrun with them and have to go to bed and wake up listening to them screech, when they tear your garbage bags open and block out your skylights with their gesso-like shit, you're probably not too terribly unhappy when one gets hit by a car.

It was like watching a juvenile delinquent disembowel a rat. *Okay,* I ultimately thought, watching as the gull struck pay dirt. *Carry on.*

July 28, 2018
London

I boarded the Eurostar Thursday afternoon, and we'd just left St. Pancras when the Englishwoman across the aisle began applying nail polish. "Tell me you're kidding," I said. She was in her late sixties and was sitting with her husband, who wore shorts and had a long pink face. "That's like using...spray paint on a train," I continued. "It would be different if the windows opened, but they don't, and it's giving me a headache."

"I've only just unscrewed the cap," the woman said. "You honestly expect me to believe it's affected you *this quickly?*"

"Yes," I told her. "I'm begging you to stop."

She said she would, and then she continued. "So you're going to stop when you're *finished,* is that it?" I asked.

"For God's sake, man," the husband said, looking up from his phone. "We have to be on this train together for two and a half hours."

"I'm aware of that," I told him, watching as his wife gave up and screwed the cap back on. The polish was cantaloupe-colored and matched her face and her short, dyed hair.

"If you've got a headache, take a paracetamol," the husband said. He wasn't as involved as his wife wanted him to be, wasn't chivalrous, just tired-sounding.

I guess you could say I won, but it was a hollow victory. I don't know what it is with me and nail polish. The smell goes right to my brain, to my nervous system, it seems, and crushes it. I've never seen a Frenchwoman apply nail polish on a train. The women are always British. *Do they not smell it?* I wonder. *Has no one ever told them it stinks?*

Last night I took the Eurostar back to London. Our departure was delayed two hours due to a hailstorm, so I took a seat in the waiting area beside a fancy Englishwoman with silver hair, scooting down a short while later to make room for a noticeably unfancy Englishwoman of around the same age in the company of her husband, her grown daughter, and three grandchildren aged six and under.

The new woman thanked me for moving down and was wrenching a big bottle of water from her bag when I asked if I could ask her a question.

"Go on, then," she said.

"Would you ever paint your nails on a train?"

"Goodness, no," she told me. "All that swaying back and forth, I'd get it all over the place."

"I was thinking more of the smell," I said.

"That too." She handed the bottle of water to her oldest grandchild and supported it from the bottom as he took a drink. "It's quite strong, nail polish. No, I'd never open it on a train and do my fingernails."

When the child finished drinking, she wiped his mouth with a napkin. "Might do me toenails, though."

July 29, 2018
Rackham

I called Hugh from London yesterday morning. The phone was in his studio, and as he answered I looked into the little mirror propped up on a shelf beside his paintbrushes. "Oh my God," I said.

"What's wrong?" he asked.

"The white of my eye isn't white anymore," I told him. "It's red. My eye is bleeding!"

It doesn't hurt. My vision's not affected. According to the NHS, it's a subconjunctival hemorrhage—a broken blood vessel—something that can be caused by coughing or sneezing too hard. I don't recall doing either of those things yesterday, but I remember that this happened once before, a couple of years ago. According to the NHS, I should expect to look like this for another week, maybe longer.

"Well, you can't go *out* like that," Hugh said when he met me a few hours later at the station.

It was that kind of day. Before going to bed last night I brushed my teeth with Hugh's foot cream. I thought it was the toothpaste I got him from Paris. Then I noticed how ungrainy it was, and how tasty. That's what caused me to pick up the tube and look at it more closely. *Foot cream!*

September 19, 2018
Rackham

I was at the little Tesco in Storrington yesterday, looking at the cut-up fruit, when a kid, maybe ten years old with a backward baseball cap on his head, approached me. "Are you crazy?" he asked.

I looked down at him. "Me?"

"You're a wanker," he said. "I bet you just tossed your load, didn't you?" He turned to the man he was with. "Look at fucking Stuart Little." I guessed this was a reference to my vest and the trousers I was wearing, which were patched at the knee.

I said, "Who do you think you're talking to?"

The kid smirked and called me a wanker again.

"Someone should talk to his father," the man he was with told him—his father, I guessed, as the two looked just alike.

The pair headed to the register then, and as they left the kid loudly spouted rap lyrics with the words *fuck* and *bitches* in them.

I said to the cashier, "Who was that horrible child?"

She was around my age and snaggletoothed. "I don't think he was right in the head," she told me.

When I repeated the story to the owner of Stable Antiques, she was apoplectic. "He said what! Was he wearing a school uniform? No? Well, he should have been in school, a boy that age. And that man, his father or whoever, isn't doing him any favors, allowing him to speak to an adult like that! I don't know what I'd have done in your shoes, I honestly don't!"

I so appreciated her outrage. Still, I didn't tell her the Stuart Little part, afraid she'd look at my outfit and think, *Well, you were sort of asking for it.*

September 23, 2018
Oslo, Norway

The idea of Norway I had yesterday morning was markedly different from the one I had last night. I was stopped by gypsies twice during the walk I took before dinner, and both times they touched me, saying, "Can I ask a question?" I was on the pedestrian mall lined with chain stores, the sort you come across everywhere in Europe. I walked it again this morning and found it strewn with trash. Gulls were tearing through the empty McDonald's containers looking for McNuggets or half-eaten fries. One of them picked up a piece of hard candy, no doubt thinking, *Fuck, is this a piece of hard candy?* I saw overturned trash bins and lots of empty cans and bottles.

"That's Oslo on a Friday night," said the woman who drove us to the airport this morning. She is Polish and loves it here. "I have my passport and everything. Lucky me."

"How do you say 'Lucky me' in Polish?" I asked.

She thought it over.

"I guess it's not something you hear a lot there," I said.

She sighed. "You're right."

September 24, 2018
Geiranger, Norway

Over lunch yesterday Ronnie talked about the summer she and Hartsell waitressed on Cape Cod, back in the early 1980s. "We worked at an Italian restaurant owned by this complete bitch named Nancy Veccione who the rest of the year was a disciplinarian at a local high school," she said, wrapping her hands around her impossibly tall hamburger. "I'll never forget the time my order was ready and she shouted, 'Pickup, Fatso.'"

"She said that to *you*?" I asked.

Ronnie said, "Yes! Can you believe it?"

Later, back in the car, she looked at the road ahead of us and sighed. "Norway has its shit together. That's the thing."

Geiranger is a fjord-side village in the middle of nowhere. The hotel we'd wanted to stay in was closed for the season, so we settled for this one. The rooms were on the small side, but they faced the water and we weren't in them for very long.

The restaurant was a buffet, so we walked down the hill and ate at the Brasserie Posten, where our waiter was Scottish and answered "No worries" to everything.

"I'll have the moose fillet."

"No worries."

I noticed that the smoked whale came with "ecological sour cream."

"I guess they're trying to make up for the whale part," Hugh said.

October 22, 2018
Rackham

Hugh roasted a chicken for dinner and after telling him about the book I had just finished—*Missoula*—I asked him if he had ever been raped. Funny that we've been together so long but have never discussed it.

He told me about a Brazilian guy he met when he first moved to Paris. "I thought he was in my class at the Alliance Française, but maybe not. I never saw him again, thank God."

I told him about X and about that guy in Hood River. There was actually one other person, a man from Spain I met at a bar when I was twenty-three. *Is it because I'm small?* I wondered. I mean three, that's a lot. *Rape* is not a word I use lightly, though at the time I wouldn't have used it at all—didn't know I had the right to. It's like complaining about the blisters the ax brought on while you were chopping up the statue of Christ. Gay rape—"It's what you get," people would have said at the time. So you'd never have gone to the police.

November 6, 2018
Tokyo

It's Election Day in the U.S. and three networks along with Facebook have pulled the latest ad created to scare old people into voting Republican. We've been hearing for months that Democrats will win back the House and possibly even the Senate. If neither happens I'm going to be devastated. I can't bear the thought of this president gloating.

Whether Democrats win or lose, I will most likely spend money on things I don't need. "That's the Tokyo way!" Amy says. We started off yesterday in Harajuku, where she was stung by a wasp she'd discovered crawling on her wrist. "Oh my God," she cried, putting her hands to her throat on the crowded, tree-lined boulevard. "I can't breathe!"

It took me a moment to realize she was kidding, and in it I thought, not *My poor sister! We've got to get her to a hospital,* but *This could cost us an entire day of shopping!*

I stepped on the wasp, and Hugh gave me a look that translated to "You monster."

"It *stung* her," I reminded him. "I'm just making sure it doesn't happen to someone else."

I walked away from a lot yesterday, mainly on account of Dawn, who would frown at whatever I was thinking of buying and shake her head no. She carries a card that explains, in Japanese, that she cannot under any circumstances eat wheat. In the afternoon it was handed to our young, bearded waiter at the restaurant recommended by the owner of an incense store we'd visited. The guy took the card into the kitchen and returned with a mug of hot water, saying, kindly, "*This* is what you may have."

In fairness, it *was* a noodle restaurant.

November 12, 2018
New York
I wrote in the British Airways lounge at Heathrow yesterday morning, not realizing that I'd left my watch in a bin at the

security checkpoint, a two-minute walk from where I was sitting, eating scrambled eggs the texture of cottage cheese. It wasn't until I'd boarded the train to Terminal B that I realized its absence. "Oh, shit," I whispered.

"What's the matter?" asked a plump, middle-aged flight attendant. She was standing not far away with a number of her colleagues. "Did you lose something?"

It's funny how quickly I began to sweat. *My watch!* "I guess I'll just take the train back to the security checkpoint," I told her. "I think I have time."

The woman said that that wouldn't be possible. "You'll have to go all the way through customs and then check in all over again. What flight are you on?"

I told her and she said to her colleagues, "That's us!" When she asked for my seat number, my hopes rose. *They'll take care of it!* "Don't worry," she said. "We've got someone at the gate who can get it all sorted." She added that she, too, lost everything when she traveled.

"Yes, well, you see, I don't," I told her. "At least, not usually."

At the gate she flagged down a security guy who said that really wasn't his department; however, he could take me to someone who could—and here was that phrase again—"get it sorted."

That person was a gate agent in his late twenties. He was thin, perhaps of Indian or Pakistani origin. One half of his face was darker than the other, as if he'd been raised partly in the shade and partly in the sun. I told him exactly where I'd left the watch, and after asking the woman beside him for the number of that particular security station, the guy dialed and got someone other than security. A second number led to the same result. "You'll have to go online to www.missingx.com," he told me.

"But you didn't even talk to anyone," I said.

"That's where they said you should go to."

"What 'they'?" I said. "You didn't talk to anyone."

"Yes, but, you see, there isn't time to go back there," he said. His was the maddening British way of not doing anything but pretending that he had. Like the time the ATM in Scotland didn't give me my money, and the woman at the bank explained that sometimes the machines do this due to various reasons, so I should check with my own bank or perhaps go online.

Huh?

"Did you get your watch back?" the flight attendant who'd led me to the security guy asked as I boarded.

"No," I told her. "Actually, that person was no help whatsoever. He didn't even talk to anyone."

"My goodness," she said. "What's your seat number again?" She wrote it down for the second time. After getting settled, I used my phone to log on to the website the gate agent had given me. "What country did you lose your item in?" was the first question.

"This is bullshit," I said, moaning. I got even angrier when it demanded that I create a password.

We left Heathrow an hour late, and that entire time, parked at the gate, still connected to the terminal, I kept thinking the flight attendant was going to walk down the aisle with my watch. *Here it comes!* I told myself, realizing as it did not, in fact, come that I loved my Apple Watch. *Loved* it, and it was probably gone forever.

As I sat in my airplane seat, fuming, it never occurred to me to blame myself. Rather, I thought that, were I in America, I'd have gotten my missing item back, especially in business class. In England, though, people go by the book, which conveniently for them always says, *Nope. Sorry. Nothing can be done for security reasons, for health and safety.*

"I hope you get your watch back," two separate flight attendants trilled as we landed at JFK. I should never have listened to them, should have taken my chances and gone through customs and security a second time, should have gotten a later flight.

Should have, should have.

December 6, 2018
London

A week ago I started feeling a slight burning sensation when I peed. It was a good kind of pain, just subtle, but in time it grew more intense. My urine turned cloudy, and by yesterday morning it hurt so much I couldn't bear it. I'd tried connecting it to my flu, then remembered that it had been going on for a week already. On the train to London I did that thing that doctors hate and diagnosed myself with a urinary tract infection. The cure is antibiotics, so on arriving in London, I pulled some I had stockpiled from last year's root canal out of my suitcase.

I took the first pill yesterday at five, and by this morning it doesn't hurt at all when I pee. Hugh criticized me for diagnosing myself, and I reminded him that my first two initials *are* D. R.

Excellent work, Doctor.

December 8, 2018
Riga, Latvia

At a convenience shop in the Russian section of town, Patsy got a carton of cigarettes. As she spoke to the woman behind the counter, I looked at the single packs on display, the logos of which had been replaced by what looked like photos from a medical book: a young woman hacking up blood, lungs that appeared to have been barbecued, a heart seemingly made from roadkill.

"You came out pretty well," I said after examining the carton of Winston Whites Patsy had been given. "The worst you've got is a child laying flowers on her mother's grave."

December 12, 2018
London

Without actually talking about it, Hugh and I seem to have agreed on a New York apartment. Not a particular apartment, but just the idea of one. In our minds we see the same thing. "The kind they lived in on the TV show *Family Affair*," I said as we took seats in the waiting area after clearing security on the Eurostar last night. "Something on the Upper East Side, in the Sixties or Seventies."

It's a neighborhood you couldn't have paid me to live in when I was young. Now, though, I like its relative dullness. I'd like to overlook an avenue. Third would be good.

"Really?" Hugh asked.

"That's how old I am," I told him.

He started looking at places last week. I can see what this is—our same old real estate bandage. A project. Newness (though in this case, as we've already lived in New York, it's an old newness).

December 19, 2018
London

At the clinic Hugh and I went to in Pulborough the other day, every seat was occupied, so it was a relief to walk into the Hospital of St. John and St. Elizabeth (two saints!) last night and find that the place was practically empty. My appointment with Dr. O., a urologist, was for 7:15, and at 7:00—a full fifteen minutes early—he ushered me into his office. The doctor spoke with a Scottish accent and was, I guessed, in his early forties. I told him about the pain when I pee and admitted that I'd diagnosed myself and taken a course of antibiotics. "That's *it* with me and the internet," I swore.

He seemed pleased.

Dr. O. has a practice on Harley Street and is at the hospital only a few days per week. Perhaps that explains the coldness of his office—no photos or mementos. A curtain divided the room in half, and after asking if he could examine me, he pulled it shut.

"Would you like a nurse present?"

"No need," I told him, wondering who on earth might answer otherwise, might want a second set of eyes on his sad, slack penis and exposed ass. After cupping my balls and ordering me to cough, Dr. O. asked that I get into the fetal position. Then he put a rubber glove on and stuck a finger up my ass. Or was it his entire arm? He'd lubed up, but still, the pain was phenomenal. "I really am *the worst* homosexual in the world," I told him, shuddering. I last had something up there a few years ago when I went for my physical in North Carolina, then a few years earlier for my colonoscopy, but I was knocked out for the latter and the doctor likely stopped at the knuckle for the former.

"We'll get you cleaned up here," Dr. O. said, wiping my ass and then tossing the paper along with his rubber glove into the trash can.

Back at his desk he jotted down some lab work he wanted me to get, one a blood test and the other urine. He ordered one scan that might determine whether or not the blockage was kidney-stone-related and another that would more closely examine my prostate, which, he said, had felt strange. "It's not *big*, exactly, but it's harder than it should be," he said, adding that it was not *necessarily* cancer. "It could just be prostatitis—a swelling, thus the suffix *-itis*, like *arthritis*."

Or gingivitis, I'd have thought under other circumstances, but my mind was stuck on the word *cancer.*

Since Mom's death in 1991 I've been telling people that I, too, will die at sixty-two, the age I will reach one week from today.

"I want the tests and scans done as soon as possible," Dr. O. said, scribbling away on a form. "I can get the results later this week, but because of the Christmas holiday, the soonest I can see you again is Thursday the twenty-seventh. Might that work for you?"

Cancer! I thought, realizing that if it's not my diagnosis today, won't it be ten years from now? Fifteen? Isn't it inevitable?

"Not necessarily," Hugh says. "Look at your father."

"No, look at my mother."

Before I left the office, Dr. O. asked, "Are you David Sedaris, the author of *Calypso*?"

I admitted that I was.

"I loved that book."

That helped a bit.

He handed me a number of papers, one of which I presented on the second floor, where two women seemed to be shopping for clothes on their computers. "It would be okay, I suppose, if they had my size, but without the scalloped bit," one of them said.

I'll be billed 280 pounds for the initial consultation. The tests are another 139 pounds, which is nothing, really.

"You think not?" said the guy who took my credit card. "Well, thank you. Most people, quite frankly, moan on and on about it."

The young woman who took my blood wore a headscarf and was easy to talk to. She accepted my vial of urine as well. "Doesn't that look like it has cancer?" I asked. "Isn't it too cloudy?"

She said the cloudiness could be due to dehydration.

Next I went to the ground floor, where two women from Eastern Europe scheduled my scans. "I'm just relieved I won't have anything else shoved up my ass," I said.

The women looked at each other. "Actually, you will," one of them told me. "The one for the prostate will be quite...invasive, I'm afraid."

Fuck, I thought, saying, "You see these people in videos begging for anal sex, but honestly, I just don't get it."

The women laughed and told me to return tomorrow at five with a full bladder and an empty stomach. "Right," I said. "One doesn't want to be violated anally after a big turkey dinner, now, does one!"

They laughed again and I thought, *That's right, keep them entertained.*

Then I went outside and tried to call Hugh. By that point I was a mess. *Cancer!* The line was busy, so I didn't reach him for another half hour. By that time I'd left the M and S at Notting Hill Gate and was headed home. "I'm freaking out," I told him. "I thought the doctor would say, 'Oh, that's such and such. We see it all the time. Here, take this pill.'" Instead, I was having to undergo scans and wait an entire week for the results.

Hugh, bless him, took it much harder than me, thus I could play the role of the comforter. "Calm down," I said, "it's probably nothing."

I'm trying not to get too far ahead of myself but it's difficult. Will I have to cancel my January tour? My spring tour? A year from now, will I be alive? Will I be wearing adult diapers?

I lay awake half the night worrying. *Bladder cancer?*

December 22, 2018
London

Amy arrived from New York yesterday morning and from then on we laughed. I'm continually amazed by how quick and funny she is, especially compared to myself and everyone else I know. We're all at 2, while 10 is just her getting warmed up.

On a crowded train to Liverpool Street, I told her about my anal probe. Then loudly, in the packed subway car, she suggested I buy an inflatable doughnut. *"For people in your condition who have had a procedure like that, it's a godsend."*

After lunch we headed to the Dover Street Market, where I saw a taxidermied kiwi mounted on a thin rectangle of polished wood. Its head was lowered, and I knew immediately that I had to have it. "How much?" I asked.

Eight thousand pounds, I was told. "It's over a hundred years old."

Amy suggested I snap off the beak and then ask, "How much is it *now*?"

December 28, 2018
London

"I think I'll work backwards if that's okay," Dr. O. said late yesterday morning after I was seated in his office. "The scan for prostate cancer, I'm happy to report, turned up nothing."

Oh, the relief.

"Everything shrinks as a man gets older except," he said, repeating a line he'd used a week earlier, "*except* his prostate." The average prostate volume for a man my age is 25 mL. Mine is less than half that—12. They like your PSA level to be under 4, and again I'm lucky—mine is a lowly 2.57. Looking over the report submitted by Dr. G., the radiologist, I saw that he'd written, *Patient tolerated the transrectal ultrasound probe poorly.*

You're damn right I did. That said, who accepts it eagerly? I felt like I'd overheard someone gossiping about me. *What else did the radiologist say?* I wondered. The rat.

The bad news was that my urine had blood in it, and the blood work showed an elevated white cell count. Because of that, the doctor wants to schedule a cystoscopy. That's where they shove a camera up your dick and photograph your bladder.

You've got to be kidding me, I thought, wondering what holes he might violate next. My ears? My nose? That said, anything less than an anal probe is gravy. "We'd give you a local anesthetic," he offered, "and it doesn't take more than a few minutes."

He gave me a prescription for antibiotics before I left. The upside is that it no longer hurts when I pee. The downside is that blood is now coming out. It's not mixed with urine the way it used to be. Rather, there's blood followed by urine or urine followed by blood. It's terrifying, but what can I do but wait for the camera to be shoved up my dick?

2019

January 1, 2019
Rackham

Ingrid and I were in the kitchen late yesterday morning, her painting and me squinting at what was either a pheasant or an armless brown troll racing across the road in front of the house, when I got the idea for prescription windows. They'd be perfect for people like me who don't want to wear glasses indoors. The problem, I suppose, would be Hugh and our occasional houseguests, who have different vision problems than I do, or none at all. But it's 2019, so can't I think about myself for a change?

Yesterday was like the day before it: cold and gray. Ingrid and I had lunch at the house, then drove to Storrington to buy a few things at the Waitrose. The store was crowded and had a merry feeling. We'd just decided on brussels sprouts and I was reaching for a branch of them when an elderly man approached us. "Why are you getting *that* kind?" he asked, looking back and forth from me to Ingrid. "They charge by the pound, so you should buy the loose ones. Otherwise what you're paying for is a lot of useless stalk."

I shrugged. "That's okay. I'm rich."

I can say that in England, as no one ever suspects I'm telling the truth. They see me in rags with the sort of teeth you'd find on a neglected llama and assume I share a council house with a full-time carer.

I love it when Dawn or Ingrid visits. It's the only time I appear half normal in Storrington—"Look, he has a friend!"

January 4, 2019
Rackham

It was nice in London yesterday morning so I decided to walk to my 11:45 appointment at the King Edward VII's Hospital. It's private, so the waiting areas looked like living rooms in country estates. I'd no sooner sunk into a red sofa and reached for one of the many books piled on the coffee table when a man arrived to lead me upstairs. We took the elevator along with a young black patient who walked with a crutch. "They're going to stick a camera up my penis and photograph my bladder," I told him.

The guy crumpled. "Fuck!"

"I know it," I said, satisfied to have gotten what I thought was the right reaction.

After the cystoscopy—during which I was mercifully unconscious—I felt twenty years older. "I don't technically have cancer yet, but already I'm tired of fighting it," I said to Hugh over the phone. Part of me wanted to take a taxi home, but instead I walked to Selfridges to buy Amy the soap she'd asked me to pick up. "I just had a camera shoved up my penis," I told the salesgirl, who was tall and French and was missing a tooth on the upper-right side of her mouth.

It's a sob story you really want to save for a guy, but still, she was sympathetic.

January 12, 2019
Philadelphia

We resumed our New York apartment search yesterday morning, and by the end of the day we'd put in a bid for a Classic 7 on East Sixty-Second. First, though, we were taken to Sutton Place, where we looked at what was once Judge Judy's apartment. "This is where she raised her family," the co-agent said.

"It feels like a house rather than an apartment," our agent, Marcia, observed. She could easily pass as Judge Judy's sister—her look, her voice. It's uncanny.

"And on a beautiful day like this, can you believe the light!" the co-agent mewed. Washers and dryers are no longer allowed in the building. "But this one is grandfathered in," she said, adding that lots of people sneak them past the doormen.

"How?" I asked.

She shrugged. "Refrigerator boxes."

Next was a two-bedroom on the fortieth floor of an unremarkable high-rise. It was a weird space but the views were insane. There was nothing you couldn't see from the windows.

"It's a divorce sale," Marcia whispered.

I felt oddly vulnerable being that high up and having to rely on the elevator. And so it was back to the nineteenth floor on Sixty-Second Street, where I can take the stairs if I need to.

January 19, 2019
Over the Pacific Ocean
We're on the plane to Maui and Hugh is overcome with emotion. He found a hardcover copy of his dad's first book, *The Man Who Lost the War,* at the Strand, and it's reduced him to tears. "At least turn your screen on so people will think you're crying over a movie," I whisper.

February 8, 2019
London
It seems I have been elected to the American Academy of Arts and Letters. It's a lifelong appointment and there are no dues,

just glory and hobnobbery. I look at the list of current members and feel woozy. In the department of literature, there's Ann Beattie, Michael Cunningham, Jeffrey Eugenides, Jonathan Franzen, Amy Hempel, Jamaica Kincaid, David Mamet, Lorrie Moore, Joyce Carol Oates, Sharon Olds, Ann Patchett, Jayne Anne Phillips, Francine Prose, Marilynne Robinson, George Saunders, Wallace Shawn, Anne Tyler, Edmund White, Joy Williams, and Tobias Wolff. *Really?* I think. These people are gods to me. It's like I've been allowed onto Mount Olympus.

Then there are the departments of art (Bruce Nauman, Cindy Sherman, Jenny Holzer, Susan Rothenberg), music, and architecture. Honorary members—people whose work falls outside these categories—include Bob Dylan, Meryl Streep, Frederick Wiseman, and Martin Scorsese.

It never occurred to me back in Raleigh or Chicago, writing in the kitchen on Cuyler Avenue or reading out loud at Lower Links, that it might lead to this. Lying in bed last night, I imagined my name on the list of other authors and worried it might stand out and cause one to question the entire institution— "Wait a minute, *him?*" I suppose it's one thing to be allowed in and another to truly accept your place, to feel like you deserve it.

Lee wrote about a guy he met on a jazz cruise last week. The husband is ninety, his wife is eighty-six, and they're divorcing after sixty-five years of marriage. "We wanted to wait until our children were dead," the man explained.

February 9, 2019
London
It started raining hard yesterday so I ducked into Hauser & Wirth, the art gallery on Savile Row, where, in the main room, an old woman lay on the ground singing in a choked voice

and shaking an egg at the ceiling. Near her was a piece of toast smeared with gold and a dancing sock.

February 16, 2019
London

Hugh talked to his mother, who complained that everyone on her television is fat. "And it's a brand-new set!" Over dinner we imagined her fiddling with her knobs: *I tried the horizontal bar but nothing works!*

February 19, 2019
Paris

My father is dying, maybe. He went to the hospital saying he couldn't breathe, and they discovered that his left lung was full of fluid. This according to Paul, who started sending messages last night.

February 20, 2019
London

This morning, Hugh's eyes welled with tears for my father. "*You* want to be the emotional one on this?" I asked. "Fine by me."

I talked to Lisa again last night. "A palliative-care nurse came by yesterday and explained that Dad's in really bad shape," she said. "He's experiencing heart failure, and with his lungs continuing to fill with fluid, it's really not good."

I ought to be freaking out, but the fact is that I feel nothing. That's why it was so odd to stand there and watch Hugh cry.

I keep getting stuck on a 2012 visit to Raleigh. Dad started in the moment I arrived and didn't let up all weekend: "You look terrible," "You have no idea what you're talking about," etc. That was when he voted for the proposition that would make gay marriage, which was already unconstitutional under North Carolina law, extra-*extra*-unconstitutional. He was just a dick.

Why can't I think of a better time? I wonder. For surely there *was* one, wasn't there? Was there ever a moment I didn't expect him to turn on me, sort of like a cat you've been stroking who sinks his teeth into your hand? Was there ever a conversation that wasn't banal or didn't end in an argument? I know there were times we'd get off the phone and I'd think, *Oh, he's not so bad, I should call more often.* Then I would call and he'd just berate me until we hung up. Then, too, it really hurts that he cut me out of his will. It's not the sum but the fact that nothing—nothing—means more to him than money, and in denying me an inheritance, he's kicking me with all his might, saying, in effect, *I do not love you either.*

Ah, the *either.*

February 23, 2019
Raleigh

Hugh and I landed in Raleigh at around four yesterday. It was cold and raining, and rather than checking into our hotel, we went straight to Springmoor, where we found Dad asleep. His arms were flat against his body, but both of his hands were raised, like a dog's paws when it's begging.

"Are y'all looking for your family?" an aide asked. She led us to a small, sad room with a humming refrigerator in it. There, Lisa told me that Dad's aortic valve no longer works. "It's nothing they can fix, not at his age," she said. "He's in heart failure, which means that the thing that just happened— his lungs filling with fluid—is going to happen again and is going to kill him."

With that, we all went back to Dad's room for a few hours. Paul came, then Kathy and Gretchen. Dinner plans were proposed as amber-colored urine slowly collected in the bag attached to Dad's catheter. The room was sweltering.

This morning we'll all return.

February 26, 2019
New York

Yesterday morning over breakfast in the hotel restaurant Hugh coached me for this evening's interview with the co-op board. "So why do you want to live in this particular neighborhood?"

"Because it's dull," I said. "I suffer from sidewalk rage and on the Upper East Side you don't have to worry about tourists walking eight abreast. I mean, what's to see here, right?"

Amy's co-op board had thrown her by saying, "So, tell us about yourself."

"Um, I was a Girl Scout. I was a cashier at the Winn-Dixie for a while. I didn't go to college?"

"Why did you leave France?" Hugh asked me.

"I couldn't stand the sight of people kissing on trains," I said. "Next question."

At 12:30 our real estate agents, Steve and Marcia, are going to coach us as a team. "Nobody was ever turned away for saying too little" is their motto.

Meanwhile, I think about our visit to Raleigh and of how awful it was to see Dad in that condition, back in his assisted-living center but so weak and out of it. Any second I expect to hear that he's died.

March 1, 2019
Rackham

Immediately after returning to London yesterday I walked to the tailor to pick up the jacket I bought last week in Paris. It might be the craziest thing Comme des Garçons has ever made, which is really saying something. It's essentially two sports coats, one sewed atop the other. The bottom one is bubblegum pink, made of summer-weight wool, and over it is a second jacket that's linen. The pattern is a mismatched plaid, gray on the left side and yellow on the right. The second sports coat is shredded and hangs in tatters, as if the person wearing it had stepped on a land mine. The only problem was that the sleeves were a bit long, and so I'd taken it to Ari on Kensington Church Street. He and his family are Kurds and own a business called Pure Stitch that I've been going to for years.

When I entered the shop yesterday afternoon he was with a customer, a difficult one. The man was British and wanted a suit altered. "But only if it can be done correctly," he said as I handed Ari's sister Tamara my claim check. She stepped into the back to find my jacket.

"I can definitely do it properly," Ari promised.

"I mean, I need *real* tailoring," the guy continued.

"I understand completely," Ari said.

Tamara handed me my sports coat, and after putting it on, I turned to her and Ari and the asshole who was doubting him and cried, "What have you people done to my jacket!"

Oh, the look on that man's face.

March 7, 2019
London

Hugh and I were waiting for the 52 bus yesterday when I noticed a woman standing a few feet away. She was thin, with shoulder-length gray hair. Her nose was sharp, like a beak, almost, and she wore a turquoise coat over a dress the color of sea foam. The only things off about her were her bedroom slippers and the way she was talking to herself. "Just ... *move,*" she said to the two buses that had pulled up in front of us to disgorge and accept passengers. "Go on, now, *go*. What are you *waiting* for." She wasn't shouting or using foul language. Rather, she spoke in a normal volume, occasionally moving her hands the way you do when you want someone to get out of your way.

When the 52 came, Hugh and I took seats upstairs. The bus wasn't crowded, but as traffic slowed at Knightsbridge, I heard a voice coming from downstairs. "*Move,* you. Come on, now, *get going.*"

The woman's words were not easy to make out, especially when we came to a construction site, so I descended the stairs in order to hear her better. She was seated in one of the spots reserved for the elderly and handicapped and appeared to be reading a newspaper. "Bus routes are for buses *only*, not cars. They should use the motorway. Get off the road this instant or go straight to jail. This bus needs to get through, not you lot." Her voice was imperious, the sort used to order around servants. "Drive over those people. Squash them! Just...put your foot down and *go.*" She was essentially saying what most people on buses—myself included—were sitting there thinking.

"Can you not see? The light is *green*. Get moving. Those blasted cars have no business here. They must get off the road at once!"

When I rang for our stop, she said, "Stop dinging the bell! We must get on with it." If I hadn't needed to pee so bad, I'd have stayed, just to see where she was in such a rush to get to.

March 8, 2019
London

I've been looking for one of those banners you see at gas stations, the sort made of colorful plastic triangles, so I stepped into the party shop on the High Street yesterday afternoon.

"We have them in the basement," said the young man behind the counter. "But I think most of ours are nylon and spell out little messages."

I went downstairs to see for myself, and after finding several that had HAPPY BIRTHDAY and WELCOME HOME written on them, I came across one that read SORRY YOU'RE LIVING.

That's perfect, I thought, realizing a moment later, and with great disappointment, that I'd misread it and that it actually said SORRY YOU'RE LEAVING.

March 25, 2019
London

Q and As followed all of this weekend's BBC recording sessions, and at the one yesterday afternoon a woman asked how I feel when my values are challenged.

"I'm not sure I understand the question," I told her.

"For instance," she said, "whenever I fly in the U.S., some big fat American will take the spot next to me and completely spill over into my personal space."

I knew what she was saying, but the only thing I hate more than being crowded out of my seat is listening to self-righteous thin people complaining about it, so I said, because it's true, "It's actually not a problem when you fly first class."

March 27, 2019
New York

I'm still finding my way around the new apartment, which is large and laid out in a perplexing but not unpleasant way. At ten o'clock last night I discovered a new bathroom—and I'd been here for seven hours! The shipment from London arrived shortly before I did, so my office furniture, among other things, is here. Still, it's very spare. We've got two forks, and at night half the rooms are dark because we have only four lamps.

One is constantly being beeped at here. The stove top got angry this morning when Hugh's oatmeal boiled over onto it, and I was chided by the refrigerator for leaving one of its doors open. Next it was the kettle scolding me for not turning it all the way off. Then the washing machine chimed in.

I left Heathrow at ten yesterday morning, and on my flight I met a doctor who'd once had cancer. I told her I was waiting on the results of my cystoscopy and she asked if I was or had been a smoker. That, apparently, is a leading cause of bladder cancer. "So are certain types of dyes," she said.

The guy who picked me up at JFK was seventy-six and had had a cystoscopy a year ago. "I went to the doctor with blood in my urine, and he sent me to a specialist," he said. The driver's biopsy proved negative. He was just telling me about his estrangement from his father when his wife called. "Hello, my love," I heard him say, then, "Yes, my master."

March 29, 2019
New York

I stopped at the Apple Store on Prince Street yesterday for an external hard drive I can use to back up my laptop. As the salesman, who was young and bearded and dressed like all his associates in jeans and a T-shirt, was running my card through his machine, I looked across the room at a woman in her mid-eighties. She wore a wide-brimmed black hat and had socks with bright flowers on them. Everything in between was beautiful and interesting, all items a witch would wear but updated slightly. "God," I said. "Doesn't that woman look fantastic."

The salesman followed my gaze. "You should go for it," he said.

"I beg your pardon?"

"Walk over and chat her up," he told me.

"I didn't mean *that way*," I said, wondering how old he thought I was. I mean, she had to have had at least twenty-five years on me!

April 10, 2019
Providence, Rhode Island

At last night's event a woman asked me to sign a book to her daughter. "She's a whore," I announced, knowing this was risky. "A complete and total whore."

The woman cocked her head. "What did you just say?"

I repeated myself and the woman, seemingly indignant, reached for her phone. "Would you like to see a *picture* of my daughter?"

She scrolled for a moment, then showed me a photo. In it, a young woman, who was lovely and long-limbed, stood embracing an erect penis that was seven feet tall and carved of wood, with two massive balls at its base.

"I stand corrected," I said, so relieved.

April 11, 2019
Boston

A woman named Meagan approached my book-signing table to say that her mother had recently died.

"I'm sorry to hear it," I said.

"It was a difficult time," she continued, "so I was touched when one of our neighbors asked if he could say a word at her funeral. Of course I told him that I'd be honored, so he got up before us all and said, simply, 'Plethora.'

" 'Thanks so much,' I told him afterward. 'That means a lot.' "

I love it when someone sneaks in a joke like that.

A twenty-nine-year-old woman in Taiwan went to the hospital with a swollen eye, and the doctor found four live sweat bees under her lid, feasting on her tears. That was the word all the reports used: *feasting*.

April 29, 2019
Iowa City, Iowa

At a signing the other night, I met a man who was wearing the jacket of a movie star who had died a few years earlier. "How did you get it?" I asked.

He told me he knew a guy who worked at the crematorium the actor's body was sent to. "He was fully dressed and my friend thought, *Well, there's no need for his clothes to go to waste!* He took the jacket, and when he gained weight and it no longer fit him, he sent it to me!" The guy showed me the label beneath the inner pocket, which said MADE FOR and then the actor's name.

I got the feeling I was supposed to be impressed, but all I thought was: *That's stealing.* Even if the person you're taking it from is dead, you're not supposed to do things like that. Then I thought of the woman's head I'd bought a few years ago in London. I wasn't the first one to violate her wishes—there was the person who cut it off and the nineteenth-century doctor who'd used it as a model in his medical-school classroom, but still, I doubt she'd wanted to wind up in my curio cabinet employed as a bookend. So who am I to judge?

June 1, 2019
Rackham

I'd just sat down at my desk last night when Lisa called. It seemed she'd just gotten a phone call from Dad, who has left the hospital after his most recent stay and returned to Springmoor, his assisted-living place. "You say you like to read and that you have a lot of friends," he said. "But what kind of existence is that? What have you really done with your life? Nothing."

He's back!

June 13, 2019
Fairhope, Alabama

On our drive from Pensacola to Fairhope, Katharine and I passed a billboard that read THE BEAVER IS IN BAMA.

"Did you see that monkey in a trench coat that got loose at an Ikea, I think in Germany?" she asked. "It's the weirdest-looking thing. You should YouTube it if you get a chance." She laughed. "In a trench coat!"

A car passed with a bumper sticker that read GOT JESUS? Then we saw a Zaxby's. "What's that?" Katharine asked.

She's very easy to spend time with. The afternoon passed quickly and I was at the bookstore by six. Many of the people I signed for were loud and drunk. The majority, though, were just Southern and pleasant. I talked to one couple and learned that they had two kids. "One caused the marriage and the other saved it," the woman told me.

I met a teacher with a student named Jaquarius and another with a student named Jedarius. Other student names included Janasia and Eudolphinique, which is pronounced "You-dolphin-eek." For a town so small and conservative, it surprised me to meet two trans women, one of whom is an astrophysicist who now works as a "box girl."

"What's that?" I asked.

She giggled. "You know, silly."

I was in bed by one and woke at six with the song "We Need a Little Christmas" in my head.

June 16, 2019
Phoenix
When I went through security this morning my ID was checked by a trans woman in her late sixties who had dull gray hair pulled into a ponytail. The top of her head was bald and she wore a pair of sparkling earrings; zirconium, maybe. She'd slapped some rouge on her cheeks, not much, and wore a name tag that identified her as McKenzie.

You're transitioning for that? I thought. *The name McKenzie?* I recalled Madison, whom we'd had Thanksgiving with, and then considered Caitlyn Jenner. All transitioned at roughly the same age and took the names of much younger women. *Where are the Gladyses?* I wondered as I approached the X-ray scanner. *The Louises, the Millies?*

July 6, 2019
Rackham
I walked home from the train station and found a pigeon on the patio outside my office, standing stock-still on the metal table. You'd think she would have flown off at my approach, but she just stood there, looking neither injured nor frightened. On closer inspection I saw that she had a green band on one of her ankles. Out of curiosity I threw down some food, but she ignored it. Her expression wasn't one of uninterest. Rather, she seemed to be awaiting further instructions.

"Hugh," I called.

He'd been wrapping his swollen elbow and came out of the house squinting against both the sun and his pain. "What are you doing? Don't feed that thing."

"She has a band on her leg," I said. "Look, she's not afraid of me."

"Well, stop scaring her." This is him all over. Every time I

497

find an animal, be it a hedgehog or a turtle, he immediately takes over. "Leave it alone!" "You're feeding it too much."

I walked six miles into Storrington and back, and when I returned the pigeon was still there. "Hugh!"

He was in the kitchen, shelling broad beans despite his bad elbow. "What?"

I told him the pigeon was still here and he got on the horn and called animal rescue, who must have been thrilled to be phoned over a pigeon. "They said it's a racing bird," Hugh reported after hanging up. "They say it'll probably continue its journey in the morning."

The pigeon had moved to the ground by this point, but neither of us thought it terribly wise for her to stay there, not with foxes around. Animal rescue suggested Hugh put her in a box and keep her in the shed overnight, but when he approached, she hurried away, looking frightened for the first time since her arrival. When I got in on it, she flew into the pasture, then doubled back and perched on top of the house.

"Well," Hugh said, the empty box in his hands. "At least we know she's not wounded."

By this morning she'd gone, thus sparing us a long day of argument:

Stop looking at her.
I'm not!
You are too.

August 6, 2019
Saint John, New Brunswick

Seth woke yesterday morning with a toothache. The pain was bad, so I gave him a handful of Oxycontin tablets I had in my suitcase. "Are the pills working?" I asked as we headed into Saint John from the airport a few hours later.

"It still hurts," he said. "But now I don't care."

That's such a good description of what that drug does.

August 16, 2019
Emerald Isle

Yesterday morning Hugh drove me to the DMV in Morehead City so that I could get a state ID card. It was overcast and muggy, and the building, which was unremarkable and made of brick, stood alone on the side of the busy highway. I'd expected a long wait, but we sat there for only ten minutes or so before my number was called. The agent I was assigned to was black and middle-aged with clear polish on her nails. In her station was a statue of two white children being watched over by an angel, who hovered above them on a wire. Beside it was a sign reading FAITH MAKES IT POSSIBLE.

"Would you like to be an organ donor?" she asked.

"Sure."

"What color is your hair?" she asked.

"Gray," Hugh said.

I touched my head as if my fingers might tell me. "Is 'mushroom-colored' an option?" I asked.

"I'm afraid I'm not allowed to answer that question for you."

We went with brown.

August 18, 2019
London

Before leaving Raleigh, Hugh and I went to visit Dad at Springmoor. It was around two o'clock when we opened his door and found him in his wheelchair wearing a Sedaris Hardwood Floors T-shirt and a pair of briefs. In his hands were the sweatpants he was trying to work his way into. "Well, what a surprise!" he said in his new little whisper of a voice.

His room was a lot less cluttered than I'd thought it would be. The curtains were open. Bills weren't piled atop everything. Most surprising of all, the TV was off. I was struck within the first few minutes at how easily Dad laughed. I'm not sure if it was a ruse—the easiest way of pretending he understood us—or if he was just being jolly.

There's a little garden in the courtyard, so Hugh wheeled him outside and we sat and talked for an hour. "So, you've got an apartment in New York now?" Dad asked. "What about the old place in the Village?"

Hugh explained that Thompson Street was rented out, and not long afterward, Dad repeated the question. "So, do you still have that other apartment in the Village?"

There was an aide on break sitting not far away, and as I talked I imagined what I sounded like to her—a sixty-year-old man trying to impress his father. "Oh, I won't be home long. After unpacking I'm off to Norway for a show, then Austria and Germany and Sweden."

Pathetic.

He looked good, Dad did, much younger than ninety-six. He seemed sharp but said several times that he didn't like the food at Springmoor and was looking forward to returning home. "I've got myself into a real...situation here," he said, "and until I resolve it, I'm pretty much stuck."

While he talked I could hear a man ranting in one of the rooms behind him. "Goddamn...and your stupid...then you come in here..."

At 3:15 we wheeled Dad back to his room and left him there. "See ya," he said after shaking our hands. It was so sad to see him like that.

September 8, 2019
Bergen, Norway

During the day, central Bergen is calm and beautiful. Then night falls, or at least a weekend night falls, and it becomes a hellscape of roving drunks. It's like Reykjavík that way, and Oslo. I went out late to mail a letter and passed a young woman doubled in half vomiting onto her shoes while a friend held her hair back and made comforting noises. Streets I had admired for their cleanliness were now smeared with garbage. All of the young people I saw were in loud, staggering packs. I'd just passed a knot of six college students when a woman approached me. She was perhaps fifty and looked like she cleaned restrooms at the airport. "You want six?" she asked me.

She wasn't a native-born Norwegian, I could tell by her accent. Romanian, maybe? Bulgarian? I said, "I beg your pardon?"

"You want six?"

On the third go-round I realized that she was saying *sex*.

"Oh, no," I said. Then, afraid I sounded rude, I added, "Thank you...no, thank you."

It was chilly out, and the woman wore a black down jacket. She had loose pants on, and sensible shoes. Does she work as a prostitute full-time or did she just see me and think, *What the hell. I could use it as mad money*?

Regardless, it always depresses me to be approached like that. I must look like I'm single or like the type who cheats on his wife. And what if I'd said yes? Then what? Where would we have gone? Perhaps she wasn't a prostitute herself but just a representative, someone who'd lead me to the poor woman who'd have to have sex with me. *What a way to ruin my vacation,* I thought, continuing on to the letter box.

September 16, 2019
London

At a museum gift shop in Berlin the other day I got a rabbit-shaped candle to put in Amy's Christmas stocking. "It's cute and everything," I said to Hugh. "But when you light it, it smells like burning hare."

September 18, 2019
New York

"We've just been having the worst problems with our new dog," Lisa said yesterday afternoon as we were walking through Central Park. "She stands at the windows in the front of the house, and if she sees anyone walking by, she just goes nuts with the barking. Oh, it's awful. So you know what we did?"

I thought for sure she'd say she had blinded it. Not permanently—she's one of the purest animal lovers I know—but eye patches were a possibility, weren't they?

"We covered our windows with a film that frosts them," Lisa said. "That way she can't see out, which means that we can't either."

Why hadn't that occurred to me? Why had I gone straight to blinding?

Continuing on through the park, we came upon a man with a parrot on his head and a boa constrictor as big around as a fire hose hanging from his neck. Odder still was the tip jar in his hand. *You walk around like that, and we're supposed to give you money for it?* I thought. If the parrot was telling the snake to tighten its grip—*Choke this moron and we're free!*—I might consider it. Otherwise, no way.

October 15, 2019
Burlington, Vermont
A gay guy approached my signing table last night with a copy of *Theft by Finding*. He was with another man, his boyfriend, maybe. "Whatever you write in this book I'm going to get as my next tattoo," he said.

This has happened before, and though I suppose I'm meant to be flattered, I just think of it as dumb. What kills me is the permanence. I don't want to be responsible for a thing like that, and so, after thinking for a moment, I wrote, *I have full-blown AIDS in my ass.*

"There you go," I said, handing the book back. "That's what you can get tattooed on yourself."

He seemed disappointed.

October 18, 2019
Greensboro, North Carolina
The doctor who performed my colonoscopy a few years back came to last night's show and stood in line to have a book signed.

"Do you have to get up early tomorrow?" I asked.

"At the crack," he said, which I guess is a common joke among gastroenterologists.

October 21, 2019
Columbus
At last night's signing I met a woman who'd just taken her family to a haunted house. "A ghost came up from behind us and said to my twelve-year-old daughter, 'You smell different when you're sleeping,'" she told me.

That is so perfectly creepy. I think that ghost deserves a raise.

*　　*　　*

"What's the most irritating thing your customers do?" I asked the young woman who waited on Adam and me at Jeni's Ice Cream last night.

She thought. "The worst is when gross old men try to flirt with you. They say things like, 'Oh, your forearms must really be strong,' and it just creeps me out."

"She should say, when she gets that comment, 'It comes in handy when I'm fisting my boyfriend,'" I said to Adam on our way out. "That would shut a senior down really quick."

As I was walking toward the exit of the Ritz-Carlton in Cleveland yesterday, a bellman asked, "Are you Dr. Friedman?"

"No," I said, "but it's so nice that you'd mistake me for a doctor." I don't look anything like a person who spent four years in med school followed by an interminable residency, so I was feeling pretty flattered when I stepped outside. There I crossed paths with a man wearing sweatpants and a T-shirt. He looked like a child molester who worked at a car wash.

"Ah!" the doorman cried. "Dr. Friedman!"

November 8, 2019
Laguna Beach, California
At last night's signing I met a young man named Cristian who works as a standardized patient. Those are people who pretend to have specific symptoms and are interviewed by young doctors hoping to determine what ails them.

"Does it pay all right?" I asked.

"Not bad," Cristian answered. He was good-looking and nicely dressed. "Come December, the doctors in training will start giving prostate exams, and I can earn up to seventy-five dollars per finger."

I personally would charge a lot more, especially if the person had exceptionally big hands or, worse still, long nails. "And how many fingers might you have inserted into your ass per day?"

"Ten," he said.

I winced, thinking of how uncomfortable that would be. They lube you up beforehand, but then you have to wipe it off, usually while the doctor is talking to you. That's the stuff of my worst nightmares, wiping my ass in front of someone. The last time I had my prostate examined, I just pulled my pants back up, then had to spend the rest of the afternoon with cold, wet Vaseline in my underwear.

November 15, 2019
San Francisco

At the Q and A, a woman asked how she and her husband can guarantee that their children remain close to each other. "We want them to be like you and Amy," she said. "Is there anything we can do?"

"Yes," I said. "Become alcoholics."

It really was a good answer.

November 18, 2019
Detroit, Michigan

I met a girl at the signing who was college-aged but not in college. "I want to teach," she said when I asked what she would like to do with her life.

"Teach what?"

"I'd like to teach kids that they're worth something, no matter what they've been told in their life, no matter how badly they were put down, because everyone matters."

"Yes," I said. "But what if they're, like, *truly* worthless?"

December 2, 2019
Raleigh

After arriving in town yesterday I was taken to Springmoor to visit Dad. It was noon, and I found him in his room wearing a red-and-navy-striped long-sleeved boat shirt. Jazz was playing, and there weren't too many lights on. "Dad?"

"Hey!" We embraced. "I was just about to get some lunch. Join me!"

The dining room he very slowly led me to had perhaps twelve people in it, all but one of them terribly old. Dad's hair has gone almost white since I last saw him, and it was poorly cut. He should keep it short, but it was Beatles-length, which made him look thinner. "You ready for some lunch, Mr. Sedaris?" a cheerful, bulky black woman asked as we entered the room.

Dad answered but his voice was so soft, she had to put her ear right against his mouth in order to hear him. "Say what? Sure, your son can eat too! Y'all have a seat."

She put a napkin around Dad's neck that had snaps on the corners and was worn as a bib. Then she brought a bowl of tomato soup, and a monkey dish of creamed corn. To drink, there was iced tea and a miniature glass of milk. Dad suggested that I eat too, but I said I was fine. "You ate on the plane?"

I lied. "Yes, I ate on the plane."

"Hey," he said to one of the women waiting on us. "I left my glasses in my room. How about you get them for me?"

She brought them, and I asked if he was farsighted or nearsighted. "The problem is that they're too damn big for me," he said. "They've fallen into the toilet, gosh, I don't know how many times."

I don't think my glasses have ever fallen into the toilet. Is his head shrinking?

Three minutes later he suggested that I eat something. "They can make you a sandwich, can make you anything you want. Eat!"

I ordered the soup.

"Attaboy." When the woman delivered it, he asked for two straws. It took him a long time to open his. When he finally got the wrapper off, he stuck one end in his soup. "I eat mine this way," he said. "It makes less of a mess."

I wanted to cry.

A man who is only eighty-three and is named Tom rolled over from another table. He pushed himself along with his feet rather than his hands and was much more substantial than the other people in the room, thicker, with a booming voice. "Who do we have here, Lou?"

"This is my son David."

I stood to shake Tom's hand.

"Your dad and me, we're buddies here."

Dad pointed to me. "That's my buddy."

For the second time that morning I wanted to cry. I also wanted to say, *Huh?*, as the one thing Dad and I definitely are not is buddies. The word was so ... wrong.

"We talk about all kinds of things," Tom said. "The war, for instance."

"Tom was in the military, a captain in the air force," Dad said in his whisper of a voice.

"And your dad, of course, was in the navy, a sonar operator."

I never knew that's what Dad did. He never talked about it, but it makes sense.

"And of course we talk about girls," Tom said. His face and hair were the color of dried corn husks. "He's always trying to pick them up, always telling them they're pretty." He winked at me, and I thought of how wrong his humor was, at least as it applied to Dad.

"I'm sort of the joker around here," Dad said. "I see the world a little differently, if you know what I mean."

Tom folded his hands together. "We make quite a team, don't we, old-timer?"

"He lived in Europe," Dad told me, "was stationed there for quite a long while."

"Where?" I asked.

"Uhhh..." Tom looked at his lap. "I was in...uhhh." It was as if someone had unplugged him. It happened again later when I asked if he had any children. "I have four and they're all..."

Dead? I wondered. *Behind bars?*

"Professionals," Dad offered.

"Professionals," Tom said. "They're all professionals. One is an accountant for a big law firm, makes quite a bit of money."

"The others make good money too," Dad said.

"They do!"

A tall aide came over then. Dad introduced him and I stood to shake his hand. "Is you the one I saw in the paper?" he asked.

"Gosh," I said. "Maybe."

"Eat something else," Dad said. "I can have them make you a sandwich, whatever you want!"

"I'm okay."

"Baloney. Eat."

Tom has been at Springmoor since 2004, when he was sixty-nine. "Well, all right," he said, pushing himself slowly toward the exit. "If you come back and want to talk, I'm just down the hall." He adjusted his glasses. "Say, there's Doris." He gestured to the next table. "She's a hundred and six." He waved at a woman with white hair and matching skin. "*Hi, Doris!*" he yelled.

The woman blinked.

"Doris! How's it going?"

A bit of food fell from her mouth.

I walked Dad back to his room and then met Adam in front of the building.

"How did it go?" he asked.

There wasn't an easy answer. Why can't I separate the ninety-six-year-old Dad from the eighty-six- or seventy-six- or fifty-six-year-old one? Why can't I see the man in front of me rather than the one I grew up with? My heart breaks for the ninety-six-year-old, so withered in his snappy French shirt, so frail.

December 10, 2019
Portland, Maine

At last night's signing I met a woman whose mother was given a lobotomy to cure her postpartum depression. "She'd tried to jump off a bridge," she said.

"And how is she today?"

The woman thought for a moment. "Now she likes to feed ants."

December 14, 2019
Belgrade, Serbia

The first thing I noticed about Serbia was that all of the men look like slobs. Since arriving, I've seen maybe three who are clean-shaven. All of the others run the gamut from five o'clock shadow to fully bearded. It's uncanny.

The first thing Patsy noticed was that in Serbia, you don't wait for the people in the row in front of you to collect their belongings and exit the plane; rather, you just push forward.

A hotel car was waiting for us outside of the baggage claim. The driver hadn't touched a razor in at least a week and said nothing much outside of hello and goodbye. It was a Friday afternoon, not particularly cold and slightly overcast. The hotel lobby includes a café and a restaurant, and while standing at the front desk, I was surprised to see people smoking. Everyone seems to smoke here. There are signs that show a cigarette with a slash mark through it and others that just show the cigarette, and they are displayed feet or inches apart from one another. The ventilation system was pretty good, as the smell didn't hit me right away. No one asked, but our rooms are nonsmoking. There are no ashtrays in them, at least.

What we saw of Belgrade yesterday was sad. Our first stop was a bakery, where we had deep-fried savory turnovers. The guy behind the counter spoke a little English, and we ate standing at a shallow counter. The bakery was clean and busy. Most of the customers carried plastic bags. Everyone carries plastic bags. The women wear a lot of makeup.

Continuing down the boulevard, we passed several bombed-out buildings. "Who did this?" I asked.

"NATO?" Patsy said. "I'm pretty sure it was NATO."

We wandered into a number of department stores, the sort where a dress costs eighteen dollars and has a tag that says KEEP AWAY FROM FIRE. I saw T-shirts reading FOLLOW and OOPSY-DAISY and FUTURE. Later we went to the post office, where I drew a picture of a postcard and a stamp beside the number 20. There were two lines going. A woman came up behind us and spoke to me in Serbian, her voice going up at the end. A question! That happened on several occasions and caused me each time to glance down at my shoes. Do I look like a Serb? Does no one notice that I am clean-shaven?

In some cities you can't bear to return to the hotel, thinking, *There's stuff out there!* Here, it felt fine to return. In the basement fitness center, I started watching *The Irishman*.

"What's it about?" Patsy asked when we met for dinner.

"A lot of people getting shot in the head," I told her.

The concierge suggested that we eat at a place called Jam. We took a cab driven by a guy with a five o'clock shadow and it cost four dollars. The restaurant was all in one room, with a smoking section and a nonsmoking section. We sat in non-smoking beside a man who arrived just as our appetizers did and lit a cigar. The women across from me were smoking as well. I liked the light in the restaurant, and the food was good. Our waiter was tall and bearded. His mother was Bosnian, but she hadn't gone back to that country in years. "After the war, it was...well."

The entrées at Jam cost between eight and sixteen dollars.

We took a taxi back and the driver was listening to a radio station his dashboard screen identified as SLOB.

December 16, 2019
Bijeljina, Bosnia

It should have occurred to me that a hotel made to look like a village of yesteryear, one with goats and sheep and ducks and geese and chickens living free range and in pens directly below my wooden hut, would also have a rooster and that it would start to crow well before dawn—at four a.m. in this case—and continue through the rest of the morning.

My room has a spinning wheel in it but no desk. There's not even a chair. I do have a TV, which is set on a corner shelf a foot and a half off the floor. There's a wooden clothes cupboard and a bathroom with a shower. Out the window I see miniature deer kneeling in the mud while chickens strut in circles around them. The goats are a short distance away, beside a penned dog that barks at everyone who passes.

I'm going to guess that Bosnians are not particularly litigious. Were they, the stone path that winds through the property would be cleared of moss and wet leaves. At night it would be well lit, not left in near total darkness the way it is now, making stairs nearly impossible to see. The bridges are particularly slippery and have no handrails. Were they flat, one wouldn't mind so much, but they rise over the artificial lake and the many man-made tributaries that feed it in high, semicircular arches that, like the paths, are moss-covered. Patsy fell flat on her ass on our way to breakfast. You'd like to think that was the lousiest thing that would happen during the course of the day, but it got worse.

December 18, 2019
London

"Goodness, you've gotten fat," Dr. Barras said as I settled into her chair yesterday for my periodontal appointment. "I can really see it in your face."

The French! I thought of Régine, who'd said the same thing to me in Normandy twenty years ago.

"Well," I said to Dr. Barras, "I've been on tour."

"*Quand même!*" she said.

"It's only a little weight," I insisted as she tucked the bib beneath the lowest of my new chins.

"More than a little." She unwrapped the tray of sanitized hooks she would use to shred my gums with. "All right, let's get to work."

I opened my mouth, and asked if, in her opinion, my tongue had gotten fat as well.

She laughed. "Mr. Sedaris!"

"How much do you think I've gained?" I asked. "Ten kilos? Twenty?"

"I couldn't say."

Now discretion was holding her back?

December 24, 2019
London
Amy and I had just taken seats on the 49 bus yesterday when she turned to me saying, sharply, "I am *not* going to have this conversation with you today, not at Christmastime. Do you understand me? Do you? Jesus!"

Nobody looked over but I knew they were listening.

"Every year we go through this. *Every year!*"

At one of the stores we Christmas-shopped at, Amy bought herself a ring. "I am out of control," she admitted, moaning. Then she justified the purchase by saying she'd received a generous bonus check from the *Lion King* movie. "Can I take a picture of this lamp for my brother?" she asked the salesperson, who was tall and pretty.

"You can photograph whatever you like," the woman said.

"Great," Amy told her. "I want you to take your blouse off for me. I'll just need a minute—five minutes, tops."

The Japanese saleswoman at the next store we went to sat on the floor to process our transactions, and when Amy plopped down beside her, she giggled. Then I got down there—a mistake, as it meant having to get back on my feet at some point. Crawling on my hands and knees toward a bench I could hopefully use to hoist myself up, I wondered what someone looking through the window might have thought. *Oh my God, what's happening to that old man!*

December 27, 2019
Rackham
My birthday was dreary. It rained almost nonstop, so everyone stayed in. While Hugh made my cake, Amy, Daniel, and Adam sat at the kitchen table and played Sorry, with the loser having to surrender his or her freedom. At one point I walked in and

Adam was the slave. Later it was Daniel. "Get me another drink," Amy ordered. When he asked to be excused so that he could take a shower, they granted permission provided he use only cold water and allow them to watch.

They were really brutal.

"When Adam was my slave I made it a point to say 'please' and 'thank you,' but not those two," Daniel complained.

"Did I say you could talk?" Amy asked.

"What's your resolution for 2020?" I asked Adam later in front of the fire.

"I want to be more direct," he said. "I don't ever want people wishing they could read my mind."

That's such a good goal, and clearly one I should consider. Were someone to walk up with a hammer and ask if he could hit me over the head with it, I'd probably look down and say, *I once had a pair of shoes like that.*

Hugh made a côte de boeuf with scalloped potatoes for dinner, followed by my birthday cake. I opened gifts, and then we retreated to the living room, where Amy gave us facials. "This cream is two hundred fifty dollars a bottle," she'd say, smearing something or other into my skin with both hands. Twelve hours later, our faces are still soft. I look in the mirror expecting to see my twenty-year-old self and am horrified at what he has become.

2020

January 14, 2020
Brisbane, Australia

At last night's signing I met a woman who claimed that in the morning she's so ugly her iPhone doesn't recognize her and refuses to unlock. "How...insulting," I said, glad that I'd never signed up for the facial-recognition function.

February 2, 2020
New York

Hugh has the flu. This in addition to his sciatica means he's complaining pretty much all the time. And so I was happy to go downtown with him and sit in the reception area as he met with an acupuncturist. On the wall before us hung a pair of golden wings made of spray-painted feathers and displayed under glass. They looked like someone ripped them off the back of a six-year-old angel. It was Saturday, and after Hugh went in for his appointment, I was the only person in the waiting area. While sitting there, I transcribed two Spanish lessons. For the most part they follow the standard Pimsleur template: "Do you want something to drink?" "What would you like?" "I can't eat at ten o'clock. It's too late," etc. The Spanish differs from the other Pimsleur language courses in that it gets fairly gossipy: "I don't want to go with him." "Carlos talks too much. He drinks too much coffee!"

Also, unlike the Swedish or the German, there's a lot of illness talk. "I'm sick." "My wife is sick too." "All my friends and me, we're sick." "We need doctors." "Do you know a good doctor? We're sick."

February 13, 2020
Vancouver

I saw a good number of homeless men at LAX yesterday. Some were outside going through trash cans and others were asleep on the floor of the terminal. That surprised me, as did all the people wearing face masks—to ward off the coronavirus, apparently. The first case was reported in the UK yesterday. It was a man in Hove who had been in Singapore the same day that Hugh and I were.

February 14, 2020
San Francisco

At dinner last night Fawnee told me about a calendar she'd seen called Social Justice Kittens. It's by Sean Tejaratchi and is pictures of kittens combined with actual tweets by so-called social justice warriors. These include:
— "Your 'opinion' is a dangerous ideology that puts me in harm's way."
— "When I'm discussing my pain, your job is to listen."
— "Humor is one of the most vicious weapons in the arsenal of cultural oppression."
— "Every day I face microaggressions and micro-invalidations from my so-called allies."
— "You are terrified because I am Living My Truth and singing a Song of Myself."
— "Your heteronormative narrative decelebrates both my inner and outer bodyshapes."

— "I'm sorry I was born privileged. It disgusts me and I feel so much shame."

— "My self-interrogation has deeply impacted my own awareness of privilege, and I understand how contemplative practices can be supportive tools to unpack and navigate my conditioning."

— "Rational thought should be replaced with a transversal and multidimensional dialogue of knowledges."

— "Your rage comes from fear and hatred. Our rage comes from love."

— "I am creating a non-hierarchal safespace to express my intersections."

— "I am not here to educate you. Shut up, listen, and own your ancient legacy of hatred and wrongness."

How does one even begin to pick a favorite? I wasn't familiar with the term *microinvalidation* and learned by looking it up this morning that it means doing pretty much anything: If I look at you; if I don't look at you. If I speak; if I don't. Talking over someone most certainly counts, though there's probably a whole other category for that. What scares me is that there might be a reaction to these tweets that doesn't involve laughter, that there's a world out there in which these lines make sense.

February 15, 2020
San Francisco
I had lunch yesterday with David Rogier. We met at a restaurant called Marlowe and as we settled in, he told me that his grandparents met at Auschwitz. It's a sobering bit of information

and I later thought of how funny it would have been had he followed this with *Yeah, they both worked there.*

February 27, 2020
Colonia del Sacramento, Uruguay

Dawn, Matt, and I left the apartment in Buenos Aires at ten yesterday morning and took a cab to the ferry terminal. Interesting to me was that no one we dealt with once we arrived spoke English. Not the woman who checked our luggage, not the immigration officers, not even the stewards in the business-class section of the boat we later took. The boarding started right on time and in an orderly manner. While waiting, I noticed a young man in a T-shirt that read THE EVOLUTION OF BASKETBALL. On the far left side was a silhouette of a monkey that grew progressively more erect until he stood straight and held a ball in his hands. "Do you think he understands how racist that is?" I asked Dawn.

There really wasn't much to Colonia. On my afternoon walk I stopped at a bakery and had a sandwich with boiled carrot coins in it. I walked through a park where all the men were grouped together, as were the women. It was hot if you weren't in the shade, but not unbearably so. I saw a lot of stray dogs, which was interesting. When one's on a leash, Dawn will glare at the owner as if to say, *Keep that thing away from me,* but when it's a stray all she can do is glare at the dog, which cares even less than its owner would have. I bought an empanada on my walk just because I hadn't had one yet. It was nasty, so after a few bites, I tossed it into a dumpster. A minute or two later a stray with swollen teats passed, and I wished I'd given the nasty empanada to her instead of throwing it away.

March 2, 2020
Santiago, Chile

It was seven by the time I returned to the hotel last night. My eighteen-mile walk had pretty much done me in, so I took a long bath before going to the ground-floor restaurant. There I was greeted by the tallest woman I have ever seen. She must have been six five in heels, stocky, and with braces on her teeth. The giantess led me to a table and a few minutes later a young waiter came over and introduced himself. "And what is *your* name?" he asked.

I don't like it when waiters do that, so I asked if he had a brother.

"I do."

"And his name is?"

The guy looked startled. "Um, Mateo?"

"Great," I said. "I'd like to be called Mateo."

The waiter liked the idea and I basically let him order for me. The food was terrific, and while eating I answered some of the mail I'd brought with me. Included was a letter from a woman in Maryland who politely called me tedious.

I was supposed to leave for the airport at eleven this morning, and I went to the Club Lounge concierge at a quarter to in order to check out. Fortunately I'd paid for my room the night before and the only charge was my dinner the previous evening, otherwise I might still be there, searching my pockets for change. I don't know what happened but for some reason or other, my card wouldn't go through. The guy tried it as debit, then as credit. He tried pressing the numbers into his machine by hand, but nothing worked. Meanwhile there was someone waiting behind me, huffing. He was a bit older than me, and American, I'd later learn. The concierge was Chilean and handsome with carefully combed hair and buffed nails. I was sweating by this point—profusely—and likely looked like someone who was guilty. "What can we do?" I asked. "I'm good for the money, really, I am."

Were I the man behind me I'd have said, *Here, let me pay that for you. You can send me a check when you get home.* I did that at the U.S. embassy in Paris once and was shocked when the young woman I got out of a jam never paid me back.

For a good portion of my life I couldn't have afforded an expensive hotel room. It wouldn't have occurred to me to stay at the Ritz in Santiago, or the Ritz in any other city, for that matter. Now, age sixty-three, here I was. But without a working credit card, I might as well have been thirty again. The clothes I was wearing cost a fortune: the permanently wrinkled Casey Casey shirt, the Geoffrey B. Small jacket made of old linen that looks like it's stained with oil. The bandanna I was wiping off my sweat with had cost $160. For a bandanna! To an undiscerning eye, though, I looked like a tramp.

"Maybe you could go to an ATM and pay the balance in Chilean pesos," the concierge said.

I explained that there were only two banks I could use in Chile, and I imagined that, because I'd already tried my PIN six times that morning, my card had been cut off.

The concierge folded his hands. "I'm just trying to work with you."

It was then I remembered the cash deposit I'd left against incidentals upon my arrival: forty U.S. dollars. To those I added five singles from my wallet. Then I took back the super-generous tip I'd left the housekeeper. The concierge canceled my airport car, and that allowed me to keep my pesos and use them to take a taxi instead. By this time I was soaked.

With my few leftover coins, I got a coffee at the airport and boarded my plane with nothing. It's the worst feeling, being penniless. It's horrible, of course, when you *literally* have nothing, but it's bad as well when you have money but can't get to it, when you're used to being treated like a regular person and suddenly have that snatched away. I mean, why couldn't the hotel clerk just have googled me, just *known* I'd be good for it? One moment I belonged at the Ritz, and the next I didn't, me with the shitty teeth and the white knapsack from Comme des Garçons that looked like it had been dragged behind a plow horse.

Then I flew Aerolíneas Argentinas, where I have no status whatsoever. Things didn't improve until I got to Buenos Aires to check in for my New York flight. The line was grueling but the moment I showed my ticket, I was ushered to the priority counter. "Why?" I asked.

"Executive Platinum," I was told. "Please, sir, come with us."

Quite a few passengers on the flight to New York had masks on, even though the surgeon general advises against them, saying they should be saved for health-care professionals. There's been a run on them, and a run on groceries as well. Hugh spoke to a woman at Grace's Marketplace who had just bought a freezer and was now stocking it. In the *Washington Post* I read that people have stopped drinking Corona beer, afraid that it's somehow connected to the virus. I remember Ayds candy taking a similar hit in the early eighties.

March 15, 2020
New York
Nike stores have announced that they're closing. France has closed as well. Graduations are canceled, and weddings. Hotels are suffering something terrible.

March 19, 2020
New York

Lisa called with updates from Costco. "They just got a new delivery of toilet paper, but it was gone by the time Bob and I got there."

Amy came for dinner last night and showed me a *Rolling Stone* photo essay on shoppers hoarding. What I loved were the expressions on their faces, the glee mixed with victory and desperation.

"Gun sales have gone up as well," Hugh said.

Amy put her phone away. "So people can protect their toilet paper."

Cristina was at the table with us, and we told her how bad we are at hoarding. "You have to understand, David and I grew up shopping with my father," Amy said. "With a professional!"

I remembered him during the oil crisis in 1977, heading to the Shell station with empty cans and getting in line at four a.m. All our cars had full tanks, but he needed the next guy's ration as well. I don't even drive but he taught me how to siphon. I remember the shock of getting a mouthful of gas and spitting it onto the street, then thinking, *Someone could have used that.*

March 22, 2020
New York

Today's *Salon* includes an article on sex workers. Due to the virus, they're experiencing layoffs and pay cuts, so many have started Go Fund Me campaigns. I'm half expecting a report on how this is affecting pedophiles. With grade-school classes canceled and playgrounds shuttered, where are they to turn?

I imagine that prostitutes with regular customers are doing

just what Amy's Pilates teacher and trainer are: reminding clients that their services contribute to one's overall sense of well-being and offering FaceTime sessions for the same cost as regular sit-on-your-face-time sessions.

March 25, 2020
New York

Diane's husband died yesterday in Paris. He's the first person I know who got the coronavirus. Now I read that Terrence Mc-Nally has died of it as well. I met him briefly at an American Academy meeting and was tongue-tied. While he and John Murray were struggling for breath, I was writing an essay for the BBC about the lighter side of self-isolation, this as my article on hoarding was landing on the *New Yorker* site.

"And don't forget *CBS Sunday Morning*!" Katharine wrote.

"I'm on it," I told her.

I could stay busy doing nothing but this. But only until Easter, apparently. By that time, Trump promises this will all be over, and we'll have our lives back. He tested negative for the virus last week, but Rand Paul is positive. While waiting for his results, he continued to use the Senate gym. *No fair,* I thought when I heard it. My gym's been closed for ten days. Even gyms in people's apartment buildings were forced to close.

The streets on Sunday and Monday were deserted, but yesterday I noticed a bit more activity. Central Park looked the way it might have on any spring day, and for that reason I worry they'll shut it down. Groups were picnicking and playing ball. There were a lot of crazy people out. "You can buy all the guns you want," shouted a woman who was dragging a rolling suitcase behind her, "but you touch my property one more time and they ain't going to help you!"

A skinny white guy who had clearly been in prison and was out on the sidewalk drunk tore into Hugh and me the other night. "Don't be looking at my money, bitch," he said, referring to the three one-dollar bills he was holding. He turned his hand into a pistol and shot us each in the head. "Bitches!"

March 29, 2020
New York

Conservatives have begun their attack on Dr. Anthony Fauci, head of the National Institute of Allergy and Infectious Diseases. He's been appearing at press conferences with Trump, and by politely correcting him, he's signed his death warrant. It's part of the Republican war on expertise, on these "specialists" who learned everything they know from a book—or, in this case, many books and many, many years of experience. Trump, by contrast, "feels" things. He knows them in his gut. And in the time of a deadly pandemic, who would you rather go with?

April 2, 2020
New York

Dad called from his assisted-living place yesterday and we talked for half an hour. "I got that last letter you mailed and thought, *Well, he really doesn't have anything to say, does he?*" he said.

Yes, but I wrote *you,* I wanted to counter. *Who else does that?*

Actually, it was a nice conversation. Lisa and Amy both spoke to him earlier in the week and told me that he sounded terrible. "I don't know how much longer I can hold on," he'd said to them. It's always been interesting how different he is from one child to the next. With me he was lucid and full of questions, though in fairness, the questions were the ones he always asks, ones you could just as easily pose to a stranger. "So, what's going on? How the hell are you?"

April 3, 2020
New York
Hugh told me this morning that we're all supposed to wear masks now.

I was still in bed. "Everyone in America?"

"Everyone in New York City."

I rolled over. "Fuck."

They'd been telling us *not* to wear them, so now the dirty looks I've been giving people with masks will have to be reconfigured to mean "You were right all along."

April 12, 2020
New York
I walked to Amy's yesterday and cleaned her oven. She'd sprayed it like I told her to, and by the time I arrived, the Easy-Off had worked its magic, reducing the hard-baked grease to a thick, tar-colored sludge. At the start it was like the inside of a cave, this forbidding dark hole you half expected bats to fly out of. When I'd finished, it gleamed, and you literally had to shield your eyes when looking at it. "Like new!" Amy said.

It really is the easiest trick in the world. No one can believe the before and after, and it's honestly not that hard to do. As people grow older and you don't know what to get them for Christmas or their birthdays, this is the perfect gift. "Did you know that yesterday was Siblings Day?" Amy asked as I knelt on her floor with my head in her oven.

"Of course," I lied. "Why do you think I'm doing this?"

As I went at the stubborn spots with a Brillo pad, we talked about the book *Hidden Valley Road*. She's only on the third chapter, so I didn't want to ruin anything. "I love that in the first few pages the mother—one of the only family members who *isn't* schizophrenic—is sewing a bird's eyes shut," I said. "I thought she was a taxidermist. Then I learned that the falcon was alive and decided that this had to be the best book ever. I sent a copy to Lisa," I continued, "and would send one to Paul if I thought he'd read it."

Next we talked about the movie she'd suggested I watch, *Krisha,* about an alcoholic and drug addict who visits her family for Thanksgiving. "A masterpiece," I said, reaching into the very back of the oven to where the interior light was.

The movie left both of us thinking about Tiffany. She was the last family member whose oven I'd cleaned. "After I finished, she baked an apple pie," I said. "When it was done, she grabbed her pot holders and intentionally spilled a half a cup of the filling onto the floor of the oven, saying, 'Whoops,' as if she were reading it off a page. She might as well have said, *Fuck you,* as that's what she meant."

April 17, 2020
New York

Starting today, New Yorkers are required to wear masks "when unable to practice social distancing." I take this to mean in stores and on busy streets. Can't I continue bare-faced outside late at night, when I normally cross paths with no one? There's talk of this lasting another month, which wouldn't technically kill me, I suppose. It sure is getting old, though. Every day feels the same. *Didn't I already play this?* I think as I listen to a news podcast. *Didn't I already walk to Ninetieth Street an hour ago?*

Bill de Blasio has gone from calling doctors and nurses "heroes" to calling all New Yorkers heroes. What did we do that was so brave? We stayed home!

April 25, 2020
New York

At midnight I walked through Times Square to Thirty-Fourth Street. It was quiet out, and everyone I passed wanted money from me except for a beat-up-looking black fellow in his eighties who had dropped his cane down the stairs leading to the subway. I had just retrieved it for him when I came upon a man in a wheelchair who was using his feet to push himself along. "Look at this fucking clown!" he thundered. I assumed that he was referring to me, but in fact he was looking across the street. "Fucking goddamn clown!" I followed his eyes and saw...a clown with a red nose and turquoise hair. At one o'clock in the morning.

Well, all right, then, I thought.

April 27, 2020
New York

Amy came for dinner and before eating we watched a dozen YouTube videos by an outfit called Soft White Underbelly. They provide great lighting and a judgment-free space for drug addicts, prostitutes, pimps, hard-core alcoholics, and people who are just plain crazy. Then they ask them really good questions. One of our favorite interviews was with a man who was transitioning into a gender-less dragon. It had had its ears cut off, and its testicles. Its tongue was split, and it had had all but six teeth removed. The canines, I'm guessing, were implants, as they were as long as a dog's, and pointed. The dragon's face and body were tattooed with scales, and it had hornlike lumps on its head. "Next to go is my penis," it said, adding that it doesn't want a vagina, "just nothing. I want to be like a doll."

Where will it pee from? I wondered. The dragon was super-friendly, sweet, really.

Another video was of a heroin-addict prostitute named Trixie who looked to be in her seventies but was likely twenty years younger. "What do you eat?" the interviewer asked.

She looked into the camera. "Semen."

527

An alcoholic and drug addict followed and said, in regard to her father, "He murdered quite a bit of people."

I love all the surprises these videos include. "The police was called because I threw a pumpkin at my stepfather," one woman says.

"A pumpkin!" Amy and I cried.

"How old are you?" the interviewer asks a mentally ill man in a dress.

"Ten."

"Do you have any children?"

"Seven hundred. I'm a federal judge. Sean Connery was my first husband."

May 13, 2020
Emerald Isle

It's fascinating to go from Manhattan to, well, anywhere else. Here, maybe one out of every one hundred people has a mask on. The cashiers at the Food Lion didn't, and neither did the ones at the Emerald Isle Wine Market. The liquor store has a notice in the window saying that if you've recently been outside of the country or in any of the U.S. hot spots, do not enter.

A sign on the door at CVS suggested that customers wear masks, so I did. The cashier was super-friendly to the woman ahead of me but turned to stone when my turn came. Normally I'd have mentioned how different from Manhattan it is here on the island. *Back in New York, there are lines out the door!* Now, though, you don't dare.

Most of the shops at Emerald Plantation are open. The pizza restaurant was serving, and its outdoor tables were full. On my way home I passed the Fish Hut Grill. The sign in its window read OPEN. NC FREEDOM IS ESSENTIAL.

Returning home, I ran into Irene, who wears both a mask

and sunglasses when she goes into the store. The glasses are to hide her eyes. Irene is Korean-American, but most people can't distinguish one Asian nationality from another. To them she's Chinese, and the coronavirus is her fault.

May 14, 2020
Emerald Isle

The Wisconsin Supreme Court just overturned its governor's extended stay-at-home order. People in favor of reopening gathered on the capitol's steps, crowded together and maskless. In other states, armed militias are standing guard as barbershops and tattoo parlors illegally accept customers.

And no one is stopping them? I think. How can that be? If they were black people with guns, the reaction would be a lot different. I think of Ahmaud Arbery, who was shot to death in Georgia last winter. There was another article about him in the *Washington Post* yesterday, and one of the people who wrote to respond said that had he not thrown a punch, had he stopped when ordered to by the two white strangers carrying guns and waited for the police to clear things up, a tragedy might have been averted for everyone involved.

Did it not occur to the author of the letter that Arbery might have been scared or that in the year 2020, a person doesn't have to stop just because two rednecks in trucks who are not cops tell him to? Or that, after being followed and shouted at and threatened, throwing a punch was his only way of defending himself? As for the police clearing things up, where did the letter writer think that might take place? On the side of the road? *So sorry for the misunderstanding, Mr. Arbery.*

May 15, 2020
Emerald Isle

Gretchen arrived at one yesterday afternoon wearing a mutilated mask. "I cut a hole in it so I can smoke," she said when I asked about it.

May 22, 2020
Emerald Isle

Finally the sun is out again. It had rained nonstop since Monday and was getting to be oppressive, much like the news. An article in yesterday's *Times* predicted that 40 percent of the people who have lost their jobs will never get them back again. *Can that be true?* I wondered.

The heavy rain overturned birds' nests. I passed a half a dozen chicks stretched out dead on the sidewalk, resembling baby dinosaurs. I'm seeing a great many frogs and toads as well, not flattened by cars but dead nonetheless, slightly crushed, as if beneath the feet of toddlers.

In the afternoon I walked in the rain to Cap'n Willis. After bringing the fish home I headed back out in my wet shoes. The sky had almost cleared by then. I thought I'd drag myself to Coast Guard Road and had just hit Publix when I saw some movement in the grass. It was a young snapping turtle, almost black, storming toward the building as if it planned to fire everyone who worked there.

"How on earth did you get here?" I asked it.

I had a plastic bag in my knapsack, so I held it down as the furious turtle charged, tanklike, into it. It made sense to release it into the water behind the Food Lion, so I headed back in that direction, holding the bag at arm's length and shaking it every so often. I hoped I'd see a ten- or twelve-year-old boy walking out of the store, a younger version of myself who'd have loved to take the snapper home and keep it for a while. They're good eaters, much easier and more satisfying to feed than box turtles. Right now the snapper was the length of an iPhone, and I wondered how long it might take for it to grow to the size of a lunch box. A year? Three years? Then, with care, it would become as big as a suitcase.

I passed no children so I proceeded to the deck behind the Food Lion. There I saw a young woman in shorts with a missing leg. In its place was an aluminum pole that ended in a sneaker. She was pretty and blond and stood beside a stocky young man, both of them staring down into the water. "I found a baby snapping turtle and thought I'd release it," I told them.

The young man peered into my bag. "Cool." He was less cautious than me, and when I laid the bag on the deck, he reached in and grabbed the turtle by the rear of the shell. Then he flipped it over and said, "She's a female."

"How can you tell?" I asked.

"I'm from Ohio," he announced, as if that were answer enough.

"Look how cute she is," the young woman said. This struck me because if there's one thing this turtle wasn't, it was cute. Small, yes, but no more adorable than a grenade. The girl stuck her finger out, and the guy from Ohio warned her not to.

Yes, I thought, looking at her bright aluminum shin. *You don't want another missing part.*

The guy dropped the turtle into the water, which was already churning with them. "Get a load of that one there," he cried, pointing to a snapper the size of a shield. "Have you ever seen one that big!"

When I told Hugh about it later, he wondered if the young woman wasn't the one who'd had her leg bitten off by a shark two summers ago. Me, I kept thinking about the turtle and wondering if I should have kept her. All she needed was the right name, something that would essentially take the sting out of her and make her seem benign rather than menacing. Mary Katherine, I'd have called her.

May 29, 2020
New York

Earlier this week, a black man named George Floyd was killed by a police officer in Minneapolis who knelt on the guy's neck as he repeatedly said he couldn't breathe and called out for his mother. A bystander recorded the arrest on her phone, and the video, which was chilling, quickly went viral. What's remarkable is the look on the officer's face. *What?* he seems to be saying. *I can do this. I can do whatever I want.* At one point he puts his hands in his pockets, the way you might when waiting for a bus.

There were protests in Minnesota, then in Ohio, New York, and a number of other states. Last night in Minneapolis, people set fire to a police station. In Manhattan, things turned violent as well. Trump responded by calling the protesters "thugs" and tweeted, "When the looting starts, the shooting starts."

Mike Sacks sent me a book titled *1001 Best Pick-Up Lines*. You know they work because the author, a man named Don Diebel who has white hair and a black mustache, is holding a single long-stemmed rose on the back cover. The book is broken into different chapters. Favorites from "All Purpose Pick-Up Lines" include:

— "You know, if I could rewrite the alphabet, I'd put U and I together."
— "If I follow you home, will you keep me?"
— "I'm new in town. Would you mind giving me directions to your apartment?"

— "Do you have a quarter I can borrow? I told my
mother I'd call her when I met the girl of my
dreams."

From "Bars and Nightclub Pick-Up Lines":
— "If this bar is a meat market, you must be the
prime rib."
— "Do you mind if I taste your drink?" Then lean
over and kiss her.
— At closing time, approach the drunkest
woman in the place and say, "Your place or
mine?"

Most of the pickup lines simply amount to sexual harassment.
I mean, kissing a stranger without her permission? Threatening to follow her home? The most the best of these might get
you is an eye-roll.

June 1, 2020
New York

Today, like yesterday, will be glorious, a beautiful day for
setting trash cans on fire!

There was looting on the streets in SoHo. I walked Amy
partway home after dinner and came upon work crews boarding up the windows at Bergdorf's and the Apple Store. It
was the same at Dior and Hermès and Marc Jacobs, where
onlookers took photos.

Walking down Fifth, we were passed by young people, in
pairs or knots of five, coming from one part of town and
headed to another. None of them paid us any mind.

We found her a cab on the corner of Fifty-Second, and
from there I turned around and walked up to Ninetieth before
returning home. As the looting continues, I worry it will play

directly into Trump's hands. *So stop!* I want to shout from my perch on the twentieth floor.

June 2, 2020
New York

A curfew went into effect at 11:00 last night, but from 7:30 onward the sirens outside our windows were constant. I'd look out at 9:15 or 11:30 or 1:00 a.m. and see police cars driving the wrong way down Third Avenue. I couldn't see many people on the street, but there was a fair amount of traffic, much more than I'd expected.

One's inclination is to say, *Okay, I get it. Enough!*

It made me so anxious, listening to the sirens and helicopters. I wish I could say I was afraid for my safety or for the safety of those who were peacefully protesting. Instead, I was thinking of my beloved shops. Here they were just scheduled to reopen. *What'll happen if there's nothing left for me to buy!*

More than that, I'm afraid of change. There were already newspaper articles about people deciding to leave New York. The virus convinced them that city life was no longer worth it. How are they going to feel now? *The value of my apartment!* I thought.

I saw a white guy in Central Park yesterday holding up a cardboard sign that read AFRAID TO PROTEST. What followed were eight names, presumably of his friends, or ex-friends, people he felt deserved to be shamed.

Then there are the videos. The *Washington Post* is carrying one of a masked man with silver hair who's using a pickax to pry up paving stones he can throw at the nearby police. A black protester forces him to the ground and is joined by several others, all shouting, "The white guy! Get him!" Together they deliver the vandal to the police.

A similar video shows white girls spray-painting the façade

of a Starbucks in Los Angeles. "What are you *doing?*" a black woman demands. "You know who's going to get blamed for that? Me. *My* people. What are y'all even *doing* here? Who asked you for your help?"

Other videos are more disturbing: demonstrators on a bridge, shattering people's car windows and kicking their doors in; young women smashing shop windows with shovels and tire irons. There's smoke in the background, and burning trash cans, the sound of sirens; it's chaos, all overseen by the chaos president, who had a path cleared with tear gas so that he could walk to the Episcopal church down the street from the White House for a photo op with a Bible, which he held the way a monkey might, as if he had no understanding of what a book is.

The bishop of the Episcopal Diocese of Washington, DC, wasted no time in condemning the president, who didn't even warn church officials that he was coming. She saw Trump as a disrespectful opportunist.

"That's fine," I said to Hugh as we were talking about it this morning. "But his supporters saw him as a fearless cowboy walking unafraid toward his God. I honestly don't think this will hurt him in the long run—not with his base, anyway."

Hugh frowned out the window. "We just can't win."

I think he meant a universal "we," as looking out the window of your Upper East Side duplex is pretty much the definition of winning.

Conspiracists are certain that George Floyd is still alive and that Derek Chauvin, the officer who killed him, is an actor. The two of them set in motion a plan hatched and financed by, of course, George Soros.

Looters, on the other hand, are insisting that shop owners *want* their stores to be wiped out so they can claim more money from insurance companies.

David Sedaris

June 3, 2020
New York

Just before last night's curfew started, we saw a protest heading up Lexington Avenue. It was the first one visible from our apartment, and it was peaceful. We heard some sirens and helicopters shortly after nightfall, but compared to Monday night, it was nothing. Unfortunately, the looting has become the story, at least on the right. That said, I love watching the faces of people in a mob, especially when they're acting like contestants on that game show where you race to grab food off the shelves. I said to Amy, "Just because you forced your way into the Nike store doesn't mean you can find your size in the stockroom. Half the time the *employees* can't even do that. And as a looter, you've got only five minutes at best!"

Trump harangued governors and mayors on the phone yesterday, warning them to get tough. They needed to "dominate" the protesters, he said. They needed to make arrests and put people away for ten years.

I said to Hugh over dinner, "What will I say years from now when people ask me what I did to fight for justice, and I answer that one afternoon I bought our only black doorman a Snapple?"

I wanted to run out and join the protest I saw from the terrace, but the night before I'd attempted to trim the nail on my little toe and cut into it a little too deeply. Pus spurted out, and ever since then I've been limping. I tried walking to Ninetieth Street but barely made it to Eightieth. It hurts too much to wear shoes, so mainly I paced in the apartment until all the circles on my watch were filled. Last week I put on those ridiculous exfoliating socks. Now my feet look like a child's papier-mâché project. The floor on my side of the bed is littered with shed skin, some in sheets the size of postage stamps and others closer to flakes. "Enough!" I say, but it just keeps happening.

So you see, I really couldn't *do anything,* I'll say when asked what I did during the great uprising of 2020. Then, too, I'm a bit uncomfortable in the role of ally. In the end I'll do what people like me do—I'll donate some money and then tell everyone I donated twice that amount.

While I was out yesterday, my watch made the alarming noise it does just before delivering bad news. In this case it had to do with the 8:00 p.m. curfew. Everyone around me got the alarm at the same time, and it was interesting to see them all pull out their phones.

June 5, 2020
New York

By the time I finished work yesterday it was nearly 3:30. I needed a walk with a toilet at the end of it, so called Amy and asked if she was going to be at home. The route I took to her place brought me down Madison, which, like every other avenue in the city now, smells of plywood, the result of all the businesses—shops, banks, even office buildings—having been recently boarded up. I lowered my mask and inhaled, almost high. It's a comforting odor I've always associated with my childhood and all the new homes being built in North Hills. Until the doors and windows were installed and had locks on them, it was taken for granted that we—that anyone—could walk into these places and have a look around.

When we were young, these were our playhouses. "Hey," Dad would say when we got old enough to carry things. "Why don't you run up the block and get me some"—nails / shingles / a couple of two-by-fours / a sack of concrete.

He treated construction sites like free hardware stores, thinking, perhaps, that others had treated our place the same way.

A few years older, and we would vandalize these houses. Not horribly, though I do recall pushing an unattached toilet down a flight of stairs and plucking the tear-shaped pendeloques off many a chandelier, completely denuding them in some cases. Dan and I would use them to make necklaces for our mothers that weighed eight pounds and always elicited the same response: "Goodness!"

I thought of all this after Ahmaud Arbery was murdered and video surfaced of him entering a house that was under construction and seemed to have no doors on it. He's seen walking in—not creeping or skulking, the way you might if you knew you were in the wrong. He looks around for a moment, thinking, I imagine, *Nice place but terrible neighborhood,* and then leaves.

Some said he was looking for water, but even if he wasn't—so what? Video later surfaced of other people walking through the house, proof that it's hardly unheard of. I'd wager that anyone who grew up in a new suburb has walked into a house exactly the way he did.

Amy and I often talk about what we might have as our last meal if we were on death row. If I could smell one thing before I died, plywood would be right up there on my list, alongside my mother's bedsheets and honeysuckle.

I was thinking that yesterday when I neared Union Square and saw people with signs in their hands walking toward a crowd that had gathered on the south side of the park. "Water, sir?" asked a young woman as I stepped closer. "Do you need hand sanitizer? Or I have some Doritos or Cheetos if you need a little something to eat." I guessed that she was a college student and assumed she was selling these things. But no, they were free.

"That's all right, but thanks," I said, feeling I hadn't earned them.

The crowd teetering at the edge of the park wasn't doing anything in particular. Many of the people had signs that they hoisted or lazily waved. It seemed a good place to get started, and so I went to Amy's and returned with her a half hour later. I said as we entered the fray, "We look like we're searching for our children."

Grandchildren is probably more like it.

"Pretzels?" an earnest young snacktavist asked. "Do you need some chips? Some water?"

The crowd numbered maybe four hundred. Signs included WHITE SILENCE NO MORE, DEFUND NYPD, NO EXCUSE 4 ABUSE, and BLM. Someone beat a drum, and while it felt like something should kick off, nothing did.

"It's just a gathering, really," a twenty-year-old woman standing next to me explained.

Amy and I wanted to see if 45R had been looted, so we left Union Square and were in SoHo when we came upon a large march heading west on Houston Street. With ease, we joined it. "Hey-hey, ho-ho, racist cops have got to go" was the chant when we merged into the crowd. This made me cringe, as I hate "Hey-hey, ho-ho." Chanting anything makes me feel self-conscious, so I was grateful for the face masks.

Everyone had phones out, and photographers lined the curbs, as did policemen. "Whose streets?" asked the crowd. "Our streets!" came the answer. Then it was "NYPD, suck my dick!"

And I'm not sure how I feel about that one. Is someone performing fellatio on you *really* the most degrading thing you can imagine? I was thinking they might change it to "eat my ass," but that has its place as well.

One of the signs carried by a marcher read BARBER SCHOOL

LENGTH 1,500 HOURS. POLICE SCHOOL LENGTH 840 HOURS. That's the kind of message you want to get across, as it really makes you think. ABOLISH THE POLICE, on the other hand, seems a bit implausible.

The crowd turned north, and we followed until Washington Square Park, where it got bottlenecked. I walked Amy to Fifth and Ninth, then headed home.

June 12, 2020
New York

In the afternoon I went to the post office, passing along the way half a peeled banana lying on the sidewalk outside the entry to the Food Emporium. I walked by, then doubled back to kick it into the street, thinking as I did so that the city should award me a citation. How many people passed that and did nothing? Animals!

Amy came for dinner. Hugh made hamburgers and afterward she taught us to say "I am not an angry clown" in sign language. To say "clown," you act like you're gripping a ball attached to the end of your nose. "Angry" is an explosive gesture toward your face with the inside of your hand.

June 23, 2020
Emerald Isle

In New Bern we took a cab driven by a woman named Bethany. She was old enough to be a grandmother—though in eastern North Carolina, that's not saying much—and had a smudged-looking tattoo on her meaty upper arm. Beside her on a cushion was a four-month-old shih tzu named Cookie. "No, ma'am," she said when it attempted to jump into her lap.

"She's my daughter's," Bethany explained, looking down at the dog, whose bulging eyes were almost on the sides of her head, like those of a goldfish. "She works during the day so I said I'd watch her. Only, of course, I'm working as well—two jobs!"

"Where's your other one?" I asked.

She sighed. "Jim Dandy's. I'm assistant manager there."

Cookie tried scratching herself and again got scolded. "No, ma'am, you are not to do that."

"Why?" Hugh asked.

"She got bit by a flea and now we got her on Benadryl on account she's got sensitive skin and isn't supposed to be scratching herself."

Bethany's hair was dyed a weak, cola-colored brown. She had many red veins in her face. Before her, wedged into a cupholder, was a massive soda with a straw poked into it. Every few minutes the two-way radio would squawk and she'd answer with a deep sigh. "Darlin', can't nobody come for at least another half hour. We got one driver out sick and the rest is all backed up."

Bethany said between calls that not long ago she drove a doctor from Raleigh. "He reckoned a lot of these corona deaths has been inflated to get the numbers up. We've had fifty-three cases here in Carteret County, and only three has died. I said, 'You think it's all political?' And he said, 'Yes, ma'am, I do.'"

She looked at me in the rearview mirror and I saw a Trump voter, albeit a diplomatic one.

I told Bethany what things were like in New York: the refrigerated trucks for bodies, the tent hospital in Central Park, the almost constant sirens in March and April.

"All I know is what that doctor tolt me. We didn't shut down for the last few pandemics, but this one's pretty much destroyed everything." The dog jumped into the back seat. "No, ma'am!" Bethany shouted.

"It's okay," Hugh said.

"Oh, Lord."

It was around 3:00 when we got to the Sea Section. Hugh made lunch, and afterward I walked to the grocery store, noticing along the way a squirrel without a tail and a Black Lives Matter banner hanging on a house where, a year ago, I had seen a teenager in a Confederate-flag T-shirt.

June 25, 2020
Emerald Isle

Over dinner Gretchen talked about the crickets she raises to feed her turtles and tortoises. "Man, do those things stink."

I remembered the ones I bought in Paris to throw to my spiders. I only had them for a week or two but they left my office smelling like a crime scene. "How do your turtles catch the crickets?" I asked. "Aren't they too quick?"

"I usually tear a leg off," she said. "They say to use scissors, but my way's just as good."

Hugh was mean to me all during dinner. He was mean all day, actually. This was on account of a dream he'd had the previous evening. "You said you were leaving me. You'd been sleeping with other people and said you didn't love me anymore—hadn't loved me in a long time. And the way you did it, it was just so...uncalled for."

"Yes, but it was a dream," I kept saying. "Both of us were asleep."

"Maybe, but still, you didn't have to be so cruel."

"I *wasn't*," I argued. "I was asleep! So were you."

I noticed that when he doled out seconds, I got the smallest portion.

July 13, 2020
New York

Walking uptown from SoHo I passed a man my age who was lying shirtless on a corner surrounded by angry signs he had made. FUCK YOU DIAPER FACE, read one. Another claimed that COVID was a lie, and a third asked, WHAT'S THE BEST THING ABOUT REPUBLICAN WOMEN? THEY DON'T HAVE A PENIS.

So hot was his rage that passing him was like walking by a blast furnace.

July 17, 2020
London

I hadn't eaten anything since my breakfast on the plane, so I stopped at the Waitrose on Gloucester Road for a peri-peri chicken wrap. I'd just walked back onto the street when an Indian man approached. "Hi!" he said. "My goodness, you look great!"

I was wearing the striped cotton culottes I'd bought five years ago. Several people had complimented me on them, so I wasn't yet suspicious of the guy. "Have you retired?" he asked. "I bet you have. You look so relaxed and... good."

"Do we know each other?" I asked.

"We do," he said. "I'm sure of it. From work, I think. Which sector were you in?"

"Oh, no," I told him. "I work from home."

I noticed then that the man's clothes were dirty. Not filthy or smelly, but stained. "Yes, but where is that, exactly?" he asked.

"Kensington."

The man snapped his fingers. "Right, I know! I was your newsagent, had a place at the bottom of the road there. Then my wife was found dead in the shop so we...so I had to close, of course."

"I'm so sorry," I said, thinking, *Which road? You don't know me.*

He held up a finger. "May I ask a question?"

Here we go, I thought.

"May I have some money with which to purchase something to eat?"

I said no.

"Give me half your sandwich, then. I'm hungry."

"That's okay," I said, and I walked toward a bench.

The man must have hit up someone else, possibly with the same scam, for when I rounded the corner five minutes later, I saw him eating a sandwich. He noticed me as well and turned his back. Newsagent indeed!

At one point during last night's dinner, Hugh scolded me for something or other. "Okay," I said. "Now you have to say something nice about me."

He thought for a moment. "You have widely spaced teeth."

"That's not a compliment," I argued.

He tried again. "*Evenly* spaced."

August 14, 2020
London

I took a walk at one a.m. and had just passed the Notting Hill tube station when I came upon a guy spray-painting the word *mine* onto a storefront. "Asshole," I said.

"What did you say?" He was thirty, at least, white, with reddish-blond hair as long as my eyelashes. His beard was the same length, and he had a sweatshirt on.

"I said you're an asshole for doing that." I took one of my earbuds out.

"What's it to you?" he asked.

"Nobody wants to look at that shit," I said. "*Mine*. Ooooh, how profound!"

"How's it different from all these adverts?" he asked. "You're looking at those, aren't you?"

"Aw, get out of here," I said, putting my earbud back in.

"That's right," he called after me. "You can't handle the truth."

If I had it to do over again, I'd have said that I don't like the adverts either, but who's he to add to the amount of crap we have to walk by every day? Were he eighteen I might have understood it, but wasn't this a phase he should have passed out of by now? *Down with the gatekeepers deciding what gets into the Tate, deciding what we should read or watch. My TikTok video equals Goodfellas, even though it's the first one I ever shot, and it's just of me crushing a taco with the heel of my shoe.*

I wanted to say that despite all his mumbo-jumbo, the guy's graffiti was ultimately about his ego, his walking down the street and seeing his stupid tag. There are any number of people who might walk down that same block and see their names—on a movie poster, on a book in the window of Waterstones—and feel that same thrill. But they worked and studied for years, while all he did was buy a can of black paint and stay up until 1:00 a.m.

August 31, 2020
Rackham

I'd been picking up trash for three hours yesterday when I approached the White Horse pub on the far edge of Pulborough. It's at the top of a hill, a nice-looking old building with woods around it. Two men and two boys were standing outside of it, and as I neared them, one of the kids peeled the label off a bottle and threw it on the ground in front of me. He was around twelve, with a straw-colored pompadour.

It wasn't accidental, his littering. He looked at me while he did it—they all did—and he smirked.

"Why would you do that?" I asked. "Why would you intentionally throw something on the ground?"

The kid put his tongue against his inner cheek and grinned.

"Because he's a bugger," one of the men said affectionately.

No, I wanted to say. *I'm a bugger. He's an asshole.*

It was as if the men had no control over the boy, as if he were free at all times to behave however he liked.

"He wanted to watch you bend over and pick it up," the other boy, who looked to be around fourteen, said. He was chubby and if this was *Game of Thrones,* say, and I were to pull out a sword and kill only three of these people, he'd have been the one I spared.

I let out a breath, the way you do when you're exhausted, and had just walked away when the boy with the pompadour called, "Wait, sir, can you take this?"

I turned, and when I held my bag open, he smirked again and threw a wad of paper on the ground. The grown men thought this was hilarious, and I could hear them and the boys laughing as, again, I turned my back and walked away, burning. I pick up trash because I want to. It's my hobby. But for all they knew, this was my job. It was like intentionally pissing on the floor of the men's room while the attendant is mopping up. It's one thing to disparage a man with a great, high-paying job, but to them, I was lowly.

All this was churning in my head when, not far up the road, a car stopped, and a guy got out. He was in his early thirties, maybe, and was smoking a hand-rolled cigarette. His hair was short, his glasses sat on top of his head, and his trousers went very well with his shirt. *What is it now?* I thought as he approached.

"Excuse me," he said, "but are you by any chance David Sedaris?" Like most English people he pronounced it "Sed-*are*-us."

I admitted that I was.

"I was literally just listening to *Calypso*," he said. "And I saw you and thought, *Is that him?* Because I was *literally* just listening to you!"

The fellow said nice things regarding my writing, and when he was done, I pointed to where he had parked. "Is that your car?" I asked.

He said that it was.

"Could you do me a favor?"

He smiled. "Of course."

"There are four people standing in front of the White Horse, just around that curve," I said, pointing in the direction I had come from. "Could you possibly go and run them down? I'd like them all killed, please."

I'd earlier thought I would spare the fourteen-year-old, but that's too complicated if you're going to plow into them with a car—it's asking too much.

The guy laughed, which was disappointing, but still I was grateful that he'd stopped. All it takes is one incident like the one in front of the pub to convince me that all people are basically horrible. But they're not. This guy, for instance. He was lovely.

We said goodbye and a third of a mile up the road I heard horses coming up behind me. It was a pair of them, each harnessed to a metal, two-wheeled carriage, like the ones gladiators rode in but updated with a roomier seat.

"Hey," someone called. I looked over and it was the kid from the pub. He was sitting beside his father and as they passed, he held up a candy-bar wrapper and let it go. I watched it drift in the breeze over the heads of the fourteen-year-old and the other man, who were in the second carriage, looking like they'd just won something.

I told Hugh about it later, and when I got to the detail about the horses, he said, "Oh, they're gypsies, then."

I went online and saw that he was very well right about that. Not that it makes any difference, really.

September 13, 2020
Rackham

I stopped at the Tesco in Storrington yesterday to buy what I always buy there—an eighty-five p. bag of popcorn. A man with tattooed forearms was on the till and pushed the bag back at me, saying, "This is on the house."

I must have looked puzzled.

"Thanks for all you do," the fellow said.

I guess he'd seen me picking up trash in his parking lot or out on the road. Later, at the schoolhouse, I saw Josie's daughter. I had my big sack of garbage and she rolled down her car window, saying, "It's reassuring that some things never change. You're still my kid's idol!"

This is my last full day in Sussex for a while. I return to New York tomorrow and will miss having an identity. I guess I have one there as well, but I like that here I'm just the guy— possibly crazy—who picks up trash. I'm not a person people talk to so much as one who they see: on the road to Pulborough, on the road to Storrington, on Broomers Hill Lane. *It's him!* Last night I came upon a plastic bag of shit that had been run over. I'm guessing that someone defecated directly into it, for there was used toilet paper in there as well. *Idol? Well,* I thought, picking it up with my grabber, *if you say so.*

That's what I'll miss?

September 16, 2020
New York

A cabdriver named Peter picked me up early yesterday morning, and on our way to Heathrow, I learned that he'll be sixty next month. I don't remember what else we talked about, but he was good company. So was the Haitian man who drove me to Sixty-Second Street from JFK ten hours later. We didn't start talking until we reached Manhattan and I asked if he'd gone on a vacation this summer. "No," he told me in heavily accented English. "I'll go in November."

"Where to?"

After he said Haiti, we started speaking in French, and his manner changed. "Look at those girls!" he said, referring to two young women standing in front of a convenience store. "My God, how beautiful!"

They were maybe Dominican and had big butts. The one that he admired most wore jeans that were all shredded down the front.

"She has clawed pants," I observed.

"Yes," he said, eating her alive with his eyes.

"The cat claws things," I continued. "He does so with his nails!"

"Um-hm."

He was still looking at her when the traffic started moving. At the next light he moved on to someone different. "What about her!"

"Maybe she has children," I speculated. "Her shoes are black."

I said this as if women without kids wore only brown or red or white shoes. "Will there be storms in Haiti?" I asked, eager to change the subject.

He said no, the season for that would have ended. "I am no

549

friend of the storm," I confided. "I like the cold and the rain sometimes, but no big winds or thunder."

"Right," he said, uninterested.

October 5, 2020
Indianapolis

In Indianapolis Katharine and I were met by a driver named Erick, who was quiet until I asked if he'd spent all spring and summer sitting at home. "Pretty much," he said, and the next thing I knew he was telling us about a YouTube video he had recently watched. "It was one of them where a bear breaks into a party store."

I leaned forward. "Wait, a what?"

"Bear," he repeated. "They come in the back doors maybe and then they head for the candy, of course."

"You're kidding," I said.

"No, sir, there's lots of videos of bears eating candy in party stores. You should look them up."

I said that whenever I went on YouTube I wound up watching mice being thrown to boa constrictors. "There's a lot of that," he agreed. "The animal world, I'm telling you, it's dog-eat-dog. I like the shows they have about super-predators, things like gorillas that are vicious."

Aren't gorillas vegetarians? I wondered. *How can something that eats leaves be called a super-predator?*

"Course, people are pretty bad too," he continued. "Stupid. Doing things like putting a toddler on the back of an alligator. I mean, that's just dumb."

Who is doing that? I wondered. *What are you watching?*

After checking in, Katharine and I took a walk through the downtown area. One of the restaurants we passed was Italian. Bocca, it was called, and its neon sign pictured a bottle of Chianti that was tilted and emptying itself into a waiting glass.

"That type of bottle, the kind that's got a wicker exterior, is called a *fiasco*," I said. "Isn't that the best?" I thought that Bocca's motto could be "Home of the bottomless fiasco." Then I thought that it could be America's motto as well, at least America under Trump.

October 23, 2020
New York

Hugh and I met thirty years ago yesterday. How has it possibly been so long? I can still see him sitting on the sofa when I entered his loft on Canal Street that night with Lilia. He had that half smile of his and was so handsome—still is. We both forgot the date until late in the day, so all I got for him were flowers. He bought some for me as well and carved one of the two pumpkins I brought home last week. For dinner we had Wiener schnitzel and listened to a bit of the final presidential debate. It was me who turned the radio off after ten minutes; I couldn't take it anymore. Trump was more civil this time, meaning that he waited his turn before lying. My real problem was Biden and how I kept waiting for him to fuck up. "Many of you are in bed this morning" is how he began one of his sentences. That's not awful, but it's probably good for a president to know what time of day it is.

October 28, 2020
Louisburg, North Carolina

How odd to go from Dad's house to Gretchen's. Both have a lot of stuff in them but hers is like a museum while his is like something you'd see on an episode of *Hoarders*. I was struck at his place by all the scissors. I must have come across twenty pairs so far, and we haven't even reached the basement. *Who lived here, a tailor?* you might wonder. There are a lot of flashlights as well, a necessity, as fewer than half of the lights work. The house is shaded by trees, so by early afternoon, lampless, you're stumbling. Then there's the smell, which is mainly mildew with a little rodent thrown in and a dash of old paper.

Dad's driveway has two years' worth of fallen leaves on it. Paul has parked one of his vans there and at night his dump truck—the one with CALL PAUL TO HAUL Y'ALL on the side— pulls in behind it. While Hugh tried opening the front door, I wondered what a real estate agent might make of the place. We'd thought a young couple might buy Dad's house, might roll up their sleeves and make something of it. *You won't believe what it* used *to look like,* we'd imagine them telling their friends, reaching for a photo album of before-and-after pictures.

Instead, it looks like Paul will buy it, in which case *this* will be the after picture: the shed with rusty tools on the ground and more heaped on the workbench beside fifty-year-old paint and varnish cans, their contents hardened and cracked. Your eyes can't take it all in—stuff on stuff on stuff. It's like a person wearing five patterns at once and tying it all together with a hat, only the hat in this case is spiderwebs.

The chaos continues inside the house. *Why did Dad never think of weeding some of this crap out?* I wondered. Amy's first stop was his hiding place in the planter that divides the living and dining room. Hugh helped me remove the lid and inside were mainly checkbooks and bank statements. It was disappointing until I found the Danish modern silverware we used on special occasions. *Bingo,* I thought, looking like— *feeling like*—a scavenger, the wayward son who never visits until it's time to take stuff. Lisa had brought boxes and told us to fill them with what we wanted. "Do you need pillar candles?" I asked Hugh. "What about these highball glasses? They were never used."

I'm glad I had him to run things by. That said, there wasn't much that appealed to me, none of the clothes crammed into closets and dresser drawers. I took charcoal portraits of Lisa and Gretchen done at the mall in the early sixties. The painting I wanted of a man lying dead on the ground is at Springmoor, so I'll have to wait on that. I did consider a few of Dad's rings but left them there, as I know I'll never wear them. "What about his secret drawer in the bedroom!" Amy said.

I brought a work light in from the carport and we used it to look more closely in what was once Paul's room. Sheets, clothes, clothes, clothes. "Do I need this icon?" Amy asked.

"No!"

"What about these scissors?"

Hugh tried on a dozen of Dad's sweaters and left the house feeling itchy. Amy was scratching herself as well. It took almost an hour to reach Gretchen's place. Her downstairs rooms are crowded but not cluttered. Objects are in cases, contained, for the most part, everything fascinating and beautifully lit. Curated. A showplace.

October 29, 2020
Louisburg

Every time I see my father I wonder if I'll ever see him again, and yesterday was no exception. Hugh, Amy, and I had an appointment for 10:00 and arrived on time to fill out questionnaires regarding our health. A friendly woman took our temperatures and we were led to a long table arranged in the outdoor courtyard of Dad's wing at Springmoor. Before us lay a microphone that was unsecured, the sort that emcees drop at the end of their sessions. "What's this for?" Amy asked.

"So that he can hear you," the aide explained.

A moment later Dad was wheeled out, looking, I thought, a bit lost but as good as could be expected. His hair was combed. He wore a fleece with a green turtleneck underneath, though it was perhaps 72 degrees outside. "Well, golly," he said. "How are you guys?"

It was the same sort of conversation you might have with a stranger: *How's your health? What's going on? How are things...where you are?*

He tried to articulate how odd this was—the masks we wore, our distance—but it mainly came out as a chuckle and a hand gesture. It was his response as well when Amy tried getting him to vote for Biden. I'm just not sure of how aware he was. "Why can't you come inside?" he kept asking.

"Because of COVID."

He smiled.

A woman in a face mask walked by then. "I'm your father's favorite nurse!" she announced broadly, like someone in a British Christmas pantomime.

"Great!"

I thought Dad was lost, but then he learned that we were staying with Gretchen. "I've never been to her house," he said, hurt. "She never invited me."

Okay, I decided, *he's more clearheaded than I thought.*

A moment later an aide came over and said that if I was going to allow Hugh in, one of us—either me or Amy—should say goodbye. "I'll go," I offered, thinking not of Dad but of my Fitbit. I knew I'd be lucky to get my steps in, given all the work that lay ahead of us, so I left and spent the remainder of our half-hour visit pacing the parking lot. At the end of our allotted time, a woman dressed like a witch crept onto the patio and wheeled Dad back to his room. Halloween costumes must be tricky in a place where so many people are out of it. *And then a witch came out and told my children to go home!*

It was a long day, and the longer I stayed in Dad's house,

the harder I found it to breathe. The mildew in the basement is terrible, and everything smells of it. Going from room to room, each filled with trash, I found myself getting progressively angrier. God, the junk I found, the stacks of old pre-wheel suitcases, the boxes of papers from the consulting jobs he took on after he retired, the yellowed engineering magazines. There were coats chewed by mice, coats collared with mildew, books so damp they were stuck to the books beside them. Gretchen's room had become a dumping ground for odd pieces of furniture abandoned by tenants or found on the street.

All of the basement was bad, but nothing was worse than Dad's office. Everything there was covered with mouse turds, even his collection of stones with *Alaska 1977* and *BC 85* written on them.

Hugh took a dozen of Mom's pottery plates and packed them in the dining room. "When I ran out of bubble wrap, I used your father's disposable diapers," he told me.

October 30, 2020
Emerald Isle

It was 1:15 when we reached the Sea Section yesterday. The early-voting spot was on the other side of the bridge, across from Bojangles on Old Highway 58, and we arrived to find three card tables in the parking lot. Two were occupied by mean-looking, gray-haired Republicans. One group had, in addition to a Trump flag, a flag that read NORTH CAROLINA TEA PARTY.

It was like seeing the word *al-Qaeda* again. I said to Hugh, "I thought that was over!"

The Democrat table was staffed by what had to be the loneliest woman in North Carolina. She was a Yankee, around my age. "I just sit here all day and listen to lies," she said, looking to her left and right. "You wouldn't believe it!"

Hugh and I waited five minutes before entering the building. There we were handed pens wrapped in plastic. The ballots were paper, and I went to a six-sided kiosk to fill mine out. Then I fed it into a machine.

Leaving, I saw a young couple at one of the Republican tables. "You did good," a fat pink man in a MAGA hat was saying to them.

"We just voted!" I said ten minutes later to our cashier at the Food Lion.

"I did it a few days ago," the woman said. A little gray was creeping into her hair. I couldn't guess who she voted for but I'm willing to bet that the men behind us were for Trump. On our way to the house we passed a hand-painted sign that read JOBS NOT MOBS! It might have been for either candidate, really, but it was for Trump.

November 4, 2020
New York

A lot of the businesses in New York are boarded up, especially the fancy ones on Fifth and Madison. This is in anticipation of possible violence and is a first in my lifetime—to expect upheaval after a presidential election. I said to Hugh, "You shouldn't be allowed to loot until you show your 'I Voted!' sticker. Is that too much to ask?"

November 8, 2020
New York

I was in my new office late yesterday morning when I heard a sudden surge of honking. One hears this all the time in Manhattan, but these cars sounded jubilant rather than impatient, so I clicked on the *New York Times* site and saw that the AP had called Pennsylvania: "BIDEN BEATS TRUMP. Harris Is First Woman Elected Vice President."

We'd all known that this would happen, at least for the past thirty-six hours. For this reason, I'd thought that my feelings would be limited to relief: *Oh, that's nice. They finally called it.*

And so it was a surprise when my throat got tight, and tears came to my eyes. I ran to tell Hugh and found him at the dining-room window. "What's going on?"

"We won!" I said. "It's over." By this I meant that Trump was over, that the boulder on our collective chest these past four years had been pushed aside, and that two of the flea-size hands that had removed it belonged to me and Hugh. Thus, it wasn't "Biden/Harris won" but rather "We won." As we embraced, I thought of the couples I knew who belonged to different parties and thus could not enjoy a similar moment. It is beautiful to be on the same side and share in a victory. "Let's get out of here," I said. "Let's go onto the street."

In retrospect, I'm not sure the Upper East Side was the neighborhood to celebrate in. We had to walk a few blocks from the apartment before we found any openly joyous people. The first three we came upon were around our age, two men and a woman walking a dog. "Yippee!" they called. At Fifth and Sixty-Second we saw a couple on the corner shouting "Hooray!" as passing cars honked. "Where do we go?" Hugh asked.

"Trump Tower," I said. As we headed south, the streets grew more crowded, and more drivers honked, even those in service vehicles. Postmen. Bus drivers. Police had set up barricades at Fifty-Seventh Street. We could get no closer to the Death Star, but no matter. A great, merry horde had gathered and we all whooped and cheered at the traffic, which whooped and cheered back. A guy arrived with a trombone. People made signs. YOU'RE FIRED!!! read one.

A sour Trump supporter in his seventies stormed down the avenue. "Get a job," he groused.

"It's Saturday!" people shouted in response.

At around one, we headed toward home. Hugh stopped in front of the Plaza Hotel to answer a text message and I watched as three angry men sucked on their cigars beside a pile of luggage. The cheering and honking offended them greatly. *Fools,* you imagined them thinking. *You jump up and down now, but in a few months you'll be sorry.*

We had lunch on the terrace, still listening as New Yorkers honked and hurrahed in the distance. Afterward we took the train to Amy's neighborhood, where people were really going at it. It was a much younger crowd, and I guessed that for many, this was only their first or second election. Washington Square was packed, so we went around it and walked to Modernlink, where the employees were drinking champagne. Amy and I did what we always do to either celebrate or console ourselves—we spent money. At John Derian they were jubilant as well. We shopped, then Amy and Hugh headed to her place and I walked home, still to the joyful sound of people celebrating.

November 15, 2020
New York

I was being interviewed for a podcast when Lisa phoned. I couldn't accept her call, so she dialed Hugh, who was with Amy trying to wrangle three veal chops into a single skillet. My conversation lasted an hour or so, and afterward I wandered into the kitchen. "Your dad tested positive for COVID," Hugh said.

"Oh no!"

"Oh, he'll be fine," Hugh said.

"He's ninety-seven," I reminded him.

"Yes, but he's strong."

"By what definition?" I asked. "I mean, you saw him a few weeks back. The man weighs a hundred pounds. He's essentially made of paper."

"Well, a lot of people get this thing and don't even know that they have it," Hugh said, sounding so crazy I had to turn away from him. Lisa, meanwhile, had just had a number of standing metal racks delivered to Dad's house. "Why?" I asked.

"So I can hang up all of his clothes. That way, he can go to the house and pick out what he wants."

I thought she and I had settled this on the phone last week. "Lisa," I said, "Dad's not going back to his house. There's no way they'll let him out of Springmoor during a pandemic."

"Well, maybe later."

"When he's ninety-*nine*?"

Just when I worry I'm the only one in my family who's not insane, I think of Gretchen, who wanted to put the family piano in her front yard and has a pile of skulls in her living room. *At least* she's *thinking straight,* I tell myself.

Honestly, though, how can this *not* signal the end?

"Well, Trump survived it," Hugh said.

"He's twenty-three years younger than my dad."

"Still..."

"Not to jump the gun," I said to Amy shortly after midnight as we rode to her house in a cab, "but if he *does* die now, we can't even have a real funeral."

That's been the awful part for so many families, that the parent has to die alone or, even worse, via Skype.

"I remember Dad saying he didn't want to be buried in North Carolina," Amy said. " 'No one's putting me in red clay' was how he phrased it."

I think of how Mom died—on a ventilator, struggling to breathe. How awful for him to go out the same way. *Is he scared?* I wonder. He seemed a bit lost when I saw him a few weeks back, so maybe he doesn't understand what's going on.

November 16, 2020
New York

Yesterday morning, just as the photographer arrived to take Hugh's picture, Amy wrote to say she had spoken to Dad. It was a good conversation, so she suggested I call him as well. He picked up after the third ring and then fumbled for a while before saying hello.

"Dad?"

"Hey!" I told him I'd heard that his COVID test had come back positive, and he said in his soft, weak voice, "No, not that I'm aware of."

"But you took the test?"

He said that he had. "Let me tell you, there's nothing more miserable in this life or the next."

I told him I'd had one too, so we commiserated on that for a few minutes. "Boy, was it awful," he said. "I'm telling you, it was torture."

I said that my test was made all the worse by the young woman who performed it. "She had no personality at all."

"Oh," he said. "She was a zero." This is pretty much the worst in Dad's book: to be a zero, a lump.

I told him a photographer had just arrived to take Hugh's picture.

"And why is that?" he asked.

I explained that *New York* magazine was doing a story about him, and a few minutes later he asked again why Hugh was having his picture taken. "It's for a magazine article!" I shouted, worried that he couldn't hear me.

"Oh, I see." He paused. "I think they'll find he's a pretty snazzy person."

I laughed. "*Snazzy?* I'm not sure that's the right word."

He laughed too. "So why is he having his picture taken?"

Later I talked to Amy about her phone call with Dad. "He talked a lot about Yia Yia and what a great mother she was, then he told me he'd been a really good football player."

"Wow," I said, marveling at her ability to connect with him.

"We talked about drive," Amy said, "why some people have it and others don't, and he said, 'You're the best thing I ever made.'"

It's odd phrasing, but I know what he meant. Dad has always liked Amy best, and nakedly, but she's earned it, is always the first to call him, to send a gift, to put up with his nonsense. It's sweet.

November 18, 2020
New York

I've finished answering the letters Alyssa gave me a few weeks back. One was from a woman who wrote that when deaf people get their hearing, they're always surprised that the sun makes no noise. They naturally assumed it would roar, though if it did, you'd think it might have been mentioned somewhere along the way, in songs at least. Maybe that's what they thought was meant by "I was awoken by the sun."

November 27, 2020
New York

In the end there were five of us for Thanksgiving. Gretchen arrived on time yesterday morning and got to the apartment at around 9:30. Shortly afterward she was showing me a picture of a woman she knows embracing her pet snail. It's a giant one with a shell the size of a boxing glove. "Ick," I said. "What kind of a pet could that possibly be?" Later she gave me a face mask made from snail slime. "So what?" I asked. "They hold the secret of youth now?"

"I've used one of those," Amy said twelve hours later.

"Me too," added Adam, who was dressed in all the colors of a pumpkin pie (crust, filling, and nutmeg).

After looking at the picture of the snail, Hugh told us that Jane had had a baby squirrel living in her house and that she'd just discovered it dead in her trash can.

"That happens at work all the time," Gretchen said. "They crawl in and can't get out!" She took a sip of the coffee she'd just made. "Squirrels have nice skulls."

In the late afternoon she and I walked through Central Park. When we got home, Hugh was putting the turkey in a Bloomingdale's bag. That's how he cooked it this year. Maybe there was some subtle difference, but to me, turkey is always just turkey, the overweight, third-rate cousin of chicken. I liked the smell of roasting paper but it smoked up the apartment, and we had to open all the windows.

We ate at around nine. Hugh used Mom's old warming tray and surprised us all with corn. It was cooked into a soufflé and was my favorite side.

"I'd pay thirty dollars for this meal," Amy said after her second helping.

"Is that all?" Adam asked.

Amy raised her fork. "Thirty-six."

December 2, 2020
New York

Before leaving the apartment yesterday, I joined Gretchen in the living room, where she was watching a YouTube video of a cursing parrot. "Who's a good boy?" its British owner asked.

"Fuck you," the parrot answered. "Piss off."

"Hey, now," the man said, sounding very wounded. "Is that any way to talk?"

"Cunt."

"Listen, you—"

"Bollocks."

"'Under the water, under the sea, how many big, fat titties can you see?'" the man sang.

"You fat bastard."

Why is nothing funnier than a cursing parrot?

December 26, 2020
New York

As everyone headed upstairs for drinks last night, Amy told me that she'd spoken to Dad.

"He asked how everyone was. 'Where's David? That's nice that you're together.' And then, near the end, he asked if I'd seen his parents.

"I said, 'What? Where would I have seen them?'

"'Around,' he said. 'I saw them earlier today, standing outside my window. My father was smiling, so at first I didn't recognize him. He never smiled.'"

Amy didn't know what to say.

"I guess I could have been wrong," Dad admitted after a short silence.

December 31, 2020
Emerald Isle

A fellow named Kevin who is in his mid-forties and is missing a number of teeth has spent the last few days in our ground-floor laundry room replacing the chewed-up Sheetrock with plywood. It's screwed into place with the aid of a kitted-out drill and makes a wrenching noise so loud I can feel it two stories up. We're hoping this will keep the rats out, but, as he predicted yesterday afternoon, they're still likely to find a way in. "Can't nobody tell," he said. "One way is through them vents." Kevin gestured with his lit cigarette to the ceiling of the carport. "There's plenty of ways for them to cause damage. Squirrels too. I got a friend and one of 'em even took his Christmas lights."

"Wait," I said. "A squirrel stole someone's Christmas lights? What did he want with them?"

Kevin crushed his cigarette and shrugged. "Just wanted to have 'em, I guess."

Why does that seem like such a fitting conclusion to this past year? A squirrel takes your Christmas lights just because he wants them, and there's not a goddamn thing you can do about it. That said, my 2020 wasn't nearly as bad as most people's. Yes, my tours were canceled, but at least I wasn't stuck in a studio apartment with three children. I had space. The only person in my family to get the coronavirus was Dad, who not only survived without being hospitalized—and at age ninety-seven!—but shed ten pounds.

"No fair!" we all cried.

Without the tours, I still managed to make some money, but that was never what I was in it for. What I loved was the attention. How had I never realized the extent to which it sustained me? Without an audience, I exhausted poor Hugh and my family. *Look, I'm crossing the room! I've taken my jacket off! Why aren't you applauding?*

When the pandemic hit, my first thought wasn't *Oh, those poor dying people* but *What about my airline status?* Because of all my tour travel, I was Gold on United and Executive Platinum on American. Neither is a lifetime appointment. Stop flying and the next thing you know, you're boarding with group 5, a nobody.

At what point did my airline status come to determine my identity? I like to think that I haven't changed, that fundamentally I'm the same person I was forty years ago, still nervous and insecure. While the best day of the year was when the election was called for Biden, the second-best was when I found thirty pounds by the side of the road as I was picking up trash in West Sussex—free money! The more of it you have, the better you're treated, and I've grown used to that over the years. *The lounge is right this way, Mr. Sedaris.*

Thank you—squint at name tag—*Anderson.*

I found it interesting at the start of the pandemic when celebrities began broadcasting from home or sending out videos of themselves and their families "coping."

"Hey!" the public cried, outraged. "That talk-show host is living in a mansion!"

Well, yes, I wanted to say, *a mansion bought with money that* you *gave her.* There was something British in the sudden disdain people expressed. Americans always celebrated wealth and celebrity, or at least afforded it a grudging respect. Something changed last spring, though, something that was started years ago with YouTube and the growth of the internet. I remember Amy telling me about DoggFace a few months back. "He's everywhere," she said, showing me a brief video in which a grown man rode a skateboard and drank cranberry juice while lip-synching to a Fleetwood Mac song.

"Okay," I said, "but what does he *do*?"

"He's doing it!" she told me. "Isn't he great!"

It was like me trying to elicit praise from Dad after the performance piece Ronnie and I did at the North Carolina museum in 1980. "But all you did was pour sand out of a boot!" he said.

"Yes, but it was *the way* I poured it."

I didn't just turn older this year—I turned old. There wasn't a specific single moment when I slipped over from middle age; rather, it was gradual, the change not so much physical as mental. There are so many things I don't understand now. Our constant need to rebrand, for instance. Someone politely referred to me as "queer" not long ago, and I was like, *Oh no, you don't.* I was queer in the 1970s, and that was enough for me. The same people using "queer" have embraced "Latinx," which, according to a recent article in the *Washington Post,* only one in four Latinos is even aware of. Fewer still are interested in adopting it, in part because, at least in Spanish, it's so difficult to say.

I also don't get holding people who lived dozens of years ago—much less *hundreds* of years ago—to the moral standards of today. Can we really condemn Dolley Madison for not supporting trans rights? If the figure on the pedestal is wearing breeches and a powdered wig, can't we forgive him for being a product of his time, just as we're all products of our time? If you want to replace statues, I understand. But couldn't the reason be that, say, Paul Revere had a hundred and twenty years to scowl down at some godforsaken traffic circle in Palookaville and now it's time to give someone else a chance? Someone like, well, me? Or we could just choose candidates at random from the phone book. Of course, there is no phone book anymore, which brings us back to me being old.